D1326063

ROYAL

HER MAJESTY QUEEN ELIZABETH II

One of the first gestures that Elizabeth was taught as a baby was how to wave to the crowds. It is a telling anecdote of a queen who may not yet be Britain's longest-reigning sovereign, but who has comfortably earned the title of the monarch who has put in the most hours of work. In this, the year of her golden Jubilee, acclaimed royal biographer Robert Lacey paints the most intimate portrait yet of this extraordinary woman—with a particularly vivid new picture of her fifty-year marriage to the intriguing and controversial Prince Philip. A compelling narrative that takes the reader into the very heart of the royal household, Royal offers fresh insight and astonishing details of the events that have shaped Elizabeth II's life.

ROYAL

Her Majesty
Queen Elizabeth II

Robert Lacey

CHIVERS PRESS
BATH

First published 2002
by
Little, Brown
This Large Print edition published by
Chivers Press
by arrangement with
Little, Brown and Company
2002

ISBN 0 7540 1787 7

British Library Cataloguing in Publication Data available.

Printed and bound in Great Britain by
BOOKCRAFT, Midsomer Norton, Somerset

For Philippa Harrison

CONTENTS

List of Illustrations

Princess Elizabeth greets the crowds with her nanny. (Private Collection)

The princesses broadcasting to evacuated children. (Private Collection)

Princess Elizabeth on board HMS Vanguard. (Private Collection)

Queen Elizabeth II on her way to her father's funeral. (Private Collection)

Queen Elizabeth II rides to open her first Parliament. (Private Collection)

The Queen and the Princess of Wales at the State Opening of Parliament. (Private Collection)

Family tree by John Gilkes.

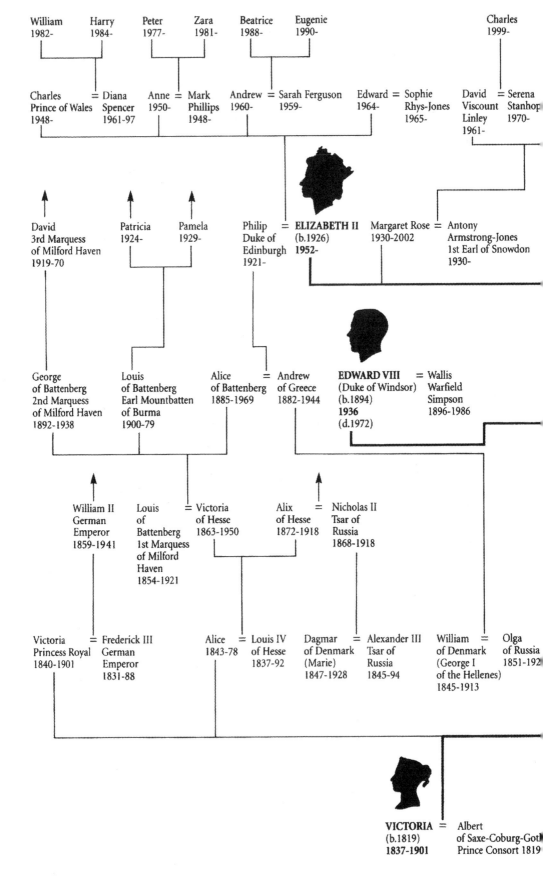

William 1982-
Harry 1984-
Peter 1977-
Zara 1981-
Beatrice 1988-
Eugenie 1990-
Charles 1999-

Charles Prince of Wales 1948- = Diana Spencer 1961-97

Anne 1950- = Mark Phillips 1948-

Andrew 1960- = Sarah Ferguson 1959-

Edward 1964- = Sophie Rhys-Jones 1965-

David Viscount Linley 1961- = Serena Stanhope 1970-

David 3rd Marquess of Milford Haven 1919-70

Patricia 1924-

Pamela 1929-

Philip Duke of Edinburgh 1921- = **ELIZABETH II** (b.1926) **1952-**

Margaret Rose 1930-2002 = Antony Armstrong-Jones 1st Earl of Snowdon 1930-

George of Battenberg 2nd Marquess of Milford Haven 1892-1938

Louis of Battenberg Earl Mountbatten of Burma 1900-79

Alice of Battenberg 1885-1969 = Andrew of Greece 1882-1944

EDWARD VIII (Duke of Windsor) (b.1894) **1936** (d.1972) = Wallis Warfield Simpson 1896-1986

William II German Emperor 1859-1941

Louis of Battenberg 1st Marquess of Milford Haven 1854-1921 = Victoria of Hesse 1863-1950

Alix of Hesse 1872-1918 = Nicholas II Tsar of Russia 1868-1918

Victoria Princess Royal 1840-1901 = Frederick III German Emperor 1831-88

Alice 1843-78 = Louis IV of Hesse 1837-92

Dagmar of Denmark (Marie) 1847-1928 = Alexander III Tsar of Russia 1845-94

William of Denmark (George I of the Hellenes) 1845-1913 = Olga of Russia 1851-192

VICTORIA (b.1819) **1837-1901** = Albert of Saxe-Coburg-Goth Prince Consort 1819

el | Arthur
1999-

rah = Daniel Chatto
64- | 1964-

Elizabeth II
and the House of Windsor

The principal line of descent from Queen Victoria

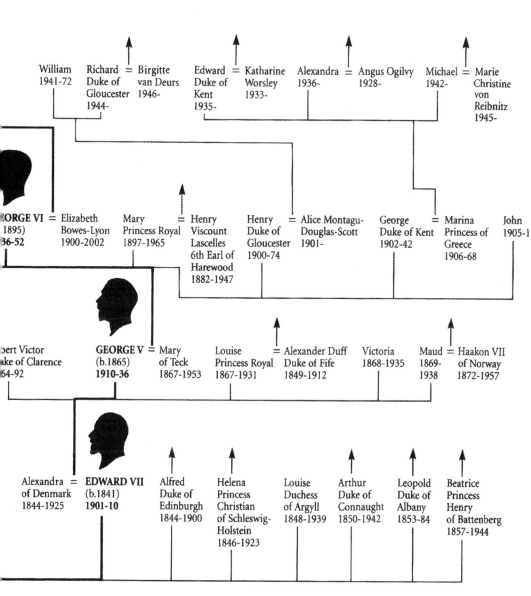

William
1941-72

Richard = Birgitte
Duke of   van Deurs
Gloucester 1946-
1944-

Edward = Katharine
Duke of   Worsley
Kent   1933-
1935-

Alexandra = Angus Ogilvy
1936-   1928-

Michael = Marie
1942-   Christine
          von
          Reibnitz
          1945-

GEORGE VI = Elizabeth
1895)   Bowes-Lyon
36-52   1900-2002

Mary = Henry
Princess Royal Viscount
1897-1965   Lascelles
              6th Earl of
              Harewood
              1882-1947

Henry = Alice Montagu-
Duke of Douglas-Scott
Gloucester 1901-
1900-74

George = Marina
Duke of Kent Princess of
1902-42   Greece
            1906-68

John
1905-1

bert Victor
ke of Clarence
64-92

GEORGE V = Mary
(b.1865)   of Teck
1910-36   1867-1953

Louise = Alexander Duff
Princess Royal Duke of Fife
1867-1931   1849-1912

Victoria
1868-1935

Maud = Haakon VII
1869-   of Norway
1938   1872-1957

Alexandra = EDWARD VII
of Denmark (b.1841)
1844-1925   1901-10

Alfred
Duke of
Edinburgh
1844-1900

Helena
Princess
Christian
of Schleswig-
Holstein
1846-1923

Louise
Duchess
of Argyll
1848-1939

Arthur
Duke of
Connaught
1850-1942

Leopold
Duke of
Albany
1853-84

Beatrice
Princess
Henry
of Battenberg
1857-1944

PROLOGUE

'As your Queen, and as a grandmother'

It was on a cool September Thursday at Balmoral that Queen Elizabeth II realised she would have to change course. She had read the newspapers over breakfast that morning, digesting their angry sermons with the long-practised pensiveness which caused her eyes to narrow. Her jaw would firm slightly as her thought processes started, shifting her chin forward a fraction—a signal to her staff to think one more hard thought before they opened their mouths. Then, soon after nine o'clock, the phone calls from London started.

Diana had died the previous Sunday—the last day of August 1997—and it had been pressure and decisions ever since. Helping the two boys had been their grandmother's first priority, applying her own therapy in times of trouble: lots of exercise and fresh air.

'We must get them out and away from the television,' said the Queen as she clicked across the sad images of the princess being run non-stop on every channel. 'Let's get them both up in the hills.'

The fact they were all together as a family, away from everything in the rugged beauty and peace of Scotland, had seemed such a blessing at first. Peter Phillips, Princess Anne's bluff and burly rugby-playing son, had gone out with William and Harry on the moors each day, jollying them along with stalking and the odd fishing expedition—plus lots of mucking around on the brothers' noisy all-

1

terrain motorbikes. The two young princes both loved the outdoors. In that respect they were very much Charles's sons.

The weather had been balmy, with just a hint of autumn crispness, and the whole family had driven out most evenings in the Land Rovers to eat. Ever practical, ever tinkering, Prince Philip, the Duke of Edinburgh, is the proud deviser of a bulky, wheeled contraption that is the centre of these cherished rituals: a picnic trailer. With the grilling rack and pots and pans stowed neat and ship-shape, and padded drawers filled with carefully segregated types of fortifying alcohol, the trailer is towed to the shooting lodge selected for the family barbecue. No staff are present and the royal paterfamilias becomes chef. In that first week of September, the Duke's patent barbecue wagon had come into its own as never before. Cooking and carving and cleaning up afterwards, the shared chores and rituals of the self-help meal had kept the whole family busy and had helped create the feeling there was something everyone could do. It was practical therapy.

At fifteen, William had seemed to take it bravely, on the outside at least. But he was insisting that he would not walk behind the coffin at the funeral. Not quite thirteen, Harry had been more obviously upset. Was everyone quite sure Mummy was dead, he was heard to enquire? Could it not be checked to make sure there had not been a mistake?

Gently helping the brothers to cope was, like everything royal, more than just a private, family matter. If the two young princes did walk through the streets of London on Saturday, their composure would be the hinge on which the whole occasion turned.

Working out the details of the funeral had been the other big job since Sunday: the style of the service, the length of the route, as well as the role that William and Harry would play. There had been family arguments in the small hours as the bad news came through. The Spencers—Diana's mother, brother and two sisters—had wanted a private funeral, a small family affair, and to start with the Queen herself had favoured that. But by Sunday evening it was clear it would have to be a full-scale ceremony in the Abbey, and since Monday the fax machine had been processing hymn sheets and processional timetabling non-stop. Princess Margaret disapproved, but the Queen Mother had got quite excited about the prospect of listening to Elton John.

Then came all the fuss about the flag.

*   *   *

Downing Street was the first to sense that something might be awry. Sitting in his media command room at Number Ten, Alastair Campbell, the Prime Minister's press spokesman, caught a cable television news bulletin that worried him. It was Wednesday morning, and the long lines of mourners waiting in the Mall to sign the condolence books for the princess were spending as many as five hours looking down through the trees towards Buckingham Palace.

People were not just signing their names when they got to the head of the queue. Most wanted to pen some special tribute of their own, and after

3

half a day on their feet everyone wanted to sit down.

'In retrospect,' says an official of the Lord Chamberlain's office, 'it was clearly a mistake to have supplied chairs.'

Some people were spending as long as half an hour over the page, composing their essays. So the lines waiting outside in the Mall grew longer; and, as people shuffled slowly forward, they had been struck by the absence of any flag flying at half-mast over the Queen's principal residence.

It was a technical matter. The Queen's presence is signalled, wherever she may be—palace, car, boat or plane—by the Royal Standard, a luscious and ancient confection of heraldic lions and symbolic harpstrings that follows her everywhere, like a battle standard, and is never lowered, not even when the sovereign dies. 'The King is Dead; Long Live the King.'

But the tradition had developed at Buckingham Palace—though not at any other royal residence— that, in the absence of the Royal Standard, no other flag should fly. So while flags all round the country, including those over Windsor Castle and over the royal country residence of Sandringham in East Anglia, were now flying at half-mast, Buckingham Palace itself was conspicuously bare of any sign of mourning for Diana.

'I've just been watching Sky News,' said Campbell in a phone call to Robert Fellowes, the Queen's private secretary, who was also Diana's brother-in-law, married to her elder sister, Jane. 'Now, it's just a straw in the wind, but I think they're going to make some mischief over this thing of the flag.'

4

Rupert Murdoch's Sky News had been running dramatic vox pop interviews from the Mall in which mourners complained about the bare flagpole over the Palace. It made for compulsive, angry television, and Campbell guessed it was only a matter of time before the other bulletins followed suit.

'I hear what you're saying,' replied Fellowes. 'But it's a curious business, the flag at Buckingham Palace. There are certain things, you know, that I can deliver straight away. But I'm not sure it's going to be as easy as it looks, even if it's right, to please the public on this one.'

Fellowes rang Balmoral to pass on Downing Street's concerns to his deputy, Sir Robin Janvrin, who was running the private secretary's office there, and also to the Queen. But he did not argue Campbell's case very strongly. 'The alarm bells,' as one participant put it, 'did not jangle.'

Sir Robert Fellowes, today Baron Fellowes of Shotesham in the county of Norfolk, was a royal retainer and the son of a royal retainer. His father, the bluff Sir Billy Fellowes, had run the royal estate at Sandringham and had been a shooting companion of the Queen's father, King George VI. In his time as private secretary, Fellowes had overseen some important changes in the monarchy, and there was a mildly subversive twinkle behind his horn-rimmed spectacles. 'We don't have protocol here,' he liked to say when talking of Palace etiquette, 'just bloody good manners.' But Fellowes had breathed tradition all his life. It was a key element in his job as private secretary, and protocol had always provided a sure fall-back in times of difficulty.

Elizabeth II felt the same, only more so. For the Queen, tradition and protocol represented something greater than oneself—deep values approaching the sacred. It could be compared to how non-royal people feel at their children's Christmas carol concert, or when the bugle sounds on Remembrance Day—the tingle of nobler things. It is easy to smile condescendingly at the scarlet-tunicked and bearskin-clad Guards parading so formally outside Buckingham Palace until, in the aftermath of a terrorist attack on New York, these very British soldiers stand to attention while their band plays 'The Star-Spangled Banner'.

Tradition is one of the cornerstones of the royal mystery. The most troublesome time in the otherwise tranquil childhood of the young Princess Elizabeth had begun when she was just ten, when her sparky and original Uncle David had ascended the throne as King Edward VIII. Shrugging his shoulders at precedent, he had spent a hectic year insouciantly overturning tradition in his quest to make the monarchy modern, and it had ended in tears. The abdication crisis of 1936 had been the darkest moment in her family's recent history.

If Prince Charles, and not his ex-wife, had died in a car crash the previous Sunday, the Queen would not now be flying the Union Jack at half-mast over Buckingham Palace. She had not done it for her beloved father, George VI, and it was not then planned for the Queen Mother, who, for all her personal popularity, had always understood how the institution of monarchy ultimately transcended any individual. A personally modest spirit, the Queen would certainly not expect such a gesture for herself. So why should tradition be overturned for a young woman, who, Uncle David-like, had put herself before the family and had come to be the focus of such bitter and divisive trouble?

Elizabeth II had been one of the first in the family to fall out of love with Diana.

'The Queen is a very good judge of character,' says one of her staff. 'She was very quick in "sussing" the less fortunate sides of the princess's personality.' The Queen had tried to be fair to her daughter-in-law, taking her side on occasions in the bitter separation battle with Charles. But Diana's open sniping at what she had publicly derided as the stuffy Palace establishment made her the last person for whom the Queen—or, still less, her strong-minded husband—would command such a change. Only days previously Diana had been parading the Mediterranean with her Egyptian playboy lover, the couple draped over each other half naked, to the horror of the royal family and the agonised embarrassment of her sons.

Fellowes got the answer he expected. There is a long-standing mistrust in Buckingham Palace towards making quick concessions to the concerns of the moment, especially when voiced by the tabloid media. 'It's like feeding Christians to the lions,' says a former press secretary. So the royal reaction to the televisual straws in the wind was exactly the opposite to Alastair Campbell's. Unhappiness over the flag was something that the enduring monarchy should rise above in a world of trendy gestures. No flag except the Royal Standard had ever flown over Buckingham Palace. 'It just needs to be explained,' insisted the royal private secretary.

Campbell did not push the point. Never one of nature's monarchists, he felt in alien territory. In his days as political editor and columnist for the *Daily Mirror* he had been famous for his scathing attacks on the misbehaviour of the young royals. Now, as he walked through the crowds that Wednesday morning to confer with Fellowes and the other members of the Lord Chamberlain's funeral committee at the Palace, he felt he could sniff mutiny in the air. 'There was almost that football crowd fear, you know, when you're coming out of the stadium and your team has lost, and you're not quite sure what you'll find round the next corner.'

But this lager and baseball cap analogy clearly did not fit the arcane world of deep precedence. There were echoes of the Northern Ireland peace process with which Tony Blair was just beginning to grapple, with all its sticking points of flags and badges and emotion-charged symbols.

'There were times in that week,' says one of Number Ten's more radical insiders, 'when you could not believe what was coming down the line from Balmoral. You wondered if they were living in the same century.'

Campbell went back to Downing Street to confer with Blair, then rang Fellowes at the Palace. 'How would it be,' he asked, 'if Tony went out publicly into the street, outside Downing Street, and said, "Look, these are ordinary people going through circumstances that none of us can imagine," you know, a "They are human beings" strategy?'

At the end of that Wednesday, the Prime Minister did just that.

'All our energies,' he said in front of Number

Ten, 'are now directed to trying to make this [the funeral] as tremendous a commemoration of Princess Diana as possible . . . I know those are very strongly the feelings of the royal family as well.'

Deploying New Labour's famed mastery of PR techniques, Blair's appeal was timed to catch the evening news bulletins, then command the next morning's front pages. But only the left-leaning *Guardian* followed the Prime Minister's lead. The tabloids went for the jugular. 'Show us You Care,' demanded the *Express* over the photo of a flinty-faced Queen. 'Your People are Suffering,' proclaimed the *Mirror* 'Speak to us, Ma'am.' With the broadsheets only moderately more restrained, Elizabeth II was confronted by an unprecedented chorus of newsprint criticism over her Balmoral breakfast that Thursday morning. Rupert Murdoch's *Sun* put it most powerfully. 'Where is the Queen when the country needs her?' demanded an open letter on the paper's front page.

> She is 550 miles from London, the focal point of the nation's grief. Her castle at Balmoral is about as far away as it is possible to get from the sea of flowers building up outside the royal palaces . . . Every hour the Palace remains empty adds to the public anger at what they perceive to be a snub to the People's Princess. Let Charles and William and Harry weep together in the lonely Scottish Highlands. We can understand that. But the Queen's place is with the people. She should fly back to London immediately and stand on the Palace balcony.

*   *   *

There was some convenient relief in the energy with which Britain's newspapers turned on Elizabeth II that Thursday morning, 4 September 1997. Three days earlier, they had been the objects of bitter blame. Photographers who ventured too close to mourners laying flowers outside the palaces had been shouted at and menaced, the butt of public fury at the role of the paparazzi in hounding the princess into the Alma Tunnel in Paris. The announcement by the Paris police that Henri Paul, the driver on the fateful night, had had more than three times the legal limit of alcohol in his blood had let the editors off the hook, and they wasted little time diverting public anger away from their own role in the tragedy.

But the idea so beseechingly stated in the *Sun*'s open letter, that royal people exist as vehicles for the collective emotions of the communities they head, was undeniable. And emotion was one aspect of the royal job that Elizabeth II—unlike Diana— had never handled with any ease. 'She has a deep mistrust,' says one of her advisers, 'of what she calls "stunts".'

Elizabeth II is not an actress. At the heart of Britain's performing monarchy is a serious, matter-of-fact woman who is an obstinately performance-free zone. Blessed with a ravishing natural smile, she finds it impossible to switch on that smile to order. She had issued a statement of regret on the morning of Diana's death and was now supervising a practical family effort to comfort the two boys who were most intimately affected. Rather shy, and quite the opposite of her outspoken husband, she had never been a step-forward-and-open-her-mouth type of person—and her staff had taken their cue from that.

'We got a day behind the game,' admit more than one of those at the centre of that week's activities.

How to catch up was the urgent theme of the discussions that Thursday morning in Buckingham Palace—and, as the ideas bounced around in Robert Fellowes's office, the flag suddenly became the simplest issue. After the tabloid front pages and the tone of that morning's radio coverage, there could even be a question of public order at stake. Some concession would have to be made, and it seemed obvious that, protocol or not, the Union Jack would need to be flying at half-mast over the Palace on the day of the funeral. Members of the royal family would have to show themselves in public before that, and, most important of all, the Queen would have to speak to the nation.

This was what had been lacking—anyone from the royal family personally expressing their feelings. The family had been planning to stay in Balmoral until the last possible moment, coming down on the royal train on Friday night to arrive in London on the morning of the funeral itself. 'How can we coop the boys up in a gloomy old palace all covered with dustsheets?' Prince Philip had asked. But it was now clear that the royal journey south would have to be moved forward as a visible concession to public sentiment—even though 'concession' was not a word that the press office would use. The Queen's arrival in London would be turned into a significant event, and it would also provide the moment for her to face the television

11

cameras.

Robert Fellowes and Geoffrey Crawford, the Queen's Australian-born press secretary, got on the squawk box to Balmoral to talk the problem through with Robin Janvrin and with the Queen herself. There was a need for a fresh and clearly proactive policy, the two men in London argued, a visible change of direction—and, faced with the facts, Queen Elizabeth II, guardian of unchanging tradition and protocol, agreed to it all, virtually on the nod. Suddenly the arcane details of what flag flew where counted for nothing.

'The Queen has ruthless common sense,' says one of her private secretaries. 'If you can explain clearly why something has to be done, and she agrees, that's the end of the matter. She doesn't say, "Well, last time when we looked at this . . ." She has an extraordinary ability to listen, absorb and come to a decision immediately.'

Five years earlier, at the time of another crisis, the Queen had decided with similar abruptness that standing arrangements could be discarded, and had agreed to surrender the royal tax immunity which she had until then considered an article of faith. If you have got to move on, you have got to move on. That is the bottom-line motto of the House of Windsor. They are a tough bunch. Their anachronistic persistence and ability to flourish in the modern world derive from an unsentimental ability to sense when the dynasty's existence is threatened, and to adapt, backtracking and reinventing themselves if necessary. They have an uncanny nose for survival—and this in turn stems from a still more profound understanding that their power and significance derive ultimately, and entirely, from the people. Being royal has no meaning or function without that. If the people do not want a stoic, stiff-upper-lip figurehead, then let the lip wobble a little.

The Queen told her private secretaries to start drafting the speech she would deliver the next day.

*   *   *

Early in her reign, Elizabeth II was due to visit the Yorkshire town of Kingston upon Hull and asked one of her private secretaries to prepare a first draft of her speech.

'I am very pleased to be in Kingston today,' the draft confidently started.

The young Queen crossed out the word 'very'.

'I will be pleased to be in Kingston,' she explained. 'But I will not be very pleased.'

Elizabeth II has always found it impossible to be what she is not. Her staff say this is her greatest strength, her inability to pose or act. She is bleakly and appallingly honest, trained by a lifetime inside the prison of courtly waffle and flattery to detect insincerity, and dismiss it in a regal and disdainful blink of the eye.

'I am *not* a politician,' is her standard response to modern press advisers who try to get her to jump through hoops.

So, as her private secretary sat down to draft the most important speech of her reign, he was faced with two problems. He knew that the Queen would not say anything that she did not mean. And he knew that Elizabeth II was definitely not mourning Diana in the way that most of her subjects were.

The condolence-book queuers and the mischief-

13

making editors were correct in their hunches. Their emotionally controlled sovereign considered that there were several more important things in life and death than the passing of Diana. At the top of that list was the Queen's own idea of enduring royal dignity, which she had upheld for forty-five years and which she was not prepared to compromise with empty gestures.

To those who knew Diana personally, the princess's saintly public aura—massively magnified in death—was compromised by a private wilfulness on a major scale. It extended far beyond self-indulgence to a pattern of deceit and narcissism that poisoned her relations not only with her royal in-laws but with her charities, her most loyal servants and even her own blood family, the Spencers. In the last summer of her life she had had bitter rows and had been in a state of prolonged 'no speaks' with both her mother and her brother Charles.

For many years Elizabeth II had done her best to keep working with what she called her daughter-in-law's 'difficult side'. She was genuinely admiring of Diana's idealistic impulses and empathy with the public, and she gave full weight to the princess's role as a future queen and mother of a future king. But the previous year, at the beginning of the Wales's divorce negotiations in 1996, Diana had engaged in a sally of deception at the expense of the Queen herself. She had lied about what she had said face-to-face to the Queen, and her blatant dishonesty had shocked Elizabeth II and angered her profoundly.

The important issue in the Queen's eyes was the institution of monarchy that she was pledged to protect—and by the end of Diana's life she had come to feel that the princess was undermining it. From that perception stemmed the difference between the Queen's feelings and those of many of her subjects. A dangerous gap had been created, and tomorrow's speech would have to close it.

*   *   *

The royal plane touched down at Northolt at 2.00 p.m. on Friday 5 September, the afternoon before the funeral. Helicopters were hovering overhead, and their cameras followed the royal car as it threaded its way through the suburbs of west London, past the BBC in Shepherd's Bush, through Paddington and across Hyde Park, finally to bring the Queen back to her palace.

'I had some trepidation,' confesses one royal aide, 'as to what was going to happen when they got out of the car. Perhaps people would jeer or hiss at her.'

Geoff Crawford had sketched out the route she would follow down the barricade of flowers against the railings, and there were plain-clothes police looking for trouble in the crowd. In fact, the mood of people around the gates was warm and welcoming—'a universal saying,' as one participant remembered, 'of "Well, at last you're back."'

Peter Edwards, the sound technician who had worked on the ground-breaking *Royal Family* television documentary in the late 1960s, had been rung at lunchtime and had driven straight to the Palace. Since 1969 Edwards had recorded all the Queen's Christmas broadcasts for both television and radio, and had a knack for putting her at ease.

She would be doing a piece to camera around four or four-thirty, he was told, to go out later in the evening, and he arrived to find the BBC's engineers in the process of setting up.

The atmosphere was tense. Philip Bonham Carter, the freelance cameraman who normally worked with Edwards on royal assignments, had not been able to make it, and Edwards worried that the lighting being set up by the BBC's cameraman was too strong. The hastily rigged circuit of lamps and electrical connections was audibly 'buzzing', both in the room and on the sound man's tape, which was crackling with interference. Press office staff were working on last-minute changes to the teleprompter.

Behind the scenes the broadcasting strategy had still not been finalised. One option was for the Queen to 'do live', talking direct to the camera in a live insert that would break dramatically into the evening news bulletins. A second-best would be for the Queen to speak 'as live', making a recording which would then be broadcast within minutes. But that would lessen the impact, and those who knew Elizabeth II's unease with rehearsals and fake occasions knew that she needed to be put on her mettle. 'It was a psychological thing,' said one aide. 'She goes flat when she knows it's being recorded. When she knows it's real, she rises to the challenge.'

To go totally live was a high-risk strategy. The Queen had never before spoken so directly and unshielded to such a major audience. Her only previous 'address to the nation', on the eve of the Gulf War in 1991, had been recorded. But Fellowes and Crawford felt it would work, and they walked to the Belgian Suite at the back of the Palace where the Queen and her husband were having tea.

'Do you think you can do it?' Fellowes asked the Queen.

'If that's what I've got to do,' she replied.

The Queen looked through her script one last time and suggested some final alterations. Fellowes went to his office to get the changes transcribed and, with only ninety minutes left before transmission, Geoff Crawford walked back into the reception-room-turned-studio.

'Can we do it live?' he asked.

There was a scrambling of BBC riggers as they ran sweating up and down the stairs, running leads to connect up with the outside broadcast links trucks outside.

'Are you sure you can say every word in this speech and really believe it?' someone had asked the Queen during the drafting process.

'Certainly,' she replied. 'I believe every word.'

At twenty to six she did a final run-through with the autoscript, looking into the camera as Fellowes and Crawford watched. One rehearsal was enough, they decided. Then, at 5.55, the countdown started. As the clock ticked round to six, the technicians turned their attention to the two television monitors in the corner. One showed the early evening programming on the BBC. The other displayed the interior Palace shot of the Queen looking intently into the lens. The floor manager was counting down—'Five, four, three, two . . .'— then he made a motion to the Queen, mouthing 'Go!' Suddenly both monitors were showing the same image, and Elizabeth II began to speak live to the nation.

Robert Fellowes had talked his first draft over with Geoff Crawford and David Airlie, the Lord Chamberlain, and had then faxed it to Balmoral, where the Queen and Robin Janvrin worked on it together. The final version had been sent to Downing Street in line with the procedure prior to the Queen's Christmas broadcast, when the Prime Minister's comments are invited as a matter of courtesy. 'It was not for the Prime Minister's approval,' stressed an aide. 'We're always a bit of a stickler for that. It was her own speech. She wasn't speaking "on advice".'

'On advice' is the constitutional term for speeches made when the Queen is acting as the government's mouthpiece, for example when greeting a foreign head of state, or, most obviously, when reading out the government's avowedly political agenda in the Queen's Speech at the State Opening of Parliament. Her address in September 1997 was infinitely more challenging. Normally it was her royal job to be plain vanilla. This Friday evening she had to do the opposite of what she had been trained for and had practised all her life: she had to show at least a little of her personal feelings.

'Since last Sunday's dreadful news,' began the Queen, 'we have seen throughout Britain and around the world an overwhelming expression of sadness at Diana's death. We have all been trying in our different ways to cope. It is not easy to express a sense of loss, since the initial shock is often succeeded by a mixture of other feelings—disbelief, incomprehension, anger and concern for those who remain. We have all felt those emotions in these last few days. So what I say to you now, as your Queen, and as a grandmother, I say from my heart.'

The words 'as a grandmother' had come from Alastair Campbell.

'Alastair was quite tentative about it,' remembers one Palace insider. 'He said, "The Prime Minister has only one comment, which is, would it be right for the Queen to say *speaking as a grandmother*?" We grabbed it and used it.'

The speech's other masterstroke was the live crowd backdrop. As the Queen spoke, viewers were able to look through the window behind her to where people were moving about like matchstick figures in a Lowry painting, coming and going, still laying their flowers.

Peter Edwards had been struggling all afternoon to get an uncluttered soundtrack, and the decision to go live had made his problem worse. The heat and sweat in the room had added further interference to the whistle of the lights. 'Can't you get a clearer sound?' the BBC control room were shouting down the line. Edwards opened the window to get a few minutes of fresh air and heard an extraordinary sound outside—the quiet murmuring of ten thousand or more people as they milled around in the traffic-free arena outside the Palace.

'Prov. Town Atmos.' is how the sound man today remembers the noise, referring to the BBC title of their standard canned sound library tape, used to create the atmosphere of a provincial town. 'But it was also a sound of its own, like nothing I'd quite heard before. This was London. *Then*. At that very particular moment. I shivered when I heard it.'

Edwards had the solution to his sound problem. He stationed a microphone outside the window to pick up the wind and the shuffle of the crowds, blending it strongly into the audiotrack from the Queen's microphone. The electronic interference was masked, and the living noise of London gave physical texture, and a brooding background meaning, to what she said.

'I admired and respected her,' the Queen was saying, 'for her energy and commitment to others and especially for her devotion to her two boys. This week at Balmoral we have all been trying to help William and Harry come to terms with the devastating loss that they and the rest of us have suffered. No one who knew Diana will ever forget her. Millions of others who never met her, but felt they knew her, will remember her . . .

'I hope that tomorrow we can all, wherever we are, join in expressing our grief for Diana's loss and her all-too-short life. It is a chance to show to the whole world the British nation united in grief and respect. May those who died rest in peace and may we, each and every one of us, thank God for someone who made many, many people happy.'

It might have made a snappier and more fluid ending to thank God for someone who had 'made us all so happy'. But this was a speech delivered by the woman who had refused to pretend that she was *very* pleased to be in Kingston. The strength of her words was that they did not flirt with exaggerated or false sentiment. Her reservations were clearly there, for those who cared to look for them, along with her sternness and her unwillingness, in Britain's number one acting job, to act.

Elizabeth II had searched her heart—a key word that she had used near the beginning of the

20

speech—and, with the help of her private secretaries, she had set out all the good things that she did feel about her late daughter-in-law. She would be genuinely grieving at the funeral next day, albeit in her own undemonstrative and queenly way. The head of a thousand-year-old monarchy had rallied the troops in traditional style, while also managing to tell her people that, in a contemporary idiom, she could feel their pain.

'She's turned it around!' exclaimed the *Sun* photographer Arthur Edwards, jovial King Rat of the journalistic royal rat pack, who had taken a break from his duties outside the Palace and retired to a pub to watch the broadcast on television. 'It brought a lump to my throat. "Thank God," I thought. "She's back in charge."'

'It was uncanny,' remembers Alastair Campbell, who had watched the broadcast in Downing Street. 'I was out in the Mall soon afterwards with all the crowds still milling about. And most of them had not heard the broadcast or even known that it had taken place. But the change in atmosphere was palpable. The pressure was being let out.'

A contingent of senior police officers had gathered in St James's ready for the transfer of the princess's coffin to Kensington Palace, where the funeral procession would start next day. Eyes that had been tense and watchful were relaxed. Their men in the crowd were telling them—and they could feel it—that the moment of crisis had passed.

Elizabeth II had taken her time about it. But when it really mattered, the Queen had done her job. Setting her personal reservations aside, she had managed to express genuine emotion. Taking command and using modern media to assert her ancient and mysterious authority, she had also acknowledged, through her willingness to change her plans and to make her speech, that she listened to her subjects—and that they were, in one sense, her ultimate boss.

*   *   *

This book is published to mark the Golden Jubilee of Queen Elizabeth II—the fiftieth anniversary of her accession to the British throne in February 1952. It seeks to tell her story while also trying to explain the nature of her monarchy, a stirring and irrational symphony of emotion between the national figurehead and her people, which enchants its many believers, and mystifies those who are tone-deaf to its music.

This private and straightforward woman is celebrating fifty years in one of the world's most public and paradoxical jobs. The British crown long ago lost the political powers it once commanded, but in their place Elizabeth II commands a potent role in the emotional life of her country—and of the wider world. Thanks to the embrace of the mass media, the personalities of the House of Windsor occupy prominent armchairs in that corner of our consciousness inhabited by presidents, film stars, television show hosts and all the variegated heroes, fraudsters and villains of the celebrity culture. We 'know' them all. The family's marriages, births, divorces and, in the dramatic case of Diana, death, have stimulated some of the late twentieth century's most intense global experiences of communal joy and sadness.

This process developed its momentum more

than a century and a half ago in the reign of Queen Victoria, whose fascinating venerability Queen Elizabeth II is now approaching. From the sylph-like slenderness of her youth, Elizabeth II moved into comfortably rounded middle age, and at seventy-five the royal silhouette is heading for the stocky authority of the first jubilee queen. With her own Golden Jubilee of 2002, the Queen's parallels with Victoria become ever more intriguing. 'Lilibet' was born in Queen Victoria's shadow, and the grand and gaudy business of royal celebrity at which she has worked so dutifully all her life first took shape around her formidable great-great-grandmother.

Part 1

'To live in the hearts of my people'

CHAPTER ONE

The First Queen of Hearts

God bless our Queen,
Not Queen alone, but Mother, Queen and
    Friend.

Jubilee salutation to Queen Victoria
22 June 1887

On 29 May 1842 the young Queen Victoria was returning to Buckingham Palace after an afternoon's carriage ride with her husband Prince Albert, when a shortish man stepped from the crowd and took aim with a pistol.

'I heard the trigger snap,' Albert later related, 'but it must have missed fire.'

The police failed to arrest anyone—even to notice the incident. The rangy and athletic Albert, a few months younger than his wife, who had just celebrated her twenty-third birthday, dashed up to the Palace balcony to see if he could spy the culprit. Seeing nothing suspicious, he wondered if he had imagined the whole incident. So next day, with a courage verging on foolhardiness, the royal couple decided to flush out the would-be assassin and set off again in their carriage along the same route. Sure enough, their assailant, John Francis, a 22-year-old Londoner, made a second attempt. Standing at almost exactly the same spot beneath the trees at the entry to Green Park, he managed to let off his pistol—and this time a policeman caught him. It turned out that Francis, a compulsive but ineffectual young man, had omitted to put any shot in his barrel.

The nation's relief was reflected in a flood of loyal addresses and press coverage couched in language of high emotion. 'Let us . . . swell the torrent of loyal and exhilarating congratulation,' exhorted the *Illustrated London News*. This pioneer of the modern picture magazine portrayed the young Queen as a romantic heroine who was the 'embodiment of the people's affections', the central focus of 'the love of her people' and the main source of happiness of 'the beating bosom of the land'.

Victoria responded with equally explicit sentiment.

'My first desire,' she declared in her reply to the University of Oxford, one of the several hundred organisations that composed loyal addresses on her deliverance, 'is to live in the hearts of my people.'

*   *   *

Sentiment was the new ingredient that Queen Victoria brought to the British monarchy. Britain had felt little affection for her immediate predecessors, her degenerate old uncles George IV and William IV. But her 63-year reign, from 1837 to 1901, saw the developing of the pattern with which we are familiar today—a royal figurehead whose significance does not reside in the relatively small role they play in the practical running of the country, but in their ability to inspire communal affection and love.

Love is a profitable commodity, and it proved

irresistible to the popular press of the nineteenth century. Aged only eighteen when she came to the throne, Victoria visibly symbolised a fresh start, and her marriage three years later to the handsome Prince Albert of Saxe-Coburg-Gotha increased the popular mood of tenderness. The *Morning Post* portrayed the marriage romantically, with touches of the recently fashionable fairy-tales, as a love match to 'the young prince of her choice'.

Sentimentality took a wide hold. Words of courtly homage had always played with the sweet nothings of romance; now the treacly language of the charmed circle was appropriated and mass-produced for the growing number of middle-class and working-class readers. The steam-powered printing press and mechanically produced paper were creating a profitable new industry of popular communication through mass media that forged direct links between monarch and people. Everyone who could read could feel in contact with the attractive young Queen and her family, and thus become a new sort of courtier. You might be physically distant but you were made spiritually intimate, thanks to the power of print and the entitlement of love.

Pictures intensified the process. The *Illustrated London News* owed its recent creation to new steel engraving and electrotyping technology that also spawned the *Pictorial Times* (1843), the *Illustrated Times* (1855) and the *Penny Illustrated Paper* (1861). These black-and-white great-grandmas of *Hello!* and *People* magazines charmed large readerships with alluringly lifelike line drawings, which gave way, once the halftone process had been developed, to an innovation that significantly enhanced the sentiment—photography. The world's first photographic portrait studio opened in London in March 1841, and the following year Prince Albert sat for the first ever photographic royal portraits. By the late 1850s it was possible for the general public actually to possess their own commercially reproduced photograph of the Queen and enjoy the sense of closeness created by the accuracy of the image. Her Majesty could sit on your mantelpiece alongside the pictures of your nearest and dearest. You could almost imagine her one of the family.

Madame Tussaud started exhibiting British royal effigies in wax soon after her arrival in 1802 from Paris, where she had taken her models from the heads in the guillotine basket. In London she copied from paintings and engravings, buying up old coronation robes to add authenticity, and in the 1840s her Baker Street gallery unveiled its most ambitious display ever: 'The Royal Family at Home—Her Majesty and Prince Albert Sitting on a Magnificent Sofa Caressing their Lovely Children'. This multi-figure tableau was a three-dimensional version of the recently completed painting by Franz Xaver Winterhalter, which would previously have been seen only by those in the court circle. Thanks to Madame Tussaud's prototype Disneyland, the lush image could be ogled by tens of thousands in all its voluptuous domesticity: the loving husband and his doting wife, with a riot of children gambolling around that Magnificent Sofa. People who came to London on the expanding new railway network could go home and say that they had seen the Queen—and had even caught a glimpse of her home life. By the 1860s they could send home a postcard of Victoria as well.

The power of modern celebrity derives from graphic images that enter people's lives and minds, creating the illusion that we are in personal touch with the famous, that we 'know' them and are entitled to relate to them with personal feelings that can sometimes be intense. This fantasy erodes the traditional etiquette between the powerful and the powerless, and John Francis's abortive shooting of Queen Victoria in 1842 was a dramatic example of that breakdown. It was the second of at least seven attempts on Victoria's life in the course of her reign, all by young men displaying the fixated characteristics of the modern stalker. Most had strangely failed to pack any shot with their gunpowder, and one had even loaded his pistol with tobacco. Not until attempt number six, in 1872, did a young Irish Fenian appear. As a campaigner for Irish home rule, he might have been assumed to have some coherent political motivation, but he too turned out to be wielding a pistol that was unloaded, and was later diagnosed as 'weak-minded'.

Celebrity culture stimulates imaginings which both confuse and entice certain types of psychotics, and while Queen Victoria's generally incompetent assailants were roundly punished—one was deported to Australia where, in later life, he became a pioneer republican—they were perceived as half-wits in their own time. Following John Francis's two failed attempts in Green Park, the law of treason was actually changed in recognition that the death penalty was inappropriate for people whom we would today identify as psychologically unstable drifters, lost in the wage-slave

31

disconnections of the world's first industrialised society.

Queen Victoria's stalkers were both a reflection and a perversion of the new climate of sentimental royal coverage. The only previously recorded examples of fixated pursuit of a royal figure had involved her grandfather, King George III, following the detailed newspaper reporting of his mental troubles, which had helped turn him from a distant and aloof figure into an all-too-human being. Far from reducing his stature, the royal madness had actually increased national affection for the once unpopular monarch—in the same years that the French monarchy was being destroyed.

In the age of revolution, humanity was replacing divinity as the underpinning for royal figureheads—and the lost souls who misinterpreted and presumed on the new familiarity were heralds of the modern world. Surviving their blasts of tobacco and shot-less gunpowder, Queen Victoria herself became quite blasé about her trigger-happy fan club, and even derived some enjoyment from the popular outbursts of sympathy provoked by their attacks. 'It is worth being shot at,' she reflected in 1882, after the seventh failed attempt, 'to see how much one is loved.'

*   *   *

The young Victoria's wish 'to live in the hearts of my people' was not accompanied by a wish to get very close to them. When the royal yacht dropped her in Edinburgh in September 1842 an hour or so earlier than scheduled, the Queen and her party took advantage of the empty streets to ride straight to their destination in Dalkeith Palace outside the city, not bothering to wait for a planned procession. When the Lord Provost, city fathers, bands, cannon-firers and loyal citizenry turned out later that morning as arranged, they discovered there was no one to cheer. It was only after they enlisted the help of the Prime Minister Sir Robert Peel, who was of the royal party, that Victoria grudgingly agreed to alter her timetable and process through the streets two days later. There were limits to being the people's monarch.

The civic authorities of the west country encountered a similar problem when the royal yacht cruised down the Channel coast the following summer. Mindful of the Edinburgh fiasco, the ports of Weymouth, Falmouth, Penryn and Truro kept anxious watch on the royal progress. Whenever Her Majesty hove to offshore, the mayors had themselves rowed out, three miles in one case, complete with mace-bearers and chains of office, to struggle up the side of the ship and find out 'if it was the Royal pleasure to land'. In each case the answer was 'No.'

Nor did media friendliness come naturally to Victoria. When 'one of that ubiquitous genus, the London reporter' was discovered sneaking round Osborne House, the royal retreat on the Isle of Wight, in the 1840s, he was handed over to the oarsmen of the royal barge. They transported him across Portsmouth Harbour in an open boat in freezing conditions, then rowed him five miles upriver before finally dropping him in the mud.

The Queen's reluctance to become public property stemmed from an autocratic and blue-blooded enjoyment of her royal status, coupled with a paradoxical shyness and lack of self-confidence. No one realised how much she had come to rely on the support of her energetic husband until Albert's death of typhoid, aged only forty-two. 'Day turned into night,' lamented the Queen in an inscription that she wrote beneath a photograph showing her, with her daughters, contemplating a bust of her beloved Albert. She withdrew into a seclusion that lasted, in some senses, for the rest of her life.

Despite her feelings of loss, Victoria kept working zealously at her official paperwork, reading and initialling the government documents that came to her in red, leather-bound despatch boxes. But the outside world did not see this, and as the Queen avoided public appearances, discontent grew. 'These commanding premises to be let or sold,' read a large poster affixed to the railings of Buckingham Palace in March 1864, 'in consequence of the late occupant's declining business.'

'The Queen,' commented Walter Bagehot, editor of *The Economist* from 1860 to 1877, 'has done almost as much injury to the popularity of the monarchy by her long retirement from public life as the most unworthy of her predecessors did by his profligacy and frivolity.' A shrewd and sceptical journalist, Bagehot noted how the vanished executive powers of the crown had come to be replaced by a sort of magic—'that which is brilliant to the eye; that which is seen vividly for a moment, and then is seen no more; that which is hidden and unhidden.' He defined this as the 'dignified' part of government, existing to generate social reverence and loyalty, while the 'efficient' parts—the Prime Minister, Cabinet and Parliament—got on with running the country.

This insight formed the theme of Bagehot's book on *The English Constitution*, written in the mid-1860s as Victoria's popularity was spiralling downwards through her failure to fulfil the 'dignified' side of her duties. Bagehot was not impressed by the monarch's self-pitying seclusion. He introduced his chapter on the monarchy with a scathing reference to 'the actions of a retired widow and an unemployed youth'—a less than sentimental description of the Queen's eldest son, the dissolute Albert Edward, Prince of Wales, who was already an object of gossip and scandal.

The radical press of these years had a field day. Papers like the *Republican*, *Reynolds's Newspaper* and the *National Reformer* couched their attacks on the Queen in anything but the language of love. Thriving on cheap wood-pulp newsprint and the removal of stamp duty on newspapers, they deployed the sturdy, libertarian vocabulary of the country that, two centuries earlier, had cut off its king's head and operated without a monarchy from 1649 to 1660.

A particular target was Victoria's fondness for vanishing to Balmoral, the turreted Scottish retreat she had created with her beloved Albert. September 1997's drama of a monarch taking refuge in the Highlands while the newspapers demanded her return to London, had its precedent in the 1860s—though in Victoria's case the criticism was sharpened by the Queen's closeness to her dour Scottish retainer, John Brown, whose plain-speaking manner had endeared him to her late husband. 'Balmoral, Tuesday—Mr John Brown walked on the Slopes,' ran *Punch*'s spoof version of the Court Circular in July 1866. 'He subsequently partook of a haggis. In the evening, Mr John Brown was pleased to listen to a bagpipe.' Defamatory pamphlets referred to the Queen as 'Mrs Brown', and as Victoria's uncle, King Leopold of the Belgians, received news of the swelling tide of disrespect, he tried to coax his niece back to public life. 'The English are very personal,' he wrote. 'To continue to love people, they must see them.'

The journalistic Robert Cecil, who as Marquess of Salisbury was later to serve as Victoria's Prime Minister, saw how the curiosity and power of the new mass media had actually removed from royal people the right to privacy that their subjects enjoyed. 'Seclusion', he wrote in the *Saturday Review*, 'is one of the few luxuries in which Royal Personages may not indulge. The power which is derived from affection or from Loyalty, needs a life of almost unintermitted publicity to sustain it.'

In 1871 Charles Bradlaugh, the free-thinking proprietor of the *National Reformer*, toured the country filling lecture halls with scathingly anti-monarchical satire, and on 6 November that year Charles Dilke, a Liberal MP who was tipped for government office, roused cheers in Newcastle for his denunciation of the 'waste, corruption and inefficiency' of the monarchy.

Three days later the Prime Minister himself, William Gladstone, appeared to place his considerable prestige behind Dilke. The worthy and ponderous Liberal leader used the platform of the Lord Mayor's Banquet in London pointedly to defend the right of any Englishman to speak out 'without any limit at all' on matters relating to 'the institutions under which we live'. This was the 'democratic' type of utterance that had already made Gladstone Victoria's least favourite Prime Minister.

But within a few months it was Gladstone's populist instincts that were to bury republicanism in Britain for a generation—while also locating the means by which Victoria and her descendants would be restored to the affections of the people.

*   *   *

In November 1871 Queen Victoria's 'unemployed' eldest son—'Bertie', the 30-year-old Prince of Wales—fell ill and nearly died. The future King Edward VII collapsed at Sandringham, his Norfolk country home, with typhoid fever. It was almost ten years to the day, 14 December, that his virtuous father had been carried off by the same disease, and as the royal family sped to Bertie's bedside, newspapers rushed out editions in a profitable nineteenth-century creation—the special royal supplement.

Just a few weeks earlier the press had carried reports of Sir Charles Dilke's attack on royal degeneracy. Now it wallowed in sugary descriptions of warm family reunion—though according to Victoria's sardonic private secretary, Henry Ponsonby, many of the party spent their time keeping a healthy distance from one another. The royal family sniffed suspiciously in corners for the foul odours that Victorians believed to be the cause of disease. The prince's doctors issued as many as five bulletins a day, and the nation came to a halt as crowds gathered outside the new electric telegraph offices waiting anxiously for the news, described in the memorably un-ironic lines attributed to Alfred Austin, later Poet Laureate:

Across the wires the electric message came:
'He is no better; he is much the same.'

Churches and chapels of all denominations filled for prayer vigils. As a nationwide ordeal experienced by people everywhere, through telegraphy and the newspapers, at the same time, and virtually as it was happening, the Prince of Wales's illness was Britain's first exposure to what we would call a media event. The joy when the portly reprobate pulled through against the odds was unconfined, and Victoria hoped that the national trauma might inspire some reformation in her fun-loving heir. Bertie's job now, she wrote, 'must be to become more and more valuable to the country who have shown him such love'.

The Queen was concerned with her son's behaviour; Gladstone was concerned with the country's. As a young man he had planned to take holy orders, until he calculated that he could propagate more virtue through politics. Much concerned with 'the principles which bind society together', he saw the state as a moral agent with a conscience. Since the nation had demonstrated its finer feelings by praying in its diverse ways for the welfare of the prince, he now proposed that the country should unite to praise God formally for sparing the young man.

Having raised the idea in Cabinet, the Prime

Minister met the Queen on 21 December 1871, to discuss a National Service of Thanksgiving. As Gladstone saw it, the grateful royal family would ride in state through London to St Paul's Cathedral, to kneel and give thanks, surrounded by several thousand of their subjects.

Victoria was horrified. Widowhood had intensified her dislike of displaying herself in public—though she eventually conceded that she might be prepared to consider a service if it were held in Westminster Abbey rather than St Paul's. She had been crowned in the Abbey, after all, and it was 'more convenient'—just down the road from the Palace and not requiring so long a drive.

Gladstone held out for the larger venue. 'There are in these times', he wrote in his diary account of what he said to the Queen, 'but few occasions on which great national acts of religion can be performed, and this appears to be one of them . . . Feeling has been wrought up to the highest point.' The emotional state of the country demanded royal communion. In the first recorded attempt by a British Prime Minister to define the role of a monarch whose powers were more psychic than political, he pointed out that the character and duties of the crown 'had greatly changed among us in modern times'. This was dangerous territory, since Victoria retained a staunch belief in the monarchy's old-fashioned political powers. But perhaps, argued Gladstone, 'in the new forms they were not less important than in the old'.

Her Majesty was pleased to give way. On 6 February 1872 an announcement from the office of Viscount Sydney, the Lord Chamberlain, outlined the plans for a huge thanksgiving service at St

Paul's in three weeks' time. A congregation of between seven and eight thousand was envisaged, ranging from peers, peeresses and Members of Parliament, via local sheriffs and Lords Lieutenant, to members of the armed services, the Bar, the Civil Service 'and other bodies and persons selected to represent the nation'. Sydney had already allocated the bulk of seats in the cathedral on the basis of his own view of who or what was 'National and Representative'. But, taking his cue from the astonishingly widespread popular response to the prince's near-death experience, he now invited applications from the general public.

That very day the Friendly Society of Ironfounders, established in 1809 and the country's oldest national labour grouping, sent in its application. 'It would be a gracious act on the part of the Authorities', wrote the executive committee, 'to present Tickets to 5 or 6 Bona Vida [sic] Working Men's representatives. It would go a great way in breaking down prejudice . . . and would help to Cement that good feeling which ought to exist between the governing Classes and the people.'

George Potter, a radical publisher and founding member of the three-year-old Trades Union Congress, wrote in the same post on the elaborately embossed notepaper of *The Bee-Hive*, *The People's Paper*, Established 1861. Potter requested tickets 'in a position that will enable me to witness the ceremony and report upon it for our working class newspaper'.

It was less than a year since trades unions had been accorded legal status, and Potter was a champion of labour. But he saw the constitutional monarchy as an ally in the people's cause. 'As a matter of fact,' he wrote in *The Bee-Hive* in 1870, drawing from an old strand in British radical thought, 'our Government at the present time is in reality, though not in name, a republic, with an hereditary President.'

The Lord Chamberlain took the trouble quietly to check that these socialist applicants were as *bona fide* as they claimed, contacting Edward Levy, the proprietor of the *Daily Telegraph*. But once Levy, a well-connected printer, had confirmed that Potter and the other applicants were 'perfectly safe', Potter and Robert Applegarth, another labour leader who was one of the Ironfounders' nominees, found themselves called in for meetings with the Comptroller of the Lord Chamberlain's office. Half a dozen tickets? The Lord Chamberlain had decided that the Working Men should have a full hundred. And so the guest list of peers and peeresses in the files of the Lord Chamberlain's office was augmented by eighteen handwritten pages of working men's names and addresses: J. Newell, ironfounder of Bermondsey; M. Morton, painter of Pimlico; J. Leicester, glassmaker of Lambeth—shoemakers, bookbinders, bricklayers, a sailor. Those who were married also received tickets for their wives.

The working men were selected from the ranks of the loyal and pro-monarchist—it was made clear that overtly republican radicals would not be welcome—and it was decided to scatter them in pockets throughout the cathedral, with their exact positions noted on the roll-call of guests; the Lord Chamberlain was taking no chances in this first ever injection of ordinary people into the inner sanctum of a royal and state occasion.

The newspapers began to take an interest in precisely who was receiving the coveted invitations, and as the days went by, the make-up of the congregation became ever more democratic. Invitations went out to the St Paul's gas fitter, to the cathedral organ builder, and to no fewer than 277 shopkeepers representing the principal trading streets of London. The original seating plan for a congregation of up to eight thousand had been based on an allowance of 24 inches per backside on the benches of St Paul's. But then it was discovered that more than thirteen thousand mourners had been squeezed in for the funeral of the Duke of Wellington in 1852 on the basis of just 18 inches per derrière. Democracy clearly meant cosiness. On the great day itself, 12,558 crowded into the cathedral, while hundreds of thousands lined the streets in an unsurpassed display of enthusiasm. The new railway 'excursion' tickets brought in throngs to rival those who had attended the coronation of 1837, and they equalled the ardour of that occasion in their cheers for the Queen and her still sickly-looking son.

'The deafening cheers never ceased the whole way, and the most wonderful order was preserved,' wrote the Queen. 'We seemed to be passing through a sea of people as we went along the Mall.'

*　　　*　　　*

Despite her wish to avoid fuss and show, Queen Victoria had found herself presented with a majestically powerful, old-fashioned way to marshal the loyalties of a new-fangled society— street theatre and the pageantry of affection.

Public ceremony gave solid form to the royal cult of sentiment fostered by the press. Britons clearly derived deep satisfaction from crowding together and cheering their heads off, and a royal person provided the ideal focus for that—with sublime disregard for the yawning gap between the scale of the rejoicing and the stature of the idle young man whose recovery was being celebrated.

Radicals sneered at the 'gush' of royal pageantry. Monarchy, sniffed *Reynolds's Newspaper*, was 'more adapted to a barbarous than a civilised state'. Uneasy with emotional display, the intellectuals' complaint was of bread and circuses—manipulation from above by a superior elite. Yet it was pressure from below that got working men and their wives inside the cathedral. In all its emotional excess, the national upsurge of sympathy was an essentially human reaction to the image of the country's mother figure at the sickbed of her son. The St Paul's service—which was replicated by thanksgiving services all over the country—demonstrated the banal but profound truth of human behaviour, that people love having someone to love.

Like love itself, the relationship between crown and people is fundamentally irrational. It is a matter of faith, its parades, waves and cheers expressing the conviction that mutual affection exists at the core of the social process. In that moment of excitement and in its enduring memory, rational calculation and self-interest take second place to emotion.

The great Thanksgiving of February 1872 also yielded some very practical results. When Charles Dilke rose in the Commons the following month to call for an inquiry into the royal finances, he was defeated by 276 votes to 2. Thanks to the electric telegraph, special supplements and Mr Gladstone's belief in 'great national acts of religion', serious talk of a republic in Britain was laid to rest for nearly fifty years.

CHAPTER TWO

Jubilee

Lord help our precious queen,
Noble, but rather mean.

Golden Jubilee salute,
Sydney Bulletin, 19 June 1887

Jubilees were originally Jewish festivals. The book of Leviticus, chapter 25, contains the details. Held every forty-nine years in Old Testament times, the Jewish jubilee was a year-long religious celebration, the *Jobel*, taking its name from the ram's-horn trumpet that ushered it in. Slaves were freed, sins were forgiven, faith was renewed. The Catholic Church took up the concept in the middle ages, and to this day a visit to Rome in a jubilee year (most recently 2000) can earn you remission of sins.

In Britain the idea of a royal jubilee took off at the beginning of the nineteenth century as the troubled King George III approached his fiftieth year on the throne, and it was principally promoted by the newly mechanised and rapidly multiplying regional press. There is no record of central government inspiring or organising any jubilee events, and it certainly provided no finance. Stealing and reprinting each other's stories, and encouraging their readerships to compete with the civic display planned in other towns, the newspapers managed to prompt celebrations in more than 650 communities on 25 October 1809, the start of the fiftieth year of the old King's reign.

George III himself was poignantly absent from Britain's first ever royal jubilee—blind, almost senile, and in the care of his doctors at Windsor. But that did not stop the nation giving itself a party which, like the 1872 Service of Thanksgiving for Prince Albert Edward, was extravagantly out of keeping with the current achievements of the individual celebrated. Oxen were roasted and plum puddings consumed. Prayers were offered up in church, and there was much charitable largesse, with legs of mutton and flagons of cider being distributed wholesale to the poor.

'All was harmony, gentleness and joy,' according to an account of the 1809 festivities in the village of Highgate in Middlesex, where the band of the local volunteers played those great eighteenth-century hits 'Rule Britannia' and 'God Save the King'—the latter just becoming known as the national 'anthem'.

*   *   *

Seventy years later you could almost hear the trumpets being tuned for another national party as the prospect of Victoria celebrating her jubilee drew near. Letters had started appearing in The

45

Times as early as 1885, drawing attention to the forthcoming fiftieth anniversary of the Queen's mounting the throne, and once again the festival was media-led, since, as in 1809, the government declined to get involved.

'It has been decided,' wrote Lord Granville, the Liberal leader in the Lords, responding to an enquiry in March 1886, 'the government had better not take any initiative.'

But the volume of press coverage mounted, and on 20 June 1886, the forty-ninth anniversary of Victoria's accession, loyal editorials looked forward to the big commemoration that lay twelve months ahead. Proposals ranged from the erection of stone cairns on mountaintops to grand military parades.

Up at Balmoral, Queen Victoria was scanning these reports with some pleasure, and she clipped two articles that she particularly enjoyed to send to her daughter Vicky in Germany.

'I don't like flattery,' she wrote, 'but I am pleased to see loyalty and *Anerkennung* [appreciation].'

That summer's general election yielded a new Prime Minister, the Marquess of Salisbury, but his Conservative government was no keener than its Liberal predecessor on the complications of a royal celebration—or the likely cost. So the Queen conferred with Sir Henry Ponsonby, her private secretary. If she had to open the Privy Purse, she would mark the occasion in her own way, with a relatively short, intimate and convenient service in Westminster Abbey, as she would have preferred back in 1872.

The Abbey was much smaller than St Paul's, with room for only 2,200. But the seat allocation reflected the growing importance of both the people and the press. When George Potter, recently elected president of the London Working Men's Association, wrote in for seats, he and other union representatives were allocated eighty-four tickets—five times, proportionately, the size of their 1872 allocation, and in a prime position. No longer scattered around the congregation, the working men were assigned seats together in the West Upper Gallery, immediately above the seats reserved for luminaries from the Foreign, Colonial and Cabinet Offices and the royal family's personal guests.

The newspapers also did better, as befitted their role in whipping up the nation's enthusiasm. Ninety seats were assigned to reporters and illustrators, proportionately four times the 1872 allowance, and the assembled hacks were all grouped together in the north transept near the peers and MPs in an area described as the 'Press Gallery'—the first known reference to such an official facility at a royal occasion.

*　　　*　　　*

Queen Victoria's Jubilee provided a peg on which the media seized eagerly to look back and weigh up national progress over the previous half-century— with an emphasis on moral advance. 'Slavery has been abolished. A criminal code which disgraced the statute book has been effectually reformed,' wrote Gladstone in the January 1887 issue of *Nineteenth Century* magazine.

A flood of self-congratulatory books and supplements catalogued the improvements in technology and the conditions of life, from railways and postage stamps to the reform of the labour laws and the ending of duelling. Reviewing one such volume, *Fifty Years of a Good Queen's Reign*, an anonymous critic in the *Pall Mall Gazette* expressed his astonishment at the 'superstitious loyalty' which placed the monarchy at the centre of all these developments. 'Were a gust of wind to blow off our Sovereign's head-gear tomorrow,' he observed scathingly, ' "the Queen's bonnet" would crowd Bulgaria out of the papers.'

The unnamed sceptic was the aspiring young socialist playwright George Bernard Shaw—Irish, republican and atheist. He ridiculed the media's tendency to create news as much as report it, but he still felt compelled to pay tribute to the widespread emotional impulse that was 'the real support of thrones'.

A. M. Ferguson, a colonial official who had devoted his life to Ceylon, argued more loyally. Ferguson had come out to the colony as a young district officer in 1837, the year of Her Majesty's accession. If anyone had then predicted, he recalled in a speech in 1887, that a member of the local native community would be sitting on the bench of the Supreme Court fifty years later, he would have been certified insane. But here, in Jubilee year, Ceylon now had its own Sinhalese Chief Justice. Proud of the world's first empire to be created by a democracy which had not been afraid to pass on its own enlightened values, Ferguson felt that the virtues of British rule had received inspiration from the humane character of the empire's female figurehead.

At home, Victoria's womanhood made the

Queen a heroine to many of her sex, and particularly to the temperance societies. These were precursors of the women's liberation movements of the following century in their attempts to wrest female safety and power over the family income from drunken, violent husbands; at a temperance rally in the Waterloo Road in May 1887 men were banished to the gallery. Jubilee medals and rosettes were distributed and a resolution was passed unanimously praising the Queen's interest in 'the increased dignity of women's position and women's work'.

In a nationally organised collection, all women were invited to make a contribution, from one pound to one penny, and vast numbers contributed. Most of the money went to fund an order of nurses. Less in accordance with modern ideas—though thoroughly in harmony with Victoria's—the balance of the subscription was spent on a handsome statue of the Queen's late husband.

Committees multiplied as people banded together to arrange their local celebrations for 21 June, Jubilee day. Municipalities, schools, churches and communities all over the empire planned parades, firework treats for the children and charity for the poor. In the provinces and the colonies the emphasis was on solid utility—'a more permanent memorial than that of mere holidaymaking', as the Maharajah of Oodeypora (Udaipura) put it in dedicating a new library and reading room in the Queen's name. A proliferation of drinking troughs reflected the Queen's well-known love of animals. In Jamaica, a Queen Victoria Lying-in Hospital was inaugurated to benefit 'women of the poorer classes'.

Pleading age and tiredness, the Queen decided that Bertie could represent her at many Jubilee events. But she did find time to visit the People's Palace, a working men's college in the East End of London (today part of Queen Mary College), and was ill-rewarded for her pains. The celebration was 'damped' by what she described to Lord Salisbury as 'a horrid noise'; she had never heard the sound before, but she understood that it was known as 'booing'. 'A few Socialists' was the explanation—along with 'the worst Irish'.

It was as bad as sentiment in Australia, where a meeting of Sydney citizens voted that Jubilee celebrations would be 'unwise and calculated to injure the democratic spirit of the country'. Australia's already well-organised republicans had contrived to pack the first meeting convened by the mayor, so a second gathering was convened at which he marshalled the forces of loyalism to get the vote he wanted. As geographically removed as it was possible to be from the magic of monarchy, Australians were destined to operate on the cutting edge of royal agnosticism.

*   *   *

By 21 June 1887, Europe's heads of state had flocked to London, filling the city with an unprecedented concentration of kings, queens and grand dukes—and creating a problem with lodgings. Buckingham Palace and Windsor Castle were filled to overflowing with royal guests, and the Queen turned to her aristocracy. Many had space to accommodate a whole royal entourage, with all its gradations of attendant personnel from chamberlains and vice-chamberlains down to valets and dressers. Across Green Park, Earl Spencer volunteered to fit in two—an unusual gesture from a family of mavericks, unkindly noted over the generations for their unhelpfulness and troublemaking.

On the day itself, the visiting royalties in flowing plumes and medals paved the way for Victoria as she rode to the Abbey in an open carriage. 'The crowds from the palace gates up to the Abbey, were enormous,' she recorded later, 'and there was such an extraordinary burst of enthusiasm, as I had hardly ever seen in London before.'

The next day, thirty thousand schoolchildren gathered in Hyde Park to salute their sovereign and receive a bun and a cup with the faces of the young and old Victoria on either side. Commissioned from Royal Doulton, the cup was in better taste than many of the souvenirs on sale in the Strand, where one could purchase Jubilee teapots, a Jubilee walking stick with the Queen's head as the knob, and a Jubilee bustle that played the national anthem as the wearer sat down upon it. No doubt about it, these were objects of vulgarity—but the word vulgar comes from *vulgus*, Latin for 'the common people'. As a mass-market phenomenon, Queen Victoria's Golden Jubilee demonstrated the growing potency of popular culture as an alternative to the conventional mechanisms of political and social power. It created a bypass around old protocols, confronting the establishment with a raucous and increasingly influential lowbrow rival which would, in due course, obliterate many of the traditions that seemed set for ever in 1887.

Queen Victoria had no hang-ups about her own

sometimes lowbrow tastes. Whenever Buffalo Bill Cody came to England, she tried to attend his Wild West Show, going to Earls Court to watch him a few days before the Golden Jubilee. The Deadwood Stage Coach had careered around the arena filled with four of the monarchs (of Saxony, Denmark, Belgium and Greece) who were in town for the celebrations. The middle-aged Prince of Wales rode shotgun and at a subsequent performance allowed himself to be captured by the Indians, so that Buffalo Bill had to rescue him.

Republicans were not too superior to enter into the spirit of the folk-fest. William Michael Rossetti, who had written a sonnet in praise of regicide, took his young son strolling through the lights and throngs in Oxford Street and Regent Street, where huge arches had been constructed reading 'Victoria—All Nations Salute You'. Father and son did not get home until ten-thirty.

Out on the polyglot island of Zanzibar in East Africa, a missionary called Harriet Smith described the thrill of wandering through the night-time streets hung across with fruit and arches, while different races and religions mingled contentedly beneath the warm moon in shared enjoyment of the occasion. Trying to put into words the epiphany she experienced, the missionary realised for the first time that the colony's Hindus lived under the same Queen as she did.

'I quite loved them for it,' she wrote home, describing how she had gone to bed feeling happy and had woken up in the same mood. 'It seemed as if Zanzibar never could go back to what it was.'

Historians might dispute Harriet's euphoric view of Zanzibar's future. But the sentiments of the uplifted and humanised missionary were close enough to those of people all over the world who got home on Jubilee night 1887 with a happy grin on their faces.

*   *   *

The following decade saw the launch in 1896 of Alfred Harmsworth's *Daily Mail*, Britain's first truly popular newspaper—written 'by office boys, for office boys', in the disdainful opinion of Lord Salisbury. With its blend of pictures, snappy stories and jingoism, the *Mail* had a keen nose for anniversaries, and in the September of its first year the paper noticed that the 77-year-old Queen Victoria was about to pass George III's record of fifty-nine years, three months and four days on the throne to become the longest-reigning sovereign in English history. Letters poured into Buckingham Palace to suggest how the landmark might be celebrated.

Victoria, as ever, was 'not personally desirous of any festivities', wrote Lord Pembroke, her Lord Steward, to the Treasury. 'They are going to take place solely because the nation evidently expects them.' She wanted no fuss until she had completed her full sixty years in June 1897, and this time the government would have to pay for everything.

Lord Salisbury, in his third term as Prime Minister, was happy to comply. After the massive success of the 1887 jubilee, he could see the usefulness of another blockbuster occasion, particularly one that highlighted the empire and Britain's military potency.

The question was, what should the celebration

be called? 'Jubilee', pointed out the Home Secretary, Sir Matthew Ridley, 'came from "the old Jewish law"', and the term was 'inseparably connected with a notion of 50 years'.

'The Queen's Year' and 'Jubilificence' were suggested as alternatives, but Ridley had to admit that the latter, at least, would certainly not catch on. It seems to have been Victoria herself who borrowed a wedding anniversary concept popularised by greetings card manufacturers to come up with a new hybrid: 'Diamond Jubilee'. Asked to vet and approve the official account of the occasion after the event, the Queen altered the draft text to make sure that history gave her full personal credit for this invention. Thus a term of deep religious significance to Jews and Catholics— both still suspect minorities in Victorian Britain— found itself hijacked by Victoria herself for the raffish circus of British royal spectacle.

Spectacle was the guiding theme in the preparations for the Diamond Jubilee. A key figure in the planning was the elegant and theatrical Reginald Brett, later Viscount Esher, a bisexual who revelled in the classical homo-eroticism beloved of late Victorian empire builders. Both a courtier and a government official—he was secretary of the Office of Works—Esher worked in the great tradition of the stylishly camp impresarios who have helped give the monarchy its ceremonial flourish. His choreography of the Queen's London procession, the main public event of the Jubilee calendar, had a distinctly stagey character, with urgings to consider the 'scenic point of view' and insistence on the deployment of splendid and inspiring uniforms. With his gay sensibility, Esher understood that style is more than just a surface matter and can convey messages of the deepest identity.

The problem was the fragility of the almost immobile and elderly Queen. Victoria consented to be driven through the streets, but she adamantly refused to descend publicly from her carriage. Plans to hoist her into St Paul's with a hydraulic lift, or for sailors to pull her carriage up the steps, were rejected. In the end it was decided she would halt outside the cathedral and sit in her carriage while priests, choir and dignitaries gathered outside on the steps to sing a *Te Deum* and pray with her in a brief ceremony.

This essentially religious clustering would have no room for working-class representatives, but, taking up a suggestion from the Bishop of Southwark, Esher and his committee came up with a better solution. Instead of returning to Buckingham Palace by the usual ceremonial route, it was decided that the Queen would break with precedent by crossing London Bridge to process south of the river through the working-class districts of Southwark, the Elephant and Castle, and Kennington, before heading back up to Westminster.

Victoria needed no persuading. Her only anxiety arose when news of the surprise southerly route prompted landlords to evict their low-income tenants from well-located rooms, with an eye to packing in fee-paying spectators on the day. 'The Queen is anxious to know', wrote the Home Secretary, 'that everything is being done to prevent accidents from the insecurity of the roofs & parapets of the poorer houses along the Royal

Jubilee Route.'

By now the details of royal ceremonial were taking on a professional character. A palace groom was sent out to plod around the course twice at a deliberate pace, so it could be calculated that Victoria would have to spend precisely two hours and twelve minutes in her carriage.

'Is this too long for the Queen?' her private secretary was asked.

In her seventy-ninth year, the mother of nine, grandmother of thirty-eight and great-grandmother to thirty-one, let it be known that she could cope.

*   *   *

The Diamond Jubilee was a worldwide event. The ticket touts were waiting for the visitors as they came through Port Said. An American who sniffed the freshly sawn green pine from the countless stands being built in the streets thought he must be walking through a California gold rush mining camp. It was the grandest celebration the world had seen since the days of ancient Rome, and with one and a half million visitors expected, it was almost certainly bigger than anything the Caesars had contemplated.

As she rode out of Buckingham Palace on the great day, the Queen paused and leant out of her carriage to press a button. Through the miracles of the electric telegraph, a message of Jubilee greeting was sent to every corner of her empire, and within sixteen minutes the first answer—from Ottawa in Canada—came clicking back. The procession of sailors, military bands, clattering horses and colourfully garbed fighting men from every corner of the world was forty-five minutes long. The empire literally passed by.

The bells of St Paul's fell silent as the Queen's carriage drew up before the steps of the cathedral, where the assembled clerics, choir and dignitaries prayed and sang lustily on what was, fortunately, a day of royally clement weather. As the brief service ended, the plan had been for the Queen's carriage to move off during the final hymn.

'But the other carriages waited,' recalled the Bishop of London, 'and when the hymn was over there was a pause of intolerable silence. The Archbishop of Canterbury, with splendid audacity and disregard of decorum, interpreted what was in everyone's mind, and cried out "Three cheers for the Queen!"

'Never were cheers given with such startling unanimity and precision. All the horses threw up their heads at the same moment, and gave a little quiver of surprise. When the cheers were over, the band and chorus, by an irresistible impulse, burst into "God Save the Queen".'

Scarcely was the Queen round the corner when 'one of the choir boys, unable to restrain himself any longer, dashed from his place, leapt down the steps and filled his pockets with the gravel on which the wheels of the carriage had rested.'

As the boy sought to grasp and preserve the fleeting magic of the royal moment, engineers of the recently invented cinematograph process were, for the first time, doing precisely that. More than twenty rival newsreel companies set up camera positions along the ceremonial route. Pondering the challenge of capturing the moving procession, they came up with a swivel device so the camera could swing on top of what had hitherto been the immovably fixed tripod. Thus the cinema's staple panning shot owed its origin to Queen Victoria.

London had only one purpose-built cinema in 1897, but newsreels were becoming big business. They were projected in 'bioscope' tents in fairgrounds and most frequently in music halls, usually in the first ten minutes after the interval. One enterprising Bradford firm hired a special railway carriage to process its film on the journey back from London, so the citizens of Bradford could watch moving pictures of the royal procession on the very evening of the event. To judge from the frequency with which the Jubilee featured on variety programme bills, just about everyone who went to a music hall in 1897 had watched the procession on film by the end of the year—though the newsreel, of course, had no sound track. So most people saw and happily celebrated the solemn ceremony to the tinkling of a vaudeville piano in an atmosphere of beer, sawdust and Woodbines.

*   *   *

The Diamond Jubilee cemented Queen Victoria's position as the first modern international celebrity. The invention of the postage stamp early in her reign had transported her image almost everywhere, and by the 1890s the rotogravure press was ensuring that her plump, partridge-like features were known to people all over the globe with an intimacy never imparted by coins or statues. When Mr Colman wished to boost sales of his mustard, he put Queen Victoria on the label.

Mr Cadbury did the same with his chocolate, Mr Lipton with his tea. Rules regulating the use of the royal likeness were not formalised until the next century, so the royal profile was broadcast as prolifically in the advertising pages as in the editorial. Thanks to placards and posters, the national icon featured on virtually every railway station and omnibus. With the possible exceptions of Jesus and Mary, no single person's image had been reproduced so many millions of times before.

There were indeed times when the cult of Victoria and her monarchy took on the characteristics of a religion. Ideas on evolution promulgated by Charles Darwin were ushering in the secular age. In 1882 Nietzsche had announced that God was dead. But His anointed representative in Britain was more hallowed than ever—and by the ordinary people. Queen Victoria was beatified with a new style of royal sainthood: canonisation by the masses. It was the way saints were made in ancient times, by grass-roots, communal acclaim, before the medieval church hierarchy got its hands on this potent method of mass manipulation.

The expanding and hugely profitable mass media were the key go-betweens in this process, and towards the end of the century Buckingham Palace negotiated the appointment of the first royal correspondent, George Morton Smith of the Press Association. But this genteel precursor of the modern royal rat pack coaxed few exclusives from the Queen. Smith had another job. He was registrar of births, deaths and marriages for the north London borough of Finchley and Friern Barnet, and his journalistic duties took up so little time that he also worked as an insurance agent on the side.

By the end of Victoria's reign the average Briton was richer than ever before, voting rights had been extended to virtually every adult male in local and national elections, while landmark Education Acts had made literacy available to all. But it was not the politicians who were glorified for these massive extensions to the power and potential of ordinary people. True to Bagehot's shrewd distinction between the 'dignified' and the 'efficient', the nation focused its affection on the human symbol, the little black-garbed widow of Windsor, while their hearts were stirred by traditional symbols like pipes and drums and the marching of red-coated soldiers.

Amid all this hyperbole, it was the poet of empire who voiced a reservation. Rudyard Kipling sensed the dark side of this self-regarding orgy of pride—for, if the monarch represents the people, there is a sense in which adulation of the monarchy is a form of self-congratulation. Invited to pen an ode for the Diamond Jubilee, he composed 'Recessional', a doom-laden work which foretold for Britain not glory but decline:

> *The tumult and the shouting dies –*
> *The captains and the kings depart . . .*
> *Far-called our navies melt away—*
> *On dune and headland sinks the fire . . .*
> *Lo, all our pomp of yesterday*
> *Is one with Nineveh and Tyre!*
>
> *Lord God of Hosts be with us yet*
> *Lest we forget—lest we forget!*

'Lest we forget' was the refrain to every verse, and it prompted a friend to question the poet's foreboding. Kipling responded that he saw war threatening the whole overblown superstructure, with Britain's only hope being the masses. 'It will', he said, 'be the common people—the third-class carriages—that'll save us.'

Arthur Ponsonby, the youngest son of Victoria's long-serving private secretary, maintained that the old Queen could not 'conceive the meaning of democracy'. But something in her sensed it. It was during Victoria's reign that the British monarchy made its crucial shift from resting on the summit of a social pyramid—Commons supporting Lords supporting the crown—to becoming a free-standing populist institution. Through street theatre and the burgeoning mass media, its appeal was being made directly to, and its survival depended ultimately on, the goodwill of the third-class carriages.

CHAPTER THREE

Performing Monarchy

What can you expect? Yours are amateurs and ours are professionals at this game.

> Sir Frederick Ponsonby, explaining to a French official why the French President and his wife had failed to match the style of King Edward VII and Queen Alexandra at a reception in 1907

King Edward VII—'Bertie', the former Prince Albert Edward—finally succeeded his mother, Queen Victoria, on 22 January 1901 at the age of fifty-nine, and one of his first tasks was to open a new parliament. Lord Salisbury's Tories had just fought the 'Khaki election' on their handling of the Boer War, and had been returned with a huge majority. The re-elected Prime Minister wrote out his government's proposed programme of legislation in the King's Speech, and sent it over in draft form to Buckingham Palace.

Queen Victoria had neglected this important, symbolic centrepiece to the ceremonial Opening of Parliament. For the last forty years of her reign she had delegated the reading of her speech to the Lord Chancellor. But Edward VII was planning to do more than just read the speech; he wanted to help shape its contents as well, and early in February 1901 he dictated a list of alterations which he sent off to Downing Street. 'Why was nothing proposed for the "Aged Poor" . . . so valuable a domestic reform?' he asked, among a number of queries and suggestions.

Lord Salisbury had deployed all his tact to humour Queen Victoria's belief that it was part of her job to influence government policy. But he decided to put the new monarch firmly in his place. It was customary for the sovereign to suggest word changes that would improve clarity or the public reading of the speech, but trying to shape policy was another matter. If the King was known to have interfered just once in the working of government, he wrote in a sharp note to Edward's private secretary Francis Knollys, 'it will amount to an admission that He regards interference as part of his duty.'

Aged seventy-one, the venerable statesman was about to retire, and he had no compunction in delivering a basic lesson in kingly limits to his monarch. 'If a popular Bill does not appear in the list of proposed measures,' he wrote, 'the question will be asked "Why did not the King insist upon its being mentioned?" If an unpopular Bill appears, the question will be asked "How came the King to allow such an announcement to appear in his speech?" In either case I see endless embarrassments for a constitutional monarch.'

Lord Salisbury could not have more clearly expounded the concept of the cipher sovereign. It has been said that if those old adversaries, George Washington and King George III, had come back to life in the twentieth century, Washington could have resumed his work as US President with little difficulty, while George III would have found the

63

role of king transformed beyond recognition. Edward VII fought hard to cling on to the monarch's old role in government policy, most notably in the area of foreign relations, where his visit to Paris in 1903 would pave the way for the Entente Cordiale. But he had scarcely prepared himself for the hard slog of being an executive ruler—nor had he been prepared for it. While allowing him to see state papers in her later years, Queen Victoria had been reluctant to let her playboy son get involved with weighty matters, relegating him to what she saw as fripperies like the stage management of her Jubilee ceremonies.

It was Bertie's, and Britain's, good fortune that ceremonies were, literally, right up his street, and this was to provide the historic theme of his reign. Through the combined disapproval of the old Queen and her last Prime Minister, Edward VII stumbled on a role that satisfied him personally— and sustained his position and that of his descendants. Monarchs who became involved in politics were to have little future in the twentieth century, but glorious ceremonial was to help lodge the British crown at the very centre of national life.

*　　　*　　　*

King Edward VII had a 'curious power of visualising a pageant', declared Lord Esher, the Diamond Jubilee impresario, and Esher became the new monarch's chief executive in a wide-ranging royal restyling that modern historians have labelled 'the invention of tradition'. After the old Queen's dowdy and black-garbed seclusion in the rural backwaters of her kingdom, it was her flamboyant son's ambition to bring the monarchy back in all its glory to the capital—and in particular to Buckingham Palace. Giving his mother's home at Osborne on the Isle of Wight to the nation as part of an accession gesture that included the opening of the former hunting preserve of Richmond Park to the public, the King called in the finest decorators to Buckingham Palace. Out went his mother's dark and heavy furnishings, and in came gold leaf, cut glass, Venetian mirrors, gigantic chandeliers, red velvet, baroque swirls, cherubs in profusion, and an imperial colour scheme of white, gold and crimson.

It was a look echoed in the Ritz Hotel going up just across Green Park, and also in the multitude of London theatres built and restored in these years. Spectacle was their keynote, thanks to the moving scenery and special effects made possible by the new power source, electricity. Along with their crimson velvet interiors and their glittering chandeliers and balustrades, their names made clear their palatial pretensions—Her Majesty's, the Prince of Wales, the Victoria Palace, the Queen's Theatre and two Theatre Royals. Until the opening of Buckingham Palace to the public in the 1990s, the best way of catching the flavour of being inside the Palace's state rooms was to visit the Ritz, or sweep down the staircase of one of London's plush and gilt turn-of-the-century theatres.

The whole of central London was becoming something of a stage set as architects like Aston Webb composed monumental, soaring white stone buildings in the style now known as 'Imperial London'. The new ministries in Whitehall; the crescents of the Aldwych, leading to Kingsway;

Canada House, South Africa House and the great palaces of the old dominions around Trafalgar Square—all these formed the perfect backdrop for the pageants of a modern Rome.

From the royal point of view, the crucial street improvement was provided by widening and extending the ceremonial avenue of the Mall into Trafalgar Square to create a direct link with Buckingham Palace. When Queen Victoria had ridden out from her palace, she had had to swing right at Spring Gardens, a nondescript group of buildings blocking the end of the Mall, to join up with Whitehall via the long, dark and narrow Horseguards' Arch. Edward VII's reign saw Spring Gardens demolished, to be replaced by Imperial London's most emblematic structure, a tall, curved, white-pillared building that symbolised Britain's maritime might, and was actually designed to have processions pass through the middle of it— Admiralty Arch.

At the opposite end of the Mall, creating a showy new landmark outside the gates of Buckingham Palace, rose a mini-mountain of masonry featuring a statue of Queen Victoria looking rather like Britannia. Built of 2,000 tons of white marble brought from Italy and 7 tons of bronze, the Victoria Memorial was financed entirely by public subscription and provided another vehicle for imperial symbolism. 'I conceived the idea of making a great base,' said its sculptor, Thomas Brock, 'placing upon it figures symbolising Peace, and Progress, Courage and Patriotism, Labour and other attributes of the British people.'

Edward himself took the closest personal

interest in the new semicircular plaza that remains the national amphitheatre of royal ceremonial to this day. Under the King's plan, it was essential that the 'pageant would have an imposing clear start from the Palace, and crowds of sight-seers would find space on the two sides of the Mall'.

The final touch was a face-lift for Buckingham Palace itself. In the late 1840s Queen Victoria had built a lumpish, workaday front to the palace. It looked like another of the new railway stations that were then shooting up in the capital. Something altogether more stirring was required, and Aston Webb came up with the solution with which we are familiar today. Completed in 1913, three years after Edward's death and just in time for the vast crowd gatherings that marked the outbreak of the First World War, Webb's stately embellishment of flat columns—with an enlarged and more prominent balcony in the middle—transformed Victoria's railway terminus into an uplifting physical focus for national feeling.

*   *   *

For Edward VII, being a king meant looking like a king. His portly figure seemed to swell visibly whenever he put on his regalia. 'He was never tired', wrote Wilfred Scawen Blunt, 'of putting on uniforms and taking them off, and receiving princes and ambassadors, and opening museums and hospitals, and attending cattle shows and military shows and shows of every kind.' The show in which his influence lives to this day is the State Opening of Parliament, which he restored, after the neglect of his mother's later years, to all its

Alice in Wonderland glory. Unable to shape the content of the King's Speech, he lavishly reshaped its setting, with heralds in ruffs and tabards, Gold Sticks walking backwards and Black Rod knocking on doors. He even had George III's elaborate Gold State Coach of 1762, every child's idea of the enchanted pumpkin that bore Cinderella to the ball, brought out of the mews. Restored and redesigned, the coach trundled him in splendour to Parliament.

A young visiting Australian was not impressed. 'It was all a beastly humbug,' wrote the 22-year-old Keith Murdoch, a would-be journalist from Melbourne who was in London on what proved an unsuccessful mission to get employment on Fleet Street. Returning to Australia, he had better luck building up a newspaper empire later inherited by his son Rupert.

Edward VII's coronation itself was something of an anticlimax, postponed for six weeks after the new King went down with appendicitis on the eve of the ceremony. By the time he got to the Abbey on 9 August 1902, most of the principal foreign guests had gone home. But it was still a lavish spectacle. Taking a personal interest in every detail from the minting of the ceremonial medals to the coachmen's new costumes, Edward choreographed a visual feast—and his crowning inspired another of his enduring memorials. Soon after his accession, Edward's ear had been caught by a recent musical composition, the first of Edward Elgar's 'Pomp and Circumstance' marches. Couldn't some words be set to the tune, the King suggested? The task was entrusted to the Eton tutor A. C. Benson, and the result was 'Land of

Hope and Glory', first performed in 1902 as part of Edward VII's *Coronation Ode*, and Britain's reserve national anthem ever since.

Given the effort Edward devoted to imparting swagger to his epoch, it was only appropriate that it should carry his name. In France, they called their high-style turn-of-the-century years the *Belle Epoque*. Across the Channel, Britain went Edwardian.

*   *   *

If being Victorian meant being solemn and sober, being Edwardian meant exactly the opposite. Over-eating, over-smoking, and indulging himself systematically from billiards to boudoir, Edward VII was, as J. B. Priestley put it, 'a typical Englishman—*with the lid off*'. The King was fantasy fulfilment, and the popularity he achieved in his comparatively short reign suggested he was doing what most of his subjects wished they could have done if they could have afforded it—and got away with it.

At just 5 feet 7 inches tall, Bertie weighed 16 stone (224 pounds) and had a stomach girth of forty-eight inches as a result of eating five meals a day. To a generous and multi-course breakfast, lunch and dinner he added a late-night supper and afternoon tea—a full-scale occasion when he liked to wash down his cake with a glass or so of claret. He smoked twenty cigarettes a day and around a dozen cigars, which provoked loud coughing fits and a uniquely royal 'No Smoking' order. Seeing the King light up after dinner one night, another guest got out his own cigar—to be asked by an equerry to refrain from smoking for the sake of His Majesty's health and bronchial comfort.

Social inequality loomed large in Edwardian politics. In the 1906 general election the recently formed Labour Party increased its parliamentary representation from two to twenty-nine (fifty-three including joint Lib–Lab MPs), and the Liberals secured a massive mandate for social reform. In 1909 their fiery Chancellor, David Lloyd George, introduced his 'People's Budget', designed to support state-funded provisions like school meals and old age pensions, as well as the arms race with Germany, with a whole series of new taxes on the rich. But while politics grew more polarised, the childlike gusto with which Edward VII enjoyed his privileges endeared him to both ends of the social scale—and possibly more to the lower than to the upper. Crowds cheered the achievements of his racehorses. As the King swaggered into the winner's enclosure he was Charles II in a top hat, the embodiment, like the beloved 'Merry Monarch', of the pleasure-based nature of monarchy. It was the Puritans who had cut off the head of King Charles I.

An ancient paradox of the British class system was the capacity of those at the very top to get on quite naturally with those at the bottom, and vice versa. They knew their place; it was the jostlers in the middle whose insecurities provoked trouble. Edward VII worked in this uncomplicated tradition of *noblesse oblige*. As Prince of Wales he had been an active member of the Royal Commission on the Housing of the Working Classes, disguising himself one day, like some medieval king dressed up as a woodcutter, to sample the squalor of tenement slums in Clerkenwell and St Pancras. He struck up a special friendship with Henry Broadhurst, a stonemason and the first working-class MP, who sat with him on the Royal Commission. Edward invited Broadhurst to Sandringham, where the working man was unable to dine with the family, since he did not own a dress coat.

'In order to meet the difficulties in the matter of dress,' recorded Broadhurst in his memoirs, 'dinner was served to me in my own room each night.' Broadhurst took this as a courtesy, not a snub, and he joined the prince on an excursion to the estate's not-for-profit village pub, where the two men drank beer together and chatted with the locals. 'I left Sandringham,' he wrote, 'with a feeling of one who has spent a weekend with someone of his own rank in society.'

A critic might have argued that Sandringham was no more than a rich man's sporting estate, but there was an unspoken compact between the King and his wealthy shooting companions. They paid for their pheasants and the prestige of his company with lavish donations to his charities and philanthropic associations, of which there were more than five hundred, with the rest of the royal family supporting five hundred more. Edward VII's shifting of the monarchy to identify with the voluntary strand in national life and to cultivate what Esher—quite a thinker in this area—described as society's 'altruistic ideal' was deeply significant. It was not obviously in keeping with the King's hedonistic lifestyle, but the royal swagger was tempered with humility. Few things pleased King Edward more than being asked to give his name to a newly devised variety of potato.

It seems to have been Edward VII who started the royal custom of sending congratulatory telegrams to centenarians. In 1908 the earliest recorded recipient, the Revd Thomas Lord, a congregational minister of Horncastle, Lincolnshire, was so inspired by his royal message that he ascended the pulpit of the local Primitive Methodist chapel and preached, despite his one hundred years, in a strong voice for no fewer than thirty-four minutes.

*   *   *

We are looking here not at the breaking down of social barriers but at old-fashioned paternalism. Like most of his contemporaries, Edward VII believed class distinctions to be ordained. He revelled in his prerogatives, enjoying them most fully and famously in his love life, where his compulsive infidelity to his long-suffering and sweet-natured wife, Queen Alexandra, earned him Henry James's dismissive retitling as 'Edward the Caresser'.

By the time of his accession in 1901 the main recipient of Edward's caresses was Mrs Alice Keppel, great-grandmother of Camilla Parker Bowles and last in a long line of handsome, intelligent, young—and almost invariably married—paramours. Edward would go to visit his mistress at teatime: cake, claret and Keppel. Her children remembered the fat, balding gentleman they knew as 'Kingy' coming down from their mother's upstairs drawing room. He wore rings set with rubies, he smelt of scent and cigars, and he took them on holiday with her every spring when he went to Biarritz for the month of April in a ritual that was unshakeable. When Henry Campbell-Bannerman resigned in 1908, the new Liberal Prime Minister, Herbert Asquith, had to travel out to Biarritz to kiss hands on his appointment.

'Little Mrs George' was Edward's term of endearment for his last and most domesticated mistress, suggesting that the cuckolding was part of the fun—and her husband complaisantly acquiesced in the adultery which gave him a status and lifestyle he could never have attained on his own merits. In fact, the Hon. George Keppel, 6 feet 4 inches tall, with curled, waxed moustaches, came from a family whose fortunes were founded on the supply of sexual favours to the crown. Arnold Joost van Keppel, the 16-year-old lover of King William III, had come over with William from Holland in 1688 and was rewarded for his affections with the earldom of Albemarle and a clutch of other titles.

Alice Keppel had a gift for amusing and mothering her spoilt royal lover, laughing him out of his moodiness and tantrums. The King, observed the Duchess of Sutherland, was 'a much pleasanter child since he changed mistresses'. Her appeal was based on what her daughter Sonia described as 'my mother's ripe curves . . . I can picture her as she lay back among her lace pillows, her beautiful chestnut hair unbound around her shoulders.' As Sonia remembered it, her mother's bedroom was always scented by flowers, 'and a certain elusive smell, like fresh green sap, that came from herself'.

The vague and gentle Queen was reluctantly reconciled to her husband's infidelity quite early in their marriage. Alexandra was popular for her own beauty and good nature, but detached from the world on account of the deafness that she contracted in her early twenties and which became worse over the years. When Easter came around, she went off on stoic holidays with her Kodak for company—she became rather a good photographer. Her consolation was her children— they called her 'Motherdear'—and, like a later beautiful and abandoned Princess of Wales, she was driven to seek comfort in the sympathy of strangers.

'Queen Alexandra', recalled Fritz Ponsonby, 'had a charming way of treating the crowd as if they were intimate friends.'

Philanthropy assuaged Alexandra, as it was to bolster the self-esteem of Diana. To this day the Queen's name lives on in Britain's first-ever national charity flag day, the Alexandra Rose Day: an idea from her native Denmark, when well-born ladies, usually chaperoned, took to the better-class streets to sell cottage garden roses from baskets to help the poor. Strikingly taller than her faithless husband and distinguished by an angular, strong-nosed beauty, Alexandra 'always looked', wrote Ponsonby, 'as if she had stepped out of a band box'. Popular eagerness to imitate her style had some eccentric consequences. The rheumatic fever which had damaged her hearing at the age of twenty-two also left her permanently lame, and the 'Alexandra Limp' became fashionable for a time.

But Edwardian celebrity worship was highly selective. The King's infidelity was not reported, and there was no hint, let alone discussion, of the inner suffering that must be the lot of a woman whose husband so systematically betrayed her. The private reality of royal family life did not correspond to the public image, and the small minority of insiders who were aware of the contradiction colluded in the hypocrisy. Most of the upper crust operated their own lives within the same value system, while the vast majority who knew nothing were kept in happy ignorance by a courtier press.

*   *   *

King Edward VII planned his funeral with loving detail; he did not want to make the same mistake as his mother. Before her death Queen Victoria had typically requested that her passing should not be the occasion of excessive national ceremony, and that her interment should be a low-key matter at Windsor. She then sabotaged her own plans by dying at Osborne, in the Isle of Wight, allowing her son and Lord Esher to work their processional mischief. When her coffin arrived by rail in London, the long and florid column that processed from Waterloo to Paddington, the railway station for Windsor, was as full-blown as any cortège from Palace to Abbey.

Determined to avoid this last-minute scramble, Bertie devised another of his new-fangled 'ancient' rituals. After his death on 6 May 1910, his body was transported for a public lying-in-state—Britain's first ever such ceremony for a monarch—beneath the oak rafters of Westminster Hall, the historic heart of the Houses of Parliament, where it was solemnly greeted by the assembled MPs and peers. In the middle ages the rites of royal mourning were the prerogative of the King's lords and knights.

Now the ordinary people—over a quarter of a million of them in the course of three days—were admitted to the hall, and kept vigil outside in a huge queue that snaked back more than two miles up the river beyond Chelsea Bridge. With the aim of keeping the homage as democratic as possible, the hall was opened at 6 a.m. every day, so that labourers could attend on their way to work, and there was a strict prohibition on servants reserving places for their employers in the queue; the wealthy had to stand in line like everybody else.

The private farewells had been made earlier, even though the details were not to emerge for another seventy-six years. 'I am sure you always had a good influence over him,' said Queen Alexandra as she shook hands with Mrs Keppel. There had been three of them in the marriage— and considerably more, if Mrs Keppel's predecessors were tallied in—but that had never been a reason, in Alexandra's eyes, to disrupt the institution whose *raison d'être* was to rise above human fallibilities. When her husband's last mistress requested the chance to say farewell, she reluctantly acceded. Now, as the King dozed fitfully through his final days, she accepted the presence of the Other Woman with graceful forbearance, and waited discreetly by the window as 'La Favorita' said her farewells.

Thus, both in private and in public, the defining Edwardian actor enjoyed the ultimate curtain call. No twentieth-century monarch was to derive such glorious enjoyment from the job. In comparison with Edward VII, every one of his successors, from George V to Edward's great-grand-daughter, Elizabeth II, have proved relatively nervous sovereigns, earnest but obviously cautious performers on the grandiose stage set which he bequeathed. It was Edward VII's achievement to polish and embellish the monarchy for the age of entertainment. He was, literally, a hard act to follow.

CHAPTER FOUR

House of Windsor

'Are we going to keep the King?'
'Of course we are . . . In England the King does what the people want. He will be a socialist King.'

Left-wing agitators debate Britain's socialist future in the summer of 1913

Every day of his adult life, King George V dutifully wrote up his diary—unlike his father, who never kept one; Edward VII had better things to do at bedtime. Bound in successive volumes of green leather, the diary of King George V is the journal of a very ordinary man, containing a great deal more about his hobby of stamp collecting than it does about his personal feelings, with a heavy emphasis on the weather. The simple, round schoolboy hand scarcely changes from the age of fifteen, when he started it, until the last entry, completed three days before his death, and its artless clarity is an immense improvement on the imperious and indecipherable scrawls of his predecessors, Queen Victoria and Edward VII. Simple handwriting that ordinary people could understand provided something of a metaphor for the style of George V and his reign.

The outbreak of the Great War in August 1914 prompted royal worry and trepidation. The King recorded how the royal family were called out on to the new balcony at Buckingham Palace five evenings in succession, and on three occasions in one evening. 'It is a terrible catastrophe,' he noted of the declaration of war which he had to sign, 'but it is not our fault.'

Digging and planting vegetables supplemented stamp collecting as the King recorded the hours he spent working in the potato patch which the royal family started at Windsor as a contribution to the war effort. Then, with revolution, the diary really came alight.

'Bad news from Russia, practically a Revolution has broken out in Petrograd,' he noted on 13 March 1917. Two days later he recorded the news that his cousin Nicky, Tsar Nicholas II, had been compelled to abdicate. 'I am in despair.'

In the weeks that followed the tone grew more personal and bewildered, as the King pondered the fate of his Russian relatives. Good Friday fell on 6 April that year, a day on which it both rained and snowed. 'The weather has gone mad,' wrote the King in his diary, '& so has the world.'

*   *   *

The Russian Revolution struck a chill into monarchies all over Europe. Within eighteen months two other emperors had vanished, along with eight ruling sovereigns—all victims of military defeat. But even the monarchs of victorious countries felt the repercussions, and in Britain the dreaded word 'republic' made a comeback. On the face of it, the stolid George V was not the man to repel the challenge.

Forty-four years old when he succeeded his father in May 1910, the new King had spent much of his youth as a naval officer and he was proud to retain simple, quarterdeck attitudes throughout his life. When reminiscing over the port about his naval career, he liked to raise an imaginary biscuit between his fingers and tap it fondly to show how he used to knock out the weevils in his days as a midshipman.

He had been sent to sea early as a support and companion for his feckless elder brother, Prince Albert Victor, the heir to the throne. George was only fifteen, but already his steadiness was recognised by his parents. Bertie and Alexandra agreed with their sons' tutors that Prince George had the strength of character needed to prod along his torpid elder brother, around whom lurid rumours of degeneracy were later to float. The family's grief at the death of Albert Victor from influenza in 1892, at the age of twenty-eight, was mitigated by the general feeling that his younger brother was actually much better suited to the job. Prince George inherited the succession—and also his brother's fiancée, Princess May of Teck. May, who would take the title of Queen Mary when her husband came to the throne, had been hand-picked by Victoria for her steadfast qualities. Thus the two buttresses recruited for royal damage control found themselves brought together—and a very solid partnership they made.

They received a crash course in kingship. 'I hope that you will brush up and practise Georgie's French and German,' wrote Queen Victoria to Princess May in 1893, 'for you *must both* be able to speak it with foreigners.' To learn the constitution, George received lessons from the distinguished Cambridge historian J. R. Tanner, who set him to studying the essays of Walter Bagehot. Queen Victoria was not amused to hear that her grandson's constitutional thinking was being shaped by so irreverent a commentator, but Bagehot's pragmatic analysis contained much to fortify King George V as he faced the challenges posed by the Russian Revolution in 1917.

Some of the journalist's thinking was encouraging. 'The existence of the crown', wrote the trainee King in his 1894 study notes on Bagehot's *English Constitution*, 'serves to disguise change, and therefore to deprive it of the evil consequences of revolution.' But in trying to illustrate the politically passive character of the constitutional monarchy, Bagehot had also employed a more alarming metaphor. Constitutional monarchs, he once explained, must sign their own death warrant if it is presented to them.

*   *   *

The British government's first reaction to the fall of the Tsar in the spring of 1917 had been to offer asylum to an old friend and ally, and initially George V supported this fully. Britain's main objective was to keep Russia fighting for the Allies on the Eastern Front. In March 1917 Russia was still run by a parliamentary government, and it was felt that removing the Tsar and his controversial wife from their country might help bolster the democrats against extremists like the Bolsheviks. In Petrograd, Sir George Buchanan set about arranging the details for the Tsar's departure.

But the news that the Russian royal family might be given asylum in Britain was greeted with general dismay. The Tsar and his German wife were controversial figures, whose prewar visit to England had been criticised. There was a feeling that they had brought their troubles on themselves. The prospect of the British crown sustaining discredited autocrats gave out quite the wrong message. 'There is considerable discussion going on in the clubs . . .' wrote Lord Charles Beresford to the King early in April. 'There is only one opinion expressed upon the matter, that is, it would be a fatal mistake.' 'If the Ex-Czar and Czarina come to live here,' ran another letter which a courtier showed to the King, 'we shall have a Revolution and remember that I warned you.' This alarmist view was confirmed by Colonel J. Unsworth, a Salvation Army officer from Essex, who sent in some grass-roots intelligence. 'I have noticed, since the news came to hand of the Russian revolution, a change has come over a certain sector of the people in respect to their attitude towards the King and the Royal family. In the streets, trains and Buses, one hears talk . . . A friend of mine saw written in a second class Railway carriage, "To hell with the King. Down with all royalties".' Railway second-class carriages were the equivalent of business class in aeroplanes today. So what was being written in the third-class carriages?

The King studied the letters with his private secretary, Lord Stamfordham. They were at Windsor for the Easter weekend, holed up in the castle by the freakish weather that the sailor king had noted in his diary. George V personally liked his cousin Nicky, to whom he bore a remarkable facial resemblance. But he shared the general mistrust felt towards the Tsarina, Alix, and he was developing misgivings about taking responsibility for relatives whose care could prove both costly and troublesome.

'Every day,' wrote Stamfordham to the Foreign Secretary, A. J. Balfour, on Good Friday, 'the king is becoming more concerned about the question of the Emperor and Empress coming to this country. His Majesty receives letters from people in all classes of life, known or unknown to him, saying how much the matter is being discussed, not only in clubs, but by working men, and that Labour Members in the House of Commons are expressing adverse opinions to the proposal.'

As royal private secretary, Lord Stamfordham was much more than a mere letter-writer or mouthpiece. Born Arthur Bigge, the son of a country parson, he was ennobled Baron Stamfordham in George V's coronation honours in 1911, proudly taking the name of the small Northumbrian village where he had grown up. Sixty-eight years old in 1917, Bigge had started in royal service as an assistant private secretary to Queen Victoria, succeeding Sir Henry Ponsonby as her principal private secretary in 1895. On the old Queen's death, he had transferred sideways to become mentor to the future George V.

In the course of the nineteenth century the office of private secretary had evolved far beyond its primary function of serving as the administrative link between monarch and government. Its occupant had become the curator and, in many ways, the guardian of royalness. Filtering whom the monarch would and would not receive, where she might visit, and what activities it was appropriate for her to shun or encourage, the private secretary had become a mixture of grand vizier and high priest. Thinking day and night about royal responsibility and how to define it, the private secretary came in many ways to know more about the throne than its occupant.

Seldom was this supervisory role embodied more effectively than in the tutelage which Stamfordham exercised over George V. During his father's reign George had sometimes startled politicians with his crude, unthinking denigration of government ministers with whom he disagreed. With a political vista that extended from the quarterdeck to the grouse moor, he had little sympathy for the Liberal Party, let alone their Labour allies. After a dinner party at Lord Londonderry's house, Edmund Gosse described the future King, then in his early forties, as 'an overgrown schoolboy, loud and stupid, losing no opportunity of abusing the government'. It was Stamfordham's achievement to tame this young bull in a china shop, shaping him into a polished and meek constitutional monarch. As George V himself put it, 'He taught me how to be a King.'

One of the private secretary's techniques for keeping his master in tune with public opinion was to scour the press for material with which to prepare briefing sheets, on which the clippings were pasted and annotated. Stamfordham made a particular effort to search out radical thinking, and it was an article from one radical journal that played a crucial role in the discussions between King and private secretary on the Easter weekend of April 1917.

The previous day a prominent left-winger, Henry Mayers Hyndman, had summoned up the dreaded prospect of 'a British Republic' in an article published in *Justice—the Organ of Social-Democracy*. Hyndman's article had been clipped and pasted by Stamfordham, and the private secretary had scored dramatic red marks alongside the passages he particularly wished the King to read.

'If the King and Queen have invited their discrowned Russian cousins to come here,' thundered Hyndman, '. . . they are misinterpreting entirely the feelings of us common Englishmen.' Hyndman was, in fact, anything but a common Englishman. Independently wealthy, he had become one of the country's best-known socialist voices, the more feared for his high-born and wealthy origins. 'It would be very easy to establish a British Republic,' he wrote. 'The old objections to Republicanism have quite died down. I cannot imagine anyone sacrificing himself or herself to safeguard the Crown.' Recalling the founding in 1881 of his Social-Democratic Federation, Britain's first socialist party, Hyndman described how the party members had been generally in favour of a republic, but how they had decided to keep that out of their manifesto. There were few votes in attacking Queen Victoria, they acknowledged: 'the abolition of Monarchy remained as a point in our programme, but we deferred its realisation to a more convenient season.'

War had now brought that season. The Armageddon in the trenches meant the end for 'the circle of kings' whose feudings had brought about the hostilities now raging. 'Not the few but the many are winning this war,' wrote Hyndman. 'It is the England of the people that has gone forth to fight . . . Shall we common folk in Britain, then, alone remain enslaved when the great battle is won?'

The idea that a postwar land fit for heroes might not include a king was an alarming prospect—particularly for the King himself. On the basis of the royal postbag, Stamfordham had already sent one letter to the Foreign Secretary about the Tsar that day. Now he and George V felt that another letter must be penned at once to cover what the papers were saying, and the private secretary took the unusual step of sending the second missive off by courier that same Good Friday afternoon. 'He [the King] must beg you to represent to the Prime Minister,' wrote Stamfordham to Arthur Balfour, 'that from all he hears and reads in the press, the residence in this country of the ex-Emperor and Empress would be strongly resented by the public, and would undoubtedly compromise the position of the King and Queen.'

The Foreign Secretary pondered the two letters. 'I think the King is placed in an awkward position,' he agreed in a minute he sent that same night to David Lloyd George in Downing Street. '. . . I think we may have to suggest Spain or the South of

France as a more suitable residence than England for the Czar.'

Four days later Stamfordham took another unusual step. He went round in person to Downing Street, where he was not a very popular figure. The private secretary never had any compunction standing up to the steamrollering style of Lloyd George, and the Prime Minister's dislike of this inconvenient individual had spread to his staff, who liked to keep the King's emissary waiting out in the hall on a wooden chair.

Undaunted, Stamfordham had brought along the Hyndman article that had been so decisive in the royal thinking, and he flourished the *Organ of Social-Democracy* to emphasise his arguments as he pushed the reluctant Lloyd George to do as the King wanted. The Prime Minister agreed to look into the possibility of getting the Tsar sent to France, and from that moment the plans to get the imperial family out of Russia ran into diplomatic quicksand. Six months later, in October 1917, the Bolsheviks seized power, and the last hopes of a rescue foundered. In July 1918 the Tsar, his wife, five children, doctor, valet, cook, parlour-maid and dog were shot and bayoneted to death in the cellar at Ekaterinburg.

*   *   *

The story of George V's role in the abandoning of his Russian cousins was successfully kept secret for more than sixty years. In his memoirs Lloyd George was silent about the crucial role played by the King. Harold Nicolson's official biography of George V, published in 1952, similarly glossed over the truth.

But the King's more comprehensive and adventurous biographer, Kenneth Rose, obtained transcripts of the documents on which the official biography had been based. They were lent to him by Nicolson's son Nigel, and Rose used these and other archives—including the Lloyd George and Balfour Papers—to piece together the whole story in his book, which was published in 1983. When Rose showed his text to the Queen's librarian, Sir Robin Mackworth-Young, at Windsor, he received a relaxed and even encouraging response. But at Buckingham Palace Sir Philip Moore, Elizabeth II's private secretary from 1977 to 1986, was more protective. He felt that Rose should be dissuaded from publishing the revelation, and sent a draft copy of the chapter to the Queen.

King George V's granddaughter was on a state visit abroad when Rose's draft chapter reached her, and she returned it to her private secretary without changing a word. 'Let Him Publish', she wrote in large letters across the top of the opening page.

When *King George V* appeared later that year, uncensored, it was placed on the trolley of new books that Mackworth-Young would assemble and wheel into the Queen every July so she could select her holiday reading. That summer, Rose's biography of her grandfather was the only book she picked. 'I think I'll take that one with me to Balmoral,' she said.

*   *   *

In June 1917, George V's financial adviser Lord Revelstoke, a director of Baring Brothers, suggested that the King should be better briefed on the nature of antimonarchical and republican sentiment in the country. Lord Stamfordham was indignant.

'I can unhesitatingly say', he responded, 'that I do not believe there is any Sovereign in the World to whom the truth is more fearlessly told by those in his immediate service, and who receives it with such goodwill—and even gratitude—as King George. There is no Socialistic newspaper, no libellous rag, that is not read and marked and shown to the king if they contain any criticisms, friendly or unfriendly, of His Majesty and the Royal Family.'

Ample witness to the truth of Stamfordham's claim resides today in the Royal Archives, in a file entitled 'Unrest in the Country'. Inside are the carefully marked articles of radicals like Hyndman—and the project went beyond press clippings. Stamfordham assembled a floating brains trust of experts who were felt to have their fingers on the pulse of the country, and the deliberations and reports of this group—part intelligence network, part think tank—are also included in the file.

One gathering of the group took place at the end of April 1917 when the Bishop of Chelmsford, John Watts-Ditchfield, was preaching at Windsor. Watts-Ditchfield had made his name working among the poor of Bethnal Green, and had a reputation as a plugged-in cleric 'thoroughly in touch with the working classes'. The conservative George V enjoyed Chelmsford's company and preaching, even though Stamfordham had the bishop down as 'a strong Liberal in Politics, with even Socialistic tendencies'.

The talking point that weekend was an inflammatory letter to *The Times* from the novelist H. G. Wells. While claiming that he was not proposing the removal of George V, the novelist had none the less called for the creation of 'a Republican Society for Great Britain'. Wells proposed a network of local clubs that would demonstrate British support for antimonarchist movements in countries like Russia and show that 'our spirit is warmly and entirely against the dynastic-system that has so long divided, embittered, and wasted the spirit of mankind'.

Press response had been indignant. 'If there is a "trade union of kings",' declared the *Daily Mail,* 'our King does not belong to it and Great Britain is a "non-union house".' But it was worrying that *The Times,* of all papers, should have provided a platform for such subversive views, and the Windsor house party sat down to thrash the problem out. Joining in the discussions, along with the Bishop of Chelmsford, were Lord Curzon, the one-time Viceroy of India, who was Lord President of the Council; H. H. Asquith, the former Prime Minister; and Lord Revelstoke.

The bishop felt that criticism like Wells's should be taken very seriously. The men returning from the war 'must have so far as is possible good conditions of life', he argued. The King should show himself in working-class areas like the East End, and in munitions centres such as Sheffield. It must also be brought home to the rich that 'taxation, reduced profits and income for the happiness and prosperity of the masses is as essential for the welfare of the Nation [in peacetime] as taxation for war'.

Asquith was not happy about this. It would be quite unconstitutional, said the former Prime Minister, for the King to give public utterance to such sentiments, which were of a contentious and party political character. Stamfordham, acting as clerk to the gathering, duly noted the objection; but the idea of the King visiting working-class areas was approved by all. In the prewar years George V and his wife had paid well-received visits to the industrial regions of Scotland and the coalfields and mines of south Wales. Queen Mary had been a particular success, carrying out an early version of what today would be called a 'walkabout' among the cottage wives. The firebrand Labour leader Keir Hardie, the Queen remarked with satisfaction after one successful visit, 'will not have liked it'.

With the coming of war these visits to industrial areas had intensified. In the military field, the King had made visits to the Western Front, while the Queen toured military hospitals. The trips were extensively filmed by the newsreel companies, and cinema historians record 1917 as the year when the newsreels showed royal close-ups for the first time. Distant shots of shuffling grandees were supplemented by closer, more informal images of the King and Queen smiling and talking, and since no new lenses were developed at the time, this can only have been the consequence of a decision to loosen etiquette and allow the cameras closer. Royal documents do not relate whether this reflected a conscious central decision; the 'Unrest in the Country' file shows no awareness of the potent messages that could be conveyed by newsreels. But the notes and letters show a general wish to increase contact between King and people, and Stamfordham had the satisfaction of filing clippings which reflected the success of his policy. 'There is more real freedom in this country than in America or France,' commented the *Clarion* in late June 1917, as it noted the success of the royal popularity tours. 'There is as much class privilege and as much snobbery and jobbery in France and in America as here . . . It is a sheer waste of energy to whip up a revolt against a king who is no more a Kaiser than Old King Cole.'

The *Clarion*'s reference to the Kaiser, however, touched on the real heart of public unhappiness about the royal family: the fact that they were Germans, and had been since the arrival of George I from Hanover in 1714. British setbacks in the war had prompted an atmosphere of hatred towards all things German. People with German surnames were denounced as traitors and imprisoned without trial, and it was not even politic to be seen exercising your pet dachshund or drinking German white wine. The hard-driving First Lord of the Admiralty, Prince Louis of Battenberg, who had been naturalised British at the age of fourteen, had been compelled to resign and retire into private life. The 'Unrest in the Country' file contained ample evidence of how people felt about 'the Hun'. According to one clipping, the Kaiser should be flung 'out of the circle of Queen Victoria's family, and consequently out of the pale of humanity, to herd with the wolves and hyenas, whose company is the only fit society for such as he'.

In fact, like all the British royal family, George V had developed a deep dislike of his cousin, the German emperor Wilhelm II. 'Willie' had distinguished himself on his first appearance, aged four, at a British royal ceremony—the marriage of his uncle, the future Edward VII, to Alexandra—by sinking his teeth into the calf of one of his English cousins. George V could not understand why anyone should imagine for a moment that he sympathised with 'the d—d Germans', as he described them in his diary, deploring their 'loathsome and wanton destruction'. He was particularly incensed by H. G. Wells's jibe that the British court was 'alien and uninspiring'. 'I may be uninspiring,' he remarked to a visitor, 'but I'll be damned if I'm alien.'

But the complaints continued. By the summer of 1917 it was clear that the clutch of German-named royal relatives would have to be camouflaged, and Stamfordham discussed the problem with another member of the 'Unrest in the Country' think tank, the former Prime Minister Lord Rosebery. In a letter of 15 May Stamfordham came up with the idea of an English surname—'Tudor-Stewart' was his suggestion—that could be used by the entire royal family, Battenbergs and Tecks included. At a meeting two days later, Rosebery suggested 'Fitzroy', and over the weeks that followed Plantagenet, York, Lancaster and even England were canvassed.

After some discussion, the Tecks and Battenbergs chose to go their own way, the Battenbergs becoming 'Mountbatten' while the Tecks became 'Cambridge'. But by this stage the search for a new royal surname had become an end in itself. Pondering all the alternatives one day, Lord Stamfordham hit upon 'Windsor'. 'Do you realise', Rosebery congratulated him, 'that you have christened a dynasty?'

It was an extraordinary leap of imagination. No royal clan had done as much before. Newcomers and usurpers had taken over old names; but for an ancient family which could trace its roots back a thousand years coolly to peel off one label and rebrand itself with another reflected hard-eyed realism and flexibility—and a certain measure of fear.

On 17 July the Privy Council announced the change, along with the royal family's renunciation of all 'German degrees, styles, dignitaries, titles, honours and appellations'. A new dynasty had been created to meet public demand. The decree gave no explanation for this extraordinary reinvention, but the reason was obvious, and would become the bottom line and guiding principle of the new House of Windsor. It was what the people wanted.

*   *   *

Five weeks after the christening of the people's monarchy came the people's honours list. After bitter years of warfare cruelly dominated by machines, it had become obvious that those who produced munitions were as crucial as those who used them. But while soldiers got medals, there was no means of acknowledging the civilians—many of them women—who endured the grind, risk and continuous tension of working long hours in a munitions factory.

Over the centuries, governments had purloined the glamour and romance of the medieval orders of chivalry to dignify public service. After forty years of toil, a Treasury clerk or Foreign Office functionary knelt down Bill Bloggs of Accounts, the sword touched his shoulder, and he arose Sir William, in a tradition evocative of the Knights of the Round Table. The Order of the Bath derived its name from the ritual cleansing of knights elect, while the Order of St Michael and St George conjured up dragon-slaying. Retiring with a title, or at least letters after the name, helped compensate government servants for the inadequacies of their pension.

The summer of 1917 saw the creation of the Order of the British Empire, the product of deliberations involving the War Office, Downing Street and Buckingham Palace. 'Never before have the rank and file of the workers, the heroes and heroines of industrial life, had their courage and devotion recognised,' declared the *Leeds Mercury*, welcoming the new order on 25 August 1917.

A major purpose of the new order was to honour women along with men, and its framers in the War Cabinet and the Palace deliberately set out also to embrace another excluded group—the socialists. Worrying that the trades union leaders and the increasing number of socialist mayors would shun distinctions that involved titles and orders of precedence, they devised an extra 'democratic' order, the Companions of Honour, specifically 'to meet the wishes of those who did not desire these distinctions'. The first seventeen Companions of Honour, entitled only to the letters CH after their name, included William John Davies, Secretary of the Brass-workers and Metal Mechanics Union, G. J. Wardle of the National Union of Railwaymen and Henry Gosling, President of the Transport Workers' Federation.

The CH carried no social precedence. Its holder remained plain Mr, Mrs or Miss, and within just a few years it became apparent that this held little attraction for most Labour stalwarts, who much preferred a knighthood, or better still a peerage. Nowadays CHs tend to go to writers and intellectuals who are lily-livered about distinction—along with politicians keen for extra letters after their names. But in 1917 the levelling implications of both orders were widely praised. 'We are all socialists now,' declared the *Darlington North Star*.

On 19 September 1917 King George V held the first investiture of the new orders—not in Buckingham Palace but on the pitch at Ibrox Park in Glasgow, the home of Glasgow Rangers Football Club. A dais was raised where the goalposts normally stood and the gates were thrown open at 1.30 p.m. to admit seventy thousand spectators—ten thousand of them female munitions workers who had been given the afternoon off and were attired in their working uniforms. The King was on a tour of the Clydeside shipyards and ammunition factories, and as he drove on to the football pitch the crowd gave hearty voice to the national anthem. In front of the dais were seated rows of wounded soldiers in their hospital blue, and as Private Harry Christian of the Royal Lancashire Regiment was carried forward on a stretcher to have the Victoria Cross pinned on his chest, the cheers ran round the ground.

But before the soldiers it had been the turn of the civilians. 'The first tremendous cheer', reported the *Dundee Courier*, 'came when Miss Lizzie Robertson, in her natty khaki overalls, stepped forward to receive the Medal of the British Empire Order "For devotion to duty in a national projectile factory." She has not lost any time in a whole year's service at the factory, although the factory has recently been working at very high pressure.'

So, one month before the October Revolution brought the Bolsheviks to power in Russia, an anointed British king placed himself at the centre of a proletarian liturgy as potent as any devised by a Supreme Soviet. 'The visit of the King', declared the *Aberdeen Daily Journal* next day, 'draws attention to the wide difference that exists between a constitutional and an autocratic monarch.' While Europe's doomed sovereigns spent their last months parading in their swords, spurs and shiny helmets, a sober-suited George V stood on a football pitch shaking hands with Lizzie Robertson in her natty khaki overalls.

Part 2

Model Family

CHAPTER FIVE

New Blood

Kings are not born. They are made by
universal hallucination.

George Bernard Shaw

It had seemed at the time just a casual aside. When
George V summoned the Privy Council in July
1917 to break the momentous news that he was
dropping the German name of his dynasty, he
mentioned that he and his wife had been thinking
that their children should also stop marrying
Germans. 'I also informed the Council', he noted
in his diary, 'that May and I had decided some time
ago that our children would be allowed to marry
into British families.'

The King clearly thought that he was breaking
new ground. The rule of the great nineteenth-
century royal family of Europe had been that royal
blood must marry royal blood, which meant in
practice that husbands and wives were usually
sought abroad. But this was a Germanic concept
brought into Britain by the Hanoverians, the
Protestant dynasty imported by Parliament in the
early eighteenth century to replace the unreliably
Roman Catholic Stuarts. In fact, King George V
was reverting to traditional English practice. Many
medieval kings took English brides, and four of
Henry VIII's six wives had been non-royal English
women. As late as 1660 the future James II had

married Anne Hyde, daughter of the historian the Earl of Clarendon.

The newspaper campaign of 1917 against Germanness had fulminated particularly against the baleful influence of 'Hun princesses'. The papers argued, with some justice, that many of the Tsar's problems had been made worse by Alix, his arrogant German wife, and there were similar complaints about the influence of the Greek Queen Sophie, the Kaiser's sister, blamed for the unpopularity of the troubled royal family of Greece. So the change of marriage policy was widely welcomed. In 1922 the wedding of the King's only daughter Mary to the north-country nobleman Henry, Viscount Lascelles was the media event of the year, covered by more than sixty cameramen from the competing newsreel companies; and a year later there was widespread rejoicing at the announcement that George V's second son, 'Bertie', the 27-year-old Prince Albert, Duke of York, had become engaged to the 22-year-old Lady Elizabeth Bowes-Lyon.

Long before she lived to be a hundred, the future Queen Elizabeth the Queen Mother was recognised as a remarkable woman, whose enrolment into the royal family had a profound and positive impact on its fortunes. Winsome, dutiful and outwardly unpretentious, she brought the common touch to the House of Windsor. Yet while hailed as a 'commoner', Elizabeth Angela Marguerite Bowes-Lyon was hardly born one of the people. Her parents, the Earl and Countess of Strathmore, owned a large London town house, two ample country estates and a healthy chunk of the Durham coalfields. The last but one of ten children, she did much of her growing up in Scotland at Glamis Castle, the legendary home of Shakespeare's Macbeth. Apart from six months at a Sloane Street academy, she never went to school. But her upbringing left her poised and cultured—and also media-friendly.

The archives of Glamis show that Elizabeth Bowes-Lyon was posing for photographs from an early age and made her first press appearance at the age of three, in the *Dundee Advertiser*. She was one of the guests at her grandparents' Golden Wedding celebration at which, it was reported, 'the young scions of the house mingled with the crowd on the most genial terms'. The press coverage made much of the relaxed and friendly attitude of the Strathmores towards their staff and more than eight hundred tenants, accurately reflecting the family charm which Elizabeth inherited in such generous quantities. 'The Strathmores were so grand,' recalls a family friend, 'you never realised they were grand at all.'

With the status and trappings of aristocracy increasingly becoming an object of criticism, it made good sense for a grandee to cultivate the neighbourhood. Newspapermen were welcome visitors to Glamis; Elizabeth's youth can be traced through the press clippings which log the Strathmores' role as the figureheads of the local community, and particularly their converting their castle into a convalescent home for wounded soldiers in the Great War. The teenage Elizabeth, dressed in nurse's uniform, took the walking wounded for walks and picnics, and got all the soldiers to sign her autograph book. Being happy and spreading happiness was much more than a matter of personal fulfilment—it was duty, the noblewoman's equivalent of the menfolk going off to war. All four Strathmore brothers of fighting age volunteered: one was killed, one was taken prisoner and Elizabeth's eldest brother, Patrick, the heir to the title, came home with shell shock from which he never recovered. Elizabeth's growing up through the traumas of the First World War gave her a lifelong dislike of Germans, and an inflexible belief in the value of sacrifice to a higher cause.

Upper-class Britain was both diminished and hardened by the slaughter of the Great War, and this loss of innocence was particularly obvious in young women. The bob-haired flapper of the roaring twenties smoked cigarettes, drank cocktails and lived for the moment with intimidating ferocity. But when Elizabeth Bowes-Lyon came down to London in 1919 to be formally introduced to society, she retained something of the innocence of the prewar days. 'Mildly flirtatious in a very proper, romantic, old-fashioned, Valentine sort of way,' recorded the diarist Chips Channon. 'She makes every man feel chivalrous and gallant towards her.'

It was hardly surprising that she attracted the attention of the shy young Prince Albert. Four and a half years older than Elizabeth, 'Bertie' was an unprepossessing character on first acquaintance, handicapped by a stutter which derived, it is thought, from being compelled by his tutors to suppress his natural left-handedness and write with his right hand. When he came courting in the early 1920s, Elizabeth turned down his first two proposals of marriage. Apart from her personal feelings, her leisured, aristocratic family considered the royal round of launching ships and opening bazaars to offer a middle-class and rather hard-working prospect. 'As far as I can see,' her mother once remarked, 'some people have to be fed royalty like sea-lions fish.'

But the young prince's persistence won the day. When Bertie summoned his resources for one last effort in January 1923, Elizabeth accepted him— and next morning the first reporter arrived at the door of her parents' London home at 17 Bruton Street.

'You see how busy I am trying to answer all these!' Elizabeth happily told Harry Cozens-Hardy of the *Star*, a London evening paper, pointing at the letters and telegrams piled up on her desk. 'I had no idea our engagement meant so much hard work!'

The journalist's ring on the doorbell had been received frostily by the butler, and Elizabeth's mother, the countess, had been even less welcoming. But the 22-year-old took command. 'Mother, leave this gentleman to me,' she said firmly, leading Cozens-Hardy into the breakfast room.

As the doorbell continued to ring through the day, the royal family's new conscript displayed a deft talent for giving the papers a story without giving much away. 'I just thought it over for a minute,' she told the *Daily Mail* about the prince's proposal. She told the *Daily Sketch* that she couldn't get used to reading about herself in the newspapers, and she told the *Daily News*, 'I'm just too happy for words.' 'Mr Gossip', the *Sketch*'s social columnist, could not believe the young lady's chattiness. 'Never before has the bride-to-be of a prince of the blood royal established such a link between the teeming millions and the private affairs of the exalted few,' he wrote. 'But I shouldn't be at all surprised to find a complete cessation of these interviews in the very near future.'

Mr Gossip was proved correct. King George V despatched an equerry round to Bruton Street with instructions that no further interviews were to be given; and Elizabeth observed the ban for the rest of her life. She never gave another on-the-record interview. But, seemingly instinctively, she channelled her charisma into a silent form of communication that would be described in later years as 'emotional broadcasting'—the capacity to provoke warm feelings with a single gesture or look. As the novelist John Buchan would later enthuse, the product of George V's change of marriage policy had 'a perfect genius for the right kind of publicity'.

*   *   *

On 26 April 1923, the newly married Duke and Duchess of York rode through cheering crowds to celebrate another twentieth-century invention—the mass media royal wedding, marked by balcony appearances and a flurry of lavish supplements in the newspapers and illustrated magazines. Queen Victoria had tried to keep the marriages of her many children and grandchildren relatively low-key events in the royal chapels at Windsor and St James's. But George V had responded to popular enthusiasm by staging his son's wedding in

Westminster Abbey, the first marriage of a royal prince in the Abbey since 1382.

The King had done the same for his daughter Mary's wedding the previous year, and had been disconcerted by the presumption with which the nation had taken over his family occasion.

> It is now no longer Mary's wedding [he complained], but (this is from the papers) it is the 'Abbey Wedding' or the 'Royal Wedding' or the 'National Wedding' or even the 'People's Wedding' (I have heard it called) 'of our beloved Princess' . . . as far as I can make out the 28th is going to be a day of national rejoicing in every conceivable & inconceivable manner.

Royal romance was big business. In April 1923 Topical Budget, one of the 'big three' newsreel companies, along with Pathé Gazette and Gaumont Graphic, paid out nearly £3,000, the equivalent of around £106,000 today, to secure prime camera positions for their nineteen cameramen along the wedding route of the Duke and Duchess of York. H. G. Wells sniffed disdainfully that he had stopped going to the cinema because of the snobbery of the newsreels.

What was snobbery to a novelist was intrusion to a king. Many years later, the fears of both Wells and George V were vindicated by the treatment that the much celebrated union of the Duke and Duchess of York received at the hands of a later generation. In 1997 the American writer Kitty Kelley alleged in her book *The Royals* that the couple's first child, the future Queen Elizabeth II, was a product of artificial insemination. According to 'a royal family friend' who was not named, her father's sperm had been mechanically injected into her mother's uterus because, the friend added helpfully, but without additional evidence, the 30-year-old Prince Albert 'had a slight problem with his willy'.

The diminishing boundaries of personal privacy were to demythologise royalty drastically in the twentieth century. It was a measure of how far standards could change in one lifetime that, while Kelley's book was not published in Britain, its intimate and uncorroborated allegation was given wide coverage as a news story in the British press.

The available evidence does not sustain the allegation. Prince Albert, Duke of York, lost his virginity relatively late by modern standards, aged twenty-two, on a trip to Paris, according to his brother David, the Prince of Wales, to whom he confided that 'the deed was done'. But then Bertie more than made up for lost time. His wild oat sowing has been detailed in the recently discovered letters which David wrote to his mistress, Freda Dudley Ward, the half-American wife of the Liberal MP William Dudley Ward. On his return from France, Bertie took up with a married woman of his own—Sheila, the racy young Australian wife of Lord Loughborough—and the two princes and their mistresses formed a clique that they dubbed 'The Four Do's'. 'What marvellous fun we 4 do have, don't we, Angel?' wrote the Prince of Wales to Freda, '& f— the rest of the world.' The two brothers were roguish co-conspirators in their high jinks with other men's wives. 'After tea', wrote David in June 1919, 'I managed to lure Loughie away on the pretext of wanting to play a few more holes of golf . . . so as to give Sheilie a chance of being alone with Bertie . . . I'm sure Loughie doesn't suspect Bertie at all!'

It was in the following year that Bertie started courting Elizabeth Bowes-Lyon, and the prince is conventionally depicted as a rather bedraggled supplicant for the favours of this dazzling young woman. The dramatic handicap of his stutter has been seized on as the defining aspect of his personality. But a photo of Bertie in these years, hands on hips, crunching his heels confidently into the gravel of Glamis Castle, the Strathmores' Scottish home, presents a keenly handsome and purposeful young prince. With his slicked-down hair, direct gaze and sharply cut kilt, he is every inch the laird-about-town. Bertie's letters to his trusted aide and mentor, Louis Greig, make clear that by his mid-twenties he had enjoyed flirtations with a trio of chorus girls, Madge Saunders, Marjorie Gordon and Ruby Miller, and had possibly conducted a more serious liaison with a fourth. Bertie met secretly in rooms in Half Moon Street with the vivacious musical comedy star Phyllis Monkman, and was rumoured to have sent her love tokens of jewellery. When Phyllis died in 1976, her effects were found to include a small leather wallet with a single photograph mounted inside—of Prince Albert in his wartime uniform.

We obviously cannot know the details of the prince's varied premarital adventures, but there is, surprisingly, first-hand testimony that he consummated his marriage successfully, and with some style, on his wedding night. 'Everything was plain sailing,' he reported to Louis Greig in April

1923 from his honeymoon, 'which was a relief. You know what I mean. I was very good!!'

This cheery report from the front, while ending in triumph, does hint at past anxiety. Greig was a naval doctor, Bertie's senior by some fifteen years, who had watched over the prince in his service days and had done wonders for his physical and psychological health. It was Greig who organised the stage-door bouquets and the rooms in Half Moon Street. The prince had no secrets from Greig, and this may be why Elizabeth, 'the smiling Duchess', made sure that the over-helpful aide departed her husband's service within a few months of their wedding. It is not impossible that Bertie and Elizabeth did seek medical help with conception, and if so, how practical and progressive of them.

*   *   *

The future Queen Elizabeth II was born in the small hours of Wednesday, 21 April 1926, a few days earlier than expected. She had not been due until the end of the month, and her theatre-loving mother had been spotted in the West End catching a new play the previous week. But on Tuesday night the doctors were summoned to 17 Bruton Street, where the Duchess's parents had set up a bedroom for the birth. The baby's arrival was logged at 2.40 a.m., and that afternoon the King and Queen motored up from Windsor to London to visit their first grand-daughter.

'Such a relief and joy,' noted Queen Mary in her diary. '. . . Saw the baby who was a little darling with a lovely complexion & pretty fair hair.'

It had been a difficult birth. 'I am so proud of Elizabeth at this moment,' wrote Bertie, 'after all that she has gone through during the last few days.' The medical complications were described in the official bulletin as 'a certain line of treatment', and the newspapers repeated this vague-sounding phrase without explanation—'Success of a Certain Line of Treatment' ran a heading in the *Daily Sketch*. In fact, the code was generally understood: it was the way in which a more reticent era revealed that the child had been born by caesarean section.

The birth of the little princess provoked great public interest. Large crowds gathered to catch a glimpse of the King and Queen and the other visitors who came to the Strathmore house to welcome the baby. There was much cheering. The occasion engendered warm feelings and the popular press tried to play up the significance of the new arrival. 'A possible Queen of England was born yesterday at No. 17 Bruton-street Mayfair,' declared the *Daily Sketch*. The new baby was third in line of succession, the paper explained, after her father and her uncle, the Prince of Wales, the immediate heir, who had not yet chosen his bride. But Queen Victoria had been the daughter of a king's fourth son, so 'it cannot be forgotten that our new Princess is a possible Queen-Empress'.

The serious papers did not get carried away with such remote speculation. It was taken for granted that Elizabeth's uncle, the Prince of Wales, would do his duty and get married—and there was every possibility that the baby's own parents would produce a son who would take precedence over her. The broadsheets also left it to the popular picture papers to brighten their readers' lives with some vicarious participation in the happy event. Next day the Sketch headed its front page with a rear view of the young Duke of York walking away from the camera. He had not spoken to any reporters, but he was confidently described as 'profoundly happy yet rather fearful of being in the way at home', as he set off on his own for a long, early morning walk. 'So like a father!'

*   *   *

The nation's spirits stood in some need of brightening, for the new princess had been born on the brink of a serious crisis. A proposed reduction in miners' wages had provoked bitter, countrywide confrontation that seemed to some once more to threaten revolution. 'Not a penny off the pay, not a minute on the day' was the slogan that inspired the Trades Union Congress to call a general strike of Britain's vital services on 3 May 1926.

'Damned lot of revolutionaries!' remarked Lord Durham, a prominent coal owner, when he had encountered George V at Newmarket races a few days before Princess Elizabeth's birth.

'Try living on their wages before you judge them,' retorted the King.

The ever-conservative monarch did not favour strikers holding the country to ransom. But his vision of a national community did not smile on greedy capitalists either. He told one of his ministers, Leo Amery, that, in his opinion, no coal owner or investor should be allowed to receive a dividend of more than 10 per cent.

The King took national disagreement very personally. 'I never seem to get any peace in this

110

world,' he had written in his diary when the dispute started the previous year. 'Feel very low and depressed.' He was horrified in May 1926 when the gung-ho Winston Churchill, the Chancellor of the Exchequer, publicly suggested that the army should be turned on the strikers, and, as the crisis persisted, he held a meeting with the Home Secretary and Attorney-General to emphasise his doubts. In some creative lateral thinking, he drew his ministers' attention to a recent football match that had been organised in Plymouth: Police versus Strikers. This was the atmosphere to engender, he suggested. On the King's instructions, Stamfordham clipped and sent to the Prime Minister, Stanley Baldwin, a front-page leader from the *Manchester Guardian* which warned how extremism on either side could endanger 'the wholehearted and healthy relations of classes in this country'. 'Perhaps it may have escaped your notice,' wrote the private secretary to the Prime Minister's office, 'so I enclose a copy. One must remember the circulation of the "Manchester Guardian" in the North of England.'

On 12 May the TUC called the strike off. Volunteering to drive buses and trains and enrolling as special constables, most of the country had supported the elected government, not the strikers—and outside Bruton Street there were some people for whom the strike might not have happened at all. When Mabell Airlie, Queen Mary's lady-in-waiting, arrived at no. 17 to deliver the bottle of Jordan water from the Holy Land with which the baby would be christened, she had to pick her way through a crowd of spectators. Prince Albert told her it was a larger crowd than usual, but that spectators had gathered outside every day for the last three weeks. People had been thronging the street in such numbers, in fact, that his little daughter had had to be smuggled out of a rear door for her daily airing.

On 29 May the christening took place in Buckingham Palace. The child was baptised Elizabeth Alexandra Mary after her mother, great-grandmother and grandmother, and the ceremony went off traditionally in every sense. 'Of course,' noted Queen Mary, 'poor baby cried.' The future Elizabeth II cried so much, in fact, that she had to be dosed with dill water. It was the last recorded instance of her surrendering to anything like a tantrum.

The ceremony was a reminder of how much the royal family still lived in the shadow of Queen Victoria. The gold font used for her children's baptisms was brought up from Windsor, and the baby princess was robed in the satin and lace gown made for the great queen's first daughter and worn by royal children ever since. But though Queen Victoria had ordained that children in the direct line of succession should be named in memory of either her beloved Albert or of herself, King George V felt the rule could be waived for this new arrival. 'I hardly think that necessary,' wrote the King to his wife. The little girl was not, after all, likely to accede to the throne.

CHAPTER SIX

Model Family

Real people live in Buckingham Palace, but always smiling, perfectly dressed . . . It is a consolation to know that such beings exist. If they live, then we too live in them vicariously.

Virginia Woolf, 1939

Early in January 1927, King George V despatched the Duke of York and his attractive little wife, now routinely referred to as 'the smiling Duchess', to Australia to open the new Parliament building in Canberra. Their new baby was just eight months old.

'It quite broke me up,' confessed Princess Elizabeth's mother, recalling the moment of parting. 'The baby was so sweet, playing with the buttons on Bertie's uniform.' As she and her husband headed for Victoria Station, the Duchess had to be driven twice around Grosvenor Gardens to compose herself for the public farewell ceremony.

It was to be nearly six months before the infant Princess Elizabeth saw her parents again, in which time she celebrated her first birthday and took her first steps—to the applause of servants and grandparents. She sat for monthly photographs that were sent out to her parents, and her nanny worked hard to preserve the parental presence. Showing the baby a picture of her mother, she coached her to say 'Mummy'. But her earnest pupil seems to have thought the word referred to the object rather than the person portrayed, for she started welcoming all and sundry as 'Mummy'— and even issued greetings to a few family portraits which pleased her.

Her nanny, Clara Knight, a large, square-jawed countrywoman, had nursed many a young Strathmore, including Princess Elizabeth's own mother. Her small charges, who had difficulty getting their tongues around 'Clara', knew her as 'Alla'. Though a spinster, she was given the courtesy title of 'Mrs' like all senior nannies in high-society households of the day. Photographs show her as an unmistakable authority figure in her nurse's uniform, amply bosomed, a faint and knowing smile on her lips. With her square frame and square black hat pulled down to her ears, she seems uncannily similar, to a modern eye, to Robin Williams in his role in the film *Mrs Doubtfire*.

Alla was old-fashioned and firm in the tradition of the professional nanny, ruling her nursery like an absolute monarch and instilling discipline and regularity in everything from mealtimes to bowel movements. In later years Princess Elizabeth was to be noted as remarkably neat and tidy, going to great trouble to line up her shoes and toy horses with military precision. She had entered Alla's kingdom on the day she was born, and it had been in Alla's firm embrace that she was smuggled out to take the air in Berkeley Square in her earliest weeks.

As the Duke and Duchess sailed around the world, travelling to Australia via Panama and returning via Suez, their daughter was also on her travels, her time divided between her two sets of grandparents; so the adults closest to the baby were all significantly senior and definitely formal folk. Even her beloved Alla was from the same generation as her grandparents. Small wonder that contemporary reports should depict the princess as a solemn and self-contained little girl, not so much a child as a tiny adult.

For the last three months of her first year, she had the uniquely formative experience of being the centre of attention at Buckingham Palace. She camped in borrowed quarters in an upper wing, and the highlight of her day was tea with the King and Queen. Every afternoon she would be reverently groomed for the occasion, her nurse brushing her hair and clothing her in a white gown and fringed sash before bearing her in to the royal presence.

The contemporary account of this occasion makes much of Queen Mary's human response to the infant's arrival. 'Here comes the Bambino!' the normally stiff Queen was reported to cry out with delight. But one can only guess at the veneration imprinted in a year-old child by the daily sensation of being ritually prepared, then swished down long corridors to the holy of holies by servants who were positively tingling with awe and homage.

Moulding her in another way was the experience of being driven out in the park most days with Alla in an open carriage from the Royal Mews. Spectators would wave at the famous baby, and one of the first gestures Princess Elizabeth learnt was to wave back. From her earliest coherent consciousness she was an item of public interest whose affection was confidently claimed by the knots of curious and friendly strangers who peered and cheered. At the sight of the little princess they would leap into happy animation, as if a child of their own were riding by in a royal carriage, and though she had no personal acquaintance with these maniacally waving adults, she responded as if, in some way, she did.

By the time her mother and father got home at the end of June 1927, the princess had spent almost half her life without them. Her mother returned a royal trouper par excellence—to meet another in her fifteen-month-old baby. When mother and daughter met, we are told, the little girl was 'almost as pleased' to see her mother as if the Duchess had been 'quite a large crowd'. The Duchess's authorised biographer, Lady Cynthia Asquith, seemed to think this a good thing and, unaware of the chilling implications of her comparison, she described the young princess's reaction to both crowd and mother as identical: 'her round face breaks into a wide smile and her arms go out.' Inside this much-scrutinised little creature the strands of public and private were already getting intertwined—and, perhaps, confused.

In the autumn of 1928 Winston Churchill was invited up to Balmoral, where he encountered the young Princess Elizabeth, by then aged two and a half. '[She] is a character,' wrote the 54-year-old Chancellor of the Exchequer to his wife. 'She had an air of authority and reflectiveness astonishing in an infant.'

*   *   *

At the age of three Princess Elizabeth appeared on

the cover of *Time* magazine, presented in a role with which she would seldom be credited in later life, as a setter of fashion trends. Children all over America were being dressed in yellow, it was reported, instead of the usual pink or blue, because it had been revealed that yellow was the colour favoured by the princess's mother for her daughter's clothes and the walls of her nursery.

The Duchess of York enjoyed getting details like this published about her daughter. Within a month of her return from Australia in 1927, the Duchess had embarked on an unusual project with the writer Lady Cynthia Asquith, daughter-in-law of the Liberal leader Herbert Asquith and secretary to J. M. Barrie, the creator of Peter Pan. Lady Cynthia had been born into the Wemyss clan, old Scottish friends of the Strathmores who were regular guests at Glamis, and the plan was for her to produce an 'intimate and authentic' life of the Duchess, with an emphasis on her motherhood and new baby. In July 1927 Lady Cynthia met up over tea with the Duchess, who handed over a selection of family photographs and instructed her servants and relatives, including her closest brother David, to talk freely to the author. The result was a doting and syrupy volume, serialised in women's magazines in Britain, America and all over the empire, particularly in the white dominions of Canada, South Africa, New Zealand and Australia.

In 1930, a similar exercise produced *The Story of Princess Elizabeth: Told with the Sanction of her Parents—By Anne Ring, formerly attached to H.R.H. The Duchess of York's Household.* By now the princess was four. The family had been settled for some time at 145 Piccadilly, an imposing double-fronted stone house that looked out across Green Park, and with royal sanction Ms Ring took her readers on a tour of the plum-carpeted premises. Readers were taken up to the nursery floor, saw the rocking-horse on the landing, and could almost touch the little scarlet brush and dustpan with which the young princess was taught to keep her room tidy. They were even invited inside the bathroom to imagine the naked splashings of 'a damp, pink cherub who seemed to be finding this bathing business the perfect end to what had been a perfect day'.

The smiling Duchess of York took the precedent set by Queen Victoria's best-selling *Leaves from the Journal of my Life in the Highlands* to new levels. Staid biographies of senior living figures like Queen Mary had been attempted, along with picture albums based on the spectacularly successful foreign tours of the Prince of Wales. But with naked babes in the bath and a voyeuristic emphasis on domestic furnishings, Lady Cynthia and Ms Ring developed a new style of intimacy one would have called intrusive if it had not been encouraged by their royal patron. They were to spawn a whole new genre of mass-market Windsor fan books, which went through numerous editions and regular updatings, plus accompanying replays in the women's magazines. Their uncritical snippets of harmless and adoring gossip suggested that the Duchess had thoroughly absorbed her mother's thoughts on royalty, sea-lions and fish.

In 1969 the BBC's *Royal Family* documentary film was to turn equivalent material into television, developing the relationship between the monarchy and the corporation that went back to April 1924, when King George V opened the British Empire exhibition at Wembley. His speech was broadcast by the new popular medium of wireless and attracted an audience of no fewer than ten million, with crowds gathering around loudspeakers in the city centres of Manchester, Leeds and Glasgow. The King's hoarse voice, 'as if roughened by weather', as A. C. Benson described it, was warm and intriguing when broadcast, and through the 1920s the BBC regularly transmitted his speeches on ceremonial occasions.

It was in 1932 that he made his first Christmas broadcast.

'I speak now from my home and from my heart to you all, to men and women so cut off by the snows, the desert, or the sea, that only voices out of the air can reach them.'

The royal eloquence owed much to Rudyard Kipling, who had drafted the King's 251 words. Subsequent broadcasts never quite recaptured that first magic—perhaps because the drafting was taken over by the Archbishop of Canterbury. The King himself hated the Christmas broadcast and was only with great difficulty persuaded to continue it. He was a nervous performer. The BBC had to cover his desk with a thick cloth to deaden the sound of his papers rustling. It ruined his Christmas Day, the King complained. But it made everyone else's.

*　　　*　　　*

On 21 August 1930 a new character was added to the royal cast—a younger sister for Princess Elizabeth, born in Glamis Castle. In accordance

119

with custom, the Home Secretary of the day was summoned to be present, and since Britain now had a Labour government, this duty was performed by one of the several working-class members of the Cabinet: J. R. Clynes, a self-educated cotton-mill worker. Clynes thoroughly enjoyed his five days waiting for the call to Macbeth's haunted castle, and he entered into the fairy-tale spirit in his description of the local welcome. 'The countryside was made vivid with the red glow of a hundred bonfires,' he wrote, 'while sturdy kilted men with flaming torches ran like gnomes from place to place through the darkness.'

The gnomes and bonfires masked a certain disappointment. There had been a hope that the new arrival would be a boy. The baby's parents had not given much thought to what to call a daughter, and it was September before the new princess got a name—Margaret Rose. With the Prince of Wales still unmarried, the feeling was growing that the succession might actually slip sideways to his younger brother and thus to his children, and, acknowledging that possibility, King George V commissioned a special investigation of an issue that was raised by the newspapers. Which of the Yorks' two little daughters had precedence? Nothing in law explicitly gave Elizabeth succession rights over Margaret, or even prohibited the unusual prospect of a sisterly throne-share.

The formal decision confirming Elizabeth's seniority raised the profile of the four-year-old. She made her debut in wax at Madame Tussaud's riding on a pony. Her face featured on a stamp in Newfoundland, and as geographers carved up Antarctica, a slice of frozen ground around longitude 80 degrees east was named Princess Elizabeth Land.

Talking to the poet and essayist Osbert Sitwell one night in the early 1930s, the Duke of York compared his elder daughter to Queen Victoria—then gave Sitwell a very direct and meaningful look. 'From the first moment of talking,' said the prince, 'she showed so much character, that it was impossible not to wonder whether history would not repeat itself.'

The more immediate consequence of Princess Margaret's birth was a reorganisation of nursery management. Alla's duties were shifted to full-time care of the new arrival, and Princess Elizabeth's new mentor was the senior nanny's assistant, Margaret MacDonald. The daughter of an Inverness railway worker who had grown up in a company cottage beside the railway line, Miss MacDonald had entered the Yorks' household at the age of twenty-two when Princess Elizabeth was born, and in best nursery tradition she had been rechristened Bobo.

From 1930 onwards, Bobo MacDonald was to become closer to her charge than anyone outside the princess's family. This plain-spoken, red-haired young Scotswoman shared the princess's bedroom through much of her childhood, and in adult life was to become her dresser. Bobo was to remain the most intimate companion and confidante of Queen Elizabeth II, accompanying her on all her tours and living in some state in Buckingham Palace. A legendary figure by the time of her death in 1993, aged eighty-nine, Bobo was credited with everything from her mistress's notoriously unmatching handbags to her frugality. The railwayman's daughter trained the princess to save the wrapping paper from her presents after Christmas and birthdays. This would then be neatly smoothed and stored away in a special box, with the gift ribbon rolled up for future use.

Such parsimony was in keeping with the times. Princess Margaret was born ten months after the great crash on Wall Street; another year on, in September 1931, the ever-weakening British economy was forced off the gold standard and the pound was devalued by 30 per cent. Until this point, Britain's deepening economic depression had had little effect on Princess Elizabeth's charmed and sheltered nursery life. But now King George V decided that the royal family must tighten its belt like the rest of the country. He decreed a 50 per cent cut in his income from the government, the Civil List, with corresponding cuts for the rest of the family—to the fury of his eldest son, who was phoned with the news while dancing in Bayonne with his latest married mistress, Thelma, Lady Furness.

Bertie was also compelled to make economies. The Duke of York gave up hunting, his great winter pastime and pleasure. 'I must sell my horses, too,' he wrote to the master of the Pytchley Hunt. 'This is the worst part of it all, and the parting with them will be terrible.' That November Bertie watched his six beloved hunters sold in a Leicester auction ring for a total of 965 guineas (just over £1,000).

For his daughters, the prince's economies actually proved a bonus. Their father had been in the habit of renting winter homes in draughty Midlands hunting counties, but now they acquired a cosier, closer and permanent country base. Royal Lodge in Windsor Great Park was one of the rent-free 'grace and favour' residences available for royal family and friends, and the Duke and Duchess of York devoted their energies to turning it into a country weekend home. The only reminder of the harsh reality of how 1930s Depression life was lived away from the coppiced woods and riding paths of the royal Great Park was a miniature cottage in the grounds of Royal Lodge, 'Y Bwthyn Bach', 'The Little House', a present from 'The People of Wales'.

Built of Welsh materials by Welsh craftspeople, some of the most cruelly hit labourers of the Depression, the little house was a propaganda make-work project. It was first exhibited at the Ideal Home Exhibition, then transferred to Windsor where it was relentlessly photographed for upbeat magazine features, with its two princessly occupants acting out the role of apprentice housewives. Everything was meticulously constructed to two-thirds scale, from the wireless set on the miniature dresser to the packet of Epsom Salts on the bathroom shelf beside the heated towel rail.

Model house, model family—the messages were manifold. Welsh labour could do it. The royal family sympathised. Domestic virtues were worth celebrating and would triumph. The Little House was a parable not just for Wales, but for the economic distress of the whole country. As fairy-tales tame frightening realities, so the Goldilocks scale of the cottage helped to make a desperate situation seem more secure and manageable—and the little princesses solemnly played their part.

Busily dusting and cleaning, they were exemplars of the same industrious values as their subjects.

The spectacle of little girls dusting for Britain would not impress a modern feminist. But in the depths of the Depression, the sight of princesses turning their hands to the duties of domestic servants seemed forward-thinking and thoroughly salutary. The effect on the two girls themselves, was, perhaps, less pondered. Princess Elizabeth was to emerge from a childhood of symbolic exhibitionism with her humility intact. She appears to have understood the purpose of the performance and to have absorbed it into her ever more dutiful persona. In her sister Margaret, however, the photography and attention had exactly the opposite effect. Being told to play in order to edify the world encouraged a sense of self-importance that was to bedevil her adult life—and her sister's as well.

'Setting an example' was the increasingly insistent theme song of the young York family as the 1930s advanced, for, quite apart from the country's economic difficulties, there were troubles inside the House of Windsor itself. In January 1932 the Prince of Wales had first invited Mrs Wallis Simpson and her husband Ernest to Fort Belvedere, his own weekend home at the edge of the Great Park, a few miles away from Royal Lodge. The romance between the Prince and Mrs Simpson would take some time to develop, but the heir to the throne's rackety lifestyle of night-clubs and mistresses was starting to cause disquiet within the family and gossip outside. As King George V contemplated what his children had made of their royal legacy, there was little to encourage him. The

King's rustic third son, Harry, Duke of Gloucester, was an undistinguished army officer whose passion was fox-hunting. His fourth son, George, Duke of Kent, was strikingly good-looking, but was said to be bisexual and had had a nasty brush with drug addiction.

In this unsatisfactory cast of characters, Bertie, Elizabeth and their two daughters were the stars. Their affectionate and tight family grouping had become the very epitome of middle-class values in the age of the suburban nuclear family. They lived in a grand, but none the less terraced townhouse with a number on the door, just a few yards away from a bus stop—the neat, hard-working husband, the adoring mother and the two well-behaved little girls in ankle socks. They were a dream model of domesticity, for all the world, as the author John Pearson has remarked, like the characters in an Ovaltine advertisement. The imagery of Victoria and Edward VII had emphasised the splendour of royal folk; the canny Duchess of York followed the logic of her father-in-law George V to construct a new mythology of ordinariness.

By now the women's magazines had revealed King George V's name for his favourite grand-daughter—'Lilibet', derived from her first babyish attempts to pronounce her own name. America had Shirley Temple; Britain had its own princess—'utterly unspoiled and in every respect a typical English child', as one of many admiring articles described her early in 1935. The nine-year-old princess's composed youthfulness was a prominent feature of King George V's Silver Jubilee, celebrated later that year. Dressed in pink, she sat on a chair just behind her grandparents in St Paul's

Cathedral and rode with her sister and parents through the cheering crowds—'the greatest number of people in the streets', wrote George V in his diary, 'that I have ever seen in my life.'

It was the first royal jubilee to depart from the festival's original half-century concept to celebrate as few as twenty-five years on the throne. Henry I, Henry II, Henry III, Edward I, Edward III, Henry VI, Henry VIII, Elizabeth I, George II, George III and Queen Victoria all achieved twenty-five years, but none marked the occasion with a Silver Jubilee. George V's decision to do so showed how the modern, mass-media monarchy had come to rely on street pageantry and public ceremonial, giving traditions that seemed time-honoured an alertly calculating twist.

In 1935 the ceremonial urge contained a strong dash of politics. With a general election in the offing, Ramsay MacDonald's coalition National Government had foreseen the usefulness of some national enthusiasm—which might yield foreign policy benefits as well. 'This'll show 'em,' thought Neville Chamberlain, as he looked across St Paul's at the row of foreign ambassadors. The Chancellor of the Exchequer felt uplifted by the spirit expressed that morning by a Westminster flower seller—'Ain't it glorious to be an Englishman?' The royal focus galvanised loyalty and people power. There is no evidence that this was remarked in the chancelleries of Hitler and Mussolini, but the French ambassador René Corbin noted 'the cohesion and power which the family of the British Democracies draw from their attachment to the Crown'. George V, he reported to the Quai d'Orsay, had made himself 'the father of his peoples, and to that loyalty he has added the warmth of love. That is the secret of the personal and living emotion which today fills the heart of this Kingdom and Empire.'

'How can I express what is in my heart?' asked George V as he broadcast live from Buckingham Palace that night. '. . . Words cannot express my thoughts and feelings. I can only say to you, my very dear people, that the Queen and I thank you from the depth of our hearts for all the loyalty and—may I say?—the love with which this day and always you have surrounded us.'

His emotion-charged language reflected an emotion-charged day. Walking through London's flag- and bunting-bedecked streets, George Orwell noted placards that read 'Long Live the King. Down with the Landlord.' 'It was even possible to see', wrote the old Etonian who had once chosen to live as a beggar in the East End of London, 'the survival, or recrudescence, of an idea almost as old as history, the idea of the King and the common people being in a sort of alliance against the upper classes.'

The King certainly had the plain man's view when it came to religious pomp and circumstance. 'A wonderful service,' he told the Dean of St Paul's as he left the cathedral. 'The Queen and I are most grateful. Just one thing wrong with it—too many damn parsons getting in the way. I didn't know there were so many damn parsons in England.'

CHAPTER SEVEN

Abdication

Old men who never cheated, never doubted,
Communicated monthly, sit and stare
At a red suburb ruled by Mrs Simpson,
Where a young man lands hatless from the air.

John Betjeman,
'On the Death of King George V'

Late on the evening of Monday, 20 January 1936, King George V's doctor, Lord Dawson of Penn, picked up a menu card in the household dining room at Sandringham and wrote a medical bulletin on the back. 'The king's life is moving peacefully towards its close.'

Regular programming was suspended as the weighty and well-turned words were read out on the BBC. Dancing stopped in West End restaurants, and crowds gathered outside Buckingham Palace.

The 70-year-old King had been sinking for some weeks. He had not been out shooting since 14 November, and had complained of chest pains over Christmas. Dozing by his bedroom fire in a faded old Tibetan dressing gown, he needed oxygen bottles to aid his breathing at night. It was clear to Lord Dawson that his patient's heart was weakening, and when he discussed the King's decline with the family in the middle of January, the doctor was given clear instructions. Neither the

128

Prince of Wales nor his mother Queen Mary, said the prince, wished 'the King's life to be prolonged if I [Dawson] judged the illness to be mortal'.

Dawson's careful notes of his royal patient's final illness remained private for fifty years. But in 1986 they were published by his biographer Francis Watson, revealing a dramatic new dimension to the famous medical bulletin—and, in particular, the doctor's confident choice of the words 'peacefully' and 'close'.

'At about 11 o-clock', ran Dawson's narrative of George V's final evening, 'it was evident that the last stage might endure for many hours, unknown to the Patient, but little comporting with that dignity and serenity which he so richly merited and which demanded a brief final scene.' Dawson therefore decided to inject a lethal dose of morphia (3/4 gram) and cocaine (1 gram) into the King's distended jugular vein. 'Breathing quieter,' he noted a quarter of an hour later, 'appearance more placid—physical struggle gone.' The doctor then called the Queen and family into the room to make their farewells and to observe the end, which came with little delay, according to his notification of death, at 11.55 p.m.—within an hour of his injection.

'Hours of waiting just for the mechanical end,' Dawson later wrote, 'when all that is really life has departed, only exhausts the onlooker and keeps them so strained they cannot avail themselves of the solace of thought, communion or prayer.' But the royal doctor added a further explanation of his frankly admitted euthanasia. 'The determination of the time of death of the King's body,' he unblinkingly recorded for posterity, 'had another object in view, *viz.* the importance of the death receiving its first announcement in the morning papers rather than the less appropriate field of the evening journals.'

Dawson's concern was such that he phoned his wife in London, asking her to let the editor of *The Times* know that the paper should hold back publication for as long as possible. In the 1930s 'The Thunderer' was still the monumental and unchallenged newspaper of record, with the evening papers tending to a less starchy and more informal style. The passing of the monarch was a weighty and historic event that deserved better company, in the doctor's opinion, than cooking tips and racing results. Thanks to Dawson's tip-off, *The Times* slowed production, prepared its obituary copy, and had managed to restrict its output to only thirty thousand copies by the time the news of the King's death reached London before midnight. 'The change was quickly and smoothly made,' recorded Geoffrey Dawson (no relation), the paper's famous editor. 'We got the leader, the pictures, and the memoir into 300,000 copies.'

So, with the help of his considerate doctor, who did not entertain a moment's doubt that he was doing the right and dignified thing by his royal patient, George V performed the ultimate duty of the media monarch. He died in time for the morning editions.

*　　　　*　　　　*

Princess Elizabeth had been staying at Sandringham during her grandfather's final weeks. The stiff old King relaxed with his grand-daughter as he never could with his own children. She had cheered him with games in the evening and had accompanied him outside on at least one occasion.

'Out of the mist came the King, mounted on his white pony, Jock,' recalled a household servant of his final, dream-like sighting of his master, a few days after Christmas. 'Walking by the head of the pony, as if leading it along, was the little figure of Princess Elizabeth. She was taking her grandfather back to the house.'

Lord Dawson recalled the little girl dealing adroitly with an invitation from Cosmo Lang, the intimidating old Archbishop of Canterbury, who enquired if she would care to take a walk in the grounds. 'Yes, very much,' the self-assured nine-year-old was reported to have replied. 'But please do not tell me anything more about God. I know all about him already.'

On 23 January 1936 the King's body was brought down to London to lie in state beneath the beams of Westminster Hall, continuing the tradition inaugurated by Edward VII. As in 1910, it was a nation-stopping event. Huge crowds of mourners queued and filed along the banks of the Thames for five days and five nights to shuffle past the flag-draped coffin. At each corner of the catafalque stood a Guards officer in bearskin and full dress uniform, his head bowed, hands clasped on the hilt of his drawn sword. But on the final night of the vigil, the relays of officers stood down, to be replaced for a while by the four sons of the dead monarch—the Dukes of York, Gloucester and Kent, and the new King Edward VIII—each dressed in the uniforms of their respective services.

The 9-year-old Princess Elizabeth was allowed

to stay up late. Dressed in a black coat and a black velvet tammy, she was brought by her mother to stand in front of the coffin in the sombre and silent medieval hall and witness the unforgettable sight.

'Uncle David was there,' she reported on her return to 145 Piccadilly, 'and he never moved at all ... not even an eyelid.'

*   *   *

The dramatic vigil of the princes had been the idea of the new King. Edward VIII, forty-one years old when he came to the throne, had a gift for imaginative public gestures. The hatless young man of John Betjeman's poem, who used aeroplanes and had no time for old-fashioned headgear, was fizzing with ideas for making what he described as the 'old hat' monarchy more in touch. But he was also preoccupied. By January 1936 Mrs Simpson had been at the centre of his life for two years, and his spirit was consumed by his passion for the polished and demanding American divorcee—'as necessary to his happiness', as Winston Churchill commented, 'as the air he breathed.'

The King's dogged love for Mrs Simpson was haunted by an ineradicable lack of logic that was comparable to the magic of royalty itself. Edward VIII's accession to the throne, which should have been a culminating moment for him, confronted him with dreadful problems. The rest of 1936 was to be dominated, and would come to be remembered historically, for the King's attempts to reconcile his compulsive personal priorities with the equally powerful requirements of his public duty.

132

The conflict went back long before Mrs Simpson. Handsome, fluent and charming, David had been set to public duties from an early age. He spent the Great War in uniform, the model royal soldier, showing himself up and down the front, conscientiously distressed that he was being kept away from the risks of real combat and could offer no more than what he called 'propaganda' and 'stunts'. With peace, his father had assigned his eldest son the job of travelling the world to thank the empire for its help, and these much fêted tours completed the process that made the prince, as Sir John Simon, the Home Secretary put it, 'the most widely known and universally popular personality in the world'. He was the jazz age prince, the first young British royal to be a media celebrity.

Fifty Thousand Miles with the Prince of Wales was the title of one of the feature-film-length reports on his tours, released in the autumn of 1920. Cinema-goers watched the prince hand-shaking his way from the West Indies via Panama across the Pacific to New Zealand and Australia, meeting Maoris and Aborigines and going through the rituals of the 'crossing-the-line ceremony' at the Equator. His nervous smile was endearing. At home the cameramen gathered around the first jump of the point-to-point steeplechases in which he competed with more enthusiasm than success. 'Can't you buggers go to the second jump for a change?' he shouted as he climbed to his feet after yet another first-jump débâcle.

'What an unnatural life for a poor little boy of 25 . . .' he wrote to Freda Dudley Ward in October 1919, while touring Canada. 'I do get so terribly fed up with it & despondent about it sometimes &

begin to feel like "resigning"!!' A month or so later he wrote to his mistress from New Zealand. 'Each day I long more & more to chuck this job & be out of it & free for YOU, sweetie.'

There was more to this disenchantment than pining for a distant lover. From an early date, the prince separated his concept of personal fulfilment from what he called his 'job', a brisk, modern word that had professional connotations, but which also carried a 'nine to five' dimension for the young man. Happiness started when the job was over. 'The more I think of it all,' he wrote to Freda, 'the more certain I am that really . . . the day for Kings & Princes is past, monarchies are out-of-date.'

David's male confidant was Godfrey Thomas, a young diplomat who had joined his staff at the beginning of the Great War, and to whom the prince poured out his heart in letters that indicated soul-searching along with his discontent. 'How I loathe my job now,' he wrote on Christmas Day 1919, 'and all this press "puffed" empty "*succès*". I feel I'm through with it and long to die.'

The prince wrote this after his tour of North America. The trip had been a spectacular public success, with vast crowds waiting and screaming for him. The royal visitor had secured blanket coverage in the picture magazines—a Hollywood star before the concept had been invented. But the adulation left him feeling empty and desperate. For David, the confluence of royalness and celebrity was an eroding and debasing experience. 'I can put up with a certain amount of contact with officials and newspapers on official trips', he wrote later to Thomas, '. . . It's when they get in on my private life that I want to pull out a gun and kill.'

This was the cry of a young man in pain—a remarkably self-centred young man, whose egoism has been amply documented, but one who also represented everything towards which the British royal family had been heading since the reign of his great-grandmother Queen Victoria. The Prince of Wales had been the youthful family pace-setter of George V's revolution-proofing strategy. David's war work on the Western Front, his postwar tours of the empire, and his later visits during the Depression to stricken working-class areas were all carried out directly on the orders of his father. The old King grumbled frequently about David's modern failings, from plus-fours to his fondness for 'weekends', but that did not stop the King relentlessly exploiting his son's modernity to buttress the Windsor vision of a people-friendly monarchy. The result was the world's first and most spectacular case of celebrity burnout.

Long analyses of the abdication have been devoted to showing how the episode was considerably more complicated than the sentimental legend of the king who gave up his throne for love—and so it was; but 'love' remains the fundamental and decisive explanation. Through a succession of married women, from Mrs Dudley Ward to his gamy and engulfing obsession for Mrs Simpson, the charismatic prince who became King Edward VIII was searching for someone—not so much a cause as a pretext—who would provide him with release from the fearful destiny of being royal.

Ratcheting up the tension was the constant threat of press exposure. As the dénouement approached in October 1936, when Mrs Simpson's petition for divorce from her husband Ernest went into open court, thus leaving Wallis legally free to remarry, Britain's newspaper proprietors were corralled by the Express owner Lord Beaverbrook. They agreed among themselves to limit coverage of the case. But for the previous two years there had been no formal press agreement. The British media, national and local, had maintained silence, and distributors had declined to handle the 'irresponsible' foreign publications who revelled in the scandal, on no other basis than deference.

The editor and newspaper director Sir Edward Pickering, then a reporter on the *Northern Echo*, recalls covering the visit of the Prince of Wales to the Durham coalfields in the early 1930s. The prince was charm itself in his dealings with the miners; but Pickering was astonished at his persistent rudeness to the local mayors and civic worthies he encountered. Nowadays, such blatant snubbing would be the story. In 1934, the cub reporter no more dreamed of describing such royal discourtesy than his editor would have dreamed of publishing it. 'It was the code,' says Pickering.

When the London papers did, finally, break the story of the King's love for Mrs Simpson on 3 December 1936, the main issues of the crisis had already been defined behind the scenes. In an emotional confrontation on 16 November at Buckingham Palace, Edward VIII had told his Prime Minister, Stanley Baldwin, that he intended to marry Wallis as soon as possible and that he was prepared to abdicate the throne if the government opposed the marriage.

In law, the King did not require his ministers' consent to make his marriage legal. The Royal

Marriages Act applied to all members of the family except the sovereign. But Edward conceded without argument the unwritten principle that the government had a say in his choice of consort, appearing to believe he could convince his Prime Minister of Wallis's virtues. The King's face, Baldwin told his family later, 'wore, at times, such a look of beauty as might have lighted the face of a young knight who had caught a glimpse of the Holy Grail'.

Many noted the trance-like state that the King appeared to have entered once he had made his decision—win or lose. 'The King was jolly, gay and full of cracks,' wrote Chips Channon of the royal mood on Thursday, 19 November 1936. On this occasion David felt confident that he could accomplish everything, telling his youngest and favourite brother, the Duke of Kent, that he was going to marry Wallis and make her 'Queen of England . . . Yes, and Empress of India, the whole bag of tricks.' The previous day the King had been standing among the unemployed steelworkers at Dowlais in South Wales, listening to them sing old Welsh hymns amid the ruins of their steelworks. 'Something must be done,' he had famously uttered, and next day, before his return to London, he had received a tumultuous welcome from the people of Pontypool. With newspapers writing leaders praising 'The King Edward Touch', he felt that nothing was impossible. 'He imagines', said Ramsay MacDonald on 30 November, 'that the country, the great warm heart of the people, are with him.'

It was the reaction of the press when the news became public that brought Edward VIII down to earth. The idea of the King marrying a commoner was widely welcomed, and there was no written objection to her being American. Several papers insisted that they liked the idea, and Edward's flair as monarch was warmly praised by the *Daily Mail* and the *Daily Express*—reflecting the King's acquaintance with their proprietors, Lords Rothermere and Beaverbrook.

But all the editorials stopped well short of advocating that Mrs Simpson should become Queen. Not even the King's allies could argue for that, since Wallis's two divorces and the fact that both her husbands were living were held to be insuperable obstacles. The nonconformist *News Chronicle* proposed a morganatic marriage—the Teutonic device for regulating a love match by giving the wife a lesser status and removing any children from the succession. Not a single national newspaper was prepared to argue that Wallis Simpson should be consecrated Queen.

The evening and provincial press were overtly hostile. 'Whatever other position in society she may adorn,' declared the *Birmingham Post* in a scathing editorial, Mrs Simpson 'is not the person to become Queen of England.' The influential Midlands paper argued that the King himself had condemned Mrs Simpson: Edward's request to Baldwin to consider the second-best device of a morganatic marriage proved 'the fact of her unsuitability'. 'They don't want me,' the King said, crestfallen, to Baldwin, as he showed the Prime Minister the editorial.

MPs went off for the weekend to take the measure of their constituents' feelings. 'Our people won't 'ave it,' declared Ernest Bevin for the TUC, endorsing the opinion that Labour Party leader Clement Attlee had already given to Stanley Baldwin: No to Mrs Simpson, Yes to Abdication. Attlee later noted in his memoirs that this position was duly endorsed by virtually all his Labour MPs—'with the exception of the intelligentsia, who can be trusted to take the wrong view on any subject'.

Baldwin had been tough and shrewd. As it became clear that his Cabinet, along with the leaders of the dominion governments whom he consulted by telegram, were unwilling to accept Mrs Simpson, either as Queen or as some sort of morganatic, unofficial wife, he manoeuvred the King into a corner. Securing assurances from the opposition leaders of the Labour and Liberal parties that they would refuse to try to form an alternative government if conflict with the King led to the Prime Minister resigning, he held the key political cards—and also made explicit a previously unresolved principle. In the final analysis it was not the King who chose who would be Queen. It was the people.

'The Throne is Greater than the Man' read the caption of a *Punch* cartoon which depicted Baldwin confronting Edward VIII with 'The Choice'. At ten-thirty in the morning of 10 December 1936, at Fort Belvedere, King Edward VIII formally signed the document by which he renounced his crown and went into exile.

A few days earlier Harold Nicolson had met Stanley Baldwin's son Oliver and heard the story of the Prime Minister's final and crucial negotiation with the King, walking round and round the garden at Fort Belvedere, in the course of which Edward

VIII had finally yielded to reality and agreed that he must go.

As one looks back today from 2002, when the question of whether Prince Charles could make Camilla Parker Bowles his queen is commonly said to involve the attitude of the Church of England, it is worth recalling that in 1936 the church played no formal part in events. Cosmo Lang, the pious Archbishop of Canterbury, made himself a brooding presence on the sidelines, and delivered a controversial sermon after the event. But church law and doctrine had no formal role in a decision that boiled down to the Prime Minister's own assessment of what the electorate wanted and would be prepared to support.

'Stanley Baldwin was feeling exhausted,' wrote Nicolson. 'He asked for a whisky-and-soda. The bell was rung: the footman came: the drink was produced. S.B. raised his glass and said, (rather foolishly to my mind) "Well, sir, whatever happens, my Mrs and I wish you happiness from the depths of our souls."'

At which point, according to Oliver Baldwin, both the King and his Prime Minister, sitting side by side on the sofa, burst into floods of tears.

*   *   *

The whole nation was overwrought. People felt betrayed that Edward VIII could value anything more than being their king. The correspondence files of Stanley Baldwin contain boxes packed with agonised letters expressing their writers' pain at the abdication and, for the most part, their gratitude to the Prime Minister for resolving the tragedy so quickly—in the eyes of some, quite miraculously.

It was another of those national moments when the country stood still, its whole destiny seeming to depend on the actions of the royal family. In reality, the opposite had been the case. The crucial decision had been taken by the politicians. The expulsion of Edward VIII had been ruthless, a stark reminder of the powerlessness of the cipher monarchy. The Duchess of Windsor later wrote of

my failure to understand the King's true position in the constitutional system. The apparent deference to his every wish, the adulation of the populace, the universal desire even of the most exalted of his subjects to be accorded marks of his esteem—all this had persuaded me to take literally the ancient maxim that 'the King can do no wrong'. Nothing that I had seen had made me appreciate how vulnerable the King really was, how little power he could actually command, how little his wishes really counted for against those of his Ministers and Parliament.

$$*\qquad*\qquad*$$

Bertie and David parted on affectionate terms.

'Thank you, Sir, for all your kindness to me,' the ex-King said as he bowed respectfully and kissed his younger brother's hand, refusing Bertie's embarrassed protests. 'It's all right, old man,' said David, 'I must step off with the right foot from the first.'

But the goodwill rapidly evaporated as the practicalities of their reversed roles hit home.

Money was the principal irritant, for the ex-King had failed to disclose his substantial personal savings in negotiating the financial package that accompanied his departure. As Prince of Wales he had accumulated nearly £1 million (over £30 million in today's values) from his revenues from the Duchy of Cornwall, and he regarded this as his private nest-egg. When the new King George VI and his advisers discovered this a few weeks after his departure, they were horrified. David had accumulated the savings as a function of his royal position. This had constitutional implications, and the sum should have been openly put on the table in the complicated negotiations which involved both public funding and private complexities like the ownership of Sandringham and Balmoral. While state-owned palaces like Buckingham Palace and Windsor went with the job, these two large country estates, purchased privately by Queen Victoria, had been left to David by his father. So the new King had to dig into his own pocket to buy them back from his brother.

The stirring tragedy of the abdication was reduced to a distasteful family squabble over money. The row that ensued could be summed up in three words—Knight, Frank and Rutley. Surveyors from the London estate agents were despatched to value the royal estates in Norfolk and Scotland, then sent back again when the brothers failed to agree on a price. Amid a stream of recriminations and ever more bitter long-distance phone calls, relations went rapidly downhill. Christened Albert Frederick Arthur George, Bertie had chosen to be known as George VI, according to his official biographer, to mark 'a return in great measure to the criteria and traditions of the reign of King George V'. But unable to bring themselves to talk of George VI as 'the King', Wallis and David developed their own private codes for him—'York', as if he had never been crowned, and, more sneeringly, 'Mr Temple', as if he were the faceless father of that perfect little royal star, the English Shirley Temple. Before long the two brothers were on 'no speaks', communicating only through lawyers.

The arrangements for the ex-King's marriage to Wallis provoked the final severance. The couple were due to be married in France on 3 June 1937. But on 28 May George VI let it be known, via letters patent, that while the title of 'His Royal Highness' should continue to apply to the ex-king, it was explicitly denied to 'his wife and descendants, if any'. Six days before his marriage to the woman for whom he had made such colossal sacrifice, David discovered that she was to be perpetually condemned to an inferior status. If the couple were, for example, to visit a British embassy on their travels, the effect of the letters patent was that the ladies and gentlemen of the embassy should bow and curtsey to the Duke, but withhold that courtesy from the Duchess.

From this massive and quite deliberate snub flowed a lifetime of recrimination. When the writer James Pope-Hennessy met the Duchess of Windsor in 1958, he noted that she had a particular facial expression 'reserved for speaking of [Queen Elizabeth] the Queen Mother', and that this expression—'a contortion', he called it—was 'very unpleasant to behold'. The Duchess had correctly identified her smiling sister-in-law, along with

143

Queen Mary, as the decisive influence in denying her royal status. The royal women blamed Wallis for leading David astray. They could not believe that Wallis would stay faithful. And behind it all lay the question of duty.

'You did not seem able to take in any point of view but your own' wrote Queen Mary to her son two years later. '. . . It seemed inconceivable to those who had made such sacrifices during the war that you, as their king, refused a lesser sacrifice.'

The new Queen Elizabeth felt this particularly strongly. She had been brought up to believe in duty. She had seen all four of her brothers go off to war and only three come back. She had made herself a royal star, but understood that her celebrity derived ultimately from a cause she was happy to acknowledge as greater than herself. She could not forgive Wallis for threatening this cause, nor understand what drove David to put his personal happiness above it. In 1970, the 21-year-old Prince Charles thought that sufficient years had passed to effect a reconciliation, only to discover that his kindly grandmother remained quite immovable on the subject.

The machinations that led up to the abdication crisis had been conducted by adults behind closed doors. But the subsequent row over the Windsors was an unconcealed family dispute which was to affect the 11-year-old Princess Elizabeth for the rest of her life. She was an eye witness to a once friendly family tearing itself apart. Uncle David's phone calls interrupted mealtimes, and the distress they caused her father was impossible to miss. Even the composure of her normally serene mother could be ruffled when the subject of the exiles came up. 'Who's got the lines around his eyes now?' the Queen snapped on one occasion when a visitor mentioned how well the ex-King was looking in his new life.

The row over the Duchess of Windsor's title, which was to find an echo in the surrender of the same status by Diana, Princess of Wales, as part of her 1996 divorce, begged an important question. Royalness was not, strictly speaking, in the royal family's gift, for it had not been the royal family who forced the issue over Edward VIII's choice of wife. David's own family had looked the other way over his relationship with Mrs Simpson, grumbling behind their hands, but hoping it would just go away. It was Stanley Baldwin who had grasped the nettle. On the basis of his reading of the popular will, the Prime Minister took the decisive action and then told the royal family how things must be. It smelt of pettiness, and was rather late in the game, for the royal inheritors now to make the stand they had been too cowardly to make the previous year. Money aside, David had behaved with decency in his renunciation. The kernel of honour in the crisis had been his personal sacrifice—David's wish to marry his wife fully and to give Wallis whatever status he had, or was allowed to keep. His brother's wives were all HRHs, and, as Duke of Windsor, he had voluntarily become a sort of younger brother. It was difficult not to sympathise with the sense of grievance that he and Wallis nursed to the end.

The royal family, for their part, could not accept that the pain and anger of the abdication stemmed from David's own complex character and the tyranny of the royal mould, in which they had a certain complicity. It was much easier to see him as a fallible man misled by a wicked woman. They demonised Mrs Simpson, and their extraordinary level of hostility towards her was to bedevil royal life for nearly half a century.

*   *   *

This dark reality of anger behind the smiling façade of the model royal family provided the backdrop to Princess Elizabeth's youth—and it loaded her with a heavy responsibility. As David and Wallis sensed in their sly digs at 'Mr Temple', the princess's role in the family dynamic was to make herself the embodiment of everything that they were not. As much as her father, she was faced with the duty of redeeming Uncle David's sins. 'That is what's behind the slavery of the boxes,' says a family friend. 'Her uncle let the side down, he put personal pleasure before his duties. She has deliberately done the reverse.'

Edward VIII's laziness in dealing with his government 'boxes' of official papers was a failing to which his family frequently referred, as if he had lost his throne through not doing his homework. 'It must be very trying for Bertie,' wrote his great-uncle, the Duke of Connaught, in January 1937, 'to find himself suddenly plunged into this new unexpected work. David never did it. And when he abdicated, Bertie found all the Sovereign's work in a frightful muddle.'

Elizabeth II was never happy with the family rift. Her mother and her grandmother, Queen Mary, the two female lodestars of her life, were at the root of a vendetta which it was not in her nature to

146

maintain. But since it was not in her nature to rebel either, she honoured it none the less. She learned to live with the tension in her own dutiful, phlegmatic way, and she maintained the façade until the very end. On 24 April 1986, the body of Wallis, who had died aged eighty-nine, was brought to England to be buried beside her husband, who had predeceased her in 1972. It was a short, dispassionate service in which the Duchess's name was not even mentioned. Elizabeth had scarcely met the woman, and had no personal reason to grieve. But at the end of the service it was noticed that the usually imperturbable Queen was in tears. It was finally over.

CHAPTER EIGHT

A Haze of Wonder

When I broke the news to Margaret and Lilibet that they were going to live in Buckingham Palace, they looked at me in horror. 'What!' Lilibet said. 'You mean forever?'

Marion Crawford, *The Little Princesses*

It was shortly after lunch on 11 December 1936 that the ten-year-old Princess Elizabeth became next in line to the British throne—at 1.52 p.m. that Friday, the moment when her father was proclaimed king from the balcony of St James's Palace. She was at home in London at the time, at

147

145 Piccadilly, being polite to Lady Cynthia Asquith who, with her writer's sense of timing, just happened to have come to call. The little girl saw a letter on the hall table addressed to Her Majesty the Queen. 'That's *Mummie* now, isn't it?' the princess enquired solemnly of Lady Cynthia.

The destiny now awaiting the child was in many ways more portentous than the role of consort that lay ahead for her mother, but in the rush of events, Elizabeth's upgrading of status was not dwelt upon. Coping with Daddy's extraordinary elevation was the issue of the moment. Next morning Elizabeth and Margaret gave their father a hug as he went off to his Accession Council, looking grave but handsome in his dark blue and gold uniform as an Admiral of the Fleet.

In the hour or so that he was away, the children's governess, Marion Crawford, nicknamed 'Crawfie', gave her charges some rapid curtseying lessons. 'When the King returned,' she wrote, 'both little girls swept him a beautiful curtsey. I think perhaps nothing that had occurred had brought the change in his condition to him as clearly as this did. He stood for a moment touched and taken aback. Then he stooped and kissed them both warmly.'

Bertie's first reaction to the news that he would be King had been to break down in tears. 'I went to see Queen Mary,' he wrote in his personal account of the crisis, '& when I told her what had happened I broke down & sobbed like a child.'

Getting the top job was a problem—and Princess Elizabeth took her cue from her father and uncle. 'When our father became King,' Princess Margaret told the historian Ben Pimlott, 'I said to her, "Does that mean you're going to become Queen?" She replied "Yes. I suppose it does". She didn't mention it again.'

In the middle ages, men schemed and fought and murdered to become King of England. In the twentieth century they abdicated or burst into tears, while a ten-year-old heiress presumptive preferred not to discuss the matter. According to Princess Elizabeth's grandmother, Lady Strathmore, when the little girl heard the news she started 'ardently praying for a brother'.

One of the princess's first public engagements in the spring of 1937 was to accompany her parents to the opening of the new National Maritime Museum in Greenwich. The royal family travelled by boat down the Thames, and with rumblings of war in Europe, the maritime nation found the occasion significant. Crowds lined the river banks cheering. But it was an incident inside the Great Hall at Greenwich which stuck in the princess's mind. A pigeon got trapped inside the high beamed chamber and throughout the inaugural ceremony flew frantically round and round, beating its wings and trying to escape. Finally, panic-stricken and exhausted, it dropped to the floor, dead. The eleven-year-old watched its fall with fascination. Now, every time the Queen goes to Greenwich, she tells the story of the pigeon.

*   *   *

Moving into Buckingham Palace was hardly a more joyful matter.

'People think', wrote Crawfie, 'that a royal palace is the last word in up-to-date luxury . . . Nothing could be farther from the truth.'

On her first night the governess discovered that her bedroom light could be turned on and off only by a primitive switch two yards outside her doorway down the passage. The upper floors of the Palace were very little changed from the days of Queen Victoria. The King took Miss Crawford to inspect the dark and gloomy schoolroom overlooking the Mall, where he had been tutored and where a heavy stone balustrade outside the window blocked the light like prison bars. The King stood in the doorway, looking at the room in silence. Then he turned away slowly, shutting the door behind him.

'No,' he said, 'that won't do.'

The Palace's long and ill-lit corridors—service thoroughfares up and down which servants shuttled at all hours—gave life a surreal quality, like living directly off a busy main street. To go to the bathroom every morning, Princess Elizabeth had to walk some way down the corridor past a lift, with every chance of meeting the Palace postman doing his rounds. Mealtimes involved a long trudge down even longer corridors. 'People here need bicycles,' remarked the princess, in one of the dry comments that were to become her trademark.

The princess was probably less disconcerted than her governess by the spectacle of her mother the Queen at mid-morning, dressed in tiara and full evening dress, wafting down the corridor to a portrait sitting. It was routine for the adults in her family to get overdressed at odd times of the day. The bizarre nature of her destiny was brought home to her more forcefully when she and her sister went out on 'the hill', a raised hump of soil and grass in the Palace gardens that rose above the walls, looking down on the traffic in Buckingham

Palace Road. They could see children on their way to the park with their nurses, and scraps of conversation floated upwards.

By her own account, the princess spent some time wondering about the outside world. Nearly twenty years later, when she was sitting as Queen for the Italian painter Pietro Annigoni, she told him that as a child she had spent hours looking out of the windows. 'I loved watching the people and the cars there in the Mall,' she said. 'They all seemed so busy. I used to wonder what they were doing and where they were all going, and what they thought about outside the palace.' She seems to have said this without complaint. Quite unlike her uncle, Elizabeth demonstrated from the first an unflurried capacity to accept her unusual lot in life.

Her parents did their best to get her mingling with other children. They organised a Palace group of Girl Guides which met on Wednesday afternoons—Elizabeth was second-in-command of the Kingfisher Patrol—but it was hardly possible for the Buckingham Palace Company to be just like any other. Elizabeth's twenty or so companions were courtiers' daughters and other well-bred Belgravia girls. Like Girl Guides everywhere, they learnt semaphore signalling, but when it rained they took their flags indoors and practised in the Palace corridors.

In April 1937, Elizabeth celebrated her eleventh birthday. She was now at the age when most girls were starting secondary school; but the high responsibility that now faced her did not alter her parents' feeling that she remained better off being educated at home. Her mother, who had had a wonderful childhood growing up around the

151

Strathmores' numerous residences, felt that the most important thing about childhood was that it should be fun. George VI, for his part, had suffered bitterly from his parents' purposeful preparation of him for his royal duties—being compelled, though left-handed, to write with his right hand, and to spend agonised nights with his legs locked in metal braces that were supposed to correct his tendency to knock knees.

It is interesting to wonder what the King and Queen would have arranged educationally for a son. A royal boy would almost certainly have gone to Eton, like the princesses' uncle George, who had boarded at the school like any other pupil. In this sense the future Queen and her sister were victims of gender discrimination. The upbringing of the future Elizabeth II was that of a young Edwardian lady, a couple of generations out of date. Princess Margaret often complained about it. She would talk bitterly at dinner parties—within earshot of her mother, if possible—about how poorly she and Lilibet were educated, stimulated by nothing more than Crawfie, corgis and rides in the Great Park.

Marion Crawford fought hard to inject real life and relevance into her charges' formation. Her passion was child psychology, and it had been her plan to work among disadvantaged children in Edinburgh, where she had trained in behavioural science. She tried both to stiffen and to broaden the princesses' curriculum, and received welcome support from the girls' grandmother, Queen Mary, who sent the governess a long note debating the relative virtues of arithmetic and history. The old Queen urged that the princesses should spend some time learning poetry by heart. While other members of the family, particularly Uncle David, would give Elizabeth indulgent presents like dogs and ponies, Queen Mary sent gifts with a stringent and educational tinge—a box of wooden building blocks, for example, each wood coming from a different country in the British Empire.

Queen Mary did some school-teaching herself in the run-up to the great event of the year, the coronation. The twelfth of May 1937 had been the date arranged for Edward VIII's crowning, and the new King took it over. Queen Mary arranged for a full-colour panorama of George IV's coronation of 1821 to be placed on an easel in the schoolroom, and she ran through the role and symbolism of every participant. It was an old tradition that the widow of a previous king should not attend his successor's crowning, but in the special circumstances of David's departure Queen Mary thought it important to show her support for her second son. It was agreed that she would travel to and from the ceremony with her grand-daughters, and would also sit with them in the Abbey. So she made sure that her team for the day understood their part to perfection.

In the Royal Archives, tied in pink ribbon, is Princess Elizabeth's own account of her parents' coronation, written in her neat, rounded hand— 'To Mummy and Papa, In Memory of Their Coronation, From Lilibet. By Herself.'

Her day had started at 5 a.m., with the band of the Royal Marines striking up outside the window of the room that she shared with her maid, the railwayman's daughter. 'I leapt out of bed,' wrote the princess, 'and so did Bobo. We put on dressing-gowns and shoes and Bobo made me put on an eiderdown as it was so cold and we crouched in the window looking on to a cold, misty morning. There were already some people in the stands and all the time people were coming to them in a stream.'

The princess wrote in a fluent, self-confident style for an 11-year-old, describing her quick breakfast and how, having dressed, she and Margaret showed themselves off to the visitors and housemaids.

'Now I shall try and give you a description of our dresses. They were white silk with old cream lace and had little gold bows all the way down the middle. They had puffed sleeves with one little bow in the centre. Then there were the robes of purple velvet with gold on the edge.

'We went along to Mummy's bedroom and we found her putting on her dress. Papa was dressed in a white shirt, breeches and stockings, and over this he wore a crimson satin coat. Then a page came and said it was time to go down, so we kissed Mummy, and wished her good luck and went down.'

The girls found the carriage that took them from the Palace to the Abbey 'very jolty, but we soon got used to it.' At the Abbey they processed down the aisle to enter the Royal Box with Queen Mary. 'I thought it all very, very wonderful and I expect the Abbey did, too. The arches and beams at the top were covered with a sort of haze of wonder as Papa was crowned, at least I thought so.'

Some observers thought that the King and Queen, both sincere churchgoers who had prayed for weeks before the ceremony, were in a state of semi-trance as they went through the coronation rituals. Their elder daughter seems to have been

154

imbued with similar mysticism. Her account of the service is remarkably down-to-earth, but she also accepted the high-flown magic as a given. As she looked up at the 'haze of wonder' in the arches of the Abbey roof, she would clearly not have been surprised if the Holy Grail itself had appeared.

'When Mummy was crowned and all the peeresses put on their coronets it looked wonderful to see arms and coronets hovering in the air and then the arms disappear as if by magic . . . What struck me as being rather odd was that Grannie did not remember much of her own Coronation. I should have thought that it would have stayed in her mind for ever.

'At the end the service got rather boring, as it was all prayers. Grannie and I were looking to see how many more pages to the end, and we turned one more and then I pointed to the word at the bottom of the page and it said "Finis". We both smiled at each other and turned back to the service.'

The boredom was understandable. The coronation service lasted a full two and a half hours, and by the end of it everyone was in need of the refreshments laid out in the royal robing room in the temporary annexe built next to the Abbey. 'We had some sandwiches, stuffed rolls, orangeade and lemonade,' noted the princess of the church hall fare. 'Then we left for our long drive.'

The morning trip to the service had been relatively direct. But the afternoon route home had been designed for maximum crowd exposure on a huge circular excursion that ran down the Thames, then up through Trafalgar Square and Piccadilly Circus and along Oxford Street, before returning to

155

the Palace. The princesses and their grandmother had been travelling ahead of the grand golden State Coach, and the moment they arrived they dashed back to see it crunch in across the gravel of the Palace courtyard.

'Then we all went on to the Balcony where millions of people were waiting below,' continued Elizabeth, matter-of-fact about the extraordinary spectacle that she had first been held up to witness at the age of fourteen months when her parents came back from Australia. 'After that we all went to be photographed in front of those awful lights.'

*   *   *

Four months earlier, on 30 January 1937, a letter in the left-wing weekly the *New Statesman* announced the creation of an ambitious new project to chart national feeling: Mass-Observation. The brainchild of Charles Madge, Humphrey Jennings and Tom Harrison, respectively a surrealist poet, a documentary film-maker and a young anthropologist just returned from studying cannibals in New Guinea, Mass-Observation proclaimed its ambition to assemble 'an anthropology of our own people . . . a sounding of the English collective unconscious'.

George Gallup's public opinion polls had arrived from America the previous year, but the left-wing founders of 'Mass-Obs' were contemptuous of information gained by ringing doorbells, armed with a clipboard, and asking questions in an Oxbridge accent. Overtly hoping to use their information to break down class barriers, they decamped to the Lancashire cotton town of

Bolton, which became 'Worktown' in the directives they sent to their volunteer observers. The coronation of May 1937 seemed an ideal occasion to test their theories and methods, and around the country 132 volunteers went into action, noting down their own reactions and experiences as well as the feelings of their friends. These observations were to be supplemented with eavesdroppings in pubs and crowd situations which were soon to earn 'Mass-Obs' a not-unjustified reputation for snooping.

Their reports went back to Worktown, where they were assembled in a book, *May the Twelfth*, the first systematic attempt to chart Britain's feelings about royal ritual and the royal family. The recent abdication gave a special edge to the occasion, with Bradford businessmen reported to be betting against a coronation taking place, and a south London landlady declaring that she 'wouldn't give a thank you to be there, not after the dirty trick they had played on the old Duke of Windsor'.

By the standards of professional market research, the findings were unscientific in the extreme, but shrewd reporting brought the occasion alive as no mere poll could have done. At points along the processional route, loudspeakers were bringing the BBC broadcast of the Abbey service to the waiting crowds, and one observer noted people's uncertainty at sacred moments— Should one smoke? Is it all right to eat a sandwich while the King is being anointed? There was some indecision at the moment of crowning, when seat-holders wondered whether or not to stand and only a few took their hats off. But then the Abbey cheering came through over the speakers, and people took their lead from that.

Most interesting to a modern susceptibility are the reports from some of the republican observers, who found themselves swayed by unexpected emotion.

'I was surprised how much I responded to the atmosphere of the crowd, the cheering etc.,' wrote a 39-year-old typist who took her left-wing principles very seriously. 'I felt a definite pride and thrill in belonging to the Empire, which, in ordinary life, with my political bias, is just the opposite of my true feelings. Yet I felt a definite sense of relief that I could experience this emotion and be in and of the crowd. One becomes very weary of always being in the minority, thinking things silly which other people care about; one must always be arguing or repressing oneself, and it is psychologically very bad. Therefore you will understand that the carnival spirit of the actual Coronation Day *really* was a holiday for me, and I say this without cynicism.'

'Poetry ought to be made by all, not one,' was one of the tenets of Mass-Observation's founders, and some volunteers found poetry where they least expected it. A bicycling republican from South Norwood decided he would take advantage of the deserted roads to go for a spin along the Kent–Sussex border, but found it was hard to get away from the fervour of the moment. 'Every habitation decorated, and from every cottage came the sound of cheering,' he reported. 'Very few people about in fields or gardens—evidently all listening to the broadcast commentary. At each village there were celebrations in the open air— dancing, sports, brass bands. Somehow the countryside seemed to purify even Coronation emotionalism of its unhealthy fever. It was spontaneous merry-making that we saw, probably little changed from what it was centuries ago.'

A Blackpool republican encountered his own version of Princess Elizabeth's haze of wonder. 'A strange thrill—apparently quite disconnected from everything—passed through me,' he recorded. 'I was annoyed, and a little afterwards wondered why.'

CHAPTER NINE

Apprentice and Master

He just smiled at me as if he'd known me all his life,
The day I met His Majesty the King.
He talked and we spoke
Just like two ordinary folk
The day I met His Majesty the King . . .

Second World War popular song,
quoted in *Time* magazine, 2 July 1941

From the outside they look like any other set of dry, discarded schoolbooks that you might find at a rummage sale—*Anson's Law and Custom of the Constitution* in three volumes. But they are kept under lock and key in the College Library at Eton, and when you open Volume I (*Parliament*, 5th edition) you discover a signature—Elizabeth, 1944—followed by swirlings of annotations, accompanied by neat, pencilled notes in a round and still childlike hand. These fading, brown, fabric-covered volumes are the textbooks from which Princess Elizabeth studied constitutional history for six years, and the earnest jottings that run around the academic text are her teenage notes on how to be Queen.

She started the lessons on her thirteenth birthday in April 1939, and her parents did their best to ensure that a subject dreaded by most schoolchildren should be taught in a stimulating fashion. Her tutor, Sir Henry Marten, the vice-provost of Eton, was a beloved and whimsical character, known for sucking on his handkerchief, comforter-like, as he lost himself in his subject. He had a vivid ability to bring the past to life. 'He was the first of my teachers', said Lord Home, later one of Elizabeth II's Prime Ministers, 'to make me realise that the characters of history had once been human beings like us.'

To start with, Sir Henry cycled up to Windsor Castle to see his pupil. Later, the princess would cross the river to Eton for tutorials in the cheerful chaos of his college study. 'Books cascaded from the shelves, surging over tables and chairs in apparent disorder,' recalled one of his pupils. As a final touch of eccentricity, Sir Henry kept a pet raven that would demonstrate its affection with occasional pecks at his ear.

This wizard's cave was the closest that the future Queen ever came to 'going to school', and some years later her Merlin made a revealing disclosure. Whenever in her early lessons Sir Henry posed a question to the thirteen-year-old, he noticed that she did not reply directly. The princess was so unaccustomed to being quizzed that she would not at first answer, but would turn away from her teacher and 'look for confidence and support to her beloved governess, Miss Crawford'. The answer, when it came, was 'almost invariably correct', and it was not as if Princess Elizabeth lacked social confidence in a public forum. When the President of France came to London on a state visit that summer, the teenager who was so privately shy that she could not give the kindly Sir Henry a direct answer commanded the public poise to deliver a polished speech of welcome in well-rehearsed French. The princess's social skills were exactly the inverse of those of an 'ordinary', run-around-the-playground child of her age—but she was, perhaps, already better honed for her unique destiny than even her constitutional trainer realised. Not blurting out a personal response, but turning to others for advice, is the cautious, sideways style to which the figurehead monarch is constitutionally condemned.

From the marked volumes we can reconstruct the principles that Sir Henry stressed to his pupil. Here was a job description of monarchy that went far beyond just waving graciously and opening things. Anson picturesquely introduced the British constitution as 'a somewhat rambling structure . . . like a house which many successive owners have altered'. This was a clue to its essential characteristic, explained a passage which attracted the princess's first pencil marking: the more complex a constitution, the more guarantees of liberty it offered. The Chinese Empire was held up to the student as an example of crude and simple autocracy; the United States of America as an example of the subtleties and complications that liberty requires in order to flourish.

There were relatively few notes on the prerogatives of the crown, and some passing glances at constitutional history. The Anglo-Saxon monarchy was described as 'a consultative and tentative absolutism'—the princess underlined the words 'consultative' and 'tentative'. The witan, the royal council of great landowners and bishops, was portrayed as an early form of Parliament. 'If the King had a strong will, and a good capacity for business, he ruled the witan; if not, the witan was the prevailing power in the State.'

Kings emerged favourably from Anson's pages. They were depicted as generally benevolent figures, with an instinct for the common weal. But the principal focus of the thirteen-year-old's pencilled attention was the power of Parliament, where she got scribbling seriously. She marked the basic principle that 'what touches all . . . should be approved by all,' and that Parliament had the power to effect any change it wished, to such an extent that no particular parliament could foresee the future and bind its successors irrevocably. Reflecting different circumstances and the will of the people, a new parliament could always undo the work of those who had gone before.

Pupil and teacher clearly worked hard at mastering the abstruse technicalities of legislation, leading up to the Royal Assent at the end of the parliamentary process, which formally turned bills into law. The princess's notes traced the procedures for the passing of money bills, and noted the observation that, when it came to practical transactions, 'every change of recent times has tended to enhance the power of the Cabinet'.

162

The longest passage of all, a full page of pencilled notes where Sir Henry had evidently abandoned Anson's text to deliver a lesson of his own, traced the day-by-day events of James II's ignominious flight from his throne in 1688, which culminated with the King throwing the Great Seal into the River Thames—the seventeenth-century parallel to the twentieth-century abdication.

The message of Anson and Marten was clear: Parliament ruled. The era when monarchs called or dissolved parliaments without the advice of elected ministers was dismissed as 'the days before responsible government' (Princess Elizabeth's underlining). But responsible government was a complex business, and leafing through the pages of earnestly inscribed detail, a modern reader comes away with constitutional overload. The future Queen has carefully noted, and presumably committed to memory, the differences between dissolving, proroguing and adjourning Parliament. It was as if she were studying to be Speaker, not Queen. Her notes precisely trace the procedural minutiae that should fill the head of the ultimate civil servant—which, in one sense, is just what this little girl was to become. Here, in this painstaking annotation of dry-as-dust data, are the roots of Elizabeth II, diligent Queen of the red government boxes. No sovereign in history has read and marked more sheets of paper more dutifully.

Taking his cue from Walter Bagehot, Marten laid particular stress on how the flexibility of the British monarchy had helped it to survive and find a role in a world where the people had assumed power for themselves. By embracing the new technology of radio broadcasting, for example,

King George V had established a vital and direct link between himself and his people not just in Britain, but all over the world. In the constitutional field, the Statute of Westminster of 1931 had given independence to the dominions of Australia, Canada, Ireland, New Zealand and South Africa, transforming the old idea of imposed imperial authority into the concept of a voluntary Commonwealth of Nations 'united by a common allegiance to the Crown'. This paralleled the evolution of the monarchy from authoritarian executive to consent-based symbol. The empire was starting to dismantle itself as a compulsory power bloc, and was moving towards what Sir Henry—apparently anticipating the happy liberation of Britain's non-white domains—cheerily described as 'one big family'.

The princess took these lessons particularly to heart. In Sir Henry's crib notes we see the Elizabeth II of the future—the sovereign who would one day be crowned truly in the sight of all the people, through television. She would also become the monarch who, it sometimes seemed, was the only person left in Britain with any belief in the Commonwealth. The Queen was to labour doggedly to maintain the concept of 'one big family' of British nations, against the odds, for more than fifty years.

The one element that was specifically lacking in Sir Henry's teachings was the ultimate spiritual purpose of the system. Life, liberty and the pursuit of happiness? The British constitution lacks any overt statement of intent to match that of the United States, so while Anson's fact-packed volumes clearly assumed liberty and democratic power to be very good things, he did not discuss the uses to which liberty and democracy should be put. What values is a representative monarch actually supposed to represent? What makes for a virtuous and civilised society? Is the ceremonial figurehead no more than an impartial referee? Should she not rather be deploying the considerable power of her symbolism to inspire the nation and swell the general stock of virtue and civilisation? These are primary questions, philosophical starting points. But on these matters, to judge from her surviving notes, the princess's tutor was silent.

*   *   *

In one sense, Hitler's invasion of Poland in September 1939 provided the answer.

'The cause which binds together my peoples and our gallant and faithful Allies is the cause of Christian civilisation,' declared George VI that December in his Christmas broadcast. He concluded with a snatch of poetry which one of his staff had picked out of his mailbag. 'I said to the man who stood at the Gate of the Year, "Give me a light that I may tread safely into the unknown." And he replied, "Go out into the darkness, and put your hand into the Hand of God. That shall be better to you than light, and safer than a known way."'

Delivered in George VI's wavering voice, so different from his father's gruff tones, but just as affecting, it was Britain's most uplifting call to arms until Churchill replaced Chamberlain as Prime Minister in May 1940.

The modern folk memory of the Second World

War has been profoundly shaped by the extraordinary longevity of Queen Elizabeth the Queen Mother, with the annual birthday reminders, sixty years after the event, of her picking her way through the rubble of the Blitz in hat and high heels. 'I'm glad we've been bombed. Now we can look the East End in the face.'

This comment on the bombing of Buckingham Palace in September 1940 was actually quite a shocking thing to say at the time, and there is no evidence it was circulated during the war years. The earliest published reference for this remark— along with her equally legendary statement that she, her daughters and her husband would 'never' leave London—comes nearly a decade and a half later, in 1955. There is no reason to doubt that the Queen Mother made either comment, but they have created the impression that she was the royal mouthpiece and figurehead, while the contemporary evidence leaves no doubt that this role was played by the King.

'Never in British history', reported *Time* magazine on George VI's role in the war effort, 'has a monarch seen and talked to so many of his subjects or so fully shared their life.' Two of the hit songs of the Blitz, the magazine reported, were the jaunty ballads 'The King Is Still in London' and 'The Day I Met His Majesty the King', which recounted the powerful fantasy of meeting the King and being greeted by him as a long-lost friend.

George VI took his representative duties very seriously. As a young man, he had drawn his own lessons from 'Unrest in the Country', and his enthusiasm for visiting factories had earned him the nickname 'the Foreman' from his brothers. His particular cause was promoting and raising funds for the Industrial Welfare Society, which campaigned for canteens, medical care and other benefits to improve relations between workforce and employers. In 1940 the Trades Union Congress awarded the King the signal honour of the TUC gold medal, citing his contribution to labour relations and praising him, with perhaps a little hyperbole, as 'Britain's hardest worker'.

His most famous initiative was his annual Duke of York's Camp, founded in 1921, at which two hundred public schoolboys came together with two hundred working-class apprentices every summer for a week of exercise, fresh air and comradeship under canvas. The high point of each camp was the arrival of the Duke—after 1936 the King—dressed in open shirt and shorts, ready for a day of Boy Scout-style fun. The monarch and his serried ranks of upper- and lower-class campers became a newsreel staple every summer as they heartily sang and waved their arms in unison, miming to the words of the campfire anthem 'Under the Spreading Chestnut Tree'. George VI took pride in never forgetting the face of a boy from one of his camps. He liked to pick out familiar faces on his tours of factories.

'You were in my camp,' he would say. 'How are you getting on?'

During the war Lord Woolton, the Minister of Food, had trouble getting Winston Churchill to face up to the coming challenge of postwar reform, and noted in his diary that George VI was more engaged than the Prime Minister was in social issues. 'The king has been brought up to do the industrial side of the royal job,' he commented, 'and he knows more about the working man than the Minister of Labour' (who, in the wartime Cabinet, was actually the former trades union leader Ernest Bevin). Thinking about how civilians should be honoured for heroism in this new style of conflict, of total war, the King himself came up with the idea of a civilian equivalent to the Victoria Cross, and it is appropriate that the George Cross and the George Medal should bear his name.

Proud, like his father, of his naval training, the King also threw himself into the military details of the war, spending hours studying the secret reports and strategies that came to him in his boxes. He saw himself as more than a symbolic commander-in-chief, keeping a careful monthly tally of aircraft production and talking imperiously of 'my generals'. Some officers of the royal protection squad, the Coats Mission, were with him when news came through of a setback in the campaign in North Africa, and they were struck by how personally the King took the defeat.

'They needn't expect any medals when they get home,' he exploded in fury. 'I shall tell them exactly what I think of them.'

As a rule, however, the King's audiences with his commanders were noted for their warmth and encouragement, and Churchill paid particular tribute to his sovereign's supportiveness. 'It was always a relief to me', wrote the Prime Minister after the war, 'to lay before my Sovereign all the dread secrets and perils wh. oppressed my mind.'

So, even as the Princess Elizabeth studied the theory of constitutional monarchy with Sir Henry Marten, she had a practical example of a working constitutional monarch in the intense figure of her father, stretching himself to the limit at a moment when it really mattered, and talking about 'my generals' without irony. George VI saw himself as a literal embodiment of a semi-divine institution, a democratic version of the Sun King's *'L'état, c'est moi.'* This was to be the model Elizabeth II chose for her life as sovereign. She did not go down her mother's path of the crowd-pleasing artiste, and, for all their closeness, very little of her mother's theatricality rubbed off on her. Instead, she became an engaged box-reader like her father, awed and respectful towards her position, but expecting other people to treat it with all the reverence that she did.

CHAPTER TEN

Mumps and Croquet

Whither the storm carries me, I go—a willing guest.

Prince Philip of Greece, entry
in a visitors' book, early 1946

The first year of war marked a momentous moment for Princess Elizabeth. In 1939 she crossed the threshold of womanhood. You can see her physically blossoming in the pictures.

'Princess Elizabeth is growing up' ran a picture caption that April. A sharp-eyed picture editor had spotted the changing shape of the 13-year-old princess. Two months later, in a photo showing her in swimming costume, receiving a life-saving award, the curves were unmistakable. From child to woman, from ankle socks to silk stockings—which she was also photographed wearing for the first time that spring—there was a new poise about her; and all this was happening as the world went to war.

The Second World War was to be a defining and, in many ways, constraining influence on Princess Elizabeth's adolescence. At the age when she became what we now call a teenager, events conspired to deny her many of the joys and thrills of that period of life. But just before the onset of war, she did a quintessentially teenage thing. In July 1939 she closed her books to go on holiday—and fell in love.

On the afternoon of 22 July 1939, the graceful old royal yacht *Victoria and Albert* sailed into the estuary of the River Dart in Devon on a visit to the Royal Naval College, where George VI had trained in the years before the Great War. For the King, the day was memorable in taking him back to the pink-bricked college perched dramatically above the steep wooded inlet. For his elder daughter, this rainbow day, remembered by its chroniclers for both rain and sunshine, would live for ever as the occasion when her eye was captured by Cadet Captain Prince Philip of Greece.

He was eighteen years old. Like Elizabeth, he was a great-great-grandchild of Queen Victoria, which made him her third cousin, and the young people were brought together by his uncle, Lord Louis Mountbatten, 'Uncle Dickie', who was one of the royal party. An outbreak of mumps and chicken-pox at the college prompted its doctor to suggest that Elizabeth and her sister Margaret should not attend chapel with their parents, and Philip was detailed to entertain the two young princesses.

A private snapshot records the meeting. At the top of a slope leading down to the waters of the Dart stands a slender youth in midshipman's uniform, his spiky-haired, cropped head bowed as he looks hard at the challenge of some croquet hoops. Beside one of the hoops stands a little girl in a neat, pale, double-breasted coat, holding her hands and looking hard at *him*.

*   *   *

Cadet Captain Prince Philip of Greece was to shape the British royal family with a force and style matched in the twentieth century only by the contributions of Elizabeth Bowes-Lyon and Diana Spencer. In successive generations these three very different but equally dynamic outsiders have each been invited by the Windsors to join their club, and once inside have each set about shaping the establishment according to their own strong characters. Their contributions have inevitably reflected the experiences and mishaps of their pre-Windsor years, which in Philip's case were more painful than his bluff, 'man's man' exterior might suggest. The bloodlines of his lineage were decidedly grander and more royal than those of the future Queen Mother, but the chaotic nature of his family upbringing was poignantly unsettled—and certainly more disturbed than the much-analysed background of Lady Di.

Even his appearance was an enigma. That July afternoon in 1939, as Marion Crawford, the royal governess, studied the fair hair, angular features and piercing blue eyes of the 18-year-old Prince of Greece, she decided that he looked 'rather like a Viking'. But that raised a question.

'You don't look like a bloody Greek to me,' said Mike Parker, a young Australian who had met Philip when they trained together as naval cadets in 1938.

'I'm part-Danish, part-German and part-Russian,' explained Philip. 'I can go to practically any country in Europe and there's a relation there I can stay with.'

Prince Philip came from everywhere and nowhere. He was the grandson of William of Denmark, the prince whom the Greeks had imported in 1863 to serve as their king. Following an unsettled spell of rule by a prince imported from Bavaria, Greece had applied unsuccessfully for one of Queen Victoria's younger sons before turning to Copenhagen. The Danish royal family were the mail-order monarchs of Europe, posting out ready-made kings to both Greece and Norway (in 1905), along with accomplished queen consorts like Alexandra, the wife of Edward VII.

Philip's mother was Alice, the hauntingly beautiful, deaf daughter of Queen Victoria's grand-daughter Victoria of Hesse, who had married Louis of Battenberg, the ill-treated sea lord and first of the Mountbattens. This elaborate cocktail mixed from the gene pool of European royalty lay at the root of Philip's unsinkable self-assurance, which he displayed at that first meeting on the croquet lawn, to the evident liking of Princess Elizabeth, then and ever since.

'She is shy and he is not,' says one of their intimates. 'That is the fundamental dynamic of their relationship. He gives her "ginger".'

Prince Philip actually has more blue blood in his veins than Elizabeth II. But his famous self-confidence has always been marked by paradoxical touchiness, and this insecurity is presumed by those who know him to have come from a dramatically hand-to-mouth childhood which tossed him around, dependent on the charity of his many relatives. His cousin Alexandra of Yugoslavia once compared him to a dog for ever 'in search of a basket'.

Born on the island of Corfu in 1921—and delivered, according to legend, on a kitchen table—Philip was little more than a year old when he started on his travels. His father, Prince Andrew of Greece, a liverish and uncompromising character who was the younger brother of King Constantine I, was made the scapegoat for Greek military defeats in Asia Minor and was lucky to escape Athens with his life. A British warship carried the family into exile, the baby Philip transported in an improvised cot of orange boxes. One of the requisites of being King of Greece, remarked Philip's cousin, George II, was to have a suitcase packed and ready at all times.

The exiles were stony broke. Paris was home for the first ten years of Philip's life because there was free accommodation—a cramped lodge in the garden of a rich aunt in St Cloud, Paris's version of Richmond-upon-Thames, on the river to the west of the city. 'There were always problems paying the bills,' remembered Sophie, one of his four strikingly attractive elder sisters, whose smartest dresses were hand-me-downs from Uncle Dickie's rich wife, Edwina Mountbatten.

Philip was the only boy, and by seven years the youngest child in the family. His sisters later claimed to have stopped the baby of the house from being spoilt, but the opposite seems more likely. He was a striking little boy with a jaunty smile, surrounded from the first, as his biographer Tim Heald has remarked, 'by adoring women'. Philip was to keep it that way all his life.

School was an academy for American expatriates to and from which Philip travelled on a bicycle he purchased with his own savings—his pocket money was augmented by a pound note which the King of Sweden, another of his royal relatives, sent him every year at Christmas.

In this cosmopolitan setting of poshness and privation, English was literally Philip's mother tongue. Princess Alice spoke it to her children, and at the age of nine Philip came to England when he was sent to Cheam, an archetypal boys' prep school in the Surrey suburbs. In the draft of her biography entitled 'My Cousin Philip', Alexandra of Yugoslavia suggested that the boy was switched from France for cultural reasons, but Philip offered a more unsentimental explanation. 'There were relations in England', he noted brusquely in the margin of her manuscript (published in 1959 as *Prince Philip: a Family Portrait*), 'who were prepared to pay.'

The relations were the Mountbattens, who sent their own sons to Cheam. They organised a small syndicate of rich relatives to keep Philip afloat— and it was through another family connection that the prince started his secondary education in Germany. The progressive academy at Schloss Salem on the shores of Lake Constance was the inspiration of the legendary educationalist Kurt Hahn, a German Jew, outspoken anti-Nazi and protégé of the Baden family into which Philip's sister Theodora had married.

There were obvious pastoral family reasons for the twelve-year-old Philip to be educated close to his second-eldest sister, and his cousin Alexandra set them out in her manuscript. But with the chip on the shoulder that has always marred a character which, one senses, is struggling quite hard to be gracious, Philip again explained the move in terms of money. Salem, he pencilled on his cousin's manuscript, was 'cheaper'.

In 1932, Salem was also the home of Philip's mother, who was recuperating from a severe breakdown which was bound up with the collapse of her marriage. Overwhelmed by exile and impecunity, Philip's father had become obsessed with the need to clear his name, devoting his energies to writing a self-justifying memoir, aptly titled *Towards Disaster,* before drifting off to Monte Carlo, where he found consolation with a mistress named Doris. Too impoverished to qualify for the title of playboy, Prince Andrew features in photographs at café tables looking both proud and rather lost, staring resentfully at the world through a monocle. Philip's mother, for her part, found solace in religious mania, lying on the ground in a trance-like state, to develop 'the power conveyed to her from above'. Alice had come to believe she was literally the bride of Christ, 'physically' involved not only with Jesus but with other great spiritual figures like the Buddha. Her 'neurotic-pre-psychotic libidinous condition' attracted the attention of Sigmund Freud, who advised radiation of the ovaries 'in order to accelerate the menopause'. This brutal treatment was carried out, and the princess was confined against her will in a private sanatorium on Lake Constance.

Philip saw little of his mother in these years. From the age of eight until he was fifteen he never had so much as a birthday card from her. For the cherished, autumn child, the only son, this severance from his mother left deep marks. She is not a subject he finds it easy to discuss, and his friends feel certain that his famous brusqueness is a mask for emotional deprivation. 'He just never had the love,' says one. 'There was no one really close—that day-to-day parental contact you need to smooth off the rough edges. That's where his rudeness comes from—not enough slap-down when it mattered.' As another courtier sees it, Prince Philip 'did not have the chance to learn the tricks of the trade of domestic bliss'. Lord Airlie, Elizabeth II's reforming Lord Chamberlain, has put it more positively. 'He is more sensitive than people give him credit for,' he has been heard to say. 'He has a remarkably soft spot for the underdog.'

The prince himself declines to be self-pitying. 'Suddenly my family had gone,' he told Hugo Vickers in 1997. 'My father was in the South of France and my mother was just ill. I had to get on with it.'

Getting on with it involved packing and unpacking his own trunk, and finding his own way by bus, train and boat to the various corners of

Europe where his relatives offered him hospitality. 'There was nobody to take me,' he later remembered, 'nobody to pick me up.'

The young prince did have his wider family to help him. Philip was wrapped in the safety net of his mother's relatives, the Mountbattens, as well as the continuing affection of his four sisters, who had by now all married German aristocrats and who rallied round with hospitality and holidays.

His other great support was his school, itself a sort of family. When Kurt Hahn left Schloss Salem in 1933 to escape Nazi harassment, Philip was one of the pupils who went with him. Hahn regrouped in Morayshire in northern Scotland, where he took a lease on an old stone mansion, Gordonstoun, and introduced his rigorous and unconventional educational ideas to Britain. Hahn became something of a father-figure to Philip, who flourished in Hahn's testing regime of study and social service, interspersed with cold showers and regular drenchings while sailing the cold waters of the Moray Firth.

Philip rose to be 'Guardian' or head boy at Gordonstoun, shaping for himself a rugged and self-sufficient persona which gave little hint that kings sent him Christmas presents, or that family weddings could involve a trip to Westminster Abbey—where his cousin Princess Marina married George, Duke of Kent, in 1934.

'We were unpacking our trunks in the dorm,' remembered one of his schoolmates from Cheam, 'and I saw that in his, right at the bottom under a pair of underpants or a towel, he had a photograph of King George V, which said "From Uncle George". He had never displayed it.'

177

The nine-year-old Princess Elizabeth had been one of the bridesmaids at the glamorous Kent wedding. Philip, then fourteen, was given time off from Gordonstoun to attend, and he likes to recall that it was at this family occasion, and not at Dartmouth, that he and his future wife first encountered each other. They met again at the coronation of 1937, and their wartime romance was to develop through meetings at Coppins, the home of the Duke and Duchess of Kent not far from Windsor. Philip was always sensitive to the suggestion that he owed his big break to mumps and Uncle Dickie.

It was certainly not family connections which got Philip into the Royal Navy. On leaving Gordonstoun in 1938 he went to live in digs in Cheltenham with a Mr and Mrs Mercer who prepared candidates for naval exams. The Mercers later noted that the lad was remarkably short of pocket money and that he applied himself diligently to his studies—relaxing only on Saturday nights with trips to the cinema, or radio and record sessions with the daughter of the house. Philip passed sixteenth among the thirty-four successful candidates for entry to Dartmouth and went on working hard when he got there, winning the King's Dirk for the best all-round cadet of his entry.

Self-starting and robustly independent, Prince Philip was already displaying the strong-minded characteristics that would mark his career as a British royal personality. But as he picked up his awards for leadership in the collective and detached environments of the school and the navy, he remained something of a loner.

178

'You're a poor bloody orphan, just like me,' thought Mike Parker, whose own family was in Australia. Parker noticed how, while the other cadets went rushing off home at weekends, 'we were the last blokes left on the quarterdeck.'

In fact, Philip had more weekend destinations than most, for he had learned to perform well at the house parties of his remarkable extended family. He was always a welcome guest, if he cared to get himself invited. Handsome and upbeat, with charm to match, the young man gave good value. His relatives were always pleased to see him, and in the case of his mother's brother, Uncle Dickie Mountbatten, they could recognise a rising star. His little hint of neediness, the dog in search of the basket, made people happy to invite him home— no one more so, before too long, than his cousin Princess Elizabeth.

Prince Philip himself has developed a studied 'No comment' response to romantic suggestions that matrimonial lightning struck on the Dartmouth croquet lawn in July 1939, and in his case, that of an eighteen-year-old midshipman training for a war that was only weeks away, it would have been peculiar if it had. But his 13-year-old cousin had no reservations. In 1958 Sir John Wheeler-Bennett published his official biography of King George VI. The book was commissioned and scrutinised word for word by Queen Elizabeth II, and Sir John's royally approved verdict was quite emphatic on the subject of Cadet Captain Prince Philip of Greece: 'This was the man with whom Princess Elizabeth had been in love from their first meeting.'

CHAPTER ELEVEN

Princess in the Tower

We know, every one of us, that in the end all
will be well.

Princess Elizabeth's first radio broadcast,
13 October 1940

War made Mass-Observation temporarily official.
With national morale to maintain, the government
hired the hitherto volunteer organisation to
monitor the national mood, and to report, in
particular, on the effectiveness with which the
Ministry of Information's propaganda efforts were
received.

Looking for objective standards of
measurement, Mass-Obs hit on cinema newsreels
with their patriotic soundtracks. These were
punctuated with carefully prompted applause
points as their well-spoken male commentators
mounted on clipped notes through each editorial
crescendo—'Another triumph for the boys in blue!'
So, by measuring the number of seconds of
clapping that any particular personality or event
provoked, Mass-Obs was able to attempt some
crudely standardised sampling. Mistrustful as ever
of clipboard polling, Mass-Obs speculated that
people might be more honest in the dark.

The survey's most remarkable discovery was the
increased royal content in the stories that war
prompted. In 1939 there were five competing

newsreel companies, and with the outbreak of hostilities the royal ingredient in the editorial mix of each went up dramatically. One tally by Mass-Observation showed that the proportion of stories featuring royal people rose from 23 per cent to 80 per cent. Other indexes showed more modest rises, but the trend was the same in all cinemas—until the crisis of the war was passed, when the proportion returned to more routine levels. The five British newsreel producers were fiercely independent of one another, and there was no government directive, so the switch to royal images presumably reflected an instinctive rallying round the flag—a homing in on comforting national mascots as mortal danger threatened.

The move struck the right note with audiences. In the first months of war, Mass-Obs's observers with their torches and stop-watches recorded that clapping at royal images nearly trebled, rising from 13 to 38 per cent. But within this huge increase, the observers recorded very varied reactions. In the summer of 1940 Paul Reynaud, the heroic French premier who refused to collaborate with the Germans, got five seconds' applause in one cinema, compared to just two for the King and dead silence for the Queen, while the Duke of Windsor also did better than his younger brother. Before the war the Duke had suffered visual banishment from newsreel reports, to match his physical exile. But when he was screened in uniform in August 1940, being installed as Governor of the Bahamas, his comeback appearance racked up high rates of response—seven seconds in one West End cinema.

The German bombing a few weeks later of Buckingham Palace—itself a major and much-repeated newsreel story—changed these responses dramatically. 'Now the King is clapped,' noted one observer, 'not so much as a man, but as a symbol of the country.' One George VI speech, complete with hesitant pauses, was applauded for no fewer than seventeen seconds.

In terms of royal popularity, the September 1940 bombing was the most fortunate of misadventures, and from this point forward Mass-Obs recorded almost invariably positive reactions when the royal family appeared on screen. It has been observed that the modern populations of mainland Europe's monarchies have noticeably less obsessive attitudes towards their royal families than the British do— and perhaps the Second World War played a part in that detachment. While exile or collaboration separated the monarchies of Nazi-occupied Europe from their populations both physically and emotionally, Britain's royals stayed in place. For the second time in less than half a century they were materially entwined with the national experience, embodying the ups and downs of the country's fortunes.

The little princesses, as the teenage Elizabeth and ten-year-old Margaret Rose were still known, played a vital role in the royal 'family of families'. As its youngest members, they embodied vulnerable domestic affection and hope for the future, the tender, human causes for which the war was fought. As they had swept their Little Welsh House during the Depression, now they valiantly 'did their bit' to beat Hitler, collecting tinfoil, rolling bandages and knitting socks—a particular penance for Elizabeth, who was not a skilled knitter. It was announced that they made contributions from their pocket money to the Red Cross, the Girl Guides and the Air Ambulance Fund—which cannot have left much over for sweets.

They also made their first broadcast. In 1938 the owner of the *New York Herald Tribune*, Helen Reid, had been rebuffed when she suggested that the two girls might contribute to the cause of transatlantic solidarity by broadcasting to open National Children's Week in the United States. The British ambassador had been disdainful of such 'attempts to enlist the princesses for stunts', and George VI's private secretary Tommy Lascelles agreed. 'There is, of course, no question of the princesses broadcasting,' he wrote, 'nor is it likely to be considered for many years to come.'

Two years later, with the Battle of Britain being fought overhead, Buckingham Palace took another view.

'Thousands of you in this country have had to leave your homes and be separated from your father and mother,' read Princess Elizabeth in her piping voice as she introduced a series of 'Children in Wartime' programmes in October 1940. 'My sister Margaret Rose and I feel so much for you, as we know from experience what it means to be away from those we love most of all.'

Listening to the broadcast, Jock Colville, the Prime Minister's private secretary, declared himself 'embarrassed by the sloppy sentiment' that the princess was made to express. The ending was particularly contrived and schmaltzy.

'My sister is by my side,' said the princess, 'and we are both going to say good night to you. Come on, Margaret.'

'Good night,' piped up an even more high-pitched voice. 'Good night and good luck to you all.'

But schmaltz and sloppiness got results. In America, radio station switchboards were jammed with requests for repeats, and the BBC turned the recording into a best-selling gramophone record.

*   *   *

The two princesses were officially described as living 'somewhere in the country'. In fact, after spending several months away from their parents at Birkhall near Balmoral, they moved to Windsor for the duration, and from January 1940 it was misleading to suggest that their existence had much in common with that of ordinary child evacuees in the Second World War, transported across the country to strange farms and lodgings, where they did not see their parents for months or years. The King and Queen came down from London to spend almost every weekend with their daughters.

But wartime Windsor was no cushy billet. It was 'distinctly uncomfortable', according to Hugh FitzRoy, later Duke of Grafton. In 1940 Fitzroy was a young officer in the Grenadier Guards, and half a century later he recalled the castle as a barren, draughty, prison-like place. The paintings and most of the furniture had been whisked off to caves in Wales for safe keeping, the glass cabinets turned to the wall and the chandeliers taken down. The few remaining light sockets were filled with low-wattage bulbs.

'We seemed to live in a sort of underworld,' remembered Crawfie of five years' existence in

Windsor's darkened corridors.

The governess had been ordered to take her charges from Royal Lodge to the castle in the middle of May 1940, when there were fears of bombing, and even German parachute raids. The princesses arrived as night was falling, and the huge bulk of the ancient building loomed out of the twilight like Sleeping Beauty's castle. As they walked in they found the state apartments muffled in dustsheets and the windows being blacked out by shadowy figures.

According to her governess, the princess who wore silk stockings was suddenly a frightened little girl who clung to Crawfie, like her sister Margaret. They were shown to their bedrooms high up in the fifteenth-century Lancaster Tower, where their bathrooms were carved out of the thick stone walls and where the wind whistled up and down the stone-flagged staircase. Princess Elizabeth and her sister were to spend five years in this royal backdrop from central casting—literally cloistered at a moment when most of their contemporaries were being emancipated as never before.

The Second World War was an exciting and liberating experience for many young people, given responsibility, freedom and sexual opportunity they would never have known in peacetime. But for the princesses it was the very reverse. At the moment when the royal family were most praised for being in tune with the plight of ordinary folk, Elizabeth and Margaret were being preserved in aspic, national treasures to be wrapped in cotton wool— the human equivalent of the Sèvres porcelain being bundled away for safe keeping.

They did have company. The Coats Mission was

a crack transport group which stood ready to whisk the princesses away to one of several safe houses in Worcestershire and Yorkshire in the event of invasion. The coded signal for escape was 'Cromwell', and the girls tested out the armoured cars which had been converted to include sufficient space for governess, luggage and one corgi. Elizabeth had been seven when her father had acquired the first of these stumpy, bad-tempered beasts for which she would develop an almost comical soft spot.

In the castle itself was a detachment of young Guards officers, whom Elizabeth, as weekday chatelaine of the castle, would entertain at decorous lunch parties. She chose who would sit to her right and left, gravely embarking on adult conversation, shifting from child to adult with the composure she had shown from an early age. The princess was developing a presence which pleased old Queen Mary and her friend Mabell Airlie when they attended her confirmation on the eve of her sixteenth birthday at Windsor in March 1942.

'I saw a grave little face under a small white net veil and a slender figure in a plain white woollen frock,' wrote Lady Airlie, drawn towards the comparison that all the elder members of the family and household tended to make. 'The carriage of her head was unequalled, and there was about her that indescribable something which Queen Victoria had.'

*   *   *

Lady Pamela Hicks, the younger daughter of Lord Mountbatten, remembers the first time she went out with her two cousins Elizabeth and Margaret 'in the cars'. A year older than Princess Margaret, Pammy Mountbatten had been to play and have tea with the princesses; but this was the first time she had moved out of the private dimension to encounter the phenomenon of the intimate strangers—the faces peering eagerly into the car, necks craning, frantic waving, manic grins. It was a startling and rather surreal dimension to her cousins' lives of which she had never dreamt.

They were going to Shepperton Studios to watch the filming of *In Which We Serve*, Noël Coward's patriotic rendering of Lord Mountbatten's exploits in HMS *Kelly*, and as the crowds thickened, Princess Elizabeth turned her smile out of the window and started to wave. But Princess Margaret was feeling sulky. She had come on the trip for her own benefit, not the crowd's, and she declined to wave—to her sister's unconcealed distress.

'Margaret, you must be nice,' said Elizabeth.

To the very end of the war, when Elizabeth was nearly twenty and Margaret a buxom fifteen-year-old—both girls inherited their mother's ample bosom—the two sisters regularly dressed in identical outfits. It was their own version of royal uniform, the dutifully joint identity of the little princesses that continued into the usually rebellious fringes of adulthood. But within their peer group of two, their personalities were developing in opposite directions. As the younger became more wilful and wayward, making the most of her privileged status, the elder became more withdrawn, worried about her destiny—and perhaps even guilty about it.

Princess Margaret's uneasy blend of grandeur

and rebellion was to provide one of the troubling themes of Elizabeth II's reign, and it was encouraged by the two girls' parents. George VI loved coaching his serious elder daughter as his successor, explaining the mysteries of the boxes and introducing her to visiting heads of state. But when Sir Henry Marten, who met Margaret socially and was struck by her brightness and originality, expressed an interest in teaching her, her parents saw no need.

The King and Queen presumably thought they were doing the younger sister a good turn, sparing her the dry discipline. If Elizabeth was the King's trusty squire, Margaret was his jester, winning his affection—as she learnt to attract social attention—by jokes, japes and mischief. But sometimes the mischief went too far. When the officers of the Coats Mission followed the family to Sandringham they were invited to family dinner and noted, on each occasion, that Princess Margaret had been sent up to bed. 'Got on the wrong side of His Majesty,' explained the equerry with a wink and a knowing whisper.

Black sheep, white sheep: Margaret's talent to amuse won her a niche in her father's affections; but when she overstepped the mark, she found herself dismissed, the naughty little sister—while Princess Elizabeth stayed up to dine with the grown-ups.

*   *   *

In 1942 King George VI took his daughter to the Beckhampton stables on the Wiltshire downs where the royal racehorses were trained. The King did not share the racing enthusiasm of his father and grandfather, but he had kept up the royal stables, as well as the royal studs, for the sake of tradition, and also to maintain the employment they provided.

Princess Elizabeth had been riding horses from an early age. Since 1938 she had been taking lessons from the royal riding instructor, Horace Smith, to whom she had famously confided that 'had she not been who she was, she would like to be a lady living in the country with lots of horses and dogs'. Smith had taught the princess to ride sidesaddle, a skill she would need when she was old enough to review troops, and he had also given her basic lessons in carriage driving. In 1943 and 1944 she would win first prize in the Royal Windsor Horse Show for driving a cart harnessed to her own black Fell pony.

Horse-racing had continued in Britain through the early years of war, and in 1942 the royal stables had two highly fancied prospects for the Oaks and the Derby, Sun Chariot and Big Game. Both had been bred at the royal studs, and the princess was allowed to go up and pat the magnificent Big Game. She later admitted that she did not wash that hand for the rest of the day.

*   *   *

The royal family's much-publicised willingness to share the rationing privations of their subjects was an important element in their wartime popularity. All royal bathtubs were painted with thick, black Plimsoll lines to indicate the five-inch level above which they should not be filled. Hot water was restricted to a few specified hours a day. Eleanor Roosevelt was horrified by the austerity of Buckingham Palace when she stayed there for two days in 1943. She was lent the Queen's bedroom and froze in it as draughts whistled through the bombed-out windows, while the fishcakes she was offered at dinner were equally discouraging— 'probably sawdust', admitted the Queen quite happily.

The stark picture of royal austerity which the President's wife took back to America prompts the suspicion that the lily might have been slightly un-gilded for her benefit, since the royal family actually had access to significant stocks of fresh meat. The nationally imposed food ration did not restrict the consumption of game. You could eat as many pheasants, grouse, venison and rabbits as you could catch, and slaughtered wildlife had always kept the game larders well stocked at Sandringham, Balmoral and Windsor. Like many country people, the royal family actually ate quite substantially during the war. The historian A. J. P. Taylor memorably described King George VI eating Spam off a golden plate. Make that pheasant. A member of the Balmoral staff recalled eating so much venison during rationing, 'It's a wonder we didn't grow antlers.'

When it came to clothing coupons, here too documents at the Public Record Office make clear that the royal family were exceptions. At a time when a non-uniformed civilian woman was allowed sixty coupons per year, the royal ladies asked for, and were given, an annual average of 1,277 coupons for their personal use, on top of their basic allowance. In addition to this, the royal households were allowed several thousand extra coupons annually to maintain the style of their liveried servants. Since servicemen and women were allowed extra coupons for their uniforms, the rationale seems to have been that royal finery was fighting kit, part of maintaining morale for the war effort.

A good number of clothing coupons went on the costumes for the increasingly elaborate pantomimes that the princesses staged each Christmas from 1940 to 1944. Choreographed by the master of the small Church of England school in Windsor Great Park, the casts were made up of local village children and evacuees. But the King and Queen's two daughters were inevitably the stars and, as newspapers printed photos of Princess Elizabeth in tight white satin breeches playing Prince Charming to her sister's Cinderella, public interest mounted. In the weeks before the 1943 production of Aladdin, more than 1,000 would-be ticket holders sent in envelopes containing blank cheques. All were politely returned. But sitting in the front row of the audience one night was Elizabeth's real-life Prince Charming.

'Who do you think is coming to see us act?' the princess asked her governess excitedly.

*   *   *

Prince Philip was having a good war. He had distinguished himself in the Battle of Cape Matapan in the eastern Mediterranean in the spring of 1941, being mentioned in despatches for manning the searchlights under heavy fire while his battleship, HMS *Valiant,* participated in the destruction of two Italian cruisers and two destroyers. Since June 1942 the prince had been engaged in convoy duty, escorting merchant ships up and down 'E-Boat Alley', the dangerous east coast run from Rosyth in Scotland to Sheerness on the Thames Estuary. E-boats were the lethal little 39-knot German *Schnellboote* that could hide behind headlands and whizz out of the North Sea mists with their torpedoes.

'He was greatly changed,' reported Crawfie, '. . . more than ever, I thought, like a Viking, weather-beaten and strained . . . I have never known Lilibet more animated. There was a sparkle about her none of us had ever seen before. Many people remarked on it.'

A cousinly correspondence had been maintained since the couple's 1939 meeting at Dartmouth, and the prince had been dropping in at Windsor during shore leaves. One day the ever-vigilant governess had noticed a photograph of Philip on the princess's mantelpiece.

'Is that altogether wise?' Crawfie asked. 'A number of people come and go. You know what that will lead to. People will begin all sorts of gossip about you.'

'Oh dear, I suppose they will,' the princess replied, and the picture vanished. But in its place appeared another one, showing Philip after a spell when he had grown a bushy beard which covered most of his features.

'There you are, Crawfie,' said the princess, who was never easily deflected from her purpose. At just about the first moment that she could, this cautious Daddy's girl had bestowed some grown-up, hormone-driven passion on her privileged but deprived life. She was not letting go of her own brief encounter.

On Philip's regular shore leaves in London he would stay either with the Mountbattens in Chester Street, Belgravia, or out with his cousin Marina, the Duchess of Kent, at Coppins. 'It is at Coppins,' reported the nosy Chips Channon, who tracked Philip's signature through the visitors' book, 'that he sees Princess Elizabeth.'

Walking in Windsor Great Park one day, Alexandra of Yugoslavia spotted the couple strolling together hand in hand, hastily stepping apart until they realised it was only family that had spotted them.

At the naval end of things, Mike Parker noticed that while there were always 'armfuls of girls' on the shore leaves that the two young officers enjoyed between their harrowing runs down E-boat Alley, Philip apparently stayed chaste. 'He seemed to be keeping himself,' recalls the Australian. 'And I remember thinking that whoever she might be at home, she had to be someone pretty special.'

By the spring of 1944, when Elizabeth reached her eighteenth birthday and Philip was approaching his twenty-third, the couple had been 'in love for the last eighteen months, in fact longer I think', confided Queen Mary to her lady-in-waiting, Lady Airlie. The pair were committed enough for Philip's uncle, George of Greece, to make a direct approach to George VI. Could Philip be formally considered as a suitor for the hand of Princess Elizabeth?

'We both think she is too young for that now,' was George VI's reaction. But 'I like Philip. He is intelligent, has a good sense of humour & thinks about things in the right way.' The King and Queen were not averse to Elizabeth marrying Philip eventually; still, 'she has never met any young men of her own age . . . P. had better not think any more about it for the present.'

* * *

The King was fiercely fatherly towards his elder daughter—and if George VI was worried that his heir had never met any 'young men of her own age', his own protectiveness was to blame. By 1944 there was no reason why the 18-year-old should not have been out mixing with her contemporaries, engaged in some sort of war work. Yet it was not until the spring of 1945, on the eve of her nineteenth birthday, that her father finally allowed her to join the Auxiliary Territorial Service: No. 230873, Second Subaltern Elizabeth Alexandra Mary Windsor.

The eleven young women on her Vehicle Maintenance Course at Aldershot were told it was the first time in history that a female royal had ever attended a course with 'other people'. They were under strict instructions not to reveal her identity and were bursting with curiosity to see what she looked like.

'Quite striking', noted Corporal Eileen Heron in her diary. 'Short, pretty, brown, crisp, curly hair. Lovely grey-blue eyes, and an extremely charming smile, and she uses lipstick!'

The princess was equally eager to get to know her coursemates. But while they slept in huts at the all-female base, Elizabeth was chauffeured back to dine and sleep at Windsor. Every lunchtime she

194

was 'whisked away' by the officers to lunch in their mess, and at lectures she was placed in the middle of the front row, with a protective sergeant on either side.

She did her best in the circumstances.

'When anyone is asked a question,' noted Eileen Heron, 'she turns round to have a good look at the person concerned. It is her only opportunity to attach names to the right people.'

By the end of the three-week course on 16 April, Elizabeth had managed to escape from her over-protective mentors and take tea with the other girls. 'These cups of tea are getting a nice chatty institution,' noted Corporal Heron. 'She talks much more now she is used to us and is not a bit shy . . . [She] says she will feel quite lost next week, especially as she does not know yet what is going to happen to her as a result of the course.'

The princess had been learning how to service and maintain army vehicles. Her long discourses on pistons and cylinder heads over dinner at Windsor became something of a family joke. She told Eileen Heron that she was hoping to join ATS headquarters later that summer as a junior officer, where she would have worked in an office with other young women on transport organisation.

It was not to be. Less than a month after her course ended came VE day—8 May 1945. There was ATS work aplenty in the months of demobilisation that followed, but George VI wanted his daughter back home on royal duties. He did not see her future as working in an office, even a military office, alongside other young women, and Princess Elizabeth bowed to his wish.

But she did get to wear her ATS uniform—on

195

VE day itself, as vast crowds surged around the Palace, calling for the royal family and Winston Churchill to come out repeatedly on the balcony to take their cheers. With a group of young Guards officers, the two princesses slipped away from the Palace on foot to mingle in the crowds, going down Birdcage Walk, up Whitehall and round Piccadilly to the Ritz Hotel. They linked arms with carefree revellers singing 'Run Rabbit Run', 'Roll out the Barrel' and other wartime hit songs, then made their way back to join the crowds outside the Palace shouting, 'We want the King, we want the King!' Thanks to an exceptional occasion, the future Queen briefly achieved an impossible fantasy. To be just a face in the crowd, like any other.

CHAPTER TWELVE

Welfare Monarchy

Perhaps the most profound satisfaction that Royalty provides is that it gives us a Paradise to inhabit.

Virginia Woolf, 1939

Fifteen weeks after VE day the royal family were back on the Palace balcony again, but in the company of a new Prime Minister. Waving beside them to celebrate the defeat of Japan and the final ending of the Second World War stood the modest, clerk-like figure of Clement Attlee, Churchill's deputy in the wartime government of national unity, and leader of the Labour Party. Promising reform and reconstruction, Labour had been swept to power by the election of July 1945 with a massive majority.

George VI felt hurt by Britain's rejection of its bulldog hero.

'I was shocked at the result,' he complained in one of two emotional, handwritten letters of farewell to Churchill. 'I thought it most ungrateful to you personally after all your hard work for the people.'

Fundamentally conservative like his father—and, indeed, like his smiling, people-friendly wife—the King deplored the new government's socialist programme of nationalisation, social welfare and wealth redistribution. 'I really don't see why people should have false teeth free any more than they have shoes free,' he remarked to Hugh Gaitskell, his Chancellor of the Exchequer, in 1951.

In its most extreme form, the welfare state presented an ideological challenge to the good works and philanthropy that had come to be staples of royal activity. Charity was an ancient tradition of the crown, embodied every year in the ceremony of the Maundy Money, in which the sovereign presented specially minted coins to the poor. Queen Victoria continued this tradition personally, giving as much as 10 per cent of her private fortune to charities.

But Edward VII, with his love of opening things, had widened royal giving into a broader encouragement of philanthropy—the 'welfare monarchy', as the American historian Frank Prochaska has described it. This dimension, strengthened by George V and Queen Mary with their own belief in good works, had extended, and to some extent replaced, the traditional idea that the monarchy fulfilled its charitable obligations by casting coins into the crowd. Personal giving might continue, but in the early twentieth century the crown's main focus had become the inspiring of others—coaxing those with resources to give money, while encouraging everyone else to offer time and effort to worthy causes, thus building up the voluntary side of national life.

Elizabeth Bowes-Lyon had fortified this tendency with her own aristocratic instincts of *noblesse oblige*, and by the 1940s it was taken for granted that royal people should accumulate dozens—in the case of the King and Queen, hundreds—of charitable patronages. The day-to-day 'work' of the royal family, and in particular the justification for the continuing prominence and subsidising of the lesser relatives who were not involved in official activities, came to revolve increasingly around the furthering of their patronages.

Taking their cue from Soviet communism, however, the most extreme Labour Party ideologues argued that the welfare state made private charity unnecessary and even undesirable. In the brave new postwar world, the state, by dint of central planning, would take care of everything, making local and individual initiatives redundant. 'In the case of nutrition and health, just as in the case of education,' wrote the young Labour theoretician Douglas Jay in *The Socialist Case* in 1937, 'the gentlemen in Whitehall really do know better what is good for the people than the people know themselves.'

The conflict crystallised over the many voluntary

hospitals that were due to be brought into the new National Health Service, whose formation lay at the centre of the new government's plans. Would their privately accumulated assets be nationalised? Was there any point in their volunteers continuing to give money or spare time to a government-controlled institution? And what role was left for the hospital philanthropy which the royal family had always encouraged, if the state provided for all human ills from the cradle to the grave?

The royal family's personal view was made clear by a speech delivered by the King's younger brother, the Duke of Gloucester, in July 1944. In thoughtful and decisive words, which the backwoods Duke could not possibly have drafted himself, he made a plea for preserving 'the freedom of the medical profession and of voluntary hospitals'. As reported by *The Times*, the Duke argued that 'no vote or public monies could replace the personal affection and collective interest which had been lavished on the voluntary hospitals of London and the provinces.'

Yet the King and Queen decided that, for constitutional reasons, they themselves should hold back from the fray. When the Royal National Throat, Nose and Ear Hospital invited George VI to continue its tradition of royal patronage following the death of Arthur, Duke of Connaught in 1942, the King declined the invitation. He was following the advice of Lord Dawson of Penn, who remained Royal Physician in Ordinary, and who had progressive views on the integration of the hospital system. Dawson felt that the King and Queen should remain 'independent' in this contentious area.

But that should not stop 'lesser members' of the family continuing to encourage the smaller voluntary hospitals, and in this spirit the 18-year-old Princess Elizabeth accepted the presidency of the east London hospital named after her mother, the Queen Elizabeth Hospital for Children, in Hackney. The princess made her first public speech there in May 1944. She wished 'to assure' the governors, she declared, that her service would be given 'wholeheartedly to what we all know to be a good cause'.

Her parents' most effective tactic in coming to terms with the left-wing establishment was the well-established royal ploy of being polite and smiling cheerfully. The King and Queen found it took the 'ism' out of socialism.

'In an earlier age,' says Sir Edward Ford, who joined the Palace as an assistant private secretary in 1946, 'I think that both the King and the Queen would have been classified as "Whig". They were both very open to ideas of social improvement.'

The couple entertained the ministers of the new Labour Cabinet at gatherings known as 'Dine and Sleeps', since the invitation was for dinner at Windsor and a night in the castle, with a brisk and non-ceremonial departure expected before lunch the next day. The guests, who included a fair sprinkling of trades union leaders, the new barons of the land, arrived in time for drinks with the King and Queen, then retired to change for dinner. Sir Stafford Cripps, the unbending Labour Chancellor of the Exchequer, sternly insisted on vegetarian dishes. 'Somehow,' recalls Ford, 'these always looked better than the food everyone else was eating.'

It was after dinner that the jollity started. During the war, George VI had several times reviewed the Free Polish troops stationed in Britain and had been most amused by their ceremonial march, the *parada*, a high, stiff, leg-kicking walk which was not that different from the Nazi goose-step.

'Oh, Bertie,' said the Queen one Dine and Sleep evening at Windsor, 'let's do the *parada!*'

So the King took his station by the fireplace, stiffly to attention, and the gramophone was switched on. To the scratchy tones of a military march, the assembled Cabinet ministers and guests goose-stepped past him, eyes right, the Chancellor of the Exchequer putting on a particularly good show, upright as ever, with a pair of fire tongs on his shoulder instead of a rifle.

The House of Windsor knew what was good for the gentlemen of Whitehall. Even the venerable Queen Mary, just turning eighty, would enter into the party spirit, sticking a matchbox on to her nose, then nuzzling up to the Labour grandee next to her to lodge it on to his. Appointed detective for a game of 'Murder' and groping in the darkness beneath a piano, Ben Nicolson, Deputy Surveyor of the King's Pictures, poked his finger into what he thought was a soft cushion, to discover he had located Queen Elizabeth.

The evening might conclude with a conga, led vigorously up and down the castle staircases by a member of the royal family, after which the guests would line up formally to wish Their Majesties good night. George VI and Queen Elizabeth would then take their leave through a pair of high double doors which were formally closed behind them. Except that on one occasion the catch slipped, and before the door could be closed again, the assembled guests caught a glimpse of the King and Queen, on their own, skipping down the corridor, hand in hand, towards their private apartments.

*   *   *

Nineteen forty-five was not nineteen eighteen. The Second World War left Britain impoverished, but the country was looking to the future with more unity than had been the case after the conflict in the trenches. The impulse for change was firmly channelled within the boundaries of the national consensus, and as an embodiment of this, the royal family emerged from the war stronger than they had ever been. If they had symbolised the people's ordeal, they now symbolised the people's victory; and, like his father, George VI was constitutional with a populist sense.

'Why did you join?' he quizzed Frank Pakenham, Lord Longford, the unconventional socialist peer, who was momentarily unclear whether the King was referring to his membership of the Catholic Church or of the Labour Party.

'Because I like to be on the side of the underdog,' replied Longford.

'So do I,' responded the King stoutly.

George VI had his own vision of a traditional, common-sense England of all classes, which he clearly separated from the doctrinaire prescriptions of the political elite. When his young war hero equerry, Group Captain Peter Townsend, complained that the shambling Ernest Bevin, the Labour Foreign Secretary, failed to take his left hand out of his pocket while shaking the royal hand, the etiquette-conscious King was untroubled. The important thing, he instructed Townsend, was not Bevin's manners, but the fact that he was 'a real Englishman. I like him.'

It was surprising that the King did not pass on more of this attitude to his elder daughter. As she grew older, Princess Elizabeth would accompany her father to the summer ritual of his across-the-classes boys' camp. But while she learned the hand gestures of 'Under the Spreading Chestnut Tree', she was never to be lit by this cheery, populist spark. As with Queen Victoria, the common touch did not come naturally to her.

George VI did nothing to push either of his daughters outside the narrowly ordained circle of family, friends and loyal retainers. While the King prescribed social mixing for the boys at his summer camps, it was not a prescription that he applied to his own children, as the princess had discovered in the frustration of her hopes to taste more ordinary life via the ATS. The message was very clear. It was ladies-in-waiting and a start on public engagements that the King wanted for his heir as soon as the war was over.

Queen Mary saw the dangers in this. One postwar summer's afternoon, in the garden of Marlborough House, she confided to Jock Colville her worry that her grand-daughter was 'inclined to associate with young Guards officers to the exclusion of more representative strata of the community'. Colville was about to become the princess's first private secretary, and just as the old Queen had tried to influence Crawfie's programme of education for the young Elizabeth, so she now suggested the social directions in which Colville might steer his charge. She emphasised 'the necessity of travel, of mixing with all classes . . . and of learning to know young members of the Labour Party'.

Colville was later to try out some of Queen Mary's suggestions, but he did not join the princess until 1947. For the first two years of her public life, her programme was in the hands of the King's own private secretary, Sir Alan 'Tommy' Lascelles, a stuffy man who sent her to stuffy places. The Grenadier Guards Ladies' Relief Committee, the opening of the NAAFI Club in Portsmouth and the Women's Land Army rally in Bedford were Elizabeth's first three engagements of 1946. Asked for local points of interest that might be mentioned in the princess's speech for her Bedford engagement, the Lord Lieutenant alluded to the county's proud libertarian tradition. 'Bedford and Bedfordshire have usually been on the side of liberty,' he wrote. '. . . In the Civil War all the MP's for borough and county were [anti-royalist] Parliamentarians.' Somehow the speech that Lascelles drafted for the princess quite ignored this most significant and refreshing aspect of local history—as the private secretary later turned down a request from the Minister of Fuel and Power for her to attend 'The Miner Comes to Town' exhibition at Marble Arch. She had no other public engagements that day, but Lascelles told the ministry that she was too busy, and it was the princess's habit to do as she was told.

'When in doubt,' she later explained as Queen to one of her own private secretaries, 'my father said, "Go along with the advice of your advisers—that's what they're there for."'

204

                    *   *   *

Public life was not Princess Elizabeth's first concern as she approached her twentieth birthday. Her priority in the summer of 1946 was her love for Prince Philip and her own bid for personal freedom—and she had to fight quite a battle to secure both.

While paternally unhappy about any man taking his beloved Lilibet away from him, George VI actually got on rather well with his would-be son-in-law. The two men shared the language and attitudes of the naval officer with the 'something understood' of duty and hierarchy, as well as the grounded assurance that came from their very similar royal bloodlines.

The existing family connection may have been one reason why Queen Elizabeth was not so happy with Philip. It was never openly stated, but the older, Germanic Windsor relatives retained a snobbish condescension towards the Bowes-Lyon queen who had diluted the royal bloodstock so that, in Teutonic terms, George VI's descendants were only half royal. It was not just wars that had severed the comings and goings between Windsor and schlosses in the Black Forest. Princess Marina, Philip's cousin, proud of her own descent from the Russian imperial family, would refer to her sisters-in-law the Queen and the Duchess of Gloucester—another pint-sized recruit from the Highland aristocracy—as 'those common little Scottish girls'.

If the Queen ever caught the condescension, she was too sunny to show it. But perhaps there was a little irony in her occasional references to the

205

family's 'Fabergé aunts', the grand old relatives who had ended up living in threadbare apartments with only the knick-knacks they had salvaged from a way of life that had got too grand for their own good. With her painful family memories of the First World War, the Queen had problems with Philip's German connections, and she was also suspicious of his pushy uncle, Lord Mountbatten. 'Uncle Dickie' was another of the Russo-German network, though he had married his way out of mansion-block destitution, and Queen Elizabeth mistrusted him for his former fair-weather closeness to the Duke of Windsor. So when she drew up a First Eleven of possible husbands for her daughter, Philip was by no means at the head of her batting order.

Her favourites came from her own home-based noble background—stalwart young aristocrats doing their time in the Guards. There was Hugh Euston, son of the Duke of Grafton, and Johnny Dalkeith, son of the Duke of Buccleuch, both heirs to ancient titles and to vast Strathmore-like landed estates. There was also Lord Porchester, the heir to the Earl of Carnarvon, with whom the princess had already established a firm friendship based on their shared love of horses. The princess called him Porchey, and was seen chatting intensely to him about equine bloodstock lines at the occasional debutante balls which were providing a faltering beginning to postwar social life.

These young Guards officers, of course, represented the very circle in which Queen Mary thought her grand-daughter spent too much time, and the princess certainly felt at ease in their company—too much at ease, perhaps, for the

206

earnest element inside her that cast royal life as a challenge. She laughed and danced with Euston and Porchester, developing relaxed and chatty friendships that were to last her whole life. But these young men represented what she already knew, and she had spent seven years studying the novel unpredictabilities of Philip. He was a challenge in all his complexity—pepper as well as ginger. On the well-mapped path that lay ahead for her, he offered swashbuckling and surprise. She was quite sure of her feelings. It was not in her nature to fall in and out of love, and it suited both her personality and her position as monarch-in-waiting not to engage in the emotional rough and tumble of more than one courtship.

While she liked the fact that Philip was very much his own man, his striking lack of material connections made him very much hers. He also had a seriousness about him that rather matched her own. Both, in a sense, were old beyond their years. Each had their own oblique detachment from the balls and the social whirl in which, people felt, the princess participated more through duty than inclination.

In the summer of 1946 Prince Philip of Greece, now a naval lieutenant assigned to British shore training, spent his leave at Balmoral. He later confessed to having been shamed by the look on the face of the footman who laid out his meagre and much-patched wardrobe, which included a couple of old suits of his father's. But he did not behave like a poor relation.

'Everyone was starting to say that he could be the one,' remembers the assistant private secretary Sir Edward Ford, 'but he wasn't deferential or ingratiating. He behaved with all the self-confidence of a naval officer who'd had a good war. He didn't show that respect which an English boy of his age would have had for the older people around him. He wasn't in the least afraid to tell Lord Salisbury [the eminent Tory and wartime Cabinet minister] what his own opinions were.'

The 26-year old's jauntiness did not impress the old guard.

'The Salisburys and the hunting and shooting aristocrats around the King and Queen did not like him at all,' remembers Mike Parker. 'And the same went for Lascelles and the old-time courtiers. They were absolutely bloody to him—and it didn't help that all his sisters were married to Germans.'

But none of this mattered to Princess Elizabeth. When Philip proposed to her that summer at Balmoral she accepted, and immediately set about persuading her father, whose consent, she well knew, was the key. George VI's approval would take care of courtiers, aristocrats and even her canny mother, who, for all her First Eleven preferences, had been careful to include her daughter's own favourite in the team.

Elizabeth and her father had been particularly close that September, enjoying the first family holiday since the end of the war. The King had initiated his elder daughter into his beloved sport of deerstalking, and out on the moors alone together some understanding was forged.

In fact, George VI had been quietly working for more than a year on the formalities involved in the match. In August 1945 Lascelles had been despatched to the Home Office to investigate the steps by which Prince Philip of Greece could become a British subject.

'I suspect there may be a matrimonial nigger in the woodpile,' noted the curmudgeonly private secretary in his diary.

From the King's point of view in the autumn of 1946, the horizon was dominated by a royal tour of South Africa scheduled for the following spring. It was the first of what was planned as a series of thank-you tours around the empire. The King had set his heart on this foreign foray by the neat little wartime family unit of mother, father and two daughters—'Us Four', as he liked to say—and there was no room in this picture for a son-in-law.

An accommodation was reached. The King consented to his daughter's engagement. But it must remain secret until after the tour of South Africa—when the princess would also reach the age of twenty-one. 'I was rather afraid that you had thought I was being hard-hearted about it,' George VI was to write to his daughter the following year. But Elizabeth agreed to wait the extra few months. She had won the main point, that she could get engaged to Philip, even if she had no engagement ring to flash—and no one but Philip with whom to share her triumph.

London's hit show of the moment was Rogers and Hammerstein's *Oklahoma!*, a colourful and warming tale of prairie romance. The couple went to see it together, finding their own meaning in its hit ballad, as two young people who had to keep their romance secret from a prying world:

> *Don't throw bouquets at me . . .*
> *Don't laugh at my jokes too much—*
> *People will say we're in love!*

When they went to dances and parties together, the couple had to act out the song literally, dancing with other partners, exchanging meaningful, but not too obvious, glances across the crowd. The only time they could feel safe was when Philip came to supper in the Palace nursery, where Elizabeth and Margaret still ate. 'Food was of the simplest,' reported the ever-vigilant Crawfie. 'Fish, some sort of sweet, and orangeade.'

Crawfie did her best to give the couple some time away from Margaret, who had been kept in the dark about the engagement, but the younger sister never seemed to take the hint. She would play silly games of precedence outside the Palace lifts until Philip solved the problem with naval briskness, by giving her a good push.

The 24-year-old lieutenant provided a breath of fresh air in the Palace. Philip would swing into the courtyard in his little black sports car and leap out in his blazer and open-necked shirt, heading purposefully for the nursery floor. But his regular visits soon became the talk of the Palace staff, and the newspapers picked up hints of the romance. One day Princess Elizabeth came back from a factory trip very obviously upset.

'Crawfie, it was horrible,' she said. 'They shouted at me, "Where's Philip?"'

Suddenly, going out in public was not fun any more. The rawness of private feelings being exposed so publicly—her most personal hopes and emotions annexed by total strangers—hit a nerve for which her sheltered upbringing, and her still naïve, unshielded nature left her unprepared. The governess noticed a dramatic change—'She began to dread the trips to factories and shops.'

These were the months when the outgoing, people-friendly child who had ordered her sister to wave to the crowd became shy and reserved—wooden, even. A shutter came down and stayed down. Faced with the power of popular scrutiny, Elizabeth became defensive and even sulky on occasions, more like her sister in her realisation that there were parts of herself that she was not compelled, and did not wish, to share with a greedy and intrusive world. As she entered adulthood and developed a life of her own that was private and precious, the future Elizabeth II painfully discovered how much her destiny invaded her privacy.

It was the Queen Victoria syndrome, the paradox of a reclusive individual at the centre of a social and commercial mechanism—the mass media—that relished and made much money from exposure. For understandable and largely positive human reasons, the princess's love for a brave and handsome young serviceman was of warm public interest. But the future Elizabeth II experienced 'Where's Philip?' as rough intrusiveness, not good wishes, and to protect herself she developed a hauteur that touched on the Victorian.

Her self-assured fiancé actually encouraged this, for Philip had long ago developed the artful outer carapace which protected his private feelings. He had very definite ideas on what was his own business and nobody else's, and his first gift to his fiancée was to help her make the same distinction. The young man who was disinclined to ingratiate himself with Lord Salisbury saw no need to kowtow to the general public.

This attitude stemmed originally from Philip's proud royal heritage and had been developed by his naval years into a royal version of the quarterdeck manner. Brisk, friendly and smiling, it kept the ratings at arm's length, and could serve the same function with the public.

'Everything OK, Smith?'

The only possible answer was 'Yessir.'

It was a useful way to prevent one's inner self from getting hurt by public attention—and it also provided a barrier against the seductive influence of adulation and celebrity. That was what had gone wrong with Uncle David, in the opinion of the royal family. The cheers had turned his head. His farewell broadcast was held against his memory as particularly vulgar, because it had revealed personal emotions to the public. In fact, the whole of the abdication crisis could be seen as stemming from the unseemly intrusion of private feeling into the public arena.

A 1950s document in the BBC archives which details the policy that Elizabeth II and her husband wished to adopt towards press coverage of their son, Prince Charles, explains their attitude almost totally in terms of Edward VIII. The family consensus was that the ex-King had been spoiled by 'the publicity'—the mass adulation which had placed him, in the opinion of his relatives, 'under a very considerable personal tension'. Thus the misadventures and tragedy of the abdication were linked in Windsor minds not only with issues of duty, but also with the celebrity culture that had turned Edward VIII's head. It became part of family lore that what they saw as the 'continual embarrassment' of public scrutiny had 'affected his attitude and his later life'. For a serious royal person, too much publicity—and too much fondness for it—was a bad thing.

*   *   *

Philip's bluff wartime shipmate, the Australian Michael Parker, heard the news of the engagement when he was summoned to the Wiltshire naval base where Philip was teaching early in 1947.

'This is my destiny,' Philip told Parker, 'to support my wife in what lies ahead for her.'

Parker knew something of Philip's confused family background. A few years earlier he had accompanied his friend on a poignant mission to Monte Carlo to collect the effects of Prince Andrew, who had died in 1944—a pair of cufflinks and a set of silver-backed hairbrushes. But as Parker heard Philip set out his vision of lifelong support for his wife, the future sovereign, the Australian suddenly understood something of the great European family of royalty from which the exiled Greek–Danish–German prince had come.

Parker's trip down to Wiltshire was the sign that, whatever the King's previous reservations, he was now committed to his daughter's new life with Philip. Although the engagement was to remain a secret for a further six months, George VI had authorised his future son-in-law to offer Parker a job as an equerry to the princess, and a few days later Parker came up to London to meet the King.

'You're coming to lunch with us,' said the King, after explaining how he wanted Parker to get to know the existing courtiers. 'I hope you've got time.' The King took the Australian to the dining room, where they found the Queen, Princess Margaret, Princess Elizabeth and Philip all sitting around the table, waiting to tuck in. They had just started eating when the King looked at his watch, and reached for his Roberts radio. It was time for the Richard Murdoch/Kenneth Horne comedy show *Much Binding in the Marsh,* and as the signature tune struck up, father, mother and daughters all joined in, singing along with the radio, word perfect. To their harmony, Philip contributed a lusty tenor, already a willing and cheerfully accepted recruit to 'Us Four'.

*   *   *

For Princess Elizabeth, the most attractive feature of the long, luxurious and rather insensitively named 'White Train' that transported the royal family around South Africa in February, March and April 1947 was the Post Office carriage, with its own telephone exchange. That was how she could keep in touch with Philip.

The political purpose of the tour was to shore up the relatively liberal, pro-British South African leader General Smuts against the rising power of the Afrikaner nationalists who wished to sever ties with Britain and the crown. In South Africa, racism and republicanism went hand in hand. The British visitors noticed the black and white chequerboard effect as they drove past Cape Town's segregated crowds, in contrast to the informal and more homogeneous mix that greeted them when they travelled north, to the noticeably less segregated colony of Rhodesia.

George VI grew annoyed at the Afrikaner

security police who kept him away from the 'native' sections of the crowds.

'Gestapo,' he harrumphed.

And he sniffed derisively when he noticed South Africa's motto on the tablecloth in the train's dining car—*Ex Unitate Vires*, 'Strength From Unity.'

'Huh!' he exclaimed. 'Not much bloody *Unitate* about this place!'

Hendrick Verwoerd, the architect of apartheid and at that time editor of *Die Transvaaler*, returned the compliment. His newspaper's only reference to the royal visitors was a report on the increase in burglaries in Johannesburg, caused by the police being called away to less important ceremonial duties.

The climax of the tour was the celebration of Princess Elizabeth's twenty-first birthday on 21 April, just three days before the family's departure, its high spot a broadcast by the princess to the empire and Commonwealth. The broadcast had been her own idea, and she contributed many of the ideas which Lascelles polished and embellished into sentiments worthy of Kipling.

'It has made me cry,' confessed the future Queen when she was shown the first draft on the train outside Bloemfontein. It had the same effect on many of the millions of listeners and, later, cinema-goers, who heard it, and it remains moving to this day—the clearest and most heartfelt statement of the entire purpose of her existence, as she saw it.

'I declare before you all,' she read out in her youthful, cut-glass voice, 'that my whole life, whether it be long or short, shall be devoted to your service, and the service of our great imperial family to which we all belong.'

These were words addressed to an era whose uncomplicated patriotism had recently been encapsulated in the derring-do of Laurence Olivier's film *Henry V*, and the princess conjured up the spirit of Agincourt as she talked of knightly vows. Sir Henry Marten's beloved themes could be heard in a clever paragraph which played with the idea of chivalric oaths of service being transmitted Commonwealth-wide through the modern invention of broadcasting.

Lascelles was delighted with the princess's performance. 'The most satisfactory feature of the whole business,' he wrote on the journey home, as he weighed up the general success of the tour, 'is the remarkable development of P'cess E.' The heiress presumptive did not have a great sense of humour, in his critical opinion, but she had demonstrated 'a healthy sense of fun. Moreover, when necessary, she can take on the old bores with much of her mother's skill, and never spares herself in that exhausting part of royal duty. For a child of her years, she has got an astonishing solicitude for other people's comfort.' This unselfishness, noted the hardened old courtier, 'is not a normal characteristic of that family'.

Lascelles still bore the scars of his battles with Edward VIII, whom he had served unhappily as both Prince of Wales and King—and there had been a curious echo of the ex-King in the remarks the private secretary had drafted for Princess Elizabeth's speech of dedication. 'I shall not have the strength,' the princess had said, 'to carry out this resolution alone.' But where the ex-King had called for 'the help and support of the woman I love', Elizabeth's invitation was to her people. She invited her audience to 'join in with me . . . I know that your support will be unfailingly given.'

CHAPTER THIRTEEN

Utterly Oyster

I didn't see it in person, but saw the film . . . It was a sort of epitome of all the lovely weddings that one would like every pretty girl to have—and indeed, any girl, pretty or otherwise.

Poultry farmer, aged fifty-six, Berkshire, 1947

On 10 July 1947—eight years, almost to the day, since the couple's meeting at Dartmouth Naval College—the waiting was finally over. 'It is with the greatest pleasure,' came the announcement from Buckingham Palace, 'that the King and Queen announce the betrothal of their dearly beloved daughter the Princess Elizabeth to Lieutenant Philip Mountbatten, RN.'

Philip's naturalisation had come through while the royal family was in South Africa. Giving up Greek citizenship had meant forfeiting his princely status; hence his plain billing as 'Lieutenant'. 'I'm told that he doesn't in the least mind by what title he is known,' commented Queen Mary approvingly to her friend Mabell Airlie. The ex-prince had taken on his Uncle Dickie's anglicised surname of

Mountbatten. Originally designed to please, it harmonised well with the worn and shabby lieutenant's uniform in which he was photographed—'the usual after-the-war look', as Lady Airlie put it. 'Observing him, I thought he had far more character than most people would imagine.'

The news was released at lunchtime, and that evening crowds gravitated to the Palace. Elizabeth and Philip came out on the balcony to acknowledge the cheers. The communist *Daily Worker* found it 'not to our liking', but the rest of the press was rapturous, taking particular pleasure in the evidence that it was not an arranged alliance, but could be celebrated, as the *Manchester Guardian* put it, as 'a love match'.

Nobody wanted to make any trouble about Philip's inconvenient foreign connections. Uncle Dickie circulated a helpful memo to editors which omitted any mention of his nephew's three surviving sisters and their German husbands, concentrating instead on the young man's brave wartime naval career and his many British connections, and this lead was happily followed. A provincial leader writer predicted that the marriage promised to be 'England's answer to *Oklahoma!*'— 'a flash of colour', as Winston Churchill put it, 'on the hard road we have to travel'.

But for the disenchanted, the general rejoicing was offensive. 'I think it's a damn waste of money,' said one lower-middle-class woman of thirty, recorded by Mass-Observation. 'I don't see why she should have everything when there are so many who have to make do with makeshift weddings, and others can't get married at all because they have no

218

home to go to.'

Mass-Obs had now been recording this sort of dissenting comment for ten years, and the wartime experience had encouraged it. Through six years of shared hardship and conflict, the national ethos, for all its military discipline, had played down rank, and had overtly invited rejection of the traditional class-based ideas of 'us' and 'them'. People's ordeal, people's victory—Britain was dramatically less deferential, and reaction to the expense of the royal wedding dress reflected this. While 37 per cent interviewed by Mass-Obs in a straw poll thought it was reasonable, 36 per cent of respondents considered it an extravagance. Ten per cent voted 'Let her alone.'

Nineteen forty-seven was the worst of all the years of postwar austerity. A catastrophically cold winter had provoked a fuel crisis, deepening unemployment and a financial showdown that was to prove a postwar pattern. Just as it was announced that the princess's wedding would be celebrated in Westminster Abbey, the running out of a dollar loan provoked a currency crisis, a dramatic Cabinet reshuffle and the scheduling of a national emergency budget. A group of Labour MPs formally protested to the Chief Whip at the extravagance of the royal celebration in such circumstances, and, faced with questions, the Prime Minister himself had to get involved. Attlee wrote to the Palace enquiring about the allegedly unpatriotic origins of the 'Lyons silk' that had been used for the bride's wedding dress so he could reassure its critics in Parliament.

'The *wedding dress*', replied Lascelles, 'contains silk from Chinese silk worms, but woven in

Scotland and Kent. The *wedding train* contains silk produced by Kentish silk worms and woven in London. The *going-away dress* contains 4 or 5 yards of Lyons silk which was not specially imported but was part of the stock held by the dressmaker [Norman Hartnell] under permit.'

Hartnell himself later joined in by pointing out that while some of the silkworms were Chinese, they were *nationalist* silkworms, not communist.

For Princess Elizabeth, sharing her joy with the nation meant sharing its grumbling as well. The cost and style of royal celebration provoked an undertow of national fractiousness that was to ebb and flow throughout her adult life and reign— though it was Aneurin Bevan, the heart and conscience of Labour's left wing, who put the contrary view. 'So long as we have a Monarchy,' he said in a Cabinet discussion on the subject, 'the Monarchy's work has got to be done well.'

By 20 November 1947, the day of the ceremony itself, the nation's pre-wedding nerves had been restored. Most people had determined to enjoy themselves, and the spectacle of the Household Cavalry with its plumes and breastplates leading the procession down the Mall provided all the joy that many had hoped for. The sight of so much glitter and finery created a sense of 'hunger allayed', recalled the journalist Anne Sharpley. 'White satin, especially, seemed the most exquisite pleasure. We'd looked at drab things for so long! All along the procession route people had brought out their old bits of ribbon and trailed and waved these in a kind of acknowledgement to the need of the day for smooth, beautiful, joyful, luxurious things.'

A socialist Mass-Observer in Manchester tried to buy a newspaper and was astonished to discover they were all sold out. 'The feeling is genuine enough,' wrote another female observer from Leatherhead. 'A delighted sort of family feeling. I always get it when watching any Royal Do.'

When it came to the feelings of the participants themselves, George VI was remarkably open. 'I was so proud of you & thrilled at having you so close to me on our long walk in Westminster Abbey,' he wrote to his daughter. 'But when I handed your hand to the Archbishop I felt that I had lost something very precious.'

Of the emotions of the bride herself on this, her day of days, we have no record. At the centre of an event that was all about feelings conjured up on a massive scale, the princess let the world guess about the movements of her own heart. The same went for Philip (to whom George VI had given the title Duke of Edinburgh on his wedding morning). The couple gave no pre-wedding interview of the sort that would become traditional with their children. The act of marriage itself was sufficient to demonstrate what they felt about each other—and their view of their own privacy was made plain by a statement they framed together as they left Broadlands in Hampshire, the Mountbatten home where they started their honeymoon. Their few days there had been marked by persistently curious crowds of onlookers, who had gone so far as to use the ancient gravestones of Romsey Abbey as platforms from which they could spy on the couple at prayer.

'The loving interest shown by our fellow countrymen and well-wishers', declared the couple, has 'left an impression which will never grow faint. We can find no words to express what we feel.'

The irony was ill-concealed. The joint statement had Philip's sardonic fingerprints all over it, and this set a tone for the future. Shortly after the marriage, the princess's new private secretary Jock Colville brought her a letter from the Board of Trade asking if the royal wedding dress might go on a tour to advertise British materials and workmanship. Colville thought it a good idea. The much-debated dress was now considered a national triumph. It had already been on display, along with all the wedding presents, at St James's Palace, and the national export drive needed all the help it could get.

But the princess felt quite otherwise.

'I can think of at least five reasons against,' she said, employing a naval trick of argument she had learned from her husband.

Recalling the incident, Colville could not remember the five reasons in detail, but his mistress's drift was quite clear.

'She thought that to do these things would be rather vulgarising the monarchy,' he recorded. 'It was her wedding dress. She did not wish to part with it.'

The little girl who had taken for granted the public attention that was the price of toys like her Little Welsh House was starting to develop a will of her own, and she was supported in this by her combative husband. The couple sought to draw a firm line to defend their own definition of what was private and dignified. Queen Victoria, the great-great-grandmother from whom they were both descended, would thoroughly have approved.

But times were changing. Elizabeth might not like people enquiring 'Where's Philip?' or climbing on gravestones to catch a peek of her at worship. But such intrusion came from goodwill and curiosity which the Palace had been all too happy to encourage when it suited their purpose—going to some trouble to update the royal effigies at Madame Tussaud's after the war, for example, or staging the wedding-gift exhibition at St James's when popular support was needed for the expense of the wedding. The Prime Minister himself had gone into battle for the honour of the silkworms. But now that the public relations battle had been won, the garment was apparently not the public's any more; it was the princess's wedding dress.

*   *   *

Who owns the details of a royal life? The question was to become a consuming theme of Elizabeth II's later reign, and it received a painful early airing in the opening years of her marriage, when her beloved governess Crawfie became the first modern example of a royal 'kiss and tell'.

Like several other significant shifts in the relations between press and Palace, the initiative came from abroad. Bruce and Beatrice Gould, the ambitious publishers of *Ladies Home Journal*, a mass-market US magazine, wanted to produce a series of articles on 'The Education of a Princess', and had been pulling every string they could in the State Department and the Foreign Office to gain official approval. The Palace eventually agreed, on condition that the articles would be written by Dermot Morrah, an academic and enthusiastically pro-monarchist writer for *The Times* who had ghosted some of George VI's speeches. Marion Crawford, who had just left royal service at the age of thirty-eight, was Morrah's most obvious source, but he and the Goulds found the ex-governess mysteriously uncooperative. Having completed Princess Margaret's education, Crawfie had finally married her long-term sweetheart, George Buthlay, a bank employee who had not endeared himself to the royal family by trying to persuade them to shift their accounts to his bank.

The pushy Buthlay seems to have been the reason behind Crawfie's intransigence. He felt that his wife's sixteen years of devoted work deserved more than her retirement package—a pension of £300 a year (equivalent today to £6,000), the lifetime use of a charming old grace and favour cottage in the grounds of Kensington Palace, and the letters CVO after her name. This distinction, Commander of the Royal Victorian Order—an honour in the sovereign's personal gift—was higher than that bestowed on many royal servants, but it was a rank below the clearly illustrious title of Dame, the equivalent of Sir, to which the ex-governess and her husband evidently felt she was entitled.

Getting a hint of Crawfie's bundle of grievances, and her reluctance to hand her story to another writer for nothing, the Americans promptly flew to London and offered her a deal.

'Her awe of the royal family almost paralysed her,' recalled Bruce Gould. 'Even in her own sanctuary, close as it was to Kensington Palace, she would hardly speak these words above a whisper.'

The governess took the Goulds' proposal to her

former employer and received a polite but very firmly negative response.

'I do feel most definitely,' wrote the Queen on 4 April 1949, revealing a telling royal code word for keeping your trap shut, 'that you should not write and sign articles about the children, as people in positions of confidence with us must be utterly oyster.'

This appealing use of a family catchphrase was of a piece with a long and friendly letter which deployed dire warnings and charm in equal measure.

'You would lose all your friends,' wrote the Queen, 'because such a thing has never been done or even contemplated amongst the people who serve us so loyally.'

The letter displayed no aversion to the ex-governess picking up some pin money.

'Mr Morrah, who I saw the other day, seemed to think that you could help him with his articles and get paid from America,' wrote Queen Elizabeth. 'This would be quite alright as long as your name did not come into it. If you want a job, I feel sure that you could do some teaching, which after all is your "forte", and I would be so glad to help in any way I can.'

The issue was privacy and the control of the information that breached it.

'Having been with us in our family life so long you must be prepared to be attacked by journalists to give away private and confidential things, and I know that your good sense & loyal affection will guide you well. I do feel most strongly that you must resist the allure of American money & persistent editors, & say No No No to offers of dollars for articles about something as private & as precious as our family.'

Queen Elizabeth had been in many ways the creator of the genre that Crawfie was to exploit so profitably. The authorised nursery-floor books and articles to which the Queen had given her blessing as Duchess of York in the 1920s and 1930s were little different in content or style from the sugary chit-chat to which the ex-governess would eventually put her name, for she made no scandalous disclosures. When the Queen was later asked to say exactly what she disliked in the lengthy series as it finally appeared, she came up with only thirteen minor corrections of fact.

The sticking point was the maintenance of royal control over the disclosure process, along with the danger of opening the floodgates to other royal employees—and this involved something far more important than what was written in the newspapers. It was about the royal family's right to relax and live a natural, unspied-upon private life behind palace doors on their own terms. As the Queen put it to the former governess, 'we should never feel confidence in anyone again'.

The Queen finished her letter by reiterating her invitation 'to come & see me again about a job'. But nothing she might fix could match the tempting offer of the Goulds—a lump sum of $80,000 wrapped up in a clever, capital asset tax avoidance contract. At rates of income and super-tax as high as 95 per cent, the deal was the equivalent of well over a million dollars in taxed income; and for this unheard-of fortune, Crawfie did not even have to do any writing. She surrendered to the now-familiar newspaper ghosting process of being confined in a hotel room for days on end with a journalist, who 'pumped' her mercilessly to extract her story. To satisfy the ex-governess's continuing fear of the Palace, the Goulds flew over an American shorthand typist 'recommended for discretion in recording wartime secret conferences', and they moved into the Dorchester themselves to oversee the process and airmail back the instalments as they were completed.

When the series started running in January 1950, *Ladies Home Journal* sold out to the last copy. Thousands of women subscribed to make sure they would not miss the next instalment, and in Britain *Woman's Own*, which bought British rights in the series for $10,000 more than the Goulds had paid Crawfie, put out half a million copies. Similar serialisations in Canada, Australia, New Zealand and South Africa made the fortunes of the magazines which ran them. And then *The Little Princesses* went hardcover in lavishly illustrated editions that were best-sellers around the world.

The market in royal exposure was set. 'Doing a Crawfie' passed into the royal catalogue of ultimate sins, and it was a serious mistake even to mention the name of the former governess in the presence of the two charges to whom she had once been so close. One visitor forgot the taboo, and prompted a sneer of frightening disdain in Princess Margaret.

'Crawfie? She snaked.'

*   *   *

Within three months of her honeymoon Princess Elizabeth was pregnant. The speed and efficiency of this achievement impressed her husband's critics. 'Such a nice young man,' Tommy Lascelles remarked to Harold Nicolson. 'Such a sense of duty—not a fool in any way—so much in love, poor boy—and after all put the heir to the throne in the family way all according to plan.'

The princess and her husband seem to have been a warm and lusty couple. Participants in Balmoral and Sandringham games of 'Murder' noted the unerring speed with which the pair located each other when the lights went out. Soon after their marriage a friend remarked on the princess's wonderful complexion, and Philip laughed.

'Yes,' he responded, 'and she's like that all over!'

In the upper-class tradition, the couple slept in connecting bedrooms and enjoyed the visitation rituals which that system involves. James MacDonald, one of George VI's valets, once revealed how embarrassed he was one morning to enter Philip's bedroom and discover that the Duke had had a visitor during the night. The princess was in her husband's bed, dressed in a silk nightgown. Philip, for his part, appeared to be naked. 'Prince Philip didn't care at all,' said MacDonald.

George VI's valet was used to more formality. The Queen was in the habit of discreetly knocking on the door to let him know when he could come in—when the King would be properly robed in a dressing gown. But Philip had no time for pyjamas. 'Never wear the things,' he once said, when a valet at a weekend house party remarked that the Palace had apparently failed to pack him any.

Nearly fifty years later a royal footman told a strange story. Norman Barson, a former Grenadier Guardsman, worked at Windlesham Moor, the country home near Ascot that Princess Elizabeth and her husband rented in the first year of their marriage. They were lodging at Buckingham Palace while Clarence House, previously the home of the Duke of Connaught, was being restored for them, and the couple used Windlesham to have a place of their own at the weekends.

But according to Mr Barson, Philip would also visit the house during the week, usually on a Tuesday or Wednesday, in the early evening. He would phone ahead to give warning and would come roaring down the drive in his MG convertible, accompanied by a pretty, slim, well-dressed and well-spoken young lady who was not the princess.

'I never knew the woman's name,' Barson told the *Daily Mirror* in January 1996, 'but they seemed very close. She would look longingly into his eyes.'

The couple would eat together. Barson would prepare beef sandwiches and gin and orange.

'He always poured the lady's drink,' the footman recalled. 'He hardly drank at all. I could later hear them laughing and joking, but I never once heard him refer to her by name . . . We gossiped as staff do, and jokingly referred to her as his fancy woman, or lady friend—even though I never saw them kiss or canoodle. I remember thinking he acted exactly the same with her as with the Queen. He was charming to both of them. He stared into their eyes with his head on one side and made them laugh.'

What the footman saw was just the first in a series of close relationships with glamorous women that were to mark Prince Philip's married life. His staff, friends and relatives do not attempt to deny them and call them his 'flirtations', explaining them in terms of an excessively active, demanding man who needs constant entertainment. 'The Queen', says one of them, 'knows she has a husband who takes a lot of amusing.'

A polo-playing friend recalls trips to South America and the Caribbean in the 1960s where women threw themselves at Prince Philip.

'It was amazing how obvious they made it,' he remembers. 'But I never saw him succumb. He knew who he was, and how he was expected to behave. There was lots of dancing and joking, but that was that. I never saw him go off with any of them.'

John Gibson, a footman who also worked for Philip in the early days of his marriage is quite sure that the Duke was never unfaithful to his wife.

'I just don't believe all that stuff about him having other women,' he said to the journalist Graham Turner. 'I've met many gentlemen—you do, in private service—and I had a feeling about some of them. He never gave me any other feeling than that he was devoted to her.'

With his customary forthrightness, Prince Philip has discussed this question with his relatives.

'Ruddy hell,' he once said to Patricia Brabourne, Lord Mountbatten's elder daughter, 'the way the papers write about my affairs, I might as well have done it.'

Talking as a man who moved in circles where adultery could be discreetly condoned, if played by the rules, the prince has evidently worked out a rule of his own.

'How could I be unfaithful to the Queen?' he said to one relative. 'There is no way that she could possibly retaliate.'

One support for the rumours is the exhibitionism with which the Duke dances at parties, while his wife, if present, sits glumly at the side.

'He just loves dancing,' says a woman who has partnered him, 'and he's got terrific rhythm. But he knows the Queen is too shy. It just wouldn't be dignified for her to do his Zorba the Greek act. I think it's another example of him feeling he's nothing to feel guilty of, so he doesn't give a damn what the world thinks.'

In later years, the Queen has certainly known about her husband's lady friends, not least because two of them—Princess Alexandra and Penelope, Lady Romsey, the wife of Lord Mountbatten's grandson Norton Romsey—are members of her own family.

'The Queen is perfectly happy to invite all these girls,' says a relative. 'She just shrugs her shoulders and says, "Philip likes to have them around." She knows there is no way that he will humiliate her.'

But is the Queen showing tolerance as an immensely understanding wife, or as a monarch whose duty and dignity require her to rise above imperfections? She knows she has a prickly husband who finds it difficult to live with the fact that he is a 'kept man', and she is, apparently, too wise to feel threatened by whatever he needs in order to prove his independence.

The latter years of Elizabeth II's reign were marked by the extraordinary marriage between her eldest son and Lady Diana Spencer. Yet the reign's more extraordinary marriage has been that between the Queen herself and her husband—and it has lasted. At the time of writing the 80-year-old prince is spending some of the summer's finest weekends with Penelope Romsey at carriage-driving house parties with friends around the UK. It seems impossible that Princess Elizabeth, the young woman who had loved only this man since childhood, should not have felt the deepest hurt and betrayal at the moment she discovered—either in the Windlesham days or some time later—the existence of someone else into whose eyes he stared with his head on one side. But it remains the central enigma of a woman whose achievement depends on her ability to keep secrets.

*   *   *

Princess Elizabeth's first child, HRH Prince Charles Philip Arthur George, was born, by a hard-working but normal delivery, on 14 November 1948, six days before the couple's first wedding anniversary, at a quarter past nine in the evening. Philip was playing squash with Mike Parker at the time, then dashed off to see his wife and child, while Parker went out to the Palace railings in an attempt to quieten the huge crowd that had gathered outside. The water in the fountains in Trafalgar Square was dyed blue in honour of the new arrival, but his infant style was unpretentious; the new prince began life in his mother's old pram and hand-me-down clothes from family friends.

The princess breast-fed her baby for the first two months of his life, but in January 1949 she caught measles and the doctors decreed that mother and child should be separated. With London so smog-ridden, it was also deemed that country air was preferable for the infant, so Prince Charles moved out to Windlesham with his nannies. His parents saw him only at weekends.

The separation does not seem to have distressed Princess Elizabeth greatly. Though proud of her son—she wrote in wonder to her friends of the beauty of his baby fingers—she was not especially maternal. When her husband was posted to the first destroyer flotilla of the Mediterranean fleet in the autumn of 1949, she flew out to join him, leaving her son to spend his second Christmas, the first he was likely to remember, with his grandparents at Sandringham. This was the beginning of Prince Charles's closeness to his British grandmother. His other grandmother, Philip's mother Princess Alice, had by now made a good recovery from her mental breakdown, but was still living abroad, working to raise funds for a religious order that she hoped to found.

Returning on 28 December 1949, Princess Elizabeth was in no hurry to be reunited with her only child after more than a month apart. Instead of going straight to Sandringham, she spent four days in London catching up on her correspondence and then took a jaunt to Hurst Park racecourse to watch Monaveen, a horse that she owned jointly with her mother, win at 10–1. She was back in Malta by the end of March and spent her twenty-fourth birthday there watching her husband play polo with Uncle Dickie, who was commander of the Mediterranean Fleet. It was sunny, and for the first and only time in her life she was able to do relatively ordinary things—swim off a beach, drive a car around the streets, sit in a hairdresser's salon, and do her own shopping, with real money in her handbag.

On this second trip to Malta it was announced that she was pregnant again, and she returned to London for the birth of Princess Anne on 15 August 1950. Two weeks later, Philip flew back to Malta to take up his first command, and in November Princess Elizabeth flew out to join him, leaving her newborn baby and Prince Charles for yet another Christmas with the grandparents.

It was a pattern of life which both the princess and her husband found congenial. But it was not to continue. In July 1951 they came back from Malta. George VI's failing health meant that his daughter and son-in-law were needed full-time to share the burden of his royal duties. The King had had an operation in the spring of 1949 to deal with the poor circulation resulting from his heavy smoking. But the suspicion was that he had cancer, and in September 1951 exploratory surgery confirmed it. A crowd of over five thousand gathered silently outside the Palace on 23 September as he underwent an operation for the removal of his left lung. George VI came through safely. But when the princess and her husband flew to Canada next month on the tour that the King would have carried out had he been in better health, their new private secretary, Martin Charteris, carried the accession documents that would be needed in the event of his death.

The whole royal family was together again for Christmas. Then it was back to London for the princess and Philip to prepare for yet another tour. This time it was a postwar thank you to Australia and New Zealand, to which the couple were flying out via East Africa. The King looked wan and strained as he waved his daughter goodbye at the recently inaugurated Heathrow Airport. He had taken to wearing lurid orange pan-stick for his public appearances, and photographers were kept at a distance.

'Look after the princess for me, Bobo,' he said to the assistant nanny-turned-dresser.

Bobo told John Dean, Philip's valet, that she had never seen the King so upset at a parting.

Six days later, in the small hours of 6 February 1952, King George VI died of a thrombosis in his sleep at Sandringham. Princess Elizabeth and her husband had reached Kenya by that time, and had just got back from a night watching wildlife from the branches of the famous Treetops Hotel. It fell to Michael Parker to tell Philip what had happened.

'He looked as if you'd dropped half the world on him,' Parker recalls. 'I never felt so sorry for anyone in all my life.'

Philip took his wife away from everyone else. 'He took her up to the garden,' remembers Parker. 'And they walked slowly up and down the lawn while he talked and talked and talked to her.'

Part 3

Queen

CHAPTER FOURTEEN

Dumb Tenderness

What is a nation's love? No little thing:
A vast dumb tenderness beyond all price . . .

John Masefield,
'At the Passing of . . . King George VI'

Queen Elizabeth II's response to her father's death was remarkably controlled. When Martin Charteris reached Sagana Lodge on 6 February 1952 to start discussing the practicalities of accession, he found the couple alone together, with Philip lying back on the sofa, holding *The Times* over his face like a tent. The new Queen's cheeks were a little flushed, but there was no sign of tears.

'She was sitting erect,' remembers Charteris, 'fully accepting her destiny.'

On the long plane journey back to London, Philip's valet John Dean noted how the new Queen left her seat once or twice. When she returned he thought she looked as if she had been crying. But no one saw any tears. Pamela Mountbatten remembers her apologising for spoiling the exciting long South Pacific expedition to which everyone had been looking forward. 'I'm so sorry that we're all going to have to go home,' she had said at Sagana.

Elizabeth II's difficulty in seeing herself as the top potato was to last, in some respects, throughout her reign—as would her dry sense of humour. As they taxied to a halt at Heathrow Airport, she looked out of the window at the line of large, black, official cars waiting.

'Look,' she said. 'They've sent the hearses.'

Britain's grief was far more obviously displayed. The country knew the King had been ill, but his cancer had never been mentioned publicly, and he was generally presumed to have recovered as a result of his operations. He was only fifty-six.

'I feel rather lost,' said a carpenter of forty-five. 'Don't quite know what to think about it really. When I heard first of all I felt it was a personal loss, as though some of my own people had died.'

'My husband poured himself out a brandy,' recounted a 40-year-old country woman, 'and I said, "Pour one out for me." You really felt as though you wanted it, it was such a shock. All I can say is, thank goodness we've still got Churchill.'

The historian Philip Ziegler has pointed out that all these people, if asked, would have agreed that Churchill was a considerably more weighty and significant figure than George VI, and that the great Prime Minister had indisputably had more impact on the country's fortunes than the King. But Churchill's death, albeit in the fullness of his years, aged ninety in 1965, struck no such chord of raw emotion. It was the royal role as surrogate parent that made the difference, and rationalism got short shrift in the general atmosphere of emotion.

'He's only shit and soil now, like anyone else,' declared one drinker in a Notting Hill pub—who had to be hustled out of the back door to avoid attacks from indignant customers.

The process of buying the newspapers that contained the sad news became itself a form of mourning ritual, as orderly queues formed beside news vendors.

'Nobody liked to push or shove,' reported one Mass-Observer. 'Everybody was very polite, which meant [the news vendor] didn't have to hurry and he was almost too slow.'

The greatest popular ritual of all was the public lying-in-state of the King in Westminster Hall, memorably described by Richard Dimbleby as he sat in his BBC commentary box above Palace Yard in the chilly February air:

> Moving through the darkness of the night is an even darker stream of human beings, coming, almost noiselessly, from under a long, white canopy that crosses the pavement at the great doors of Westminster Hall. They speak very little, these people. But their footsteps sound faintly as they cross the yard and go out through the gates, back into the night from which they came . . . No one knows from where they came or where they go, but they are the people, and to watch them pass is to see the nation pass.

Of that nation, 305,806 queued to pay their respects. The King had made two perfect marriages, said Geoffrey Fisher, the Archbishop of Canterbury, in a radio address on Sunday 10 February—one to the Queen and the other 'to his people'. Mourners laid posies of spring flowers beside the coffin in Westminster Hall, and the nation of shopkeepers which had not yet seen a supermarket rearranged their window displays into hastily improvised shrines of homage. A Mass-Obs survey of Kensington High Street showed that seventy-six of the ninety-seven shops presented some sign of mourning, from a hairdresser's decorated with strips of black paper to a shoe-shop which featured a large portrait of the King surrounded by a giant wreath. 'In memory of King George VI,' read an elaborate scroll, 'the well-beloved.'

Down in Kingston-on-Thames, one shopkeeper's tribute was so incongruous as to be moving. Giving it their best, the staff of a draper's shop dressed their portrait of the late monarch with swags of black bras, slips and bloomers.

Richard Crossman, the radical and antimonarchist MP, was struck by the depth and genuineness of people's emotions. 'You certainly realised,' he wrote in his diary, 'that the newspapers were not sentimentalising when they described the nation's feeling of personal loss.' He confessed that he was moved himself by the dramatic image captured by a newspaper photographer of the three queens, Mary, Elizabeth and Elizabeth II, going to the lying-in-state 'like Moslem women clothed in dead black, swathed and double-swathed with veils'.

The sharing of feelings evoked memories of the Second World War. Television cameras covered the funeral procession on 15 February 1952, but the event was experienced primarily via sound radio— the swan-song, as it turned out, for the wireless-led occasion. Many factories closed for the day, and at 2 p.m. there were two minutes of national silence, which was observed with remarkable universality. Britain had demonstrated it knew how to grieve— though some felt that the radio, still a BBC

242

monopoly, had gone too far in its suspension of normal programming and the playing of sombre music. 'You might as well take the plug out of your wireless,' remarked a forty-year-old plumber when old Queen Mary died a few months later. 'They're at that lark again.'

*   *   *

Less than two weeks after the death of George VI, his stricken mother, Queen Mary, angrily summoned Jock Colville to her presence.

Colville had transferred from royal service back to politics as private secretary to Winston Churchill, who had regained power in October 1951 with a small majority over the Labour Party. Queen Mary had heard a terrible thing, and she wanted the Prime Minister to know of it right away. She had lost her son, and it seemed she was about to lose her dynasty. Down at Broadlands, at a house party attended by distinguished guests, one of whom had brought her the news, Lord Mountbatten had boastfully declared 'that the House of Mountbatten now reigned'.

Churchill was equally horrified. Dickie Mountbatten was anything but the meek, cipher-style royal character with whom politicians feel comfortable, and his links with the previous Labour administration blackened him particularly in Churchill's eyes. The Cabinet shared their Prime Minister's outrage and addressed the matter that same day. There were War Criminals and German Finance Contributions to discuss, but right at the top of the agenda was the heading 'Name of the Royal Family'.

243

'The Cabinet's attention was drawn to reports that some change might be made in the Family name of the Queen's Children and their descendants,' recorded the Cabinet minutes for 18 February 1952. 'The Cabinet was strongly of the opinion that the Family name of Windsor should be retained; and they invited the Prime Minister to take a suitable opportunity of making their views known to Her Majesty.'

Churchill did so immediately. The question had, in fact, already been considered in the run-up to the wedding in 1947. At that time the Labour Lord Chancellor's reading of the law was that any children of the marriage would bear the husband's name, as in any other marriage, and it was presumably on this basis that Mountbatten had uttered his proud boast.

Philip himself had rather a different view of the issue. Determined to succeed, and to be seen to succeed, on his own merits, the young man had always been wary of his uncle's attempts to serve as his 'General Manager', as he once put it. He had rebuked Mountbatten quite sharply more than once on the subject. His own idea, rather gracefully taking the title that his father-in-law had bestowed on him, was that his children might take the name of Edinburgh and that the royal house might be known as the house of Windsor and Edinburgh.

This possible compromise, however, involved conventional and mildly Germanic dynastic thinking. It didn't take into account the fact that Windsor was more than just a family name; it was a popular artefact—as Churchill recognised in the speed and decisiveness with which he acted. Within two days he had secured the new Queen's consent to the status quo, which, from Philip's point of view, represented the overturning of age-old law, custom and basic husbandly rights.

'I'm just a bloody amoeba,' he exploded. 'I'm the only man in the country not allowed to give his name to his children.'

For Elizabeth II it was an agonising conflict at an already painful moment. Just as she was finding her feet in the very first weeks of her reign, her support system shattered around her. Her family elder statesman, Uncle Dickie, was at loggerheads with her venerable Prime Minister, while the argument also pitted her beloved grandmother, backed up by her equally strong-willed mother, against the pride and self-respect of her husband.

'He was deeply wounded,' remembers Michael Parker.

The injured husband sat down and wrote a paper arguing his case which annoyed Churchill so much he instructed the Lord Chancellor, the Lord Privy Seal, the Home Secretary and the Leader of the House of Commons to spend two long meetings with Colville to stamp on it firmly. According to one courtier, Philip had a stand-up argument with the Lord Chancellor when he came to stay at Sandringham. And that was nothing to the battles going on over the home hearth.

'Those few years were a purgatory,' recalls a relative. 'He deeply wanted some recognition that they were his children.'

The Conservative politician R. A. Butler later said that the only time he saw the normally placid Elizabeth II close to tears was when discussing the troubled issue of the family surname, which was to rumble on for eight more difficult years. On her wedding day in 1947, the future Queen had irritated both progressive and some traditional opinion by swearing 'to obey' in her marriage vows. 'Princess Elizabeth had always believed', according to one authorised publication of the time, 'that the principle of the husband being head of the family is the only guarantee of happiness in the home.'

In the long, strained aftermath of the row that got her reign off to such a privately fractious start, Elizabeth II tried to make it up to her wounded husband. She surrendered every power that she could in the private domain, most notably in the education of Prince Charles, who was sent in his father's footsteps to Cheam and Gordonstoun, against the fierce opposition of the Queen Mother. The Queen also put Philip in total charge of the Sandringham and Balmoral estates, which he ran, as the again disapproving Queen Mother put it, like a 'German Junker'. Visitors to family house parties were amazed by the off-handed contempt with which Philip could dismiss his wife's remarks—'How bloody stupid!' was one of his milder put-downs. Marital rows of high decibel level could occasionally be heard from behind closed doors.

Later, Elizabeth II learned to give as good as she got. But in these early years, her tendency was to keep her head down.

'I'm not going to come out of my cabin until he is in a better temper,' one courtier recalls her saying phlegmatically after a row on the royal yacht *Britannia*. 'I'm going to sit here on my bed until he's better.'

In the short term, the issue of the surname was settled with a proclamation of 7 April 1952, stating that 'I and my children shall be styled and known as the House and Family of Windsor and that my descendants who marry and their descendants shall bear the name of Windsor.'

The proclamation had been prepared and taken up to the Queen's study in Buckingham Palace by Tommy Lascelles, whom she had inherited from her father as private secretary. Lascelles was a confirmed pro-Windsor, anti-Mountbatten man, and as Elizabeth II bent her head to sign the document, he later related, he stood over her like 'one of the Barons of Runnymede'.

*   *   *

'I, whose youth was passed in the august, unchallenged and tranquil glories of the Victorian era, may well feel a thrill in invoking once more the prayer and anthem, "God Save the Queen".'

Winston Churchill had lived through six reigns, and one decisive historical consequence of Elizabeth II's early accession was to extend his tenure of power by as much as three years. Immediately before his death, George VI had been discussing with Lascelles how, at seventy-seven, the Grand Old Man could gently be eased into retirement. For both party and national reasons, many in the Cabinet felt that the government needed younger, more agile leadership. But the young Queen lacked both the track record and the stature to make the suggestion that no one else dared—and so, with her accession, Churchill had the perfect reason to stay on. He could play Merlin to the new young monarch.

The Prime Minister was entranced by the

romance of his role, dressing up in his best frock coat and top hat for his weekly audiences, where he paid remarkable attention to his young sovereign's slightest wish. In one audience the Queen let slip that she had not greatly enjoyed *Beau Brummel*, the royal film performance she had attended the previous evening. 'Churchill came out of the audience muttering testily,' remembers Sir Edward Ford. ' "The Queen has had an awful evening," he said. "This must not recur." ' Within two days the Home Secretary had been set on the problem and a royal film performance selection committee had been created.

In 1940 Churchill had articulated the mood of Bulldog Britain. Now he brought his eloquence, sentimentality and deep historical sense to bear on what was, in effect, Britain's long-delayed reward for its wartime endeavours. The coronation of Elizabeth II would be the victory celebration that austerity had spoiled, intensifying the connection between national identity and the popular monarchy. As Churchill put it, the crown had come to be 'far more broadly and securely based on the people's love and the nation's will than in the sedate days . . . when rank and privilege ruled society.'

Taking its lead from the Prime Minister, and encouraged by the youthful promise that the new Queen embodied, most of the country willingly agreed. As schoolchildren were instructed in the arcane details of the forthcoming ceremony, with its ancient accessories of crown, orb and sceptre, they were taught how the constitution had evolved. These exotic baubles had once been the tokens of a single person's absolute authority. Now they

248

symbolised the complex checks and balances by which popular power was exercised. It provided a nationwide civics lesson.

The New Elizabethan Age became the catchphrase for this potent mixture of history and fairy-tale. It linked the well-justified comparison between 1940 and 1588, when Elizabethan England had stood alone against the Spanish Armada, to the more speculative hope that twentieth-century Britain could imitate the enterprise and achievement of Shakespeare's England.

Most people still believed that Britain was in the top rank of world powers. RAF planes had recently flown alongside the USAF in defeating the Russian blockade of West Berlin, and Elizabeth II had acceded to a nation that was actively at war. Her very first investiture in the early spring of 1952 was of a Victoria Cross, won by one of the twelve thousand British soldiers fighting in Korea. Still, Britain had said farewell to its empire on the Indian subcontinent and was facing increasingly strident calls for independence in many of its remaining colonial territories. On the night she had become Queen, Princess Elizabeth had been told that the armed guard at the foot of her tree in Kenya was there to protect her from big game. In fact, he was keeping a look out for the guerrillas of the Mau-Mau, who were already active in the area, and who were to secure independence for Kenya within a dozen years.

In this ambivalence, the country took great comfort from the recently minted concept of the Commonwealth, and this empire-substitute was woven strongly into the imagery of the coronation. Along with the thistle, rose, leek and shamrock, the symbols of the Commonwealth were embroidered into the silk of the Queen's coronation dress—the wattle for Australia, the maple leaf for Canada, and a whole market garden of symbols for countries ranging from South Africa to Trinidad and Tobago.

Within weeks of the accession, the Ministry of Works had set up an elaborate organisation to co-ordinate the celebrations. Coronation liturgies going back to the Middle Ages prescribed the building of platforms so that the monarch might be crowned in sight of all the people. In the age of the mass media this involved converting central London into a ceremonial theme park, with processional arches and long, covered grandstands that gave sections of the Mall and Whitehall the appearance of a racecourse. A huge modern building like an airport terminal was tacked on to the front of Westminister Abbey as a rest and robing area, where the processions could form up. Such physical practicalities, together with the timetabling of the official guests, meant that the ceremony could not take place until the following summer, in June 1953. This created a sixteen-month period of royal-dominated anticipation, which took the emotion generated by the death of George VI and built it up to almost unbearable levels, with newspaper features and supplements on every detail and personality involved.

It might have been expected that some critical local commentator, or perhaps a quizzical journalist arriving from abroad, would have queried this mounting hysteria. But one combs the back issues in vain for doubt, criticism or even mild amusement. In 1953 the whole world took Britain's coronation very seriously indeed. While newspapers did start referring to 'coronation fever', the overheated atmosphere was almost universally accepted as a perfectly natural thing, like the excited preparations for a family wedding.

The only disagreement was over who would take the pictures. Commonwealth pressure had ensured that the ceremony would be filmed in colour by the four British newsreel companies, who among them claimed a worldwide audience of 350 million cinema-goers. Sound radio would reach some eleven million British licensed wireless sets, with a live international listenership of several hundred million. In contrast to this awe-inspiring coverage, Britain's one and a half million pioneer television owners peering at the indistinct black and white images flickering from their 9 inch by 6 inch screens seemed a minority who were scarcely worth catering for. They could see it properly next day at the cinema.

Besides, the Queen herself did not want her big moment televised.

At the time, and until quite recently, strenuous efforts were made to hide the fact that the initial decision that the coronation of 1953 should not be televised came directly and personally from Elizabeth II herself. She was shy, and she was worried that some personal gaffe would be transmitted live to the watching millions without the possibility of censorship or re-editing that film provided. It was a matter of dignity. Her father's much-repeated account of his own coronation in 1937 was a recital of prelates nearly tripping him up and the archbishop getting the crown the wrong way round. Then there were aspects of the ceremony, like her taking of Holy Communion, and the anointing of the bared upper part of her chest, which she understandably felt were private. More generally, she viewed the prospect of television covering sacred events as part of the vulgarisation of the monarchy against which she and her husband had set their face. In the early 1950s the 'telly' was widely seen as impossibly 'common'.

'The prevailing sentiment,' remembers Mike Parker, 'was that television was just the same as the gutter press.'

'Television', sniffed the Archbishop of Canterbury, 'is a mass-produced form of entertainment, which is potentially one of the great dangers of the world.'

The decision not to televise the ceremony was taken early in the summer of 1952, based primarily on 'the importance of avoiding unnecessary strain for Her Majesty', as the records of the Cabinet's discussions put it.

'It was extraordinary,' remembered Martin Charteris, 'all these elderly gentlemen having Arthurian fantasies about this fragile and delicate young woman.'

The very youthful and energetic Duke of Edinburgh, who was chairman of the joint executive in supreme charge of all arrangements, shared the concern for his wife's welfare.

'I am sure you will remember,' he said meaningfully, as he tested the heat that was radiating from the film lighting on an early visit of inspection to the Abbey, 'that everyone here will be under the lights for some hours.'

Brian Barker, a senior official in the Ministry of Works, was standing beside him. 'We understood perfectly what he meant.'

Not until 20 October 1952 was it publicly announced that television would be excluded from the ceremony. TV cameras would cover only the procession up and down the aisle, outside the Abbey's massive choir screen, before and after the service. The outcry was immediate. It was a 'bad and reactionary decision', said the *Daily Express.* The *Daily Mirror* called it 'truly astonishing'. The ban was front-page news in every newspaper, and the editorials condemned it with remarkable unanimity.

The *Daily Express*, in fact, was well aware that the Queen herself was 'the chief opponent of television'. The managing editor, Edward Pickering, had briefed Lord Beaverbrook to that effect in a confidential memo. But the Express pursued the conventional path of blaming those around her. 'If her advisors cannot understand such communion between ruler and people which television can invoke,' the paper editorialised, 'it can only remain for the Queen to intercede and have a foolish deed undone.'

Such instant national protest—both reflected and led by the media—had never happened before, though it was to happen again. Elizabeth II's reign was to be marked by such flashpoints—the Windsor fire, the death of Diana and, most recently, the undignified touting for PR business by Sophie, Countess of Wessex. In every case a press outcry would compel a royal change of direction, and 1953 set the precedent.

MPs immediately laid down questions in Parliament, and when Churchill rose in an unusually crowded chamber to respond, it was clear that the point had already been conceded. There was talk of consultations and the need for fresh lighting tests, but the real issue was working out a compromise that was personally acceptable to the apprehensive Queen. In the end it was agreed that the cameras would look away from the sacred moments of her anointing and her taking of communion, and there would be no close-up shots of the Queen at any time. But television would present on-the-spot, live coverage of virtually everything else. The gaps would be filled, the Cabinet decided, by 'symbolic shots'—an altar cross, the nave—but no images of people.

The overruling of the television ban was loyally presented as having come personally from the Queen, as if she had been offended at the attempt to stop her people joining in her sacred moment and had hastened to put things right. But what Elizabeth II really felt about the telly was made clear by her rejection of the BBC's request that her first Christmas broadcast should be televised. On 25 December 1952, television licence-holders had to be content with hearing the speech as it was broadcast on the radio, with just a flickering still of the Queen and her radio microphone to occupy their screens.

*   *   *

Winston Churchill had been most concerned that the coronation should not be presented 'as if it were a theatrical performance'. But the inclusion of television cameras made it precisely that. Film of the 1937 ceremony was studied carefully. It was noted how George VI's arrival had been shaded by

254

a heavy canopy. It was therefore decided that this canopy should be transparent in 1953—and, taking advantage of the visual opportunity, a camera position was created to take shots through the glass.

The new Queen measured out her paces between the posts and tapes that laid out the Abbey floorplan on the carpets of the ballroom at Buckingham Palace. White bedsheets were fastened together to duplicate her coronation train.

'Don't be silly,' she said to Philip when he took it less than seriously. 'Come back here and do it again properly.'

When the Queen came to the Abbey for live rehearsals it became obvious, to the horror of the cameramen, that the archbishop's robes concealed her face from their lenses as he lowered the crown, totally obscuring the main shot of the day. The archbishop tried again, raising his arms higher and subtly shifting the angle of his gesture so the camera-line was not obscured.

A more obvious alteration was the wearing of mitres by the assembled bishops. Since the Reformation the tradition had been that prelates should officiate bare-headed at coronations. But in 1953 this had to be abandoned. It was decided that hatted bishops looked more respectful on television than bald ecclesiastical pates brought out in a sweat by the heat of the camera lighting. When a lack of dignified horse-drawn carriages was identified for the procession through the streets, it seemed only appropriate that the shortage should be made up by the British movie magnate Alexander Korda, who provided five broughams and two landaus that had been used as props on his film sets.

But through all the artifice, the meaning was kept in sight. The seats in the stands which lined the five-mile processional route, carefully designed so that the timber could be reused afterwards for much-needed housing, were allocated at cost price to worthy organisations selected to ensure that 'the widest possible spectrum of our national life will be represented'. And it was decided that, during the service in the Abbey, everyone should have a chance to join in. For the first time ever, coronation singing was not confined to the choir. The whole congregation rose and sang together a special Vaughan Williams setting of 'All People that on Earth do Dwell'.

The date, 2 June, had been chosen on the basis of Meteorological Office records, showing it to be particularly blessed with sunshine. But the weather broke several days before. The vast crowds camping out overnight along the route were soaked. In describing the decorations along the route, the Minister of Works, David Eccles, had invited journalists to compare them with 'drops of dew on threads of gossamer'. On 2 June they were dripping with rain that continued throughout the day. But, sheltering beneath umbrellas and makeshift shelters, the crowds remained defiantly cheery.

For Elizabeth II herself, the rehearsing was over. This was the day of her life when she could give reality to the moving pledge of service she had made on her twenty-first birthday. Showing no sign of nerves, she was alert and composed, her dark eyes bright, relishing every detail. 'She looked 150 per cent alive,' remembers one of the participants in the service. It was as if this smooth and glamorous 27-year-old's beauty had been magnified to match the heavy sanctity of the occasion. As Elizabeth II came down the aisle after being crowned she looked Byzantine, a holy idol. The camera kept focusing on her. Her face grew bigger and bigger in the frame as she approached. The cameraman held his view on her transfixed, knowing that rules were being broken, but not willing to swing away until he got the order. It never came. The image was compelling. It was the essence of what was happening. It transcended the old rules and created a new rule of its own. Keep close. Get intimate. Television had no boundaries but the power of its picture.

*   *   *

That night the sodden, rejoicing crowds called the Queen and her family out on to the Palace balcony no fewer than six times. As they cheered, three RAF Canberra PR3 jet bombers were flying across the Atlantic at two-hourly intervals, carrying film and telerecordings for the American and Canadian viewing public. Live transatlantic television transmission was still six years away, so during the day US and Canadian viewers had had to make do with looking at a succession of still photographs, transmitted by wire and changing every two minutes. These stills were accompanied by the live radio commentary. The bombers had been equipped with film processing and editing laboratories, and when they landed in Goose Bay, Labrador, Mustang fighters were waiting to continue the relay to the United States. Canadian

CF-100s flew the Canadian packages to Quebec. NBC tried to steal a march on its competitors by hiring its own Canberra to fly direct to Boston; but the plane turned back with engine trouble, and NBC were lucky to hitch a lift on the last plane out of London.

That evening Edward R. Murrow presented a one-and-a-half-hour programme for CBS, and his rivals at the other networks did the same. Every single television set in North America—nearly one hundred million viewers—was tuned to the story from England, making Elizabeth II's coronation the top-rated US and Canadian television production of the year.

CHAPTER FIFTEEN

Mindful of the Church's Teaching

When the mobs rush forward in the Mall, they are taking part in the last circus of a civilisation that has lost faith in itself and sold itself for a splendid triviality . . . My objection to the Royal symbol is that it is dead; it is a gold filling in a mouth full of decay . . . It distresses me that there should be so many empty minds, so many empty lives in Britain to sustain this fatuous industry; that no one should have the wit to laugh it out of existence or the honesty to resist it.

John Osborne, October 1957

The spell was broken with a speed that no one could have guessed—within minutes of the new Queen being crowned. As the royal entourage moved out of Westminster Abbey at the end of the coronation on 2 June 1953, Princess Margaret reached out playfully to brush a piece of fluff from the uniform of the handsome comptroller of her mother's new household, Group Captain Peter Townsend, DSO DFC. The princess ran her white-gloved hand along the medals above his breast pocket with a flirtatiousness that caught the eye of a watching journalist, and with that gesture, the royal story slipped off the high road of pageantry and cheering. The new reign was instantly shadowed by the spectres of divorce and scandal that had marked the abdication—and all the embarrassing, newspaper-stirred turmoil that went with it.

Princess Margaret had first met Peter Townsend in February 1944 when she was thirteen, the very same age at which her elder sister had met and fallen in love with Philip. The two teenage princesses were lying in wait to catch a glimpse of the glamorous new recruit to the household—and Palace lore relates Elizabeth's reaction: 'Bad luck, he's married.'

Townsend was arriving at the Palace as a new sort of equerry, a battle hero to stand beside the King. It had been a happy idea, in time of war, to replace the conventional well-born personal attendant with a young man who had won the place by sheer valour—and who, frankly, deserved the cushiness of living in the monarch's company. An equerry was the male equivalent of a lady-in-waiting.

Townsend was a Battle of Britain fighter ace. He had led crack squadrons of Hurricanes and Spitfires in a sparkling career that included being shot down twice and a brief period of nervous collapse. He had the good looks of a film star, and could deploy his delicate, slightly nervous charm in super-abundance. 'He was like Jean-Louis Barrault,' recalls the future Surveyor of the Queen's Pictures, Sir Oliver Millar, referring to the dashing French actor of the time. 'You expected him at any moment to leap up lightly on to the nearest chandelier.'

Though not out of the very top drawer, Townsend came from an honourable, empire-building background. Haileybury, his public school, had been founded to educate the sons of employees of the East India Company. His grandfather was a general in the Indian Army, his father Deputy High Commissioner of Burma. Brought up among tiger-skins and brass gongs, he had a deeply embedded sense of service, with a tweaking of eastern musing and mysticism. His decision to join the socially undistinguished RAF in the 1930s was a form of rebellion. 'At the time,' he remembered, 'it was not at all the right place for a nice young man to go.'

His royal tour of duty was supposed to be for three months, but he stayed for ten years. King George VI, who shared both a stammer and a love of the RAF with his calm and capable young assistant, found Townsend's sensitivity a balm as he grew sicker. He treated Townsend as the son he never had, and his wife also came to lean on the new equerry.

'Peter had a rather lost quality that was both vague and glamorous,' remembers Oliver Millar. 'It somehow fitted well with the Indian summer character of those last years of George VI. He was not quite connected to reality—and when that was linked with his extreme good looks and genuine friendliness it turned out to make the situation, unintentionally, very dangerous indeed.'

The price of royal favour was the fighter ace's romantically hasty wartime marriage. His attractive wife Rosemary was rapidly disenchanted with being left alone with two small children while her husband played canasta with his grand adoptive family. After Princess Elizabeth got married, Townsend was effectively co-opted as the elder sibling's replacement in the old Windsor family unit of 'Us Four'. 'There was a sense in which the King and Queen rather encouraged the closeness,' remembers Prince Philip's friend Mike Parker.

Townsend was given the job of Deputy Master of the Household, a uniquely demanding post. It not only required supervision of the cooks and cleaners who start work in the Palace at dawn; Townsend was also expected to travel as a full-time Mr Fixit to Sandringham and Balmoral, eating every meal at the royal table, and helping to organise the clan's beloved *al fresco* picnics. A modern holder of the post has calculated that these so-called 'holiday' duties alone kept him away from his wife for ninety days and nights a year.

In the old days courtiers married women who took such separation for granted; royal service was seen as a type of military posting. Some of the most fascinating correspondences in the Royal Archives are those between private secretaries and their wives back at home. But neither Townsend nor his wife rose to the challenge. One courtier remembers a birthday party for one of the Townsend sons, at Adelaide Cottage, the Townsends' grace and favour Windsor residence. The telephone rang to ask if Peter would go riding with Princess Margaret, and, though he was not on duty, he jumped to the call.

Rosemary, for her part, looked for solace outside the marriage. When the couple divorced, she took the legal role of the 'guilty party', not contesting her own adultery with John de Lazlo, son of Philip de Lazlo, the society portrait painter. The divorce came through shortly after the death of George VI, leaving Townsend needy and available precisely at the moment when Princess Margaret was also in personal distress. 'After the King's death, there was an awful sense of being in a black hole,' the normally polished princess frankly confessed to Ben Pimlott forty years later.

Princess Margaret became notorious for her icy snubs, but they were frequently the more painful because they followed some informal episode of fun, or, on occasions, some surprisingly intimate sharing of feelings. Snootier than her sister, Margaret could also be more openly vulnerable, and it was in shared loss and pain that the princess and the war hero came together. Courtiers claimed to have seen evidence of flirtation as far back as 1947, when Townsend and Margaret were on the White Train together in South Africa. But it was not until the beginning of 1953, a few months before the coronation, that matters came to a head, when the couple found themselves alone at Windsor Castle one day, with the rest of the family up in London.

'She listened, without uttering a word,' recalled Townsend, 'as I told her, very quietly, of my feelings. Then she simply said: "That is exactly how I feel, too."'

Margaret told her sister almost immediately, and the new Queen's response was encouraging. She invited the couple for dinner at Buckingham Palace that very night to talk about the future with her and Philip. There was a friendly equality about the two young couples, each sister with her dashing and handsome military partner. Townsend later recalled an atmosphere of informal supportiveness. No one was minimising the problems that lay ahead—indeed, Philip made it his job to bring them up, with the pointed banter that he was making his trademark.

The Queen herself was more opaque. Townsend recalled her 'movingly simple and sympathetic acceptance of the disturbing fact of her sister's love for me'. But as he sat with his feet under the royal table, 'the thought occurred to me that the Queen, behind all her warm goodwill, must have harboured not a little anxiety.'

Reality impinged when Townsend went to tell the news to his de facto boss, Tommy Lascelles. 'You must be either mad or bad,' declared the old courtier, making no attempt to feign helpfulness or sympathy. His immediate advice to the Queen was that Townsend should be removed at once from Clarence House, where the Group Captain had transferred after the King's death. He should be despatched far away on some safely remote overseas posting.

Elizabeth II declined to be so hard-hearted. She

agreed that Townsend would have to leave Clarence House, but, ignoring several backroom offices to which she could have despatched him, she chose the post that brought him most visibly and frequently into contact with her. She made him one of her equerries. It was a sisterly and supportive gesture to Margaret—though, with the coronation just a few months away, it did not seem unreasonable for the Queen to ask the couple to wait for a year. She and Philip, after all, had had to wait much longer.

Margaret's careless gesture on coronation day was a poor repayment for her elder sister's understanding, for it disastrously sabotaged the agreement that the romance should remain secret. It was the ultimate upstaging by the younger sister, who, as Elizabeth once complained to Crawfie, 'always wants what I have'. Elizabeth II got her crown on 2 June 1953. Princess Margaret had her man—and, as she left the scene of her sister's great triumph, she could not resist showing off her own talisman.

A curious interlude ensued. American newspapers reported the 'tender hand' next day, in line with the speculation they had been printing for some months. Following the pattern of the abdication crisis, the British press kept silent. But the self-restraint lasted only eleven days, and when the dam broke, it was with typical Fleet Street self-righteousness, repeating the rumours of Margaret's love for a divorced man while saying that they could not possibly be true.

Down at Chartwell, Winston Churchill's initial reaction was surprisingly favourable. The course of true love 'must always be allowed to run smooth',

264

declaimed the great statesman benevolently when Tommy Lascelles arrived for a council of war. Why shouldn't the beautiful young princess marry her handsome war hero? It took Mrs Churchill to remind her sentimental husband that he had made the same mistake back in 1936, when his support for Edward VIII and Mrs Simpson had proved unpopular and politically damaging. Abdication parallels lay at the very heart of the matter. For what purpose had the Duke of Windsor been made to suffer, if his niece was now allowed to marry a divorced man?

As in 1936, exile was the solution—though this time on a temporary basis. It was decided that Townsend would be despatched as air attaché to the British Embassy in Brussels, and that Margaret would delay a decision until after August 1955, when she would be twenty-five. She would then be outside the scope of the Royal Marriages Act, which required the assent of the Queen—in other words, the Prime Minister.

Public opinion, at least as measured in the newspapers, seemed wholeheartedly in favour of the couple being allowed to marry. On 13 July 1953, the *Daily Mirror* printed a voting form on its front page which prompted over seventy thousand replies. The newspaper claimed this as a world record. Of these respondents, 67,907 voted in favour of the marriage, with only 2,235 against.

The Press Council promptly reprimanded the newspaper for its impertinence.

*   *   *

The immediate consequence of the controversy

was a change in the Regency Act. As it stood, the act laid down that, in the event of the Queen's death, the powers of Prince Charles, as heir, should be exercised until he reached his majority by the next in line of succession who was over the age of twenty-one, which meant Princess Margaret. It was obvious that the Duke of Edinburgh should be his son's regent, and displacing Margaret might help reduce constitutional controversy if she did marry Peter Townsend.

The papers speculated whether this change marked a move by Philip towards the position of prince consort that had been held by Prince Albert. It did not. Philip had read several books about Albert at the time of his engagement, and had decided he did not want the formal involvement in state papers that the prince consortship, a constitutional position, involved. The position was in any event almost certainly not on offer while Lascelles and Churchill were around, and the Duke had already worked out a role that he found more creative and free-ranging.

In the late 1940s George VI had handed Philip two responsibilities to blend in with his continuing career as a naval officer. Plans had been drawn up for a new royal yacht, and the King asked his son-in-law to represent the royal interest in the project. The vessel was intended, alongside its royal duties, to serve as a training centre for crack officers and to double as a hospital ship in time of war.

The other challenge was civilian—to take charge of the National Playing Fields Association. 'The King threw him that as a bone,' remembers Mike Parker. 'It was like a challenge. The King was so proud of his work with his boys' camps. I think the idea was for Philip to bring some help to the suburbs. After the war there were all these housing estates going up, with no room for the kids to play.'

Philip was on a naval staff course at Greenwich, and when it finished he requested his own space in the offices of the National Playing Fields Association in Victoria, going in every day on a regular nine to five basis for several weeks. 'I want to assure you,' he announced at his first committee meeting, 'that I have no intention of being a sitting tenant in this post.' Philip worked with the NPFA to get compulsory amounts of recreational space included in the planning regulations for all new housing developments, and by 1953 new playing fields were opening around the country at the rate of two hundred a year.

With the Queen's accession in 1952, her husband took over the reorganising and modernising of Buckingham Palace. His first thought was that he and the family should stay living down the road in Clarence House, leaving the non-ceremonial areas of the Palace as almost exclusively office accommodation. 'The Palace', remembers Parker, 'seemed to him the coldest and most unfriendly place to raise a young family and the Queen quite agreed. She was delighted with the idea.'

But Churchill was adamant. Buckingham Palace was the centre of the empire, where the Royal Standard flew.

'It came down from the government as a three line whip,' remembers Parker. 'I drove with her for the last time on that short trip from Clarence House and I can assure you there was not a dry eye in that car.'

Philip and Parker had to content themselves

with office reorganisation. They visited every one of the Palace's 620 or so rooms and set about installing modern devices like intercoms—and one of Britain's first ever answering machines. It was a bulky piece of equipment, the size of a small cupboard, and because of its novelty it gained uncertain results.

'Oh, my God, what's that?' was the first recorded response on the tape, from a lofty official in the Foreign Office, stunned by the mechanical invitation to leave a message. 'Oh, absolutely not. I'm sorry, no. Good-bye!'

Lascelles and the older courtiers shrugged their shoulders. But the Queen was impressed—and so was the Queen Mother, who respected the way that her bumptious son-in-law had knuckled down and kept working, despite his disappointment over the family name. Prince Philip was proving nothing if not persistent. 'Bloody workaholic!' says one of his staff. 'The man doesn't know how to take a rest.'

The prince was also proving a major support to his wife, developing the hands-on, 'welfare monarchy' side of the job, which did not come naturally to Elizabeth II. Again, the Queen Mother appreciated the way in which her son-in-law continued the social initiatives of 'the King', as she referred to George VI for the rest of her life, as if in the present tense. Philip's 'Outward Bound' adventure scheme for young men blended Kurt Hahn-style ideas of adventure training with the egalitarian traditions of the Duke of York's camps. And his most enduring and internationally successful initiative, the Duke of Edinburgh's Award Scheme, which combined outdoor endeavour for young people with involvement in idealistic social projects, was even more in the tradition of the royal 'Foreman'.

With his fluid—sometimes too fluid—style of speech, the Duke was also taking on the role of an off-the-cuff royal spokesman. In November 1954 the *Daily Mirror* criticised the royal family for its work rate, sneering that some of its members seemed to have nothing better to do than 'twiddle their thumbs'. The jibe provoked a surprisingly rapid response from Philip during a factory visit next day.

'Of course, ladies and gentlemen, you know what I am doing,' he said. 'I am twiddling my thumbs.'

The *Mirror*, which was discovering that there were readers to be won by cheeking the royal family, correctly pointed out the historic significance of the remark.

'For the first time in the present century,' it crowed, 'a member of the Royal Family publicly replied yesterday to a newspaper comment.'

It was a watershed indeed. For decades the Palace had behaved as if even reading the papers was below royal dignity. Now it was clear that it wasn't. Even the tabloids—perhaps especially the tabloids—were clearly on the royal breakfast table, and as the showdown over Princess Margaret drew closer, they would be read with increasing interest, though seldom pleasure.

*   *   *

'I am unique,' Princess Margaret was given to pronouncing over dinner. 'I am the daughter of a king and the sister of a queen.'

The chronic insecurity behind this conversation-

269

stopper summed up the unhappiness of the Queen's younger sister who never proved able to establish a satisfying identity of her own. A birthright of incredible privilege, which could have been a platform for constructive endeavour, was never to be fulfilled, leaving the princess wreathed with the perpetual grievance of the also-ran.

'There is already a Marie Antoinette aroma about her,' reflected Chips Channon on seeing the princess, aged nineteen, at a ball in Windsor in 1949. By this date the fun-loving and attractive princess was the inspiration of what came to be known as 'the Princess Margaret set'. Brittle, faintly arty, and bohemian in a safe, chinless-wonder sort of way, it was epitomised by images of the dark and elegant Margaret smoking a Balkan Sobranie through a long cigarette holder. Haunting London's smarter dance floors to the small hours of the morning, the princess's coterie revived memories of the fast set that once surrounded the Prince of Wales.

But her parents showed no concern. When Crawfie criticised Margaret's late nights, the Queen brushed her objections aside.

'We are only young once, Crawfie,' she told the governess. 'We want her to have a good time.'

In childhood, Princess Elizabeth had dutifully adhered to the family convention of being nice to Margaret. When it came to the girls' compulsory housework, a cook from 145 Piccadilly recalled how the elder sister would go out of her way to spare Margaret the worst chores by taking them on herself. The elder sibling seems to have bent over backwards to offer some compensation for her own seniority and advantages, establishing the no-argument, placatory pattern that she also adopted with her husband. It might actually have been helpful for Margaret to have had a nasty elder sister who put her in her place from time to time. Spoilt by kindness, the younger sister's fallibility became her essence.

As a later decade was to be captivated by the dysfunctional Diana, so Princess Margaret's vulnerabilities struck a public chord. Her apparent rebellion represented the other side of the 1950s— the self-obsession of Lucky Jim and the Angry Young Men. Margaret might be a princess, but her bid for personal happiness echoed the cult of waywardness that was subverting the uptight, dutiful England embodied in the coronation and in the Queen herself.

As the Margaret–Townsend romance reached its moment of decision, the princess's twenty-fifth birthday on 21 August 1955, when it was expected she would be free to marry as she wished, the attitude of the press reflected the new licence. 'Come on Margaret!' exclaimed the *Daily Mirror*. 'Please make up your mind.' At least it said 'Please'.

Up in Balmoral, more than three hundred journalists and photographers carried out the first ever royal doorstepping, and when Townsend arrived in London in September to attend the Farnborough Air Show he was pursued by posses of newshounds. Journalists besieged the succession of friends' houses to which the Group Captain retreated to communicate by telephone with Margaret, who remained up in Balmoral with the rest of the royal family.

Newspapers stirring up mayhem in the capital

while the royal family kept their heads down at Balmoral set a fateful precedent, and Elizabeth II did not thank her sister for it. Her feelings had moved far beyond the open-hearted and somewhat naïve optimism that had inspired the cheery *diner à quatre* in the spring of 1953. The Queen was tired of the fuss. She had not enjoyed having to put this family complication on the agenda with her new Prime Minister, Sir Anthony Eden, the former Foreign Secretary who had succeeded Churchill in April 1955. She had come to feel that both Margaret and Townsend had imposed on her goodwill and patience.

'She's so instinctively dutiful herself,' says a friend, 'that she can't understand why other people—and particularly her own family—do not just do the right thing.'

By the autumn of 1955 Elizabeth II herself was in no doubt: the obvious and correct course was for Margaret to give up Townsend—but she shrank from imposing that decision on her sister. As the deadline approached for Margaret to go down to London to see the Group Captain at the beginning of October, both sisters avoided the issue. After the final picnic on the princess's very last day, the Queen took her dogs out for a very long walk, arriving back with time to say no more than 'Goodbye'.

Her mother was equally evasive—'ostriching', to employ another expression from the royal repertory of animal catchphrases. The Queen Mother had come to feel quite certain that Margaret should not marry Townsend. It stirred abdication-like convictions in her. She was furious with her younger daughter for provoking such

272

vulgar publicity at the beginning of Lilibet's reign, but she shared the family's very English aversion to thrashing things out face to face. So mealtimes at Clarence House, where the two women were confined together, were marked, Princess Margaret later remembered, by long and frosty silences 'for weeks on end'.

The Queen Mother, however, now fifty-five, did make her feelings clear to her old friend 'Bobbety' Salisbury, the Fifth Marquess of Salisbury, grandson of Queen Victoria's last Prime Minister whose parting gesture had been his stern constitutional lecture to Edward VII in 1901. An annual guest at Balmoral, where he had crossed swords with the young Prince Philip, Bobbety was a pious churchman who heard a fully choral morning service in his family chapel at Hatfield each day before boarding the Green Line bus for his political duties at Westminster.

Salisbury was also a senior and powerful voice in the Eden government, and on 20 October 1955 he made a decisive intervention. If the princess persisted with her plans to marry a divorcee, Salisbury told his Cabinet colleagues, he would resign from the government rather than acquiesce in a subversion of the church's teaching. The price of his staying in the event of Margaret marrying Townsend was a bill of renunciation that would strike the princess and her heirs from the Civil List and the succession.

It would be too much to suggest that Bobbety was doing the Queen Mother's dirty work. He felt very strongly about the decay of old-fashioned standards. A few years later he would again threaten to resign, in protest against Britain's negotiations with Archbishop Makarios, the Cypriot leader, stalking out of the Cabinet when he did not get his way. But as he made his stand in 1955, the Fifth Marquess knew that one very senior figure in the royal family would sigh regretfully and remind both her daughters that it was not possible to cross the will of an elected government.

Eden had tried to stay out of the argument. The Prime Minister was himself a divorced man who had remarried. But Salisbury had forced the issue on a generally uncensorious Cabinet. Though Princess Margaret was by now twenty-five, and beyond the scope of the Royal Marriages Act, she was in receipt of £6,000 a year from the Civil List, which would rise to £15,000 when she married. Even if Eden were willing to accept a Cabinet split, he was faced with having to justify, as a matter of government policy, taxpayers' money going to support the divorced Group Captain and the new Mrs Townsend—along with her prospective stepchildren, Townsend's two sons, whose inconvenient existence was seldom brought into the matter. In political terms, the battle was simply not worth fighting, and Eden regretfully informed the Queen that the price of Margaret's marriage would be a bill of renunciation. If the royal family wished to endorse divorce, it would have to do so at its own expense.

The Queen passed on the bad news to her sister, and within four days Margaret had made her decision. On Monday, 31 October 1955 the news was made public in a statement that Townsend had helped her frame:

I would like it to be known that I have decided

not to marry Group Captain Peter Townsend. I have been aware that subject to my renouncing my rights of succession, it might have been possible for me to contract a civil marriage. But, mindful of the Church's teaching that Christian marriage is indissoluble, and conscious of my duty to the Commonwealth, I have resolved to put these considerations before any others.

'What a wonderful person the Holy Spirit is,' the Archbishop of Canterbury had exclaimed when she told him the news. Margaret had gone to see the archbishop prior to the announcement, and, since Salisbury's Cabinet intervention was not leaked, but remained secret for decades, this religious context was generally seen as the dominating factor in the whole affair. But, in 1955 as in 1936, in terms of law the church had no legal say in the matter. It was a political decision which had compelled the princess to face up to the harsh reality which Kenneth Rose would later describe as 'life in a cottage on a Group Captain's salary'. Margaret had been raised to be nothing but a somewhat ornamental princess, and she came to realise that marriage to Townsend would mean surrendering her lifestyle, her status and, in many ways, her identity.

'Let me tell you, from bitter experience,' said the former Princess Patricia of Connaught, Queen Victoria's grand-daughter, who surrendered her HRH two days before her marriage to the gallant naval officer Captain Alexander Ramsay, and was to spend fifty-five happy but obscure years as Lady Patricia Ramsay: 'It's not a good idea to give up being a princess.'

Margaret's understandable complaint was that the political obstacle placed in her path by the Eden Cabinet had already existed back in 1953 and that she had been persuaded to wait under false pretences. Her twenty-fifth birthday had not altered the underlying reality of the situation. She and Townsend had lived all that time in uncertainty for nothing, and she focused her resentment particularly on Tommy Lascelles, who, she felt, had kept this truth from her. In later years, Lascelles was her neighbour in a grace and favour apartment in Kensington Palace, and she described the moment when she saw his stooped frame trudging across the drive in front of her car. She confessed to an impulse to command her chauffeur to step on the accelerator and crunch him into the gravel.

The impression that the sympathetic British public was left with, however, was one of submission and meekness, and in many ways that was fair. Princess Margaret had laid herself on the altar of duty in the best traditions of her family, underlining an important truth of which she was to lose sight in her later life: some appearance of sacrifice is an essential element of royal homage to the people.

CHAPTER SIXTEEN

Ersatz Religion

The more democratic we get, the more we shall get to like the state and show which have ever pleased the vulgar.

Walter Bagehot, *The English Constitution*, 1867

'Is the New Elizabethan Age going to be a flop?' asked the *Daily Mirror* in a special three-part series in September 1956. 'The circle round the throne is as aristocratic, as insular, and—there is no more suitable word for it—as toffee-nosed as it has ever been.'

With average daily sales of over 4.6 million through the 1950s, the *Mirror* was Britain's pre-eminent daily tabloid. Though proudly left-wing— its masthead read 'Forward with the People'—it well knew the value of royal stories. Its sale of seven million copies on coronation day 1953 was the largest ever sale by a British daily paper. So its willingness to criticise the royal family was significant. 'The Queen, the Duke and the Princess', wrote the young northern novelist Keith Waterhouse, 'are at the centre of a Royal Circle that is out of date and out of touch.'

Critical comment on the royals was still rare. At the height of the Princess Margaret controversy the previous October, Malcolm Muggeridge, the sprightly editor of *Punch*, had been daringly disrespectful. There were a growing number of people, Muggeridge wrote in the left-wing *New Statesman,* 'who feel that another photograph of the Royal Family will be more than they can bear . . . The Queen Mother, Nanny Lightbody, Group Captain Townsend, the whole show is utterly out of hand.'

At the time, Muggeridge's comments—like the *Mirror*'s—stirred little reaction. Notwithstanding the shadow of the Margaret–Townsend affair, Britain's royal sentiments had been buoyed up by the extraordinary success of the six-month tour that the Queen and her husband had made across the Commonwealth in the months following the coronation. Huge crowds had turned out in Australia and New Zealand to greet the attractive young monarch. She had travelled less as a New Elizabethan than as an echo of Victoria, the Great White Queen, greeted at every stop by governors-general and colonial administrators in uniforms and plumed helmets. As Elizabeth II opened local parliaments on a serial basis and landed on successive South Sea islands, she received a crash course in one of the staples of her job—smiling relentlessly in the face of other people's folk dancing.

The huge tour, which ended with the royal couple sailing home up the Thames in the gleaming new royal yacht, *Britannia*, had stirred proud feelings in the dominions and colonies. As the film reports came home of the loyal welcomes at every destination, it was a reassuring reminder to Britain of how much of the atlas could still be coloured pink.

All this would change dramatically at the end of October 1956, with Britain's catastrophically bungled attempt to recapture the Suez Canal. The débâcle knocked Britain sideways. The canal, in which Disraeli had invested to strengthen Britain's links with India and the east, was, like the monarchy, a resonant symbol of Britain's imperial power. But Sir Anthony Eden's conspiracy with Israel and France to recapture the canal zone which Egypt had seized three months earlier proved a disaster. The pound collapsed as America sternly ordered Britain to withdraw, and the international ignominy that followed brought down the shutter beyond argument on Britain's postwar illusion that it belonged at the top.

For the monarchy, the political aftermath of Suez made things worse. When Eden, his health and political credit both exhausted, resigned in January 1957, there were more than four years to run before the need for another general election. The Conservatives had always shunned any mechanism for openly electing their party leader. So Eden's final advice to the Queen was that she should await the verdict of the Marquess of Salisbury ('Bobbety', Princess Margaret's Cabinet nemesis), who had been commissioned as a Tory elder statesman to take 'soundings' of the party. Salisbury did this, interviewing each member of the Cabinet individually in the presence of the Lord Chancellor, Lord Kilmuir, to ensure fair play.

The two leading candidates were Harold Macmillan, the Chancellor of the Exchequer, and Eden's deputy R. A. Butler, known as 'Rab', who was considered rather too clever to be a safe Tory. Salisbury interrogated the Cabinet one by one with a question made famous by his inability to pronounce the letter 'r'.

'Well, which is it?' he enquired. 'Wab or Hawold?'

The Hawolds had it, by an overwhelming majority, and the verdict of the Cabinet was endorsed by the Conservative chief whip, Edward Heath, who was quite clear that the majority of Tory MPs favoured Macmillan. Seeking to rally votes in the aftermath of Suez, Heath had had first-hand experience of the widespread distrust felt in the party for the talented but feline Butler.

The morning newspapers, however, had overwhelmingly backed Butler as the man who could and should lead the Tories and the country. So when the Palace summoned Macmillan, a disagreement between the political correspondents and the Tory high command was widened to embrace the monarch and her role in the process. The last significant royal prerogative, the power to select a Prime Minister, was accused of being complicit in a fix.

It is not easy to see what else Elizabeth II could have done in January 1957, given the Tories' masonic faith in behind-the-scenes 'soundings', as opposed to a transparent leadership election. If she had queried the verdict of Salisbury, which was endorsed by other senior Conservatives, including the now-retired Winston Churchill, she would have been accused of meddling in politics. Macmillan proved a most accomplished Prime Minister, who led the Conservatives to a surprising electoral victory in 1959 and took a progressive stand against apartheid in South Africa with his prophetic 'Winds of Change' speech. But the obscurity of the selection process increased people's linking of the crown with the stuffy, secretive, old-school-tie network that was coming to be identified by the Angry Young Men of the late 1950s as the source of the country's troubles—the establishment.

*   *   *

Lord Altrincham was a thoughtful and passionate enthusiast for the monarchy. His father, Sir Edward Grigg, had won his title through a career of distinguished public service which had included writing speeches for Edward VIII on some of his early travels as Prince of Wales. Politically, Altrincham belonged to the younger generation of Tories, who were campaigning to make the Conservative Party more meritocratic and less class-bound, and he was anxious to do the same for the monarchy. When the law enabling peers to renounce their titles was passed in 1963, he was one of the first to take advantage of it. He made a career until his death early in 2002 as the historian and political commentator John Grigg.

From the accession of Elizabeth II, Altrincham had been worried by the false notes and hypocrisies of the 'New Elizabethan' cult. At the time of the coronation he had written an article for the *National and English Review*, the small-circulation magazine of ideas that he owned and edited, complaining at the unrepresentative make-up of the Abbey's congregation. Every single peer, down to the most obscure, had been given a seat, but that had left fewer than one hundred places for the 625 elected Members of Parliament, who had to draw lots for the right to a seat. The new-style monarchy, with its Commonwealth links, argued Altrincham, should be reflected in an altogether more democratic audience, which should, among other things, contain an ethnic cross-section of the numerous Commonwealth states, several of them non-white, to whose headship Elizabeth II was being crowned.

His appeal was ignored. So four years later, in August 1957, Altrincham returned to the fray with an issue of his magazine that was entirely devoted to the monarchy. Learned contributors included the ever-present Dermot Morrah, royal correspondent of *The Times*, and Humphry Berkeley, the progressive young Tory MP, writing on such subjects as the role of the private secretary and royal finances. The journalist B. A. Young provided a business efficiency analysis of the Queen's public engagements from May to July, the busiest royal season of the year. He concluded that thirty or so public appearances in ninety days was 'hardly a back-breaking programme' for an enterprise whose principal *raison d'être* was the making of public appearances. Young also remarked that only three of these thirty-four engagements could be described as cultural. This lack of artistic interest, he argued, was a regrettable royal blind spot.

It was Altrincham's own criticisms, however, that hit home. He started with traditional deference, by directing his negative comments at Elizabeth II's 'tweedy advisors', but then moved beyond convention to make a scarcely camouflaged criticism of the Queen herself. Her speeches were 'prim little sermons', he wrote. Her speaking style was 'a pain in the neck', and the overall impression was of 'a priggish schoolgirl, captain of the hockey team, a prefect and a recent candidate for 'confirmation'.

Close reading of his article made clear that these comments were technically directed at the words the Queen was given to speak, rather than at Elizabeth II herself, and John Grigg was horrified at the idea he was an antimonarchist. 'That is like saying that an art critic is anti-art,' he said. 'I love the monarchy. Constitutional monarchy is Britain's greatest invention.'

Read in this light, Altrincham's article is tinged with all the sorrow and disappointment of a football supporter who feels let down by the complacency of his club. But Fleet Street had no ear for such subtleties. In the great journalistic tradition of lovingly reporting every detail of what you profess to deplore, the national press splashed Altrincham's criticisms, and had no trouble in digging out ancient aristocrats who denounced the impertinent young peer as a 'bounder' who should be hanged, drawn and quartered, or simply shot.

These sentiments were given physical expression on 6 August 1957, when a Mr B. K. Burbage stepped up to Altrincham as he was leaving Television House and slapped him hard across the face, with the cry, 'Take that, from the League of Empire Loyalists!'

As he fined Mr Burbage twenty shillings for his assault, the Chief Metropolitan Magistrate expressed sympathy with his viewpoint. 'Ninety-five percent of the population of this country', he declared, 'were disgusted and offended by what was written.'

The most significant aspect of the attack was that it took place outside the recently established Independent Television News building. The BBC had suppressed all mention of Altrincham and his views, but Britain's newly established commercial TV network, which had started broadcasting two years earlier, gave him airtime. Altrincham had been interviewed by Robin Day, and he was with Day's colleague Ludovic Kennedy, at the time of the assault.

Until now the BBC, with its broadcasting monopoly, had nursemaided the monarchy, faithfully doing its duty as a pillar of the establishment. Radio and TV were unfailingly loyal. But from now on the Palace would have to contend in broadcasting with the same competitive market forces that were already eroding the deference of the popular press.

Looking back, John Grigg deplored the 'blandness and servility' of 1950s royal coverage, quite alien to Britain's fundamental traditions of free thought and free speech, and he tellingly compared the post-coronation atmosphere to Shintoism. This Japanese worship of the obsessively revered but theoretically impotent emperor has been compared in turn by the Japanese psychiatrist Takeo Doi to the concept of *amae*—adult nostalgia and yearning for the warm, passive feeling of nurturing experienced by the infant at the breast.

Inside the Palace, some people realised there was truth in what Altrincham said. Within two days of the furore, the outspoken peer had been contacted through a mutual friend to arrange a private meeting with Martin Charteris, the Queen's assistant private secretary. Thirty years later, in the course of a political meeting at Eton, Charteris told Altrincham, 'You did a great service to the monarchy and I'm glad to say so publicly.'

*   *   *

One of Lord Altrincham's chief targets had been the debutante presentation system, whereby socially eligible young women came to Buckingham Palace to be initiated into high society. It was an investiture for the upper crust. In Edwardian times the young women flocked into the Palace in ostrich-feather head-dresses and satin dresses with long trains. Large crowds gathered round the entrance to cheer the debs as they passed through the gates for the ritual laying on of hands. Altrincham argued that this custom, which emphasised the 'social lopsidedness' of the crown, should have been quietly shelved at the end of the war. Already the debs themselves seemed to have acknowledged the incongruity of the process by modernising their costumes to afternoon dress. Without the feather head-dresses and satin trains, the snobbish, marriage-market essence of the ritual was difficult to escape.

Elizabeth II and her husband did not enjoy the debutante presentations at all. It was a barren procedure at which they sat immobile while the young ladies filed past them, each dropping a curtsey at the mention of her (frequently double-barrelled) name. The Queen much preferred the investitures where she had a chance to greet people from every class, who had won the entrée to the Palace through their own efforts. Before Altrincham's criticisms, it had already been decided that debutante presentations would be replaced by an increased number of garden parties

285

whose guest lists, investiture-like, ranged over all areas of society.

The Queen, however, did not want to be seen jumping to Lord Altrincham's command. 'We actually delayed cancelling the [debutante] presentation parties for a year,' remembered a courtier of the time.

Elizabeth II's own attitude towards Altrincham, the press and almost every vulgar detail of public relations was magnificently embodied in the palace press secretary, Commander Richard Colville (a cousin of Jock Colville). A soulmate of Lascelles and the other old-school courtiers inherited from the previous reign, Colville made little effort to disguise his contempt for Fleet Street. 'He was', remembered Martin Charteris, 'an anti-press secretary.'

With a mouth that turned down at both corners, the Commander was known inside the Palace as 'Sunshine'. Cecil Beaton, the court photographer who considered himself several cuts above the common reporter, described Colville as 'the wicked uncle in a pantomime . . . who deals so sternly with all of us who are in any way connected with the press'. In Fleet Street itself, parodying one of the running stories of the time, the uncommunicative communications officer was known as 'the abominable no-man'.

In best naval tradition, the Commander would get to his desk early and work through his papers systematically, putting on his bowler hat and going home as soon as his desk was clear. No matter if it was 3 p.m.; public relations were over for the day. One rare evening, Peter Dimmock, head of BBC relations with the Palace, happened upon the

Commander still at his desk, to be greeted with a steely stare.

'A gentleman', said the Commander, looking beadily at Dimmock's formal office outfit that was the norm in the 1950s, 'does not wear a boiled collar after six p.m.'

'Press enquiries', remembers Kenneth Rose, 'were met at best with guarded courtesy, sometimes with impatient disdain, never with good humour.'

But Colville's colleagues do recall a grimly humorous side to this lowering figure. After giving some enquirer a particularly dusty and dismissive answer, the Commander would put down the phone, pause for a moment—then throw back his head in fits of laughter.

No one had any doubt that his attitude exactly reflected the wishes of his employer and her husband.

'The Queen', the Commander told the Press Council, complaining at the serialisation of a book by John Dean, Philip's former valet, was 'entitled to expect that her family will attain the privacy at home which all other families are entitled to enjoy'. But on this occasion the usually subservient press watchdogs would have none of it. The Queen and her husband might be incensed that the valet had 'done a Crawfie', but to any outsider, his revelations were kindly and trivial.

'The private lives of public men and women, especially royal persons, have always been the subject of natural curiosity,' the Press Council replied. 'That is one of the consequences of fame or eminence or sincere national affection. Everything, therefore, that touches the Crown is of public interest and concern.'

In the autumn of 1957 the battle moved to Washington when Elizabeth II paid her first state visit to the United States. Colville insisted that the two-thousand-strong throng of reporters and television men be pushed back far behind their normal vantage points, and they meekly obeyed, with the consequence, according to Time magazine, that they 'ended up interviewing one another over nothing very much'.

This unusual submission may have reflected a recent shift of national mood. Russia had launched its Sputnik, the world's first successful space satellite, and the shocked United States was going through a Suez moment. The Queen was struck by the surprising lack of self-confidence shown by every American that she met, from President Eisenhower downwards.

'It was as if', she said, 'they all needed a friendly shoulder to lean on.' She was surprised and rather shocked by Eisenhower's anxiety to tell her his problems.

The visit was marked by the first coining of a phrase that would come to be much over-used: the royal soap opera. Malcolm Muggeridge had updated for the *Saturday Evening Post* the article he had written two years earlier for Britain's *New Statesman*. Pre-Suez and Altrincham, his remarks had not been noticed, but now the piece re-ignited the controversy.

Muggeridge's target was less the crown than British attitudes towards it. It was only because a materialistic society was losing touch with religion, he argued, that people felt the need to create a substitute, what he called an 'ersatz' religion, in the monarchy. Though these sentiments were in tune with Muggeridge's deeply spiritual, if radical, Christianity, they were greeted in Britain with the same outrage that had met Altrincham. The BBC, on which he appeared regularly, took Muggeridge off the air. But times had changed. By the time the BBC governors had reconsidered and invited him back, it was too late. The iconoclast had been snapped up by ITV.

Commander Colville encountered a different world when the royal tour moved north to Canada. The friendly dominion had been thought ideal for Elizabeth II's first ever television broadcast, but the Commander found himself sharply at odds with the local producer, Michael Hind-Smith. Knowing of the Queen's shyness, Hind-Smith proposed to put her at ease 'by creating a highly informal atmosphere'.

'Gee! You look great!' Hind-Smith exclaimed enthusiastically when the 31-year-old monarch appeared in her television make-up.

Colville was horrified. The Queen was 'the Sovereign', he said, 'and must be so treated'. Hind-Smith would have none of it. He wanted to produce a broadcast, he said, 'in which the Queen will be seen and heard as a woman with ordinary human feelings'. When the Commander ignored him during the rehearsal, and attempted to interfere in the proceedings, Hind-Smith had him ejected. Colville left the studio escorted by the floor manager.

Hind-Smith was no bumptious colonial. A BBC trainee, he had been educated at Winchester. Exactly the same age as the Queen, he now took charge of the situation, treating her as 'a contemporary facing a somewhat trying experience and needing encouragement'.

Elizabeth II responded. She and her husband seemed surprised when the young producer ventured to correct her delivery, pointing out that she presumably had different levels of feelings towards Canadian children and the Canadian currency—two rather different subjects in the speech that she was reading—so perhaps she might try to adopt different tones of voice when talking about them.

The Canadian broadcast was judged a success, and back in England, Peter Dimmock picked up the baton. The Queen had finally agreed that she would allow her 1957 Christmas broadcast to be televised—though she refused the assistance of the recently devised teleprompter. She considered this to be in some way acting. In her eyes it was almost dishonest. BBC staff were informed that Her Majesty was 'very averse from artificiality'. If she was going to read, she did not feel it right to pretend that she wasn't. The literal monarch felt that the proper, straightforward way to deliver her speech was from a sheaf of papers, not hiding anything from the viewer. So Elizabeth II's first ever televised Christmas broadcast was presented as if she were performing her radio message, with monarch, manuscript and microphone all in the picture.

This complicated arrangement to accommodate the Queen's anxieties did not, in fact, result in a relaxed delivery. In the rehearsals, Dimmock worked strenuously to get his performer at least to sign off with a smile. Philip came to his assistance, ducking down below the camera to make funny gestures at the appropriate moment. At each rehearsal their joint efforts were rewarded only with an unconvincing, watery grin, and the same went for the final live performance.

But then, when the camera light blinked off and the ordeal was finally over, Her Majesty broke into the most radiantly natural smile.

CHAPTER SEVENTEEN

New Family

I read the newspapers avidly. It is my one form of continuous fiction.

Aneurin Bevan, 3 April 1960

Lieutenant Philip Mountbatten (retired) had had enormous fun designing the royal yacht, but he felt—along with the captain and crew—that *Britannia* had never been given a proper outing. The vessel had not been completed in time for the great post-coronation tour of the Commonwealth through the winter of 1953–4, for which a liner, the SS *Gothic*, had had to be hired. So an invitation to the Duke of Edinburgh to open Australia's first Olympic Games in Melbourne in November 1956 seemed the ideal peg for an epic, long-distance proving voyage.

The trip was planned to fill in the gaps of the 1953–4 odyssey. In addition to Australia, the royal yacht would visit isolated communities like Tristan da Cunha and Ascension Island, as well as the British scientific stations in Antarctica. For Philip, along with his good mate and aide Mike Parker, who planned the details, it was also something of a jaunt—a chance to escape from the straitjacket of royal duties, organise beard-growing contests and be naval officers again. The painter Edward Seago was recruited to record the trip and also to give Philip watercolour lessons, and the Victorian character of the expedition was enhanced by the presence of James Thomas, Viscount Cilcennin, the former First Lord of the Admiralty.

Thus it was that the Queen's husband, along with the recently retired commander of Britain's naval forces, came to be cruising off Ceylon in late October 1956, when the news came through that British troops were landing in the Suez Canal Zone.

'Haven't you heard there's a war on?' telephoned Arthur Christiansen, editor of the *Daily Express* and a regular companion of both Philip and Parker at their London luncheon group, the Thursday Club. In the event it was decided that the Duke's priority remained the Olympics, so he sailed on serenely to Melbourne.

The long southern voyage of *Britannia* did not become a matter of controversy until February 1957, when Michael Parker's wife, Eileen, sued him for divorce. By the accounts of both parties, the Parker marriage, which Mrs Parker was later to discuss in her memoirs, *Step Aside for Royalty*, was uneasy from an early date, and, like that of Peter Townsend, another wartime romance, it was not helped by the demands of royal duty.

The royal yacht was heading for Gibraltar when news of Mrs Parker's petition hit the papers, and when *Britannia* docked, the press were waiting for

Parker en masse. They followed him to the airport in the new blanket style of royal scandal coverage, and occupied every seat around him on the flight back to London.

At Heathrow, Parker was delighted to see Commander Colville among the additional crowds of waiting pressmen.

'Hello, Parker,' said the press secretary, shaking his hand. 'I've just come to let you know that from now on, you're on your own.'

Elizabeth II was more sympathetic than her press secretary. When the news first hit the papers she phoned *Britannia* to tell Parker that neither she nor her husband wished him to resign. When he got back to London the Australian continued to come in to work at the Palace. But the newspapers were unrelenting. Royal news was hot news. Taking the 'doorstepping' of Peter Townsend a stage further, reporters tailed Parker around London, rummaged through his rubbish bins and even cornered his children on their way home from school. It proved too much for Philip's bluff Aussie fighting companion from 'E-Boat Alley'. Within the month Parker had admitted defeat and handed in his resignation.

Once again, the chance to link the royal family with the socially contentious issue of divorce had generated headlines and profitable stories—and it also gave Fleet Street the excuse to speculate directly about the state of the royal marriage. Four months at sea seemed a long time for a husband and wife to be apart; and if Parker had had matrimonial troubles, what did that suggest about his friend and boss?

This slender connection opened the door for

stories about the men-about-town roistering enjoyed by Philip and Parker with their fellow members of the Thursday Club, an all-male, lunchtime gathering in an upper room at Wheeler's restaurant in Soho. Along with Fleet Street editors like Arthur Christiansen, the company included such racy characters as the actors David Niven and Peter Ustinov, the American jazz harmonica player Larry Adler, the novelist Compton Mackenzie and the Italian Jewish society photographer Baron, who had organised Philip's pre-wedding stag party. The Queen referred to them collectively as 'Philip's funny friends'.

According to participants, the lunches of the Thursday Club were marked by nothing more wicked than the telling of risqué stories and the consumption of large quantities of house white wine and fish in fancy sauces. 'The qualification', remembers Mike Parker, 'was the ability to tell a good story. One week someone brought along Kim Philby [already suspected by some of being a double agent]. He was dull as ditchwater and we never invited him back.'

But early in 1957 rumour had it that Philip was involved with a woman whom he had been meeting regularly at the apartment of his Thursday Club friend Baron. In America the *Baltimore Sun* ran with the story, and it was picked up in Britain— 'Report Queen, Duke In Rift Over Party Girl'.

Elizabeth II was stung to the quick and ordered Richard Colville to issue an immediate denial. Fleet Street was astonished, especially since the denial was credited to her tightly buttoned private secretary, Michael Adeane, Lord Stamfordham's grandson, who had succeeded Lascelles at the end of 1953. The public statement can only have reflected the Queen's personal wish and instruction to set the record straight—another first.

The Times and the *Telegraph*, along with the *Mail* and the *Sketch*, followed the old-time etiquette of ignoring a story that was not technically a story. There was no evidence beyond rumour, and the tale had been denied. But the *Manchester Guardian*, *Express*, *Herald* and *Mirror* followed what would become the modern orthodoxy: no matter that there was no credible evidence; the denial itself made a story.

Elizabeth II's mending of this potentially disastrous situation showed a sensitive but uniquely Windsorian touch. She had been delighted at the chance that the *Britannia* voyage had given her hyperactive husband to be a naval officer again. She trusted him. She felt he deserved the long break after all the work and reorganisation that had followed her accession—and it was also some compensation for his disappointment over the family name, which remained a marital grievance.

'Of course they had their difficulties,' recalls a relative, 'and this was probably the most difficult time. But it was nothing like the press suggested and I think the Queen wanted to teach them a lesson.'

While at sea Philip had sprouted a fine set of ginger whiskers. He had shaved them off before the couple's reunion in Lisbon, where they were due to carry out a state visit. But when Philip sprang up the steps of the plane that had brought the royal party out from London, he was confronted by a Shakespearean tableau—his wife and her entire entourage, all decked out in ginger whiskers. As the couple emerged from the plane, the Queen was seen to be grinning broadly and a tiny smudge of lipstick was detected on the Duke's freshly shaven cheek.

The very courtly silliness of a cabin filled with beards struck precisely the fond but detached note of banter on which the royal relationship operated at its best. Tension was diffused. It showed the seldom-revealed sense of fun which was the Queen's strongest suit, and a few days later came the royal rebuke to an impertinent nation. With her government's approval, Elizabeth II announced that Philip, who had ceased to be a prince of Greece when he was naturalised British, would henceforward carry 'the style and dignity of a prince of the United Kingdom'. This was in recognition of his services to the nation, which pointedly encompassed 'the tour which had just concluded'.

*   *   *

Being a prince again helped salve the dignity of an enduringly sensitive character, and was one of several readjustments in the balance of a marriage that had been thrown out of kilter. For the new prince, there could be no more Thursday Club; and he gave way to a wish that his wife had long nurtured—to have more children.

Philip had long thought that Charles and Anne, a male heir and a feisty female 'spare', of whom he was particularly fond, were more than enough. 'The last thing the world needs,' he once said, 'is more royal mouths to feed.'

His departure with his wife's blessing on another

long *Britannia* voyage early in 1959 made clear that absence at sea was not a problem for either partner in this naval marriage. The prince returned on 30 April 1959, and Elizabeth II was soon pregnant.

It is a long-cherished article of British royal folklore that the third of Elizabeth II's children, Prince Andrew, born on 19 February 1960, is not Prince Philip's biological son. This legend, which adds a touch of spice to the Queen's formidably virtuous reputation, owes its genesis to Nigel Dempster, godfather of the modern gossip column, who first pointed out the physical resemblance between Andrew and the royal racing manager, Elizabeth II's old friend Porchey, Lord Carnarvon.

But considerably less attention has been given to Dempster's evidence that his mischievous suggestion is hugely unlikely to be true. Using the official Court Circular and newspaper reports, he has demonstrated how Prince Philip and his wife were scarcely separated after his arrival home, nine months and nineteen days before Andrew's birth. They spent an unusual amount of time together—as they did, indeed, throughout the pregnancy, which marked a new stage in their marriage.

'What a sentimental hold the monarchy has over the middle classes!' recorded Harold Nicolson when the news was announced on 7 August. 'All the solicitors, actors and publishers at the Garrick were beaming, as if they had acquired some personal gift.'

Caribbean folklore has it that babies conceived with particular enthusiasm and passion—after your husband has returned, for example, from a long sea-voyage—are blessed with 'sweet' blood that is especially playful. Such would seem to be the case with Prince Andrew. The new arrival was named after Prince Philip's father, Prince Andrew, and to mark the baby's arrival Elizabeth II had devised an even more welcome gesture of reconciliation.

Early in 1960, Harold Macmillan arrived at Sandringham for an audience with the Queen and bumped into her Colonel Mustard-like uncle, the portly Duke of Gloucester, who seemed greatly disturbed.

'Thank Heavens you've come, Prime Minister. The Queen's in a terrible state; there's a fellow called Jones in the billiards room who wants to marry her sister, and Prince Philip's in the library wanting to change the family name to Mountbatten.'

Always fond of a good story, the Prime Minister had managed to combine in his *Cluedo*-like anecdote the resolution of the two great family problems that had marred the beginning of the reign. Making clear that it was her own idea, and that her husband did not know what she was planning, the Queen asked the Cabinet to approve a compromise. Kings, queens, princes and princesses do not actually use surnames. These are needed only for those not in the direct line of succession. So while, as Macmillan put it, 'the name of the House, Family and Dynasty [is] to be Windsor—the name of any "de-royalised" grandson, etc., of the Queen and Prince Philip is to be "Mountbatten-Windsor".'

Thus did the cuckoos of nineteenth-century royalty finally win their place in the most comfortable nest of all. The Battenbergs had their origins in a love match, and Philip secured their perch through the same means.

298

'On which lake did you win those medals?' Philip once asked a gong-adorned admiral in Brazil's infrequently battle-tested navy.

'Not in the marriage bed,' retorted the Admiral with a meaningful look at Philip's equally gaudy array.

But in whatever way Mountbatten was used as a surname, the compromise of 1960 enshrined the name of Windsor as the descriptive title of the British ruling house for the foreseeable future. The designer monarchy had been branded indelibly with the label first devised to satisfy popular demand—which could be seen as reflecting another sort of love match.

*   *   *

The engagement of her sister to the photographer Antony Armstrong-Jones in February 1960 offered Elizabeth II a welcome solution to the Margaret problem. Margaret had found happiness, and, like many a photographer, the pint-sized Jones was the model of classless charm. His lack of pedigree, and the fact that he worked for his living, appealed to the Queen's unstuffy side. But unpublished passages from Harold Nicolson's diaries record grumbling by the old guard: 'I lunch with the Eshers . . . There is much criticism of Princess Margaret wanting a royal wedding. They think she should be married quietly at St George's Chapel and honeymoon at Balmoral. They do not like the *Britannia* being commissioned for Mr Armstrong Jones. The upper classes do not like Princess Margaret whom they regard as a vulgar woman . . . Tommy [Lascelles] comes to see me. . . He laments the whole thing, especially the yacht. He says that the boy Jones has led a very diversified and sometimes a wild life and that the danger of scandal and slander is never far off.'

Nicolson sympathised. 'I mind this loss of glamour, the cheapening of the mystery,' he confessed—though he was delighted to record the word from Clarence House that the couple were truly in love.

'At least,' he noted, 'Mr Jones is not a homo, which is rare these days.'

Mr Jones was to prove anything but a homo. Within days Nicolson's son Nigel was reporting that Fleet Street had uncovered a lover in the young photographer's recent past—the Chinese actress Jacqui Chan. The couple had cohabited, which in the late 1950s was still a bohemian and unusual practice, well worth a scandalised headline. There was certainly more evidence of Miss Chan's existence than there had been of Prince Philip's lady friend in Soho. But editors held back. They could not spoil another Margaret romance with scandal. It was time for a happy ending— Cinderella in reverse, with a rakish photographer to capture and heal the heart of the troubled princess.

Questions had been asked in Parliament about the cost of using *Britannia* for the honeymoon— some £60,000 (the equivalent of about £800,000 today)—but though the Queen Mother offered to meet the cost herself, the Macmillan government paid up without demur. 'You've Never Had It So Good' had been the victorious slogan of Super-Mac's recent election campaign, and the fairy-tale princess riding to the Abbey in a glass coach on a bright May morning suited the mood exactly.

'We see the bride now,' pronounced Richard Dimbleby, high priest of the occasion thanks to television. As at the coronation, the great commentator put people's sentiments into words. Dimbleby had recently been diagnosed with cancer, and, conscious that this might be his swan-song, he conveyed particular emotion to his description of the bride, 'as she looks about her at the Abbey in this lovely gown of white silk organza, with the glittering diadem on her head, the orchids in her hand, and the comforting, tall, friendly, alert figure of the Duke of Edinburgh, on whose right arm she can rely'.

If there was one figure in Westminster Abbey on 6 May 1960 whose attitude towards Princess Margaret had, on occasions, been less than comforting and friendly, it was the Duke of Edinburgh. Prince Philip did not approve of the indulgence with which his wife and mother-in-law treated Margaret, and had made his feelings obvious at family gatherings. But that was not the message of the day.

As at all royal occasions, the participants themselves provided no soundtrack. They mimed the pageant, while the rich, sonorous artistry of professional voices conjured up appropriate emotions for the onlookers to share.

'The morning was brilliant,' recorded Noël Coward, approvingly watching Britain click professionally into the motions of street theatre. 'The crowds lining the streets looked like endless, vivid herbaceous borders.'

There was nearly disaster when the well-wishers thronging the streets in the City delayed the

301

progress of the happy couple across London to *Britannia*, which was waiting beside Tower Bridge. It looked as if the yacht might miss the tide, and the delay created an unexpected void in the television schedule. But 'the gold microphone in waiting', as Malcolm Muggeridge dubbed Richard Dimbleby, came to the rescue. Deploying all his research notes, and a lifetime's love of royal lore, Dimbleby ad-libbed for nearly fifty minutes. The history of the royal mews, the details of a postilion's uniform, the complement of the crew on board the royal yacht—every detail was caressingly imparted, transforming a void into a triumphant crescendo.

The nation wanted a party; the nation got a party. It was the first big royal occasion since the coronation, covered by more cameras and watched by even more millions. It was also the first royal wedding ever to be televised. A pattern was set— though now the splendour and pageantry did not adorn a solemn state occasion, with its weighty, constitutional implications. It was harnessed to the enchanting but fallible ideal of romantic love.

CHAPTER EIGHTEEN

Swinging Sixties

Sexual intercourse began
In nineteen sixty-three
(Which was rather late for me)—
Between the end of the *Chatterley* ban
And the Beatles' first LP.

Philip Larkin, 'Annus Mirabilis'

Decades do not always start on time. The sixties took a little time to get swinging—and if 1963 was the year when the earth started to move for Philip Larkin in Hull, it was also the year when public treatment of the royal family was first marked by the new mood. The BBC's late-night satirical TV programme *That Was The Week That Was* depicted the royal barge sinking—with the royal family on board. As the national anthem played, a Dimbleby-like commentator intoned, 'And now the Queen, smiling radiantly, is swimming for her life. Her Majesty is wearing a silk ensemble in canary yellow . . . Perhaps the lip readers among you can make out what Prince Philip, Duke of Edinburgh, is saying to the captain of the barge as she sinks.'

The sketch was mild stuff by later standards, and it was aimed more at the pomposity of BBC royal coverage than at the monarchy itself. But when a West End theatre planned to include the sketch in a larger show, the management decided to drop that particular skit from the review, fearing a ban

303

from the Lord Chamberlain's office, which still had responsibility for the censorship of London's theatres. The leaky royal barge had to travel to Brisbane, Australia, to get an airing, where an actress in a revue called *Roll Yer Socks Up* made a small piece of history by performing the Commonwealth's first theatrical impersonation of the Queen—something still forbidden on the London stage.

As the permissive society took shape, the most sacrilegious suggestions raised a cheer. When Anthony Wedgwood Benn, the young Labour MP who had campaigned against hereditary titles, suggested to Oxford undergraduates in May 1963 that British postage stamps should no longer carry the Queen's head, his proposal prompted the loudest applause of the evening. Benn's other revolutionary suggestions were that Cabinet ministers might dispense with dinner jackets when they visited Buckingham Palace, and that while on official business they should travel around in the new Mini cars.

The defining event of the year was the Profumo scandal, a farrago of sex, spies and deceit that mortally undermined the credibility of Harold Macmillan's Tory government. John Profumo, his war minister, lied to the House of Commons about having sex with a model, Christine Keeler, who had also slept with the Russian naval attaché. Macmillan reformed his government and staggered onwards, but that October a prostate operation brought him low.

As the ailing Prime Minister contemplated resignation, Buckingham Palace anticipated the danger of getting involved in another messy process of Conservative 'soundings'. Elizabeth II and her private secretary Michael Adeane were determined to avoid a repeat of what had happened after Suez. They wanted no involvement in the Conservatives' decision-making, and Adeane made it clear that the Queen expected the Tories themselves to come up with a single, clearly nominated successor whom she could then invite to form a government.

Constitutionally, this detached stance—inviting the majority party in the Commons to nominate its preferred leader—would have earned full marks from Sir Henry Marten. The tricky question was, who spoke for the Tories? At the time of the controversy over Eden's successor, the Labour Party had announced that, were they to be in power in similar circumstances, they would 'proceed to the election of a new leader who would then be ready to accept the invitation of the Crown to become Prime Minister'. In advancing this mechanism, the supposedly anti-establishment socialists were showing more understanding of the constitutional crown than the Conservatives, who liked to claim the mantle of monarchy's protector. In 1963 the Tories continued to rely on their undefined process of 'soundings'—which meant, in practice, consulting 'Super Mac', the ailing but very partial party leader, lying in his hospital bed.

Macmillan was determined to keep his rival, R. A. 'Rab' Butler, from succeeding him. So when the Queen, four months pregnant with her fourth child, visited him in hospital, the retiring Prime Minister handed her the name of Alec Douglas Home, Fourteenth Earl of Home, who had been Macmillan's Foreign Secretary. Seeking to avoid the mistakes of 1957, Elizabeth II did not give Home the job at once. She invited him instead to see if he could form a government commanding a Commons majority and then report back to her. She was, in effect, pushing the Conservatives to go through a further process of consultations.

'What else should she have done?' asked Martin Charteris, her assistant private secretary at the time. 'After all, she *didn't* just allow Alec to kiss hands. She said, "Now, I want you to go away and come back within twenty-four hours and tell me whether or not you can form an administration." Which is what he did. And the answer is, he *did* form an administration. Now, if Rab had said to Alec, "I won't serve under you," *he'd* have been Prime Minister. Simple as that, I think.'

Many people did not think it was that simple. Two prominent Conservatives, Enoch Powell and Iain Macleod, refused to serve under Home. They were incensed at the 'magic circle' that had fixed things again for the grouse-shooting Tory oligarchy. And this became the general verdict, provoking even more fall-out for the Queen than in 1957. As Tony Benn put it, becoming a Tory prime minister was not so much a matter of first past the post as first past the Palace. Despite her best efforts to avoid a problem she had foreseen, Elizabeth II and the monarchy had been dragged into a political 'fix', and stood once again accused of fuddy-duddiness and reaction.

*　　　*　　　*

Alec Douglas Home, last of Britain's aristocrat prime ministers, lasted just a year. In October 1964 the Conservatives were voted out of office, to be replaced by a Labour government headed by a grammar-school boy with a defiantly non-BBC accent. When Harold Wilson arrived at Buckingham Palace on 16 October 1964 to kiss hands with the Queen, he eschewed tradition and brought along his father, his wife, his two sons, his sister and his personal secretary, Marcia Williams. This veritable supporters' club, which occupied two cars, showed his absolute confidence that the institution existed to serve his purpose. Set on shaking up Britain with fresh modern attitudes—what he liked to call the 'white heat of technology'—Wilson used the crown to play the role classically described by Walter Bagehot: the disguising of change.

Some of Wilson's radical ministers, however, found it harder to achieve change than they imagined. Richard Crossman confided to his diary that the Privy Council was 'the best example of pure mumbo jumbo you can find', and when appointed Lord President of the Council, declared that he would not attend the State Opening of Parliament. Michael Adeane responded that he could, of course, ask Her Majesty to excuse him. But the private secretary did remark that 'the Queen has as strong a dislike of public ceremonies as you do. I don't disguise from you the fact that it will certainly occur to her to ask herself why you should be excused when she has to go—since you are both officials.' The notion of the Queen as fellow servant of the people caused Crossman to think again. He duly attended the State Opening.

His colleague Tony Benn found his republicanism similarly blunted when he was appointed Postmaster General. The introduction of large-sized graphic postage stamps after the style of banana republics opened up a new philatelic revenue stream for the government, and also offered the antimonarchist Postmaster General the chance to achieve his ambition of removing the royal head from the nation's envelopes. Taking his first set of headless designs to Her Majesty, Benn was expecting resistance and was surprised to be met by apparent interest. The Queen leant over her minister as he knelt on the carpet where he spread out the designs to explain them. 'Did she get down on the floor with you?' commented Wilson with admiration when Benn recounted the story later.

The Queen did not, in fact, kneel beside Benn, but after a forty-minute audience, the Postmaster General felt assured of victory.

'I went back to the House of Commons', he confided to his diary, 'feeling absolutely on top of the world.'

But he had underestimated his adversary. Elizabeth II's ultimate professional skill is the concealing of her personal feelings—it is the essence of her job—and, as the negotiations continued through private secretaries, Benn was forced to admit defeat. The republican Postmaster General did eventually manage to shrink the royal profile to a token silhouette in the corner of commemorative issues, but that was the limit.

'The plain fact is, that I shan't get the Queen's head off the stamps,' he wrote in December 1965. 'And it is probably rather foolish of me to go on knocking my head against a brick wall.'

Benn could have forced the issue if his Prime

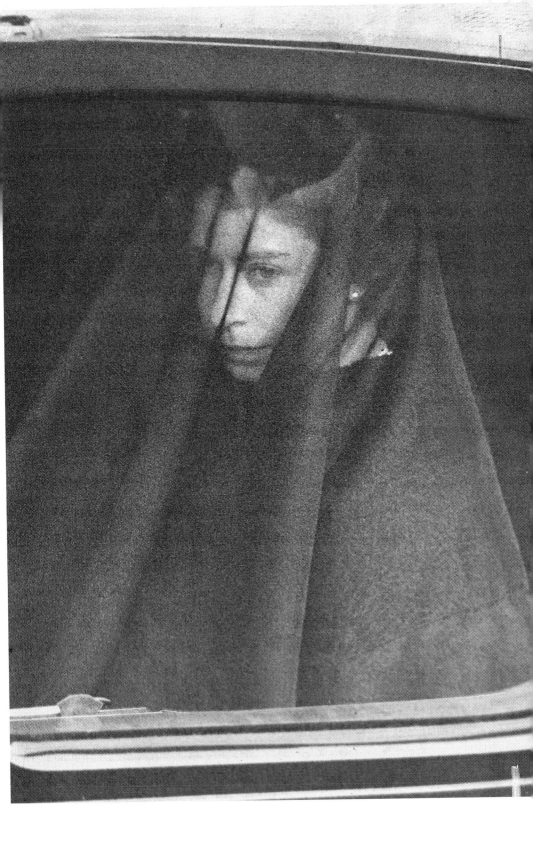

Minister and the Cabinet had been willing to back him. But Harold Wilson did not wish his administration to be remembered as the government that removed the Queen's head from British stamps.

'It is clear that Harold's intentions are that we should be more royal than the Tory party,' confided Benn bitterly to his diary. 'And he finds the Queen a very useful tool.'

*   *   *

On 21 October 1966 a mountainous coal tip collapsed on top of the south Wales mining village of Aberfan. The falling debris engulfed the village's primary school, killing 116 children and 28 adults. The Prime Minister paid an immediate visit of sympathy, as did Lord Snowdon, the recently ennobled Antony Armstrong-Jones, who drove to south Wales at once and was overwhelmed with emotion.

'Instead of inspecting the site,' wrote Harold Wilson in his diary, '[he] had made it his job to visit bereaved relatives . . . sitting holding the hands of a distraught father, sitting with the head of a mother on his shoulder for half an hour in silence.' It was the type of gesture that the world was later to associate with Diana, Princess of Wales; and, as with Diana, courtiers had different opinions of this casting aside of the normal barriers of royal stiffness. Some still sniff at the way Princess Margaret's husband 'went scampering off' to south Wales on his own account. Prince Philip went down in more measured and formal mode the very next day. But the Queen herself refused to go. 'We kept presenting the arguments,' recalls an adviser at the time, 'but nothing we said could persuade her.'

It could not be said that Elizabeth II or her family had failed to demonstrate concern. The Palace issued a statement of sorrow immediately and, following Snowdon's return, Princess Margaret had launched an appeal so that children round the country could show their sympathy by sending some of their toys to Aberfan's young survivors. The Queen arranged to have a toy each from Andrew and Edward packed up and sent anonymously by parcel post. But she held back from going herself.

'People will be looking after me,' she objected. 'So perhaps they'll miss some poor child that might have been found under the wreckage.'

Her imagining of a lost child showed the reality of her concern, and she could not imagine why her presence mattered.

'She has no vanity,' said one of the advisers involved in the daily meetings which tried to get her to budge. 'She can't understand why people *should* want to see her. And she is not an actress like her mother.'

Elizabeth II was, in fact, adopting an approach exactly opposite to that of her parents. During the Second World War King George VI and his wife had taken pride in arriving at a trouble spot the very morning after the bombs had fallen. But their daughter did not have their easy confidence that she could deal with the pain of people's grief. Perhaps it scared her. In her very English way, she had always found emotional display embarrassing—'common', even—and it seems possible that, as a teenager, she had developed some sort of block against the way her mother played the crowd with her too-easy displays of sympathy. Much more solemn and reflective than the ever-smiling Queen Mum, Elizabeth II actually felt unqualified for the heavy responsibility of ministering to people's sorrow.

'She simply has no sense or instinct', says one of her longest-serving advisers, 'for the balm that her presence brings.'

Extending personal comfort and softness was not something that the Queen did very well in her personal life, and she found it still harder in public. It was the old problem of acting and 'stunts'. The protocol of what to do at collapsed coal tips had not been laid down by Henry Marten, whose textbooks contained no instruction on the symbolic dimension of a monarch's life. And if her royal work usually involved the suppression of personal emotion, how could she be expected suddenly to put it on display?

All these dilemmas provoked a curious knotting in the impulses demanded by a crucial aspect of Elizabeth II's job. As her reign progressed through and beyond the 1960s into an ever more relaxed and touchy-feely era, the slowness of the Queen's visible response to disasters was to become a matter for criticism.

In 1966, the criticism was attached to Princess Margaret's appeal for toys, which flooded into the little village in unmanageable quantities, filling the cinema to overflowing and diverting energies from the rescue efforts—exactly the problem that had worried her more cautious and reflective sister.

In the event, the Queen finally agreed to go to south Wales eight days after the coal tip had collapsed. Rescue efforts had been abandoned by then, and the grief etched on her gaunt features was the more moving for being so clearly genuine. With its curious wartime misting, Aberfan was one of the last black and white moments in the photographs of Elizabeth II's reign.

But if the episode revealed a weakness in the Queen's aversion to gestures that she, almost alone, considered theatrical, it also revealed the considered steadiness that made up the other side of her character. Unlike many of those who reached Aberfan ahead of her in 1966, Queen Elizabeth II has been back twice to revisit the village. She returned in March 1973 to open a new community centre, and again in May 1997 when she planted a tree in the Garden of Remembrance and talked with some of the survivors for the third time in thirty years.

*   *   *

In May 1967 the 65-year-old Francis Chichester became swinging Britain's most unlikely hero. The gangly old-age pensioner arrived home in his small yacht having sailed round the world single-handed, and Harold Wilson decided that the feat deserved a knighthood.

Elizabeth II did the job as usual. But instead of performing the ceremony at Buckingham Palace in a routine fashion, she went down to Greenwich to dub the ancient mariner publicly. As Chichester knelt before her, Elizabeth II touched his shoulder with the very same sword that the first Elizabeth had used to knight another nautical Francis—Sir Francis Drake, who had circumnavigated the globe

318

in the *Golden Hind* in 1580.

The imaginative gesture, which was dismissed by some as a gimmick, was the work of a new hand on the wheel of royal public relations. Lord Altrincham's criticism of the 'tweedy' inner circle around the Queen had got results. In the late 1950s Michael Adeane had started inviting Commonwealth governments to nominate promising civil servants for tours of duty in the Palace press office, and in 1960 Australia's choice had been a 30-year-old Western Australian, William Heseltine.

'I've never had anything to do with the press,' was Heseltine's first reaction on being offered the job.

'They'll probably consider that rather an advantage,' was the dry response of his Canberra recruiting officer.

Heseltine performed well during his time in London, and in 1964 he was invited back to join the press office on a more permanent basis. He had impressed the Palace old guard with his ability to join in smoothly while retaining the perspective of a creative outsider. But it was the measure of the man that he declined the job offer until Michael Adeane intimated that, if his assignment went well, he could move on to 'higher things'. From 1955–9 Heseltine had served as private secretary to Sir Robert Menzies, the romantic, Winston Churchill-like Prime Minister of Australia, and thirty years later Sir William duly became the first ever Palace press officer—and also the first non-Brit—to earn the knighthood that goes with the position of royal private secretary.

'Bill had such an easy manner with the Queen,'

remembers one of the party on the royal trip to South America in 1968. 'He would come up from the back of the plane and plonk himself down to go through the newspapers with her. But he was never disrespectful.'

It was characteristic of Heseltine that, from the moment of his arrival, he made it his business to get on well with Commander Colville, whom he had been hired to replace. For the two years until Colville's retirement in 1967, the Australian worked amiably alongside the abominable no-man, retaining his friendship and even recruiting him to his royal PR revolution. It was actually Colville who, just prior to his departure, suggested the use of Drake's sword for Francis Chichester's camera-friendly dubbing.

'There is a distinct wind of change at the Palace,' recorded a perceptibly astonished BBC memorandum the following year. After more than a dozen years of hard pushing—the latest battle had been persuading the ever-cautious monarch to switch her Christmas broadcast from black and white to colour—the Corporation suddenly found the door swinging open. Indeed, it was the Palace which came to the BBC with the proposal that was to catapult royal press relations into a new era: the landmark documentary film that was eventually titled *Royal Family*.

The one-and-a-half-hour film originated in the mounting volume of TV and radio programme proposals to mark the coming of age of Prince Charles in 1969. Charles was already receiving coaching in television and interview techniques, but he was also studying full-time at Cambridge. It occurred to Heseltine it would make more sense to depict the life and work that lay ahead of the prince—the day-to-day existence of a family-based constitutional sovereign. He proposed it to the Queen, and it turned out to fit precisely with a remarkably similar idea that Lord Mountbatten had already been discussing with his son-in-law Lord Brabourne.

Brabourne, married to Mountbatten's elder daughter Patricia, had produced the acclaimed TV series *The Life and Times of Lord Mountbatten*. It had rivalled the success of *The Forsyte Saga* as a weekly attraction that kept middle-class Britain at home for the night. The royal family gathered to watch each instalment with avid interest, and the Queen thoroughly enjoyed it. She called it 'Dickie time'. So, when Brabourne came to her with the idea for making a television documentary about her own life and work, she did not reject it out of hand.

'Will we have some say?' she asked.

When the film was broadcast, much was made of its supposed 'editorial independence'. In fact, *Royal Family* was a tightly Palace-controlled exercise. A committee headed by Prince Philip would come up with ideas. The Queen would say what could and could not be filmed, and Heseltine functioned as the on-line producer, helping to develop sequences with the director, the BBC's top documentary-maker, Richard Cawston, whom Brabourne and Prince Philip had recruited together.

Heseltine managed to persuade Cawston not to include any field sports sequences. The long hours spent by the royal family blasting little birds out of the sky did not match the desired image of middle-class normality. Prince Philip, for his part, wanted to cut the sequence which showed the four-year-old Prince Edward bursting into tears when the string on a cello being played by Prince Charles broke suddenly and hurt him.

'Prince Philip thought it was unkind to little Ed,' recalls one of the team. 'But in the end he was persuaded that the tears added to the authenticity.'

The BBC normally worked to a ratio of shooting ten hours of film for every hour that appeared on the screen. For *Royal Family* the ratio was trebled. More than forty-three hours of film was shot and stored in high-security vaults in cans labelled 'Religious Programming'.

The Queen took some time to grow accustomed to the novel process of having her ordinary conversation recorded. While talking to a group of Commonwealth Prime Ministers, she was startled when a three-foot-long 'gun mike' popped up in front of her on its long boom. Her personal protection officer was even more alarmed, leaping forward and felling it with a karate chop.

But it was the talking that provided the fresh element. The film was an animated version of the 'off-duty' royal photographs that four decades of picture magazines had made familiar. The real novelty lay in the apparent eavesdropping on private royal conversations, and when the film was first shown in June 1969, the most remarked-upon element was the unexpected naturalness and humour displayed by a figure who had previously been seen as stiff and remote. It was exactly the result that Heseltine had been hoping for—the showcasing of the private spontaneity and naturalness of his boss, which she, more than anyone, had spent the first part of her reign concealing.

*   *   *

Royal Family proved a televisual landmark to match the coronation. Viewed in more than 125 different countries, it was seen by more people than any other documentary ever made, and by 1975 had been transmitted no fewer than eleven times in Britain and twice, coast-to-coast, at peak time in the United States. But thereafter the film was seldom seen. The Queen retained control of its screenings and firmly turned down most requests to show it again, either whole or extracted in the royal TV programmes that attempted to follow in its footsteps. It was soon realised, as perceptive critics like Milton Shulman pointed out at the time, that showing the royals to be mere mortals was a double-edged sword. Never again did Elizabeth II let the camera so near her private life. She did agree to a fly-on-the-wall documentary that concentrated on her work for the fortieth anniversary of her accession in 1992, but ten years later, for her Golden Jubilee, she was quite adamant that she was not available.

Royal Family, an enjoyable home movie of a brightly coloured and more innocent time, enshrined a moment. Its enormous royalty earnings, which the *Sunday Telegraph* loyally praised as 'a direct benefit to our balance of payments struggle', were given to a fledgling professional association, BAFTA—the British Association of Film and Television Arts. BAFTA used the money to acquire the grandiose premises on Piccadilly from which they were to organise the

British equivalent of the Oscars.

A month later saw another experiment with television's alchemy: the July 1969 investiture, or mini-coronation, of Prince Charles as Prince of Wales. Marking the prince's coming of age, it was a late twentieth-century embellishment of a very ancient 'invented tradition', dating back to a medieval exercise in regional tokenism. King Edward I first gave his son Edward the title in 1301 in a ceremony in Lincoln in England, hoping to keep the Welsh quiet while he went off to fight the Scots. Though there had been many Princes of Wales since, none had ever been actually invested in Wales until the twentieth century, when David Lloyd George, the Liberal leader, grew worried at the inroads that the new Labour Party was making into his Welsh power base. In 1911 Lloyd George devised the pseudo-medieval pageant that Edward VIII was to remember with horror all his life. The clothes-conscious young man was mortified at being compelled to wear what he called a 'preposterous rig' for his crowning in Caernarfon Castle.

The Queen entrusted her photographer brother-in-law with the task of ensuring that Charles would not be similarly embarrassed. Tony Armstrong-Jones had a Welsh father and godfather, and he had chosen to play up his Celtic connections with his title as Earl of Snowdon. He had already designed a visionary aviary for London Zoo, a soaring, dramatic and thoroughly modern structure, and he applied the same combination of design and technology to the ceremony at Caernarfon.

In 1911 Lloyd George had set the ceremony

inside his idea of a crusader tent. In 1969 Snowdon designed a sweeping canopy made of clear perspex, embossed with the Prince of Wales's feathers, so the television cameras could move in with the best possible flexibility and light. The entire ceremony was shaped and reshaped for the benefit of the cameras. Snowdon recruited the stage designer Carl Toms, who had worked as an assistant for Snowdon's designer uncle, Oliver Messel, and had designed sets and costumes for Covent Garden and the Royal Shakespeare Company.

In 1911 this new, royal ceremony had been the preserve of the heralds at the College of Arms. In 1969 the chief of the heralds, the Garter King of Arms Sir Anthony Wagner, was greatly upset by the assembled forces of trendiness invading his sphere, and Snowdon's waspish sense of humour did not help.

'Garter, dear, do be more elastic,' he purred after a particularly tense confrontation, over whether Welsh dragons have knots in their tails.

But Garter got his revenge. When it came to Charles's crowning, Snowdon had envisaged a simple circlet of gold after the style of that worn by Sir Laurence Olivier in the film *Henry V.* But Wagner sabotaged this cinematic inspiration by getting a bulbous piece of headgear made up on his own initiative. The result, the Queen later told Noël Coward, extinguished Charles like 'a candle snuffer'.

Over the faintly ridiculous atmosphere of the occasion hovered the real prospect of danger. Welsh nationalists had threatened to disrupt the ceremony. A terrorist had been killed a few days earlier by the bomb that he was transporting. In the

325

Lloyd George tradition, the Labour government had encouraged the ceremony to help subdue the Welsh separatist sentiments that were nibbling at their vote. Charles had broken off his studies at Cambridge to spend a term at Aberystwyth University, where he had learnt sufficient Welsh to deliver a creditable speech. Real issues and drama brought seriousness to an occasion that had risked bathos, and the resulting outside broadcast, which consumed most of a balmy July day, proved another popular triumph.

'It was no coronation, of course . . . no lump in the throat', wrote Maurice Wiggin, TV critic of the *Sunday Times*. '. . . But it was an agreeable spectacular, stage-managed very effectively, entirely for television. I loved it.'

*   *   *

Together, the investiture and *Royal Family* provoked what the *Yorkshire Post* described as 'a remarkable revival of interest in the British Royal Family'. Some metropolitan columnists sniffed at 'the current wave of royalty mania', but it ended the decade for the crown with a surprising flourish. The monarchy might not swing as much as the sixties, but it was generally viewed as having a refreshing and modern bounce to its step. The Carnaby Street trendiness of the times contained a fond element of royal-tinged nostalgia, from Union Jack blazers to the Beatles' *Sergeant Pepper* album, whose sleeve design was a Victorian Jubilee pastiche. Snowdon's perspex-covered ancient ceremony, allied to the family's fly-on-the-wall TV appearance, pulled off the same trick.

This public vitality matched the élan of developments inside the Palace. The talents of Heseltine, now press secretary, were matched by the sprightly wit of Martin Charteris, number two in the private secretary's office, and by Patrick Plunket, Elizabeth II's Deputy Master of the Household throughout the decade. Only a year or so older than the Queen, from an Anglo-Irish family, Lord Plunket was a good-looking former Guards officer—'one of those bachelors of easy manners and taste', as Kenneth Rose has put it, 'who are always in demand at court'.

Opinions varied on Plunket's sexuality. 'He was one of those lucky characters', says one of his friends and fellow Guards officers, 'who was just neutral.'

He devoted his talents to the service of his Queen. Never were flowers better arranged, menus so expertly chosen. Appreciating the good things of life, but not creative herself, Elizabeth II gave Plunket free rein. Before Christmas and birthdays, or when presents for state visits were required, Plunket haunted Burlington Arcade and the smarter shopping streets, bringing back a selection of classy and original gifts from which the Queen could make her choice. He knew every upmarket jeweller in London.

'He was like a step-brother to her,' remembers a friend.

He arranged adventures—trips to cinemas and discreet lunches in ordinary restaurants with groups of friends. He also danced with the Queen at parties where Philip was kicking up his heels with one of his lady friends. Plunket would dance Elizabeth II round and 'drop her off' with a new partner, who might not have dared to come up himself to ask for a dance.

When Uncle Dickie and the Queen Mother both hit seventy in the same year, Plunket invented a new sort of generational royal party. Both as old as the century, born in 1900 (June and August respectively), but not especially fond of each other, they were teamed by Plunket with Uncle Harry, the Duke of Gloucester, and the Duke of Beaufort, Master of the Horse, who was the Queen's host at the Badminton Horse Trials every spring. The resulting party for the four septuagenarians was a vast, smart, jolly evening of the sort that only a palace-dwelling family could give. The Queen was the host and the common link, giving her the central role that was certainly hers, but which she was too modest to have claimed for herself.

With two children under the age of ten cycling and chasing each other down the corridors, Buckingham Palace took on a cheerful family feel in the late 1960s. 'Goodness,' said the Queen to a friend, 'what fun it is to have a baby in the house again!' Elizabeth II spent much more time with her new children, Andrew and Edward, than she ever had with Charles and Anne. More at ease as a queen and in every area of her life, she enjoyed being a mother again. When the two boys were little, she had happily got up in the night and settled them back to sleep again. Her favourite night of the week was 'Mabel's night off', when Mabel Anderson, their nanny, took a break, and she could put the boys to bed herself.

She also had a soft spot for her sister Margaret's two children, David and Sarah, who played with Andrew and Edward at weekends. The relaxed and

328

casual atmosphere of the *Royal Family* film accurately reflected a happy home life at the Palace, possibly the happiest period of the Queen's married life. Her family provided a private reinforcement to her public duties, the very opposite of the private and public headache they would later become. Professor Jack Plumb, the distinguished historian, remembers a visit in these years when the Queen's greatest concern seemed to be whether Princess Anne would get a crucial A-level.

For the final two years of the decade, the domestic mix in the family home at the end of the Mall was enhanced by the exotic presence of Princess Alice of Greece, deaf and imperious, floating round the corridors in her grey nun's habit. Prince Philip's mother had survived her ordeals with Sigmund Freud and Swiss sanatoria in the 1930s to found a short-lived order of Greek nursing sisters, whose habit she wore until the end of her days. Her less reverent relatives found her costume pretentious.

'What can you say of a nun', asked one, 'who smokes and plays canasta?'

If Palace servants could tell that the Queen was in the offing from the scuffling of corgis, in the case of her mother-in-law the warning came from clouds of tobacco smoke, accompanied by fits of bronchitic coughing.

The troubles in Greece which finally disposed of the Greek monarchy in the late 1960s had led Elizabeth II to invite her children's other granny to come and live at Buckingham Palace, and Princess Alice added an illuminating dimension to the family dynamic. Prince Philip's staff got valuable clues to the enigmatic character of their boss through witnessing the apparently rough style in which Philip and his mother interacted. It seemed to explain the prince's discouraging way of offering affection. His mother continued to refer to her favoured only son, now in his late forties, by his nursery name of 'Bubbikins', but disagreements were quite common. Princess Anne noted how her father would go stalking off muttering after some difference of opinion, leaving her grandmother 'in her room, muttering too'.

Alice maintained a similarly astringent relationship with her brother, Dickie Mountbatten. 'He only comes to see me', she complained, 'to write letters on Buckingham Palace writing paper.'

To start with, her deep voice frightened her grandchildren, but her two younger grandsons, Andrew and Edward, came to enjoy going to her room at the front of the Palace for games of halma. She got on particularly well with her daughter-in-law, with whom she had lively conversations despite her deafness. One courtier recalls the Queen and her mother-in-law having an animated discussion throughout one of the Palace cinema sessions. 'They sat in the front in their armchairs chatting away to each other, but how the Princess managed to lip-read the Queen in the darkness I really don't know.'

Elizabeth II enjoyed the chance of getting to know her unusual husband's highly unusual mother, and she supported her religious charities generously.

'Really,' the Queen once remarked with happy resignation, 'what with my mother and her racehorses and my mother-in-law with her nunneries.'

Neither of the exotic grannies had featured in the *Royal Family* film. Along with the field sports, they hardly fitted, even in the wild and swinging sixties, with the image of everyday British life.

*   *   *

The death of Princess Alice in December 1969 led to a final revelation that shed light on the characters of both herself and her son. The fulfilment of Alice's wish to be buried in the White Russian Orthodox Church in Jerusalem took delicate diplomatic and religious negotiations that lasted nearly twenty years, and uncovered a hidden war record. Unknown to her family, the princess had given shelter, while living in Nazi-occupied Athens, to the widow and children of Haimaki Cohen, an Athenian Jew, rebuffing the enquiries of suspicious Gestapo agents by playing up her deafness, and by appearing to be less than bright. She saved the Cohens from transportation, and when they heard of the princess's burial in 1988 in Jerusalem, they started the procedure to secure her the honour of 'Righteous among the Nations', the highest Israeli award for a non-Jewish foreigner— the same distinction bestowed upon Oskar Schindler.

On 31 October 1994, Prince Philip went to the Holocaust Memorial in Jerusalem to receive the award on behalf of his mother, laying a wreath, planting a tree at Yad Vashem, and making an acceptance speech which paid Princess Alice graceful homage, but which also said something about his own personal style.

'As far as we know,' he said, 'she had never mentioned to anyone that she had given refuge to the Cohen family at a time when Jews throughout Greece were in danger of being arrested and transported to the death camps. I suspect that she never thought of it as something special.'

CHAPTER NINETEEN

Money Matters

Above all things, our royalty is to be reverenced, and if you begin to poke it about you cannot reverence it. When there is a select committee on the Queen, the charm of royalty will be gone. Its mystery is its life. We must not let daylight in upon magic.

Walter Bagehot, *The English Constitution*, 1867

'Beastly humbug' had been the verdict of the young Australian journalist Keith Murdoch when he witnessed King Edward VII's elaborate State Opening of Parliament in 1909. Sixty years later his son Rupert arrived in Fleet Street from 'down under' with the same irreverent attitude towards the British establishment.

'Titles?' he was once reported to have exclaimed. 'The only titles I want are more newspapers.'

In 1909 Keith Murdoch had failed to get a job in London, but he had returned to Australia to build up a medium-sized newspaper empire. His son

Rupert inherited this in 1953 and, having spent sixteen years expanding News International and adding television interests in Australia, he decided to get established on Fleet Street. His first purchase, the well-established *News of the World*, Britain's best-selling Sunday scandal sheet, showed his unashamedly commercial instincts.

'We are not here to pass ourselves off as intellectuals,' he once remarked. 'We're here to give the public what it wants.'

It was his second acquisition of 1969, the ailing left-wing broadsheet the *Sun*, that demonstrated his newspaper genius. He transformed the paper— a dedicated Labour mouthpiece, formerly part-owned by the Trades Union Congress—into a snappy populist tabloid that doubled its circulation to over a million within months. Using a formula of sex, scandal, sport and raucous, often disrespectful humour, Rupert Murdoch built the *Sun* into Britain's biggest selling daily in less than a decade, its circulation topping four million and overtaking the *Daily Mirror* in 1978. One of the *Sun*'s staple ingredients, the saucily topless 'Page Three Girls', entered the language, as did *Private Eye*'s inspired nickname for Murdoch, with its echoes of both scandal and the penal colony—the 'Dirty Digger'.

Murdoch's personal attitude to the monarchy was complex. In Australia he was an overt republican, encouraging the Labour Prime Minister, Gough Whitlam, in his replacement of 'God Save the Queen' by a local national anthem. But in Britain he has always denied the accusation—strongly believed by both the Queen and her husband—that he has deliberately sought to bring about the fall of the monarchy.

'I'm ambivalent about that [the end of the monarchy],' he told his biographer William Shawcross in 1991, condescendingly adding that he doubted whether Britain 'has the self-confidence to live without it'.

For the record, Murdoch has always denied wanting to see or encourage a republic of Britain. But from his days at Oxford, where he kept a bust of Lenin on his mantelpiece, he has expressed the belief that the crown should be subject to the same blast of populist scrutiny as any other institution in a democracy. As a businessman, he has unashamedly operated on the basis that stories about the royal family, especially scandalous ones, sell newspapers—and he is puritanically disdainful of the fondness displayed by his fellow press proprietors, especially those from the Commonwealth, for peerages.

'The last thing I wanted was to be a bloody press lord,' he once declared. 'I think when people start taking knighthoods and peerages it really is telling the world you've sold out.'

It was this steely lack of deference that made Rupert Murdoch different from any major press proprietor Britain had ever seen prior to his arrival in Fleet Street in 1969. He was not, as some of his detractors have depicted him, original sin. As Keith Waterhouse put it, Murdoch's great achievement was to vulgarise the existing vulgarity of Britain's newspapers. But the Australian's arrival did prompt a new aggression in British newsgathering, coupled with a ruthless commercialism that was permanently to change the ground rules between the press and the Palace.

The *News of the World* and the *Sun* swung into Murdoch mode at a moment of particular delicacy for the royal family. In 1969 Buckingham Palace was running out of money. Inflation had been eroding the financial arrangements made at the beginning of the reign, and since 1962 the annual fixed payments from the Civil List had been insufficient to meet royal expenses.

In November 1969 a carefully framed story hinted at the problem in the columns of *The Times*. Seeking to enlist sympathy among other sufferers of selective employment tax, the levy which the Wilson government had devised to induce businesses to prune their workforces, the article disclosed that the Queen had had to lay off 15 per cent of her three hundred or so full-time staff. For several years she had been drawing on private income to keep the Palace running, said the article, and an unnamed official was quoted as warning that 'it might be time for the situation to be reviewed.'

A few days later the subtlety of this démarche was totally flattened. Elizabeth II had been quietly discussing this most sensitive of subjects with the accommodating Harold Wilson, but now her husband jumped in.

'We go into the red next year,' Prince Philip cheerily remarked in the course of an interview with NBC's *Meet the Press*, while on a visit to America. 'We may have to move into smaller premises, who knows?' The prince went on to say he had already had to sell 'a small yacht' and that he would probably have to 'give up polo fairly soon'.

His casualness could not have been better calculated to provoke inflammatory headlines.

'My heart bleeds,' responded Willie Hamilton, the antimonarchist Labour MP, speaking on behalf of those who had no yachts to turn into ready cash. More loyally, a group of Bermondsey dockers organised a collection to buy the prince a polo pony.

'When we were kids he did a lot for us with the playing fields and the boys' clubs,' said Bobby Cadman, twenty-seven.

Compelled to answer inflammatory questions in Parliament—which prompted the very stories and headlines he had been hoping to avoid—Harold Wilson felt that his discretion and loyalty had been ill repaid. Discussing royal spending in Cabinet, he commented peevishly on the meanness of the royal family when compared to the generosity with which some rich people gave to charity. Nor did he waste much energy arguing with radical ministers like Richard Crossman and Barbara Castle, who had no time for pleas of poverty from 'one of the richest women in the world'.

But there was an election in the offing and Labour did not want to go into it seeming antiroyal. The *Royal Family* film had helped foster monarchist sentiment. Wilson got Edward Heath, the Conservative leader, to agree to the setting up of a select committee on royal funding, whichever party won the election, thus postponing the problem. But it meant that the price of the Queen's 'pay claim', as the newspapers called it, would be the most searching enquiry into a sphere she had worked very hard to keep private. In this respect, thanks to her husband, *Royal Family* had been for nought.

The fact that Wilson surprisingly lost the general election of June 1970 did not help the Queen's dilemma. Edward Heath was no old-style Tory from the charmed circle and, with his brusque executive manner, had little time for the romantic courtesies that Wilson so enjoyed. This may have been why Elizabeth II struck Richard Crossman as singularly unthrilled by the change of government.

'It means knowing a lot of new people,' she told the retiring minister when he enquired if she minded elections. Crossman came to the conclusion that political parties were much of a muchness in her eyes, and that 'for her all this simply means that, just when she had begun to know one, she has to meet another terrible lot of politicians'.

The Conservative victory meant that the Select Committee on the Civil List, which started work in May 1971, had an inbuilt Conservative majority and a Conservative chairman, Anthony Barber, the new Chancellor of the Exchequer. Harold Wilson demonstrated his continuing loyalty by choosing to head the Labour contingent, along with the heavyweight Roy Jenkins. But he could not exclude the backbencher who carried the flag for royal reform, Willie Hamilton, and it was the energetically republican MP for West Fife who became the loudest voice on the committee and, in many respects, its life and soul.

Hamilton had already made his position quite plain. The 'Gracious Message' by which the Queen had formally requested Parliament to consider her finances was, he said, 'the most brazenly insensitive

337

pay claim made in the last two hundred years'.

Hamilton was a Durham miner's son who traced his antiroyalist sentiments to the general strike of 1926 when he was at primary school. 'We were told a member of the Royal Family would pass our school,' he recalled, 'and we were all taken out to wave. The car came past, we duly waved and that was that. But I resented this fine car because I knew we weren't able to put a coal fire on [at home].' His parents were staunch Labour supporters who represented exactly the sort of thinking of which George V had been so afraid. They taught their son early, the MP remembered, that the monarchy was 'the very apex of something evil, of that pyramid of wealth, privilege and exploitation, at the bottom of which writhed coal miners, dock workers, textile workers and toiling masses everywhere'.

Hamilton had entered Parliament in 1950, wresting West Fife from the Communist MP Willie Gallagher. This made him one of the few Englishmen ever to represent a Scottish constituency, and critics explained his radicalism in terms of his need to hold on to the support of tough miners and working-class voters.

Like Altrincham, Hamilton became a national figure entirely on the basis of his willingness to criticise the monarchy. People said they disagreed with him, but they also liked the snook that he cocked at authority. His equivalent in these years was the moral campaigner Mary Whitehouse, similarly derided for one-issue nuttiness in her attempts to keep sex and swear words off television, but winning time on the national soapbox for finding the words to voice a widely held concern. Hamilton's passion was endearing, and his energy set the agenda for the fiercest public scrutiny and questioning to which royal business had ever been subjected.

Royal financing was traditionally dealt with at the beginning of every reign in a transaction that dated back to 1760, when George III surrendered his claim to the income from the crown lands in return for an annual allowance set by Parliament. Negotiated in the respectful optimism of the first months of a new reign, the Civil List was traditionally non-contentious and generous, calculated on the assumption that it would have to last the monarch's lifetime. But by 1971 Elizabeth II had already reigned for three years longer than her father, through a period of unprecedentedly severe inflation which had exhausted the allowance that had been calculated in 1952.

Creative book-keeping had helped stave off insolvency by placing certain categories of expenditure under the departments that administered them. Thus the costs of the royal yacht, some £839,000 per year, had always been borne by the Royal Navy, as the RAF financed the £700,000 annual cost of the planes of the Queen's Flight. The existence of these so-called 'departmental votes' had not been generally realised, and when these extra grants were added up it showed that the total cost of the monarchy was some £2.9 million on top of the £475,000 of the Civil List. The committee also gave publicity to the £100,000 a year that the Queen enjoyed from the historic estates of the Duchy of Lancaster. These obscure ancient revenues were not surrendered to Parliament, but went straight to the Privy Purse—

which was further swelled from other sources. Royal enterprise was generating healthy profits from mushroom production in the sheds at Windsor Castle, and from fifty acres of blackcurrant bushes at Sandringham. (The juice was sold to the Ribena fruit cordial company.)

Such intriguing housekeeping details were like the juicy morsels that had been disclosed by the *Royal Family* film—but the committee rapidly discovered that royal disclosure was selective. Elizabeth II's advisers adamantly refused to disclose any details of her personal wealth. Looming behind the details of blackcurrant bushes and the cost of the royal train (£36,000 a year, paid for by British Rail) was the question of the Queen's personal fortune.

The committee rapidly and usefully established that her personal assets did not include her official residences of Buckingham Palace and Windsor Castle. These were 'inalienable' assets that belonged to the nation, like the Tower of London and the Crown Jewels. Also in the inalienable category were the paintings and fabulous antiques of the Royal Collection, some 450,000 treasures mistakenly included in many of the journalistic calculations that reckoned Elizabeth II 'the richest woman in the world'. To put it crudely, if the Queen and her family were sent packing, she could not take these things with her. But she could take the huge private estates of Sandringham and Balmoral, along with private investments of unknown magnitude.

Few people shared Willie Hamilton's consuming grudge against all things royal, but the issue of the Queen's private fortune did raise eyebrows. As

Wilson's Cabinet colleagues had pointed out, there was an inescapable incongruity about pleas of poverty from a family that was so demonstrably comfortably off, and it raised a dangerous question about the cosy domestic scenes filmed in Balmoral's acres of rolling heather. How had this 'ordinary family' come by such affluent possessions?

The simple answer was: through wise economy and saving. Queen Victoria had come to the throne penniless. Her father had been so poor he had driven the family in his own carriage because he could not afford servants. But Victoria had handled her Civil List thriftily. With her savings and at least one legacy from an admiring subject, she had been rich enough to purchase the estates of Osborne, Balmoral and Sandringham, and her descendants had continued to salt money away. The royal family considered—and Parliament never questioned—that they could pocket any savings they made from their official income. It was an acceptable inducement to responsible husbandry.

But whereas any ordinary individual or family was liable to the penalties of income tax and inheritance tax on its private fortune, the House of Windsor had largely escaped these depredations. Queen Victoria and Edward VII had paid some income tax at the relatively low levels of the time, but George V and George VI had successfully pushed for exemptions which, in the early years of Elizabeth II's reign, became total. Generations of low or zero taxpaying had built up the comfortable assets enjoyed by the Queen and her family, and this was the principal reality to emerge from the national scrutiny: Elizabeth II was wealthy because she paid no tax. One telling detail Willie Hamilton discovered was that when the administrators of the Queen's stock market investments received dividends from which tax had been deducted at source, they would reclaim that tax from the Inland Revenue.

Elizabeth II herself took a certain pride in her tax-exempt status. She was personally frugal in the family tradition—in the early 1960s R. A. Butler noticed what a close, practical eye she kept on rising prices—and she had been brought up to see her tax exemption as something she should not lose. 'Not paying tax was one of the things her father told her to fight for,' recalls one of her senior advisers. 'Her mother', recalls another, 'felt just as strongly, and kept reminding her not to give in.'

Over lunch during the select committee hearings of 1971 the normally discreet Sir Michael Adeane made a telling admission. After a number of highly publicised hearings, the Queen's tax exemption was coming to be seen as the hot issue. The respected Labour Minister Michael Stewart had pointed out that the public could not be expected to judge how much to pay the Queen through the Civil List when it had no idea how much it was already paying her via the royal tax exemption. The Queen would surely grow greatly in public esteem, it was put directly to the private secretary, if she took the initiative and came clean.

'I don't agree,' replied the courtier, smiling politely. 'But even if I did, she wouldn't do it.'

Elizabeth II's personal style was not at issue. After nearly twenty years on the throne, it was generally accepted that she was a thrifty spirit. But when it came to her family fortune, she clearly went by the motto 'To Have and To Hold'. The normally mild monarch was tough and uncompromising in the defence of her dynastic position—in the slang of the time, she was the royal family's own Bolshie shop steward.

In 1971 the royal shop steward got all her members their pay rise, and they kept their perks as well. By a vote of 168 to 47 the House of Commons voted for a 4 per cent per annum rise in the Civil List—and the Queen's refusal to disclose details of her private income was accepted, along with her exemption from tax.

But now the cat was out of the bag. Money had always been a subject of conflict between crown and Parliament. As Richard Crossman remarked with relish, it had been the reason why King Charles had lost his head. In the course of the long and raucous public argument, Willie Hamilton had for the first time singled out royal individuals for personal attack. He prompted particular applause whenever he referred to Princess Margaret as 'the most expensive kept woman in the country', and newspapers had discovered in the process that royal loyalty did not always pay. On 3 December 1971, the *Sun* ran a relatively mild and supportive spread on how hard Her Majesty worked, then asked what its readers thought. Eighty per cent of the respondents said she did not deserve a pay rise.

*   *   *

In January 1972 Britain finally joined Europe. Edward Heath signed the Treaty of Brussels, admitting Britain to what was then known as the

European Community, and in May the Queen went on a state visit to Paris intended to 'improve the atmosphere' for the British membership that would formally take effect the following January.

There was, however, a family complication. Paris was the home in exile of the Duke and Duchess of Windsor, and a biopsy the previous November had revealed that the Duke was stricken with inoperable throat cancer. From the bronchial problems of Edward VII and George V to the lung cancer of George VI, smoking had claimed its fourth successive British king.

It was inconceivable that Elizabeth II should not visit her uncle. Since her accession, the Queen had made cautious attempts to heal the family rift. In 1960 she had accepted the Duke's request that he and Wallis, like other royals, could be buried together in the grounds of Windsor at Frogmore. In 1965 she had visited the Duke when he came to London for an eye operation, and there had been a public reconciliation two years later when he and Wallis joined the royal family for the unveiling of a memorial plaque to Queen Mary. When Wallis met her old adversary, the Queen Mother, it was noted that she did not curtsey.

Preparing for the Queen's May 1972 visit, Sir Christopher Soames, Britain's ambassador in Paris, summoned the Duke of Windsor's doctor, Jean Thin.

'The Ambassador came to the point,' Dr Thin recalled, 'and told me bluntly that it was all right for the Duke to die before or after the visit, but that it would be politically disastrous if he were to expire in the course of it. Was there anything I could do to reassure him about the timing of the

Duke's end?'

No Dawson of Penn, the Frenchman was unfamiliar with the British tradition of royal euthanasia, and he reacted with astonishment and outrage. Dr Thin told Soames it was perfectly possible that the Duke would die during the Queen's time in Paris.

In the event, the Duke hung on. He was determined to see his niece, and he gallantly insisted on being got out of bed and dressed up properly to greet her. Weighing less than ninety pounds and perilously weak, he sat waiting for the Queen, spruce in a blue blazer and shirt, beneath which a drip tube was hidden. The tube emerged from the back of his collar, and ran to flasks concealed behind a curtain. As Elizabeth II entered the room, the old man rose to his feet and inclined his neck in the reflex bow he had made to his sovereign since childhood. The French doctor was horrified, fearing the drip would become dislodged. But the ex-king then sat and talked to his niece quite affectionately for a quarter of an hour. As she left the room, the doctor noticed there were tears in her eyes.

The Duke died nine days later. His body was flown to Britain to lie in state in St George's Chapel, Windsor. No fewer than sixty thousand mourners filed past his coffin in the next few days. After thirty-six years, there were clearly some who still remembered.

Lord Mountbatten took Wallis to see the coffin.

'He was my entire life,' she said. 'I always hoped I would die before him.'

Prince Charles, now twenty-three, felt he should try to ease the discomfort of the situation, but when he tried to broach the subject with his grandmother, the Queen Mother, he discovered how unyielding she remained. Elizabeth II, as ever, steered a middle course. She had Wallis to stay at Buckingham Palace, but she did not invite her up to truly home territory, to her private dining room with its calm, eighteenth-century paintings around the walls. She kept the occasion formal, entertaining in the Chinese Dining Room—though the atmosphere became more family-like when everyone sat down around the television to watch Uncle Dickie's televised tribute to the late ex-King. It was 'very moving and beautifully done', wrote Prince Charles in his diary.

Elizabeth II saw no reason to cancel the Trooping the Colour ceremony, which happened to fall two days before the Duke's funeral. In the Palace discussions, she was unusually firm in insisting that it should go ahead. She was not cancelling or postponing the principal royal ceremony of the year for someone who had betrayed both the job and his family. Martin Charteris was handed the challenge of devising a proper way to mark the passing of a king who had scuttled, and the private secretary came up with a lament to be played by the pipes and drums of the Scots Guards. It was an ancient-seeming new tradition whose mournfulness could be taken several ways.

At the funeral itself on 5 June Clarissa Eden, wife of the former Prime Minister, was struck by how gently the Queen responded to the Duchess's confusion. Under sedatives and showing signs of the dementia that was to mark the final years of her life, Wallis did nervous things with her hands and kept talking: 'Where do I sit?' 'Is this my seat?' 'Is this my prayer book?' 'What do I do now?' The Queen had had herself seated beside Wallis, and she responded to the old lady's worries with what Lady Avon described as a 'motherly and nanny-like tenderness'. She 'kept putting her hand on the Duchess' arm or glove'.

Wallis was to survive for nearly fourteen more years, the last of them bedridden and totally out of contact with the world. But before she finally lost her faculties, she did fire one final salvo at the family whose hostility had so dramatically defined her life.

Dickie Mountbatten had made it his job to attempt to retrieve objects which, in the family's opinion, should not have been taken into exile by the Duke and Duchess. He even suggested that the couple's personal fortune—jewellery, art, furniture and memorabilia that were to raise nearly $70 million in auctions after the Duchess's death— might be willed back to the monarchy, or perhaps to Prince Charles and other younger members of the family. He also proposed a charitable foundation that Prince Charles might head. But, aided by her ferocious French attorney, Maître Suzanne Blum, the Duchess resisted.

'It is always a pleasure to see you,' she wrote to Mountbatten in 1974. 'But I must tell you that when you leave me I am always terribly depressed by your reminding me of David's death and my own, and I would be grateful if you would not mention this any more.'

When Wallis died on 24 April 1986, aged eighty-nine, the reading of her will revealed that she had left nothing to the royal family. The principal proceeds of her estate, including her priceless jewellery collection, had gone to support the medical research work of the Pasteur Institute, which in 1983 had announced the first isolation of the virus that causes AIDS.

* * *

The subdued dignity of the Duke of Windsor's funeral and farewell owed much to the organising abilities of Patrick Plunket. The occasion was strewn with pitfalls that could have led to embarrassment, both public and private. But, working with Martin Charteris, who had become private secretary at the beginning of the year, Plunket wrapped the whole occasion in his customary lightness and style. 'Patrick had a way', recalls one of his friends, 'of making everything memorable. He always left you smiling.'

Plunket knew how to handle the Queen, how to coax her out of her obstinacies. He brightened up her cautious and reactive nature, persuading her to take small chances and to see that some sorts of changes could be fun. If the idea came from Patrick, Elizabeth II would take direction, and even graceful contradiction, that no one else would dare proffer. 'He spoke to her like an equal,' remembers a friend.

To those who witnessed it, the Queen's relationship with Plunket was a sort of love affair, chaste and deep. He lit her up, expanding her horizons, particularly when it came to art. Queen Mary's heavy-handed tours and lectures had drained all the fun out of looking at things; Plunket gave her back the joy. At a late-night reception in the mid-1970s, Elizabeth II led a group of guests into the Palace picture gallery and gave them a guided tour which cast the philistine Queen in a new light. 'She took such delight in her paintings,' remembers one of the party. 'And she knew everything about them.'

That was all thanks to Patrick. But earlier in the decade, the Deputy Master of the Household was diagnosed with cancer. His illness was a trauma for Elizabeth II, something of which she did not like to be reminded in later years. 'It was just tragic,' remembers a friend. 'She watched him withering away.' After his death in 1975, she joined in a fund organised by friends to raise a monument to him, the only servant or courtier that she ever honoured in that particularly Queen Victoria fashion, giving the land on which a little gazebo was erected in Windsor Great Park.

Plunket's executors found a note among his papers. He wanted the Queen to have his Bonington—a small, spare, elegant coastal scene by the early nineteenth-century English painter Richard Parkes Bonington. A contemporary of Constable and Turner who died young, Bonington shared their light and fluid capacity to capture landscape. The canvas was full of sky and fresh air, exhaling space and light: a heart-touching artistic tribute to the outdoors and natural elements which he knew to be the Queen's love and her escape.

The mid-seventies saw other sadnesses. The Snowdon marriage had started splintering at a surprisingly early date. Battle lines had been drawn by the late 1960s, with both partners engaged in mutually destructive infidelities. It is not remarkable for a marriage to go wrong in such a way and, historically, the privileges of position have made royal people more prone to it than others. But, picking up the flavour of the burgeoning 'me' generation, the couple were less inclined to camouflage. Snowdon cunningly, and Margaret in a more foolhardy fashion, pursued their divergent paths. And the press watched with a predatory and newly competitive gaze.

In February 1976, a Murdoch journalist masquerading as a schoolteacher joined an upmarket group of tourists to the private Caribbean island of Mustique. Margaret was holidaying there with Roddy Llewellyn, a young man eighteen years her junior, with whom she had been involved for three years, and the resulting snap of the princess and her bare-chested toy-boy was published in the *News of the World*. The original photograph showed quite a large group sitting around a table, but it was carefully cropped to show just Margaret and Roddy.

The picture broke a new boundary in press revelation, and it was followed within days by a new departure for the figurehead family. It was announced on Friday, 19 March 1976 that the Queen's sister and her husband were formally separating—leading, two years later, to the House of Windsor's first high-level divorce.

A significant footnote to the break-up was that it occurred, by chance, at the same time that Harold Wilson, who had reached the age of sixty, was planning to retire. Since he was departing of his own free will, the Prime Minister gallantly offered to time his announcement to coincide with the Snowdons' bad news.

'He came back from the Palace with some glee,'

recalls Wilson's press secretary, Joe Haines. 'He said he made this arrangement with the Queen to blank out the separation by announcing his resignation on the same day. Having worked on popular newspapers, I was doubtful.'

Haines' doubts were justified. Wilson's resignation was announced at 11.30 in the morning, Princess Margaret's separation at 5.00 p.m. 'The papers went for the later, sexier story,' remembers the press secretary. The princess pushed the Prime Minister straight off the front page.

CHAPTER TWENTY

Silver Jubilee

I wish you could have been there for our party
   in the street,
With all the kids a-shouting and the stamping
   of their feet,
Flags and bunting flying, dancing on the green,
And Mums were even crying—What a caper!
   What a scene!

     Entry for the Michael Aspel Capital Radio
     Silver Jubilee Poetry Competition 1977

By 1976 Elizabeth II's advisers were well into the planning of her Silver Jubilee, the celebration of her twenty-five years on the throne. But Princess Margaret's marital failure added to a catalogue of bad omens. Looking back over the previous quarter of a century, the dreams of a new Elizabethan age could only be contemplated with a wry smile. Continuing inflation and balance of payments problems had eventually exploded in the early 1970s with the bitterness of industrial disruption and the débâcle of the three-day week, when the country went on part-time working. Energy was in such short supply that television transmissions were ended by government curfew at ten-thirty every night.

Conservative and Labour governments were equally frustrated and when, in 1976, the oil price explosion drove inflation up to 16 per cent, Wilson's successor, James Callaghan, had to go cap in hand to the International Monetary Fund. With the pound collapsing and one and a half million Britons unemployed, the IMF agreed to bail the country out—on the same tough terms it imposed on any third world government that could not handle its own affairs. When the loss of empire was added in, it was difficult to recall twenty-five years of such precipitous national decline. A royal celebration seemed the last thing the country needed.

There was a definite mood of apprehension among the organisers of the Jubilee. The Home Office was the government department liaising with Buckingham Palace, and the Labour Home Secretary Merlyn Rees was particularly unhappy at the Palace's proposal of a Silver Jubilee Medal. This award would be made to village postmasters, hospital matrons, charity organisers and other 'good eggs', along with the police and the military, as a one-off Jubilee supplement to the honours list.

Rees could not see the point. A new medal seemed a frivolity to a senior government minister sitting in Cabinet meetings that were trying to stave off national bankruptcy. With a high-level pessimism in the government, even Palace enthusiasts began to ask themselves whether the celebration would not turn out to be a humiliating flop.

The early soundings of Mass-Observation suggested the worst. Working with the author Philip Ziegler, Mass-Obs mounted a full scale Jubilee survey in the tradition of its previous national soundings. Two national opinion polls were commissioned, one in February 1977 and one in late May, to chart how emotions changed as the event approached, and the existing core of observers was expanded. Letters were sent to the correspondence columns of the national newspapers inviting readers to send in reports on their own experiences, and particularly any local celebrations which they observed or helped to organise.

At the beginning of the year confusion reigned. It had been forty-two years since the last Jubilee and people were not quite sure what it celebrated. Some people thought it commemorated D-Day, while others presumed it marked twenty-five years of the royal marriage.

'Does that mean that Prince Charles is illegit?' asked a precocious 14-year-old. 'I read he was twenty-seven.'

The Oxfordshire village of Shilton tried organising a torchlight procession on 5 February, the cold winter night preceding the actual anniversary of the Queen's accession, and discovered in the darkness and pouring rain why the official commemoration, like the Queen's official birthday, was scheduled for the summer months.

'Apathy Hits Plans for Jubilee,' reported the Guardian with mournful glee.

Complaints about the cost of it all were as traditional as the bunting that forward-looking Women's Institutes were starting to order, and there was some publicity for antiroyalist groups circulating 'Stuff the Jubilee' badges. The motto propagated by the Socialist Workers' Party was 'Roll on the Red Republic', while the Communist Party organised a 'People's Jubilee' at Alexandra Palace. When the results of the first poll conducted by the British Market Research Bureau came in, it showed 16.4 per cent answering 'No' to the question 'Does Britain need a Queen?' In the previous fifteen years, similar surveys had established 11 per cent as the norm for hardcore republicans.

This meant, of course, that more than 80 per cent of those polled supported the monarchy, but one perceptive 53-year-old observer, anonymous like all Mass-Obs reporters, though identified by age, gender, occupation and locality, noted the new outspokenness and scepticism in the national tone.

'What strikes me', he wrote, 'are the editorials in newspapers like the *Daily Telegraph*, discussing the pros and cons of the monarchy and the Queen's virtues and faults. Such articles, even though they are laudable to the Queen, would have been inconceivable even twenty-five years ago.'

By the time the May poll came around, however, commercial pressures were mounting. The souvenir trade was building up momentum, with the first recorded Union Jack Y-front underpants breaking new boundaries in taste. By late May, a survey of Kensington High Street showed even more shop windows dressed out in royal decorations than had been the case at the coronation. Barratt, the builders, offered a 'beautiful Royal Staffordshire Jubilee loving cup' to anyone who bought one of their houses in Luton, while Shinner's Department Store in the Surrey suburb of Sutton cashed in unashamedly:

Oh to be in England,
Now that Spring is here,
Oh to be in Shinner's (China and Glass)
In Jubilee Year.

It was, perhaps, when the satirical magazine *Private Eye* announced the Silver Jubilee plans of their fictitious Neasden launderette operator, Colonel Buffy Cohen, that the national mood could be said to have changed. The event was important enough to be made fun of—affectionately. By midnight on 6 June, Jubilee eve, crowds were bedding down with hot thermos flasks and sleeping bags in the Mall. The no. 1 chart hit of the moment, banned on the BBC, was the Sex Pistols' nihilistic rock anthem 'God Save the Queen'. But beneath the veneer of the punk seventies, the old traditions held true. By 9 a.m. on Jubilee day the crowds stood six deep along the whole route from Buckingham Palace to St Paul's, and thousands kept coming. 'Liz Rules OK!' was the slogan on one badge that was commonly seen.

Mass-Obs had stationed a special group of observers to monitor the great innovation of the day, the Queen's first ever walkabout through the streets of London. She had ridden to St Paul's in the ancient golden State Coach. But after the service she walked from the cathedral to the Mansion House, moving through the crowds in her candy-pink Jubilee outfit, topped off with an unusually successful matching pink hat.

'We've come here because we love you,' said an office girl in her early twenties.

'I can feel it, and it means so much to me,' replied the Queen, trying not to shut off direct emotion for once.

'She asked us where we came from,' said another woman, 'and we said "Lewisham" . . . We'd come from Uganda originally. We were thrown out five years ago . . . But we didn't like to tell her that.'

Tumultuous balcony crowd scenes ended a royal day as successful as any other. But the real significance of the Silver Jubilee lay in the twelve thousand or more street parties organised by local communities around the country. In parish councils and Women's Institutes, the nation's doers and organisers had got busy. The great national tradition of bazaar, raffle and jumble sale had been given royal form. Cucumbers were being sliced, sausages rolled, three-legged races organised and Jubilee Ale set out in the tradition that went back to the festivities of 1809 for King George III. The historic power of communal ritual proved as inspirational as ever.

One cul-de-sac in Worcester witnessed a knobbly knees contest and a tug of war between Mums and Dads, which the Mums won twice, to loud cheers from the watching children.

'This is great, man, just great,' remarked a long-haired student.

The party's organiser, an electricians' shop steward, took advantage of the young man's interest to explain what he was witnessing. The cul-de-sac's residents included a pipe-fitter, a factory foreman, a chemist, a garage manager, a butcher and the local Anglican priest, who had said a grace to open the proceedings. There was also a character 'who has been on social security for four or five years, refused to work and is regarded as the local layabout'. The shop steward explained to the young student that he was privileged to be witnessing 'working-class culture . . . something which is fast disappearing'. The Labour stalwart thought it quite natural that this proletarian gathering should have been inspired by a royal symbol.

'It's a pity it takes a Queen's Jubilee to make people talk,' reflected a Manchester-street party organiser, giving voice to a frequently expressed sentiment. 'New and old residents in our street began to really look at one another instead of through each other.'

'Old age pensioners were brought down in cars and given a seat. Just about everybody was there,' wrote a Southampton housewife. 'Dad's arm was aching helping children down the slide . . . With the economic state of the country, people have been feeling a bit low, and this Silver Jubilee was just what people needed to cheer them up a bit.'

This particular party in Southampton progressed through a children's fancy dress competition to an evening disco that went on into the night. 'It was lovely dancing in the fresh air instead of the stuffy hall. At midnight a police car drew up and out jumped a very jovial policeman. This was the fourth street party he had called at. He was given a pint of beer . . . The evening wound up [just before 1 a.m.] with everybody singing *Rule Britannia* at the top of their voices—and, what was so odd, really meaning it! I have never heard people sing with such fervour since the end of the war. It went on and on with everybody shouting it out again and again in a very united way.'

This description was not composed self-consciously for the benefit of the Mass-Observation survey. It was a spontaneous, private letter written to a son living in Norway, who had seen the Mass-Obs appeal in his English Sunday newspaper, and subsequently secured his mother's permission to send her account to the archive, which was now based at the University of Sussex. 'When I first read your letter,' he replied, setting out some reflections of his own,

I started wondering why the Queen's Jubilee should arouse such strong feelings of loyalty . . . The royal family have no real power and as a symbol of Britain's greatness, the whole thing is illusory in the present day. The royal family is also the peak of the class system, which from a Scandinavian perspective is one of the major obstacles to progress in Britain today. So why the celebration? Is it a type of escapism from the problems of the economic depression? Is it because the monarchy is a symbol of stability in a period of rapid change, which many people experience as disturbing and frustrating? Is it a reflection of people's disillusionment with the politicians and party politics?

Distance and the fresh Scandinavian air had evidently prompted some clear thinking in this young Englishman about his mother country.

'Whatever the motives,' he concluded, 'if the Jubilee can lead to a re-finding of the local community, it will have had a purpose.'

Part 4

'Queen of people's hearts'

CHAPTER TWENTY-ONE

Great White Queen

There is a motto that has been borne by many of my ancestors—a noble motto, 'I serve'.

Princess Elizabeth's broadcast of dedication to the Commonwealth, April 1947

One February afternoon in the mid-1970s, the Queen's private secretary, Sir Martin Charteris, received a visit from the Australian high commissioner in London, Sir John Bunting. Australia had decided to grant independence to the Territory of Papua New Guinea and although the islands, previously an Australian protectorate, had never been part of the British Empire, the inhabitants had come up with a curious request.

'They want the Queen to be their Queen,' said Bunting.

'That's very nice,' replied Charteris. 'Why is that?'

'Well,' replied Bunting, 'first of all because she's been there and they liked her very much. Then they want someone who is above the fight and will hold the ring. And above all, they want to keep on getting knighthoods and British decorations.'

'The Queen was tickled with the idea,' remembered Charteris. 'She accepted straight away.'

Papua New Guinea brought up to a full dozen the number of independent countries which, after

363

ending their colonial links with Britain, had decided to retain Britain's monarch as their head of state. Mixing tradition with inertia and a little old-fashioned snobbery, their motives were not very different from Papua New Guinea's.

The problems inherent in not having your monarch on the premises were made dramatically clear in Australia in November 1975, when Sir John Kerr, the Queen's Governor General, controversially dismissed the elected Prime Minister, Gough Whitlam, without consulting the Queen. She was actually asleep in London at the time. But illogical though it might be, timeshare monarchy struck a dozen independent countries as being preferable to no monarchy at all.

The affection that the Queen commanded was very obvious when she visited both Australia and Papua New Guinea during her Silver Jubilee visits to the Commonwealth in 1977. The sacking of Whitlam had proved a decisive step in moving Australia towards the day when it would become a republic, but most people, including Whitlam, realised that the Queen was not personally to blame for Kerr's action. 'We only had one placard thrown at us outside the Opera House,' recalls one of her aides.

The tour was one of the warmest since Elizabeth II's post-coronation progress of 1953–4, and in Papua New Guinea the welcome was even more ecstatic. The Queen particularly enjoyed her reception by the Foreign Minister, in his best European suit. A few days later she encountered him again, in native costume, which consisted of a straw apron in front and very little behind. When His Excellency advanced to the microphone to make his address of welcome, he treated Her Majesty, and everyone else seated behind him, to the impressive vista of his bare buttocks, made slightly less immodest by the adherence of several pages of his speech, upon which he had been sitting.

The Commonwealth has provided Elizabeth II with more sustained pleasure than any other aspect of her work—and an area in which her power and prestige have actually increased. In 1952, Britain's Commonwealth seemed a poor apology for a lost empire. In the course of her reign it has developed, in a quietly persistent and low-key style that rather echoes her own, into a pragmatic international organisation from which its members have generally profited. It helps its less developed members get aid, and has played its part in such events as the ending of apartheid and the coming of majority rule in South Africa.

The Queen's deep belief in the British 'family of nations' derives from the instruction of Sir Henry Marten—the only figure approaching a conventional teacher she ever had—and from the urging of King George VI.

'I am amazed by the number of times she says, "My father would have done this," "this is what my father would wish,"' says someone who is working closely with the Queen today—portraying a 75-year-old woman who is still devoutly following the principles that she learnt at her father's knee. 'That wonderful trip to South Africa in 1947 must have been the opportunity to talk endlessly to her father.'

It was in South Africa that the 21-year-old Princess Elizabeth made her speech of adult dedication in a Commonwealth context, and it was in Africa again that she became Queen. Elizabeth II has never seen herself as Queen of Britain with various foreign territories added on. Just as Queen Victoria revelled in her global dimension as Empress, so Elizabeth II is most completely realised as Head of the Commonwealth. This is a title in its own right, giving her status, at the time of writing, over an association of fifty-four independent states—nearly a third of the membership of the United Nations. To receive the homage of India, Malaysia and sixteen black African nations, as well as such geographical giants as Canada and Australia, would be good for anyone's ego. As Head of the Commonwealth, Elizabeth II exercises influence, if not power, that is significantly greater than her prerogatives as a constitutional monarch, and she is also treated with noticeably more good old-fashioned reverence and respect.

She was wearing her Commonwealth mantle when she jousted for the first time with the woman who would become her longest-serving Prime Minister, Margaret Thatcher. In May 1979 the Iron Lady won her first general election, displacing James Callaghan and starting on her programme of cutting back the state-controlled sphere of British life—a direct attack on the 'one nation' postwar balance within which both parties had been happy to work for more than three decades. In political terms the reign of Elizabeth II can be divided into the years BT and AT—before and after Thatcher.

Just six months older than the Queen, Margaret Thatcher was the first Prime Minister of the Queen's own generation, and for the entire course of the 1980s male chauvinist Britain was to be unique in the world, its female head of state teamed with a head of government who was also a woman. But they were women of very different styles. A Prime Minister who loved a row was teamed with a monarch who would do anything she could to avoid one.

Margaret Thatcher was to become notorious for being more royal than the Queen. 'We are a grandmother!' was her reaction to the news of her son Mark's first child. Her public style was epitomised for many in her stance at the end of the Falklands War in 1982, when she decided that she, not Elizabeth II, should take the march past from the victorious British troops. But this was never her attitude in the presence of the Queen.

'Margaret had the deepest respect for the Queen and all her family,' remembers her adviser Tim Bell. 'She even curtseyed to Sarah Ferguson, for Christ's sake—deliberately and visibly so.'

'Margaret was a fervent royalist,' insists one of her former lieutenants. 'When it came to anything to do with the Queen, she was no longer the Iron Lady—she was Margaret Roberts, the shopkeeper's daughter from Grantham.'

This deference played to Elizabeth II's advantage in her very first contacts with her new Prime Minister. A Commonwealth Conference was coming up in August 1979, with the status of white-controlled rebel Rhodesia at the top of the agenda. For nearly a decade and a half the former colony of Southern Rhodesia had been an ongoing embarrassment to the British government. The Unilateral Declaration of Independence by Southern Rhodesia's white settlers in 1965 and the obstinate survival of the white rebel regime was a deeply resented grievance to the black nations of the Commonwealth. Economic sanctions had failed and freedom fighters operating from neighbouring black African countries had made no headway against the white government headed by Ian Smith. In 1978, following pressure from America, Smith had even managed to broker an agreement with the less militant black politicians who stayed in the country to create an elected, black-dominated hundred-seat assembly in which twenty-eight seats would be reserved for whites.

Mrs Thatcher was inclined to accept this compromise. She had little instinctive sympathy with black Africa's leaders and their call for 100 per cent majority rule. She certainly had no appetite for going to a Commonwealth Conference, due to be held in the Zambian capital of Lusaka, where she could expect to be simultaneously lectured by third world leaders and pestered for money.

'Margaret had never been to Africa,' remembers one of her colleagues, 'and she knew she was not liked. It's not something you could say about her in many circumstances, but in this case she was truly physically scared.'

In 1979, Elizabeth II actually knew African leaders like Kenneth Kaunda, the President of Zambia (formerly the colony of Northern Rhodesia), much better than she knew her new British Prime Minister. Her relationships with many of black Africa's premiers went back to the mid-1960s when half a dozen British colonies became independent countries. She met them every time they came to London and at every

Commonwealth gathering.

'They all had these secret smiles as they would creep away from the assembly for their private audiences with her,' remembered Charteris. 'It was a personal thing.'

In the case of Kaunda, the Queen knew that the Zambian leader had been deeply humiliated by the incursions of Ian Smith's white Rhodesian troops into his territory. Through her reading of her boxes, she had also been following the proposals for a Rhodesian peace process on which Kaunda had been working with Thatcher's predecessor, James Callaghan, and his Foreign Secretary, David Owen. The long-incubated Foreign Office plan was to summon all the parties—Ian Smith along with the country's exiled freedom fighters, Joshua Nkomo and Robert Mugabe—to a top-level conference in London at Lancaster House on the Mall. The Ian Smith compromise with its white reserved seats was not acceptable to black Africa, nor to most other members of the Commonwealth. The primary purpose of the Lusaka gathering was to get Commonwealth endorsement for this Lancaster House peace process that would bring unfettered black majority rule to Rhodesia.

Whenever David Owen encountered the Queen Mother, she would twinkle at him with one of her most winning smiles.

'Now, Dr Owen,' she would say, 'you be sure to be kind to that nice Mr Smith!'

The last Empress of India was unashamedly nostalgic for the days when the map was coloured pink and grateful natives were administered by titled English gentlemen in osprey-feathered hats. 'Africa's quite gone to pot since we left it,' was a sentiment frequently expressed at Clarence House, with a sad shake of the head.

But Elizabeth II did not share the imperial nostalgia of her mother. She took personal pride in the achievements of the dozen and a half independent nations that had been born on her watch. She had visited every capital, opened virtually every new dam and university, and felt she had played a personal part in their creation.

'On the apartheid issue, she has always been on-side,' says David Owen. 'It's the one man, one vote principle. On racial matters she is absolutely colour-blind, and her non-white Commonwealth premiers were very conscious of that.'

They did not view Mrs Thatcher so kindly. In the weeks before Lusaka, the British Prime Minister had refused to provide parliamentary time to push through economic sanctions against white Rhodesia.

'Margaret was so difficult about Lusaka,' remembers one of her colleagues. 'There were Africans who regarded her as evil and she knew that. She did not want to go.'

The Queen had had to deal with a similar situation eight years earlier when Edward Heath, fearing trouble over his decision to keep selling arms to the white apartheid regime in South Africa, had refused to let the Queen attend the 1971 Commonwealth Conference in Singapore.

'It was a great pity,' said Sir Martin Charteris. 'Singapore was the one Commonwealth Conference that was really sour and bad tempered and that was because she couldn't attend. If she's there, you see, they behave. It's like nanny being there. Or perhaps it's Mummy. Anyway, she demands that they behave properly in her presence. Never by saying anything, but by looking like a Queen—"And no bloody nonsense from you!" It also works because she knows them all and they like her.'

Allowed to follow her personal inclinations, Margaret Thatcher would probably not have travelled to Lusaka in August 1979. She could plausibly have despatched her Foreign Secretary, Lord Carrington, to represent her, and, in that event, would probably have advised the Queen not to go either, citing the same grounds of security and dignity that Heath had given as his reasons in 1971.

Elizabeth II, however, was not having it.

'She greatly regretted letting Ted stop her from going to Singapore,' said Sir Martin Charteris. 'I think she was determined it was not going to happen again.'

Events like the dismissal of Gough Whitlam had caused Elizabeth II to look harder at the practicalities of her overseas authority. The success of her Silver Jubilee, coinciding with her entry into her fifties, had considerably increased her self-assurance. So when it came to her position as Head of the Commonwealth, she had come to feel by the late 1970s that she was her own best guide in certain matters.

'I have no doubt the Queen dug her heels in over Lusaka,' says an official who had been involved in the process. 'Only she and Margaret Thatcher know what went on in their audiences, and it would never have been a matter of going head to head. Knowing how she works, I imagine the Queen would have pointed out all the momentum of the Foreign Office telegrams she had been reading about the Lancaster House process and all the work that the FO had put into it—what the Commonwealth wanted, and what she felt she had to do for them, and that she really felt she should go.'

For the new Prime Minister, it was her first major foreign policy decision. Her suave and experienced Foreign Secretary, Lord Carrington, favoured the Lancaster House strategy that had been worked out by his Labour predecessor. So, only weeks into her crusade to transform Britain, Margaret Thatcher bowed to her sovereign's judgement and effectively followed royal advice.

'It actually gave Margaret courage,' remembers a prominent Conservative. 'Her monarch was going. It was her duty to go as well.'

Lord Carrington remembers that, as the plane taxied to a halt in Lusaka, Mrs Thatcher took a pair of sunglasses out of her handbag. 'She thought she might be attacked with acid thrown in her face,' he recalls. ' "Don't worry," I told her. "They're going to love you." ' She took them off, and so it proved.

'The Queen made a big difference,' remembers Carrington. 'Everybody had a little hut. She had a grand hut and she held court in her hut. It was extraordinary the effect she had on everyone.'

As the leaders slipped away successively to the grand hut—which was actually a suburban bungalow with a chiming door bell—the Queen talked to them of everything but Rhodesia. 'She would know who was in the clutches of the IMF,' remembered the Commonwealth Secretary-General, Sir Sonny Ramphal; 'who had got what political scandal raging. She'd know the family side of things, if there were children or deaths in the family. She'd know about the economy, she'd know about elections coming up. They felt they were talking to a friend who cared about the country.'

Elizabeth II's combination of homework and humanity gave tangible form to the idea of the Commonwealth being a fellowship. 'It was another bit of glue that made them a collective,' said Ramphal, 'and the Queen was very conscious of this kind of valuable role she was playing.'

Sitting on the sidelines, avoiding the subject but making people feel good, Elizabeth II was getting the job done. You could describe her skills as diplomatic, although it was not her brief to close on the deal. You might alternatively describe her as a therapist or confessor, except that she would have considered those titles much too grand. As Martin Charteris said, it was 'like nanny being there'.

'If Lusaka had gone wrong,' says Lord Carrington, 'I think it not impossible that the Commonwealth would have broken up.'

But it was far from going wrong. After the opening banquet Kenneth Kaunda tried some human chemistry of his own. 'He swooped Margaret off over the dance floor,' remembered Lord Carrington. 'She quite fell in love with him.'

Ballroom diplomacy, a remnant of the days when monarchs regulated the affairs of nations, still had its uses. From her arrival as a grudging participant, Margaret Thatcher became an enthusiastic advocate of the principle enshrined in the unanimous final communiqué—full-scale black majority rule for the people of Zimbabwe, as independent Rhodesia became known.

373

Mrs Thatcher came to feel that the Lancaster House settlement, negotiated in London early in 1980, was her own achievement. The agreement ended the fourteen-year embarrassment of UDI, restored legality, ended the war and produced democratic elections. From the Queen's point of view, her family of nations now contained one more independent country free to follow its own destiny.

CHAPTER TWENTY-TWO

Wild Oats

In the choice of a Queen, the voice of the people must be heard.

Stanley Baldwin, 1936

On 27 August 1979 the IRA detonated a massive bomb it had planted on the holiday fishing boat of Lord Mountbatten off the north-west coast of the Republic of Ireland. Uncle Dickie and his family were on their way to pick up lobster pots outside the harbour of Mullaghmore, close to his mansion at Classiebawn where he went every summer.

Mountbatten's shattered body was found floating face downwards in the water. He had been killed instantly. Also killed were his 14-year-old grandson, Nicholas, and a local boy who was helping crew the boat. Mountbatten's daughter Patricia and her husband, Lord Brabourne, were rescued from the debris-strewn water with broken legs and multiple lacerations. Brabourne's 83-year-old mother died of her injuries next day. In a linked attack in Northern Ireland, for which the IRA also took credit, twenty British soldiers were blown up by half a ton of explosive hidden in a haycart.

The Queen was at Balmoral when she heard the news. She was devastated and deeply angered. Dickie had been murdered because he belonged to her clan—because he was royal. There were times when the 79-year-old had been something of a joke in the family, forever interfering and pushing his latest hobby horse. But Mountbatten had been an elder statesman of radical and creative insight. Unlike his contemporary the Queen Mother, he was the one person willing to tell the family what they might not like to hear. His swashbuckling career in the navy and as the last Viceroy of India also made him a rare royal person—one with independent achievements to his name.

The murder was a reminder of the whole family's vulnerability. Six months later the Queen was out riding at Sandringham with her cousin and old friend Margaret Rhodes. It was a morning of quite thick mist.

'I've been informed,' said the Queen, 'that the IRA have a new sort of sniper sight that sees through the mist.' And she went on riding.

The other side of her stoicism, however, was that she found it difficult to articulate her personal grief. The Brabournes were very old and close friends, as intimate as any. Patricia had been her Girl Guide leader in the Buckingham Palace company. They had shared the joy and resigned exasperation of living in the Dickie Mountbatten forcefield. Patricia once sent a brief note of condolence to her old friend the Queen over the death of a favourite corgi, chased into a lake and drowned by the Queen Mother's pack of dogs. By return she received a four-page letter full of gratitude and feeling, spilling out what the loss meant to her. 'You can say it all about a dog,' says one of her close woman friends with a trace of sarcasm.

When it came to a letter of condolence to either Patricia or her sister Pamela in 1979, however, Elizabeth II sent nothing. It was clear from her actions that she felt for her cousins and shared in their distress. She had Patricia and her husband up to stay with her at Balmoral as soon as they were out of hospital, and her compassion for them both was evident. But, as with Aberfan, the tragedy was too big for ordinary words. The enormity of the sorrow produced, in that respect, a sort of paralysis.

Prince Philip, by contrast, dashed off a long and lyrical letter to Patricia Brabourne as she lay in hospital recovering from her wounds, unable to attend the funeral of her son Nicholas. Between teatime and dinner, while the Queen does her boxes, Prince Philip often vanishes to his quarters, wherever he may be, to deal with his personal correspondence, bashing out his thoughts in direct, frank sentences which, nowadays, he usually processes through his computer. Duke.doc—what gems have been filed on Prince Philip's hard drive? In 1979 his epistle to his injured cousin was a moving and compassionate example of his vivid writing style, a graphic description of the occasion and how everyone present had felt—exactly what a grieving mother needed to hear about the funeral of her fourteen-year-old son.

* * *

The member of the family who was most affected
by the death of Mountbatten was Prince Charles.
In the last decade of his life, the old man had
become a surrogate parent to the prince. 'Life will
never be the same now that he has gone,' wrote the
Prince in his diary. 'In some extraordinary way he
combined grandfather, great uncle, father, brother
and friend.'

Charles and Mountbatten had become
particularly close in the aftermath of the prince's
Welsh investiture in 1969. Immediately following
the ceremony, Charles had embarked on a week-
long tour of Wales, an initiation into royal whistle-
stopping that he had passed with flying colours.
With Welsh nationalism running high, there had
been fears that the trip would prove a flop, but the
young man's eagerness and energy charmed
everyone. Cheering crowds greeted him
everywhere.

It was Charles's first taste of public acclaim in
his own right, and he got back to Windsor anxious
to share the joy of achievement with his family—
only to find that no one had waited up for him. His
father and sister had gone to bed, while his mother
was at Buckingham Palace with a cold. It was his
first major venture in the family business, and the
family just took it for granted.

It is the culture of the House of Windsor to take
duty and its successful performance as par for the
course, and it is certainly not done to admit that
you might actually enjoy the warmth of public

acclaim. Windsor style is not to encourage the cult of personality. It had been the great sin of Uncle David—and Uncle Dickie had also strayed in that direction. Detachment was the recipe of both the Queen and her husband for surviving the voracity of public adoration, and they carried this style into parenting. Philip had applied his brisk naval banter to discourage his son from getting swollen-headed, and the Queen had been sparing in her 'well done's. Charles was apt to see slights where none was intended, and it was easy to interpret his parents' style as a put-down.

Uncle Dickie's 'mission accomplished' letter that arrived a day or so after the prince's return from Wales, written in slightly pompous naval style, was much more what Charles needed to hear.

'Confidential reports on naval officers are summarised by numbers,' wrote Lord Mountbatten, '. . . pretty poor 2 or 3, very good 7 or 8 . . . Your performance since you went with Fleet coverage to Wales rates you at 9 in my opinion.'

Charles responded with equal warmth, and a correspondence sprang up between two eager, naïve and obliquely creative characters who were both viewed with a certain puzzlement by their relatives. Suddenly they realised what soulmates they were. From being a great-uncle who gave good gadget-type presents, Lord Mountbatten became the most important single influence on Charles's life, the grandfather he had never had. For Mountbatten's part, he had finally found the attentive, mouldable son that Philip had always refused to be, and for the next ten years he provided the overt combination of guidance, praise and constructive rebuke that Charles had never received from his parents. The elder man drew many of his unashamedly prescriptive lessons from the life of the previous Prince of Wales—'your Uncle David'—and this played well to Charles's sense of history and of his own personal destiny.

Uncle Dickie had particularly firm ideas when it came to love, sex and the choice of a wife.

'I believe, in a case like yours,' he told Charles, 'that a man should sow his wild oats and have as many affairs as he can before settling down. But for a wife he should choose a suitable and a sweet-charactered girl before she meets anyone else she might fall for.' Charles's future Queen, in other words, must be an old-fashioned virgin.

Mountbatten encouraged the prince to bring girlfriends down to his home at Broadlands for romantic assignations. He took pride in making it possible for his 'honorary grandson' to enjoy what he boasted was a 'normal healthy sex life' out of sight of the cameras. There were girls you bedded and girls you wedded, in the old man's view—though the Catch 22 of this division of function was that any girl with whom you romped between the sheets was automatically ruled out as a wife.

By the standards of the sexual revolution that was taking shape during these years, Mountbatten's recipe was male chauvinist and outdated. But Charles welcomed his great-uncle's simplistic commandments. When it came to parental guidance, the new Prince of Wales found himself operating with a surprising lack of signposts. One would expect the heir to the throne, of all people, to be coached and given rules to live by, especially when it came to marriage, but the opposite was the case.

'You see Charles laughing and relaxing and thoroughly at ease with his parents,' says a courtier. 'And at those moments you'd think there were no problems. But, in fact, they do not have a relationship where dialogue on personal matters is possible.'

His mother held back, partly by instinct and partly because she felt it was her husband's sphere, while Charles was intimidated by his father's well-meaning but brisk attempts at constructive and encouraging advice. In the most important area of his entire life, the choosing of a partner and future Queen, the prince's parents had little input, and it was the advice of his great-uncle that the king-in-waiting followed.

Though easily ridiculed with hindsight, Mountbatten's views were not that different from conventional thinking in the late 1970s, for it lay deep in the folklore that there should be something unsullied about a princess. As Prince Charles started courting seriously, newspapers took it for granted they should burrow into the previous love life of his girlfriends to make sure they did not have what was euphemistically described as a 'past'. It was the difference between Cinderella and the Ugly Sisters—the ultimate lesson of the abdication. Uncle David had lost his throne for choosing a woman who did not measure up to the national purity test.

*   *   *

The 'bedded-can't-be-wedded' convention was to play a major role in the outcome of Prince Charles's friendship with a young woman who spent much time with him at Broadlands in the autumn of 1972. Camilla Shand was a girlfriend whom Charles temporarily succeeded in inveigling away from a young Guards officer, Andrew Parker Bowles. On her mother's side she was a direct descendant of Edward VII's mistress, Mrs Alice Keppel, and legend has it that this provided Camilla with her unique and appealing come-on line at an early meeting: 'My great-grandmother was the mistress of your great-great-grandfather— so how about it?'

Camilla had the Keppel directness with a hearty, county touch. Her father, Major Bruce Shand, was a former cavalry officer who was prominent in the Sussex squirearchy. She rode to hounds, enjoyed her drink and cigarettes, and had a clowning, infectious sense of humour. She and Charles shared a fondness for silly accents, funny faces and the Goons. They called each other Fred and Gladys, which were *Goon Show* names. Camilla also had an earthy and direct attitude to sex. A year older than Charles and appealingly lacking in either malice or ambition, she made him laugh and helped him relax. She was a fixture at Broadlands in the summer and autumn of 1972, and twenty years later Charles told his biographer, Jonathan Dimbleby, that he 'lost his heart to her almost at once'.

Memorably, however, Charles did not marry the woman he later realised that he loved. He did not propose to Camilla, nor convey to her at the time any idea of how deeply he felt. In one sense, Charles had met her too early. Young and uncertain, he was overawed by the responsibility of selecting not just a soulmate, but a future Queen of

England. Marriage and the choice of the right partner 'for the job' was an obsessive theme of the interviews that he was now giving quite regularly to the press. Uncle Dickie, for his part, had hopes for his teenage grand-daughter, Lady Amanda Knatchbull, and he made it his business to keep Charles's eyes firmly fixed on the search for the unsullied 'sweet-charactered girl'.

When the time came for the prince to join his first ship, HMS *Minerva*, early in 1973, the still diffident Charles did not ask Camilla to wait for him. He did not consider her princess material— and nor, evidently, did she. Her opening gambit suggested forwardness, and a definite pride in an ancestor who had been admired less for her purity than for her worldly wisdom as the perfect royal mistress. Extra-marital royal service was in Camilla's family tradition going back to William III. Princes bedded Keppels, they did not marry them—and Keppels organised their marital arrangements accordingly. Within months of Charles being at sea, Camilla accepted the proposal of Andrew Parker Bowles, who had his own connections with the royal family. He was a godson of the Queen Mother as well as a friend of Charles's, and had dated Princess Anne quite seriously. Andrew Parker Bowles could well have been husband material for the Queen's only daughter if he had not been a Roman Catholic.

It was several years later, in the mid-1970s, that Prince Charles started searching more earnestly for the girl whose foot fitted the glass slipper, and the British press joined him avidly in the task. The Silver Jubilee stoked British affection for the monarchy back towards the levels of the coronation of 1953—but with a difference: the media were deferential no more. The red-top voice of the tabloid was becoming more strident, and Princess Margaret's high jinks with Roddy Llewellyn, which were to continue until the couple separated in 1980, had helped establish a flourishing market in royal misbehaviour.

*   *   *

In the early 1970s the typical royal photographer had been a deferential elderly gentleman, who wore a suit, usually with a waistcoat and fob chain, and who took formal pictures from a distance with a square camera. By the end of the decade he was twenty years younger, wore sneakers so he could run faster, and carried an arsenal of long lenses and motor-wind mechanisms, together with an aluminium step-ladder to help him peer over inconvenient walls and hedges. This new species sprang up to service the glossy, full-colour celebrity magazines created in the 1970s—and the photo every picture editor wanted was the shot of the future Queen of England.

Leading the hunt from 1975 onwards, and in many ways the inspiration of the new genre, were a pair of Murdoch journalists, the writer James Whitaker and the photographer Arthur Edwards, who worked in partnership, covering royal stories for the *Sun*. Rotund and affable, both men were Falstaffian characters, thoroughly relishing the walk-on parts they were to create for themselves in the royal drama, with a ribald and cheeky good humour which masked their steely intent.

Both had something of the old-fashioned court

correspondent about them, but they had taken the tradition into fresh territory. No newspaper had ever had a writer and photographer teamed up to cover nothing but royal stories. Whitaker took to going up to Sandringham in January, traditionally a fallow time for the gossip columns, and found he could pick up five or six reasonable stories about the royal shooting parties and their young female guests. The reporter would figure out the girls' identities with the help of binoculars, and would stand drinks in the pub later in the day for the royal protection officers, who were then less suspicious than they would later become. In the summer the *Sun*'s team would go up to Smiths Lawn, in Windsor Great Park, to watch Prince Charles playing polo—where, again, it was remarkably easy to pick out his female companion of the moment cheering in the stands.

'The prince was always very relaxed and informal in those days,' remembers Whitaker. 'He'd say, "Hello, Mr Edwards, how are the children?" And of course we would be very polite. We'd never go up and say, "Who are you shagging?"'

They didn't need to. Whitaker and Edwards soon worked out the network of country houses, including Broadlands, where Prince Charles would take his girlfriends at weekends. Some were long-term relationships, others were more casual. But any girl involved with Prince Charles knew that she risked getting caught by the lenses. It was part of a game which then seemed quite fun.

One of the *Sun*'s greatest coups was the discovery of where Prince Charles went skiing. Whitaker had airport contacts who alerted him when bookings were made with the codenames that

384

were used to disguise royal travellers, and early in 1978 he tracked the prince down to Klosters in Switzerland. Charles was staying there in the chalet rented by his friend Charlie Palmer-Tomkinson; and staying with the prince, the *Sun* revealed, was the attractive red-headed Lady Sarah Spencer, eldest daughter of Earl Spencer.

'The deal was we'd leave them all day, then go and knock on their door at five, five-thirty every night,' remembers Whitaker. 'Charles's detective, John McClean, a tough Scot, would come to the door and give us the news for the day, and Sarah used to love it—don't forget, we're only talking about three or four journalists in those days, not fucking hundreds. She'd sit on the radiator, swinging her legs and just joining in the general banter. And Charles came down carrying a transistor radio with a towel around his waist, saying, "Excuse me, can I interrupt this press conference? I want to go and have a bath."'

Building on this informal atmosphere, Whitaker invited Sarah out to lunch in London and persuaded her to do an in-depth interview for *Woman's Own* magazine. In it, she spoke freely about her youthful indiscretions, which had included drinking and getting expelled from her boarding school, West Heath, which she attended with her youngest sister Diana. She also gave Whitaker a poignant and detailed account of her battle with the eating disorder anorexia nervosa, and later sent him two photographs of herself when she had weighed under 80 pounds.

'She was wearing one of those ghastly woollen bikinis,' remembers Whitaker, 'just skin and bone, looking straight on. We couldn't possibly use the pictures. They were so painful that we sent them straight back to her and never even took a copy.'

Trying to downplay her relationship with the prince, Sarah claimed that she had dated 'thousands' of boyfriends.

Prince Charles was not amused when Sarah rang him to warn him that the article was coming out.

'You've just done something incredibly stupid,' he said, and he never dated Sarah Spencer again.

*   *   *

To start with, the Queen and Prince Philip contemplated their son's succession of romantic entanglements without panic. They were *laissez-faire* parents. Guided by Uncle Dickie, they had quiet confidence that Charles might eventually settle on the Brabournes' daughter, Amanda Knatchbull, whom they had known and liked from childhood. Charles had been developing a friendship with Amanda which miraculously escaped the attention of the press.

But in 1979 Amanda, just turning twenty-two, politely said 'no' to Prince Charles, confirming the prince's fear that 'to marry into the House of Windsor is a sacrifice that no one should be expected to make.' She was the latest in a line of dashed prospects. Lady Sarah Spencer; Lady Jane Wellesley, daughter of the Duke of Wellington; Sabrina Guinness of the brewing dynasty; Lady Leonora Grosvenor, sister of the richest man in England, the Duke of Westminster—no one could accuse Prince Charles of not testing candidates who were dynastically qualified for the job.

Charles was now approaching thirty, the

threshold which he had injudiciously set in his press interviews as the age by which he should get married, and as he despaired of finding a serious partner, he was tempted more and more by flighty ones. Like a pop star with groupies, the prince had discovered by his late twenties, in the most basic and physically gratifying fashion, how willingly—and totally—many people would surrender to the allure of royalty.

'Call me Arthur!' he would tell his one-night stands, according to Luis Basualdo, his debauched polo-playing companion, who would arrange the assignation and then eavesdrop outside. By deploying the third of his Christian names, Charles Philip Arthur George might have been seeking to place a little distance between his royal dignity and the passing encounter. But those close to him were not impressed. Friends noticed how the young man once known for his gentleness and sweet nature was beginning to display the short fuse of his father, while those with a sense of history detected the 'gnashes' of his grandfather, King George VI. Charles took to changing his plans at the last minute, often in pursuit of his latest sexual conquest.

Lord Mountbatten was close enough to see the trouble developing, and to deliver his warnings in the bluntest terms. Uncle Dickie had not intended the oats to grow this wild. Before his death he more than once reproved his honorary grandson for 'beginning on the downward slope that wrecked your Uncle David's life and led to his disgraceful abdication and futile life ever after'. After one row he wrote to Charles that he had 'spent the night worrying whether you would continue on your

387

Uncle David's sad course or take a pull'.

To Charles's credit, he did not lose touch with his spiritual side during this turbulent period. These are the years when the plant-talking started. In the mid-1970s the prince had found another father-figure in Laurens van der Post, the elderly explorer and philosopher who introduced him to the ideas of Jung and his search for 'an inner world of truth'. In an implied rebuke to Philip's bracing style of parenting, van der Post suggested that Charles should be shaping his life to be 'outward-bound the inward way'. The prince also became emotionally involved, for a time, with a persuasive young Indian woman who introduced him to Buddhism and eastern philosophy. Gripped by her ideas, Charles became persuaded by the arguments for vegetarianism and against the killing of animals.

It was when the prince gave up shooting at Sandringham that his parents finally seem to have taken alarm. The abstinence did not prove permanent, but it revealed a son and heir who was travelling along a very different track.

'There are times,' says a courtier, 'when the Queen and Prince Philip are just plain baffled by this eldest son they have produced.'

It was disturbing for a woman who had so earnestly followed the example of her father and predecessor to have a son who seemed to be looking anywhere for guidance except in the old-established places. While Dickie was riding guard, they had felt reassured. Right up to his death Mountbatten had been a regular visitor for lunch or tea at the Palace, seeing the Queen at least once a month. Charles's welfare had been a regular subject on their agenda. Neither the Queen nor her husband looked with much favour on the replacement that their son had found in Laurens van der Post. 'He was entrancing company,' recalls a courtier of the time, 'but you could tell it was all Walter Mitty.'

The elderly guru's suggestion for Silver Jubilee year had been that the heir to the throne should leave Britain to spend seven weeks communing with nature in the Kalahari Desert. When one added in the eastern mysticism, the nut cutlets and no shooting, the Prince of Wales was proving worryingly unorthodox.

More specific cause for concern was the news that some time in late 1979 Charles had resumed his relationship with Camilla Parker Bowles. Now mother of two children, Camilla was living on her own in Gloucestershire while her husband Andrew carried out a tour of duty at the British High Commission in Zimbabwe/Rhodesia, helping to wrap up the details of independence that had been negotiated at Lancaster House. Charles was looking for a house in the country and had his eye on Highgrove House near the market town of Tetbury in Gloucestershire—just a short drive away from the home of the Parker Bowleses.

The Queen was told of the affair in an almost eighteenth-century fashion.

'Ma'am,' she was informed via an intermediary, 'the Prince of Wales is having an affair with the wife of a brother officer, and the Regiment don't like it.'

The message was conveyed to the Palace by a senior officer in the Household Cavalry, with the request that it be passed to the Queen.

Elizabeth II is reported to have looked down

and said nothing. Silence was her defence in any difficult situation.

Charles's own staff found he was placing them in a difficult situation. In the spring of 1980 the prince flew out to Zimbabwe/Rhodesia for the independence ceremony, and the fact that Andrew Parker Bowles was already out there prompted the suggestion that Mrs Parker Bowles should fly out on the royal plane to join him. To the embarrassment of Charles's private secretaries, Camilla and Charles made little attempt to hide their closeness. The couple remained closeted in his private quarters of the plane, prompting staff sniggerings about the Mile High Club—and also some courtly anger.

In 1928, the undisguised womanising in Africa of the then Prince of Wales had led to the resignation of his private secretary, Tommy Lascelles. In 1980, the scion of another courtier dynasty, Edward Adeane, son of Sir Michael and grandson of Lord Stamfordham, did not resign. But when the prince's ostentatious flirting with Camilla at a dinner extended to obvious fumbling below the table in her husband's presence, Adeane, Charles's private secretary and treasurer, made no secret of his disapproval, and news of this incident also reached the Queen.

What was it about being Prince of Wales that made it so difficult to locate and stick with a simple, attractive, uncomplicated young girlfriend?

*   *   *

Early in September 1980, James Whitaker was patrolling the banks of the River Dee near

Balmoral with his binoculars. He was no longer working for the *Sun*. The success of Rupert Murdoch's daily tabloid had inspired the creation of a rival, the *Daily Star.* It was Britain's first new national newspaper for nearly half a century and Whitaker had been poached to head its royal coverage.

By now the 39-year-old journalist was the acknowledged prince of the swelling band of Fleet Street royal-watchers. He took particular pleasure in dressing in the costume appropriate for the occasion. He appeared at Ascot in his own morning suit, looking like a toff in top hat and tails; at Balmoral his camouflage took the form of tweeds, deerstalker hat, shooting stick and the indispensable binoculars, which he was training this bright autumn afternoon on a bank of the river where he had spotted Prince Charles fishing.

It is a peculiarity of the royal family's country estates that they are criss-crossed by public roads and footpaths with public rights of way, and the royal family have come to treat the presence of outsiders, and even snoopers, with a tolerance that is both libertarian and disdainful. Like a lion in a safari park, Prince Charles was displaying absolutely no sign he thought he might be under observation. But then a flash of mirror from behind a nearby tree trunk belied the pretence. The prince was well aware he was being observed, and had evidently warned his companion, presumably female, to go into hiding behind the tree. On her very first public sighting—or, rather, the sighting of her compact make-up mirror—Lady Diana Spencer was craftily watching the press as they craftily watched her.

'What a cunning lady,' reflected Whitaker. 'This one is clearly going to give us a lot of trouble.'

CHAPTER TWENTY-THREE

Whatever 'in love' Means

For me it was like a call of duty really—
to go and work with the people.

Diana, Princess of Wales, 1991

Diana Spencer had been invited to Balmoral in September 1980 so that the Queen and her husband could take a closer look at the girl whom insiders were already tipping as their future daughter-in-law. Diana was no stranger to either of them. Born on 1 July 1961, she was between Andrew and Edward in age, and had been one of the group of little children who rode bicycles and came round to watch movies with the princes when the royal family went to Norfolk. Diana saw *Chitty Chitty Bang Bang* among the comfy sofas of the Sandringham 'cinema'.

Diana Spencer actually grew up at Sandringham. Her father, the future Earl Spencer, farmed several hundred acres there, living in Park House, a ten-bedroom farmhouse on the estate, leased from the royal family. In 1954 'Johnny' Spencer had travelled as one of the Queen's equerries on her great post-coronation tour of the Commonwealth, and had been sent home early because he had been so lovesick for Frances Roche, whom he married later that year in Westminster Abbey. The Queen and Prince Philip had headed a sizeable delegation of royal guests—invited by both sides of the family. The bride was the daughter of Ruth, Lady Fermoy, the talented pianist who was a friend and confidante of Queen Elizabeth the Queen Mother.

Diana Spencer's close childhood and family links to the royal family were primary reasons why the Queen was disposed to consider the young woman well qualified for the responsibilities that went with being married to her eldest son. Diana could be expected to know the ropes. She had been a guest at a royal shooting party when her sister Sarah had been going out with Charles, and she was linked to the firm in an even more integral manner: her sister Jane was married to Robert Fellowes, the Queen's bright young assistant private secretary—who had family connections of his own.

'Robert is the only one of my private secretaries I have held in my arms,' the Queen remarked on one occasion, referring to the days when, as Princess Elizabeth, she had cradled the new baby son of Billy Fellowes, her father's estate manager at Sandringham.

That September in Balmoral, Diana's own tastes and attitude appeared perfectly adapted to the robust country style of the Queen and her family.

'We went stalking together,' remembered fellow guest Patty Palmer-Tompkinson. 'We got hot, we got tired, she fell into a bog, she got covered in mud, laughed her head off, got puce in the face, her hair glued to her forehead because it was pouring with rain . . . She was a sort of wonderful English schoolgirl who was game for anything.'

The whole family liked her. Edward and Andrew

competed with their elder brother to sit at her side at evening picnics, and Prince Philip eyed her appreciatively.

Charles himself had first taken serious notice of this bright and buxom young woman earlier that summer, after a polo match in Sussex. He had been sitting on a hay bale beside her at a barbecue, and when he mentioned the murder of Mountbatten she told him she had watched the funeral on television. She had sensed his loneliness, she told him, and his need for someone to care for him. A few weeks later Charles was already telling friends he had met the girl that he intended to marry, and Diana's stay at Balmoral that September confirmed his impression. Just a year after the death of his beloved honorary grandfather, Charles felt he had found 'the sweet-charactered girl' that Uncle Dickie had told him to look for.

For the Queen and her husband, the arrival of Diana Spencer seemed to promise an end to nut cutlets—and no more complaints from brother officers in the regiment.

*   *   *

James Whitaker, of course, knew none of this as he saw a young lady's compact mirror flashing from behind a tree on the river bank. He stayed watching intently until his quarry was forced to beat a retreat, walking straight up a steep hill through the woods, keeping her face firmly turned away from his gaze.

But among the other royal-watchers on Deeside was his old partner Arthur Edwards, still working at the *Sun*. A police contact of Edwards gave

Whitaker the lead that helped him identify Prince Charles's attractive blonde house guest as Lady Diana Spencer, aged nineteen. So before he filed his story to his own paper, Whitaker picked up the phone to brief his former deputy, Harry Arnold, who had taken his place on the *Sun.* It was the least he could do to repay Edwards for his help.

So it was that Harry Arnold, six hundred miles away from Balmoral at the time, got the scoop of the century.

'He's In Love Again', proclaimed the *Sun* on the morning of 8 September 1980, in its front-page headline. 'Is this the real thing for Charles at last?'

The *Daily Star* had chosen to bury Whitaker's report from the river bank on an inside page. It was the Murdoch paper that had grasped the news value of the information and had splashed it extravagantly on the slenderest of evidence. In that very first story the *Sun* also coined the famous nickname, 'Lady Di', taking firm possession of Diana's identity and reshaping it in the paper's own chirpy style.

With her doe-like eyes and wistful smile, Lady Diana Spencer was a gift to the little-recognised spine of Britain's tabloid journalism, the 'back bench', staffed by the humbly titled sub-editors who in fact provide the sinews and spirit of a world-conquering newspaper. It is the back bench who make up the headlines, devise the front page and inspire the jokes, campaigns, nicknames and general attitude that gives a paper a personality of its own. With Diana, the back bench needed just a photograph and a dateline, and around that they were to create a legend.

By the time Lady Di returned to London from

Balmoral, Whitaker had found out where she was living—in a flatshare in Coleherne Court, a red-brick mansion block between Earls Court and Fulham that was a traditional rookery for upper-class girls getting started in town. He stationed himself outside, greeting her cheerily as she came and went. She responded with the giggling, downcast head that became her trademark and the inspiration of another nickname, 'Shy Di'.

Within weeks, Coleherne Court had become a rugby scrum of scuffling cameras, notepads and microphones through which Diana demurely made her way each day. If falling in the bog and getting covered with mud had earned her the seal of royal approval at Balmoral, it was her handling of the daily gauntlet of harassment beside the Earls Court Road that won her the admiration and affection of the country.

Mishandling the press, of course, had been the downfall of Diana's elder sister.

'My sister Sarah spoke to the press,' Diana later told Mary Robertson, the American living in London who had employed her as a child-minder for a time. 'Frankly . . . that was the end of her.'

Observing her sister's mistakes had given Diana the advantage of a dummy run that no previous candidate had enjoyed in the arduous auditioning for Queen of England. In April 1978, the month after Sarah's disastrously over-revealing interview, James Whitaker had arrived outside the Guards' Chapel to cover the marriage to Robert Fellowes of the two girls' middle sister Jane.

'I know who you are,' said a smiling young Diana. 'You're the wicked Mr Whitaker. I know all about you.'

Now, in the autumn of 1980, the candidate knew better than to exchange more than a polite time-of-day with any of the plausible charmers who rang the bell at Coleherne Court.

The Queen thoroughly approved. Diana was going through the 1980s version of the 'Where's Philip?' situation, and she was handling it with a poise that a potential mother-in-law and employer could only admire.

'In those early days,' remembers one of her friends, 'she looked out at Diana coping all on her own and she really felt for her.'

In November 1980, Elizabeth II made one of her rare interventions, instructing her press secretary Michael Shea to deny a story in the *Sunday Mirror* which had claimed that Diana had spent two nights with Prince Charles on the royal train while it stood in a Wiltshire siding. As an experienced operator, Shea's preferred technique for burying the story would have been to ignore it. But he was acting on orders—which showed how concerned the Queen was to protect the reputation of someone she was now viewing as a potential future member of the family.

In the absence of Uncle Dickie, the Queen and her husband did what they could to help steer home the match. That Christmas Sandringham was overwhelmed by unprecedented numbers of reporters and photographers, who now gloried in a new name—the royal 'rat pack'. The family's holiday was ruined, and even the woman who had ridden out into the mist the previous January unperturbed by the IRA's new sniper sight seemed to crack under the pressure.

'Go away!' shouted the Queen from the window

of her passing car; 'can't you leave us alone?'

Diana duly arrived, but cut short her visit. The atmosphere inside the besieged house was surreal. The reporters and photographers might be outside in the darkness, but their curiosity hung over tea, dinner and every attempt to pretend that this was a house party like any other. The Queen and her husband felt that the nineteen-year-old was in an impossible situation.

It was Prince Philip who put their thoughts into words in a letter that he sent to Prince Charles in the early weeks of 1981. Press interest was creating an intolerable situation, which meant, said his father, that Charles must come to a rapid decision. Either he must offer Diana his hand in marriage, which would clearly please the country—and would also, his father made clear, please the rest of the family—or he must break off the relationship. The involvement of virtually the whole world through the intrusion of the mass media had created a curiously Victorian situation. In an age when young people routinely lived together before getting married, the intensive press reporting and speculation meant that Diana's reputation risked being 'compromised' if Charles did not decide one way or the other without delay.

Charles was later to complain bitterly of what he came to see as his father's ultimatum.

'Read it!' he would exclaim furiously, whipping the letter out of his breast pocket and thrusting it into the hands of friends and family with indiscriminate indignation.

'At some stage when the marriage started going wrong,' recalls one of those who read the note, 'he dug this letter out, folded it up, and started carrying it round and showing it to everyone, burning a hole in his pocket until just a year or so ago. It was his attempt to say that he was forced into it.'

Those who have been confronted with the prince's talisman of innocence say that the tone of the letter is matter-of-fact and quite kindly, exactly the sort of advice you might expect a supportive father to impart.

'It's very constructive and trying to be helpful,' says one who read it under Charles's indignant gaze. 'It certainly does not read as an ultimatum.'

In fact, the ultimatum had come from the extraordinary pressure of the press, which Charles himself had acknowledged a few years earlier when Lady Jane Wellesley had been staying with him at Sandringham. So many newspapers had tipped her as his bride that some ten thousand people drove from different corners of East Anglia to watch the couple attending church.

'Such was the obvious conviction that what they had read was true,' the prince later remarked to parliamentary journalists, 'that I almost felt I had better espouse myself at once so as not to disappoint so many people.'

Charles took his father's letter to mean that both his parents wanted him to marry Diana—which was actually the case. His grandmother, the Queen Mother, had spoken out warmly in favour of the match, and almost all his friends had counselled him to marry the girl, albeit in an elderly, slightly patronising sort of way. One of Diana's skills was generating the impression in strangers that she needed taking care of. The one person in his circle who sensed trouble was Penelope, Lady Romsey, the wife of Mountbatten's grandson, Norton, Lord Romsey, the elder brother of Nicholas who had been blown up by the IRA along with his grandfather. Penny Romsey felt she could sense a lack of intensity in Charles's feelings towards Diana, and she suspected that Diana, for her part, was more in love with the idea of being Princess of Wales than with the prince himself. She had also noticed that while Diana joined in the general family condemnation of press intrusion, she none the less always contrived to get herself photographed in an appealing light. When she and her husband raised these doubts with Charles, however, he brushed them aside—and rather angrily.

The prince was trapped by duty, by his own best intentions, and by the relentless expectation of the press—'the first time the Queen of England has been chosen by referendum', in the words of Barbara Cartland, the romantic novelist and mother of Johnny Spencer's second wife, Raine.

'I do very much want to do the right thing for this country and for my family,' wrote the prince to a friend as he wrestled with the decision.

He proposed to Diana early in February 1981, and she accepted on the spot.

'Can you find the words to sum up how you feel today?' the couple were asked when the news became public on 24 February 1981. '. . . In love?'

'Whatever "in love" means,' was Charles's famous reply. 'Put your own interpretation on it.'

*   *   *

Taken out of context, and with the wisdom of

hindsight, the prince's uncertain response has been frequently cited as evidence of his insincerity. In fact, the demeanour and body language of both Charles and Diana showed an understandable mixture of hope and uncertainty. It was a brave and honest answer, showing an understanding that marriage, especially for a future king, involved a lot more than the platitudes of love songs. It was also a spontaneous response to an unexpected and very intrusive question. When one of the Spanish infantas and her fiancé were asked the same thing on their engagement day a few years later, a press officer intervened. The details of private emotion, he said, were not proper matters for public discussion.

The BBC's archives reveal that Princess Anne and Mark Phillips had both firmly declined to discuss their private feelings in the questions put to them on the eve of their wedding in 1973, in the first ever televised pre-royal-wedding interview. That reticence reflected both Anne's highly developed sense of privacy and her fiancé's tongue-tied shyness. Eight years later the gap between chat-show familiarity and royal events had narrowed, but the 'in love?' question crossed a boundary that only became obvious later. If the nature of a couple's personal feelings for each other was a matter for public questioning and consumption on their engagement day, then presumably it remained so ever afterwards.

The mood of happy madness that the news of the engagement engendered was summed up outside the gates of the Palace, where television cameras found the bride-to-be's father, Earl Spencer, taking snapshots of the celebrating

401

crowds with a battered old camera.

'Diana has a sympathetic face,' he declared, 'the sort you can't help but trust.'

The childlike enjoyment that this Colonel Blimp character derived from his daughter's good fortune was one of the themes of the months that followed.

An uncle on her mother's side had already told James Whitaker that the world need not worry about his niece's virginity.

'I can assure you,' he said, 'she has never had a lover.'

The royal rat pack was so dumbstruck by this open addressing of the issue that was very much on their mind that none of them requested his authority for such a confident and intimate assertion. In fact, there was little appetite in Fleet Street to look for anything that might make their girl less than the perfect princess. Her parents had separated when Diana was six and had subsequently fought a bitter divorce and custody battle, to the considerable distress of their children, particularly Diana and her younger brother, Charles. But the details were glossed over, as Antony Armstrong-Jones's oriental mistress had been ignored in 1960. Scandal-digging had been suspended for the time being. In fact, Diana's coming from a broken home was offered as proof that she was thoroughly contemporary and in touch with the real world.

Britain went Di-crazy. A first step in explaining the mass dislocation of the British psyche that occurred when Diana died is to examine the craziness that consumed the country when she married. Lady Di haircuts proliferated; magazines that put her on the cover enjoyed 20 per cent more sales; the ingredients of her 'Sloane Ranger' style were exhaustively anatomised and copied.

With colour pictures travelling around the world, the fever was international. When Prince Charles travelled to Australia in April on a long-scheduled trip on which it was judged better his fiancée did not accompany him, he was greeted with huge placards displaying pictures of Diana and incessant requests about her welfare. From the other side of the world, the prince came to contemplate his future wife through the television images and newspaper pictures that were entrancing everyone else. James Whitaker discussed this with the prince's biographer, Anthony Holden. This was the moment, they agreed, when Charles did finally contract the enjoyable emotional fever and excitement which 'in love' conventionally means.

'That was where he really got the idea of her,' says Holden. 'He saw what the world saw.'

The summer of the royal wedding of 1981 saw public excitement and celebration surpass even the levels of the Silver Jubilee. The essential car accessory of the season was a cut-out image of Lady Di to stick in your side rear window, complete with a cardboard arm that waved. The collective soppiness that overtakes most normal people at wedding time overwhelmed the entire nation.

But that summer was also marked, in the Toxteth area of Liverpool and in other deprived inner-city areas, by the most bitter and destructive race riots that twentieth-century Britain had ever seen. With unemployment mounting, urban ghettos exploded in scenes reminiscent of America's 'long hot summers' of the 1960s. News bulletins presented a bizarre combination of urban ghettos in flames alongside wedding dress speculation and the competition to bake the best wedding cake.

On 13 June 1981 they also presented a curious and alarming tale of shooting in the Mall. Marcus Sarjeant, an unemployed youth of seventeen, had fired off six blank cartridges at close range as the Queen rode to the Trooping the Colour ceremony on Horse Guards Parade. 'If there had been real bullets in that gun he would have shot the Queen,' said John Heasman, a St John Ambulance man who helped wrestle the assailant to the ground.

The young attacker, who had been wearing a Charles-and-Di lapel badge, came from Folkestone in Kent, where it was discovered he had scrawled a warning some days before on a local bus: 'Anti-Royalist Movement is going to assassinate the Queen at the Trooping of the Colour on 13 June 1981.' He was charged, and later sentenced to five years in prison, under the 1842 Treason Act that had been brought in to cope with the deranged stalkers who discharged blanks at Queen Victoria.

It was another token of an emotionally overwrought summer—though most reports preferred to concentrate on the good horsemanship and sangfroid of the Queen, as she steadied her horse Burmese and rode on to arrive at her birthday parade on the stroke of eleven. She was reported to have been 'ashen-faced' as she looked at the gunman, but kept on riding 'as cool as a cucumber'.

There was talk of closed carriages for the wedding procession six weeks later, but on 29 July 1981, the atmosphere in the Mall was relaxed and carefree again. People had slept out for several days to get good vantage points, and TV crews had arrived from all over the world.

Twenty-eight years earlier, on the morning of Elizabeth II's coronation in 1953, the crowds who had slept out in the streets had been warmed with the news in that morning's papers that Mount Everest had been conquered by an expedition of British Commonwealth climbers. The report of Sir Edmund Hillary's triumph had been sent in from the Himalayas by James Morris, a young reporter from *The Times*. On 29 July 1981, James Morris, now Jan Morris, sent rather a different despatch to the *Times* correspondence page.

'I would like to put on record,' she wrote, '. . . one citizen's sense of revulsion and foreboding at the ostentation, the extravagance and the sycophancy surrounding today's wedding of the heir to the British throne.'

Looking back with the benefit of hindsight—to which she is entitled, having placed her then most unusual and unpopular reservations on the record—Jan Morris recalls feeling that she was witnessing 'the last days of the Romanovs' as she contemplated Britain's royal wedding fever in July 1981. The vulgarity of the overblown emotion seemed 'sleazy and sinister' to her, and she was struck by how many of those who later wrote to her—nearly half—shared her misgivings.

But, writing at the same time in *Country Life*, Marghanita Laski offered a kindlier view. The Cinderella story is the most necessary female myth, she suggested. Romance is the beautiful unattainable, the fantasy of life as we would wish it to be—so much more attractive than the world as it really is.

CHAPTER TWENTY-FOUR

Permission to Kiss

It seems to me a pity that *anyone*, however stupid, can take a photographic snap.

Elizabeth, Duchess of York, 1936

'Go on, give her a kiss,' urged Prince Andrew as his elder brother went out on the balcony for yet another appearance with his bride on the afternoon of 29 July 1981. The cheering crowds, massed against the railings, were calling for it too. But Prince Charles held back. No one had ever kissed on the Buckingham Palace balcony before. The seven modern royal marriages that had ended up on the Palace balcony had all been rounded off with nothing more intimate than smiles and decorous waves. Prince Charles knew he must get his mother's permission for the extra gesture—and Elizabeth II, seduced like everyone else by the high emotion of the day, nodded her assent. So Charles and Diana went back outside, and this time shyly, momentarily, but just long enough for the telephoto lenses and motor-winds to catch the contact, they established the affectionate precedent.

Sentimental love and pageantry—the wedding day gloriously combined two of the core, tug-at-the-heart-strings elements of popular monarchy.

'The sort of thing', as the *Sunday Times* put it, paraphrasing Noël Coward, 'that we over-do so well.'

'The Royal Family of England', observed the *Boston Globe*, 'pulls off ceremonies the way the army of Israel pulls off commando raids.'

Bells, bands and youthful beauty worked their alchemy. Mass-Observation's reports of royal wedding street parties were a rerun of the collective celebration of the Silver Jubilee, with mentions of a new phenomenon—video recorders, which created an instant, home-made souvenir and doubled the enjoyment for couch potatoes. In one Oldham street the women voted for continuous reruns of the day's events, while the men opted in favour of playing Space Invaders.

Watching the video was how the royal family itself relived the fun—at Claridges, where Patrick Lichfield's sister, Lady Elizabeth Shakerley, had organised a party featuring large television screens. Dry martini in hand, the Queen watched herself intently, pointing delightedly whenever the cameras caught one of her famous glum faces. It was noticed that she beamed with particular pleasure whenever images of her new daughter-in-law appeared. Prince Philip danced a lot with Princess Grace of Monaco. He was wearing a saucy straw hat which said 'Charles and Diana' in red, white and blue around the hatband, and it was only with difficulty that Elizabeth II prevailed upon her husband to take it off before they walked out into the street. By then it was one-thirty in the morning and the Queen hitched up the hem of her skirt and did a little jig as she said her goodbyes. 'I'd love to stay and dance all night,' she said.

Three weeks later, they welcomed the couple back from their honeymoon with similar gusto.

Two hundred staff and estate workers lined the drive leading to the front door of Balmoral as the honeymooners were pulled up from the castle gates in an old pony trap drawn by four muscular Highland retainers. The Queen ran alongside, skipping to keep up, while her husband pedalled on an ancient bicycle, racing round and round, Paul Newman/Butch Cassidy-style, before shooting off ahead to be waiting at the front door.

*   *   *

The Queen's annual summer holiday in Balmoral is the high spot of her year. She could not be happier than when out in the crisp autumn setting of the hills—and it is more than a matter of leisure and renewal. Her two months in the Highlands give life to the dream of the girl whose childhood yearning was to live in the country with lots of horses and dogs.

The logistics are formidable. If there is one ritual in the life of Elizabeth II that recalls the progresses in which medieval monarchs packed up all their belongings to travel the land with their entire household, it is the annual royal migration to Balmoral. A detachment of troops spends several weeks in late July filling 40-foot-long containers with mattresses, dog baskets, brass pots and kitchen equipment to be ferried up to the Highlands, where it is all elaborately unpacked and put in place before the royal arrival.

Balmoral is not a 'second home' in the sense that the British middle classes use the term, filled with furniture and stocked with everything, down to food in the freezer, ready for the moment the key is turned on Friday night. For nine months of the year the castle is largely bare and draughty, maintained by a skeleton staff.

'There are the old wooden floorboards, and the lights are a bit dim,' says someone who has been there in the off-season. 'It smells a bit like a forgotten old country post office'—until the moment in early August when the castle becomes the royal summer camp. Then the Queen's gun dogs (Labradors) are brought up from Sandringham with their handlers, and the Queen's horses are boxed north from Windsor with their grooms. The 'Iron Huts', built to house the entourage of the Russian royal family when the Tsar came to stay in 1896, are filled with the pages, maids, cooks and cleaners from Buckingham Palace on their annual jaunt to the Highlands.

For the royal staff—split into two batches—it is part of a double holiday. You have the option of doing one month at Balmoral and then having a month off, or vice versa. While the royal family picnic and enjoy themselves, there are evening barbecues and bonfires for the retainers in the Iron Huts. Song sheets are issued—no. 36 is 'Cockles and Mussels', no. 38 'I Love to Go A'Wandering', complete with 'fol-de-rees' and 'fol-de-rahs'. Two ghillies' balls are organised which the royal family attend, one for each batch of staff, and Scottish dancing lessons are laid on for new staff. In the early 1980s many of the household were recruited, as a matter of policy, from labour exchanges in areas of high unemployment. So young Merseyside lads and Tyneside lasses were initiated into the mysteries of the eightsome reel or learnt the words of song no. 40—'Maybe It's Because I'm a

Londoner'.

During this annual summer migration the personal quarters of Buckingham Palace are deserted, with the furniture under dustsheets and the decorators roaming free. The wholesale character of the annual move to the north was part of the difficulty Elizabeth II experienced in visualising the possibility of coming down to London in the week following Diana's death in September 1997. With the exception of a few wartime summers, Balmoral has been her home base every August and September for more than sixty years. Subsidising its ancient, shooting-estate way of life costs her £1 million each year, an extravagance that dwarfs her relatively self-financing racing activities—and with the expense goes sentiment. Prime Ministers who do not enjoy their semi-compulsory autumn weekend at Balmoral have failed a significant test. These certainly included Margaret Thatcher, who was so keen to escape she would get up early on her last day and leave before breakfast.

The apparent appetite that the young Diana had displayed for Balmoral life in the September before her engagement had won her particular kudos with her future mother-in-law. It augured well for Diana's integration into the family, and seemed to promise a future queen consort who would keep up the old traditions. In August 1981, much excited discussion went into planning the welcome for the newly-weds, and the staff piled out of the Iron Huts in force.

Everyone thought Charles and Diana looked tanned and relaxed. 'You never saw a couple so much in love,' remembers one of the reception committee. On 19 August the honeymooners went down to the banks of the River Dee for a press photocall, Charles in a kilt and open shirt, Diana in a houndstooth check suit. Snuggling up together, smiling and joking, while the clattering motor-winds ran through film by the spoolful, they appeared the very image of love. Responding to questions shouted by the serried ranks of cameramen, the new princess reported that married life was something she could 'very much recommend'.

But all was not as it appeared. Diana later said that things had started to go wrong on the second night after the wedding, when Charles produced seven Laurens van der Post books, his guru's suggestion for honeymoon reading. On *Britannia* the new princess was distressed at having to make polite conversation with the captain and officers every night—and, discussing it later, Charles saw her point. He acknowledged that on the royal yacht, 'even an intimate dinner by candlelight was hardly a private affair, accompanied as it was by the camaraderie of senior officers at the table and a band of Royal Marines playing a romantic medley in the background.'

Diana's unhappiness at the all-in-a-gang character of royal life on *Britannia* continued when she arrived at Balmoral, with its stream of distinguished and largely elderly visitors, plus the supporting cast of ladies-in-waiting and equerries. As a young man, Diana's father had been one of these auxiliaries, who can bump up the routine small 'family' meal or picnic at Balmoral to a dozen or more people. 'It's tremendous fun,' says a regular visitor. 'But it is a bit like Scout camp or boarding school.'

This essentially Edwardian lifestyle had its conventions. On shooting mornings at Balmoral, the men would head off to the moors and the women would join them later for lunch. Mornings were when the Queen dealt with her boxes and correspondence with her private secretary—another permanent member of the cast. Those left in the house amused themselves in the morning, with midday or 12.15 set as the moment for them to gather in the hall. Elizabeth II would appear in headscarf, tweeds and sensible shoes, ready to lead the party to the Land Rovers waiting outside. It went without saying that no one should be a minute late.

'So there we'd all be, waiting in the hall,' recalls a guest, 'making polite conversation—and no Diana. So after a time the Queen would send off a footman, and he'd come back looking embarrassed. "Sorry, Ma'am, the Princess of Wales will not be joining the party for lunch."'

The Queen would go very silent. Friends saw the danger signs—the pursed lips, the quick extra blink of the eyes. Staying in your room at lunchtime was something you did only if you were ill or rather odd. It clearly amounted to opting out. Then the smile would return, a trifle strained, and Her Majesty would move off resolutely in picnic mode.

'The Queen's thought in those early days,' says a friend, 'was that Diana was a "new girl" who was finding it very difficult to get used to things.'

That was an understatement. For if Balmoral stood for everything that Elizabeth II loved, it soon came, for her daughter-in-law, to embody all the stuffiness and formality that upset her about royal life. Diana found it threatening, and the fact that her not-so-youthful husband clearly fitted very happily into these middle-aged rituals made her feel even more lonely and trapped. A year before, the prospect of being a princess had seemed fun. Confronted with the reality, the twenty-year-old's psyche, more fragile than anyone realised, now started to unravel. Diana later described how she would go up to Balmoral feeling strong and would 'come away depleted of everything'.

'I tune into all their moods,' she explained, 'and, boy, are there some undercurrents there!'

In search of less daunting company, she took to going through the service door to sit on the draining board, chatting with the maids and pages who were so much closer to her in age and outlook. Before she became a princess Diana had hired herself out as a house cleaner for a time.

'She was always very warm and friendly,' remembers one. 'But it caused trouble. The alarm system was switched on after dinner, and it had to be changed so she could go on coming down to visit.'

The secret that Diana hid from her friends below stairs, not to mention her husband and his family, was that she was by now spending much of her time alone in her room, putting her fingers down her throat to induce herself to vomit. The princess was suffering from the complex and deeply rooted eating disorder that had only been given a medical name two years previously—bulimia nervosa.

Bulimia takes its ugly-sounding name from the Greek words bous, meaning ox, and *limos*, meaning hunger—literally, 'bull-hunger'. For many years it

413

lurked inside the syndrome of anorexia nervosa, from which Diana's sister Sarah had suffered. But while anorexics avoid food, literally starving themselves, bulimics seek control over their diet and body image by binge-eating and then purging themselves with self-induced vomiting. Both conditions may relate to distressed early childhoods—in Diana's case the 'broken home' which people had optimistically thought of as a token of her normality.

Another characteristic of bulimia is that it is brought on by stress or pressure. Diana later confessed to some brief bouts in earlier years, but it had been straight after her engagement, when she moved into Buckingham Palace for the five-month run-up to her marriage, that the trouble really started. The designers David and Elizabeth Emanuel noticed her weight loss as they took in the seams of the wedding dress after each fitting. Their client's waist measurement went down dramatically from 29 inches at the time of her engagement to 23½ inches. Fashion commentators welcomed her developing svelteness and approvingly noted how a pudgy teenager had metamorphosed into an elegant young woman. The puppy fat was gone. The cheekbones emerged.

'You look beautiful,' the lip-readers saw Charles say as his bride reached the altar.

'Beautiful for you,' she replied, with a line that could have been crafted by her step-grandmother Barbara Cartland, whose romantic novels Diana had devoured as a young teenager.

Diana's personal insecurities had blended tragically with her ambition as she sought to make herself the perfect princess for her husband, his family and the people. By the time of the honeymoon, she recalled, 'the bulimia was appalling, absolutely appalling. It was rife, four times a day on the yacht. Anything I could find I would gobble up and be sick two minutes later— very tired, so, of course, that slightly got the mood swings going in the sense that one minute one would be happy, next blubbing one's eyes out.'

Charles ascribed his wife's perplexing shifts of mood to the pressures of adapting to her new and exacting role, the problem he had articulated so frequently when discussing his search for a future queen. He invited Laurens van der Post up to Balmoral for some Kalahari-style marriage counselling.

'Laurens didn't understand me,' recalled Diana—which was not surprising. The flawed emotional history of the guru in whom Charles placed such trust embraced three marriages and the seduction, when he was in his thirties, of an under-age girl, whose illegitimate offspring he declined to recognise.

The royal doctors guided Diana in a more constructive direction. The princess was later to blame the callous and unfeeling House of Windsor, who expected so much and tolerated so little, for what went wrong with her marriage. But when the Queen and her husband were confronted by weepings and collapses within weeks of their son's wedding, they took action. Far from pretending there was no problem, the family turned to the best medical and psychiatric help they could find, and Diana was flown down to London.

'All the analysts and psychiatrists you could ever dream of came plodding in trying to sort me out,' she later recalled. 'Put me on high doses of Valium and everything else.'

The princess told none of these doctors about her self-induced vomiting, lying to them as she also lied to her friends. At that date, people knew enough about eating disorders to wonder if Diana was suffering from anorexia, and a few friends tackled her directly about her weight loss. But the princess's response was to joke how she always cleared her plate at mealtimes, then raided the fridge for tubs of ice-cream.

The bulimic's deception is a perverse form of empowerment. The world was fooled, and that encouraged the deceit. As the newspapers delightedly welcomed the ever more slimline princess, Diana was enticed even further down the binge-and-purge path on which she had embarked when she entered Buckingham Palace. What is a princess for, if not for looking at?

*   *   *

The bottom line of Diana's recruitment into the royal family had been made unsentimentally clear when she had been sent for a fertility test prior to her engagement announcement. Within three months of marriage, it was mission accomplished.

'Fine,' she later remembered of the news that she was pregnant early in October 1981. 'Great excitement.'

But now she had to cope with morning sickness as well as her bulimia, and she looked grey and gaunt when she accompanied Charles on a three-day visit to Wales that autumn.

'Sick as a parrot, rained the whole time,' she

416

recalled.

Elizabeth II stepped in again. Knowing nothing of Diana's illness, she interpreted her daughter-in-law's nerves entirely in terms of her pregnancy and the pressure of media intrusiveness, and she reckoned she could certainly help with the second one.

A cold December morning at the end of the momentous royal wedding year saw a dozen Fleet Street editors, together with senior broadcasters from BBC and ITV, filing into Buckingham Palace. The last such summons had come twenty-four years previously in 1957, also on the Queen's personal initiative, when Commander Colville had successfully appealed to the press to stay away from the young Charles at school. Now Michael Shea, a fluent Scot with a sideline in thriller writing, expressed the concern of the entire royal family over the invasion of the pregnant princess's privacy. As the lords of Fleet Street sat either side of a long polished table, solemnly pondering like delegates at a grand international conference, the press secretary drew particular attention to a recent incident when a photographer had pursued Diana into the village shop at Tetbury, near Highgrove. The Queen, said Shea, would be grateful if the press would co-operate in not placing stress on the monarchy's delicate new recruit.

The one editor who tried to turn the peace conference into a press conference was Barry Askew, editor of the Murdoch-owned *News of the World*. Was the princess heading for a nervous breakdown, he wanted to know? Was there a risk of miscarriage? Was the word 'trauma' appropriate?

Michael Shea tried to explain that the problem

417

was more subtle than that.

'She's not like the rest of us,' explained the Queen, who joined the gathering for drinks afterwards. 'She's very young.'

'It's very difficult drawing a line between public and private,' persisted Barry Askew, unwilling to let the subject drop. 'I mean, when she's out at the shops she's in public. Why shouldn't she be photographed?'

'All she wants to do,' replied Elizabeth II, 'is to buy some winegums without being disturbed.'

'If she wants to buy winegums,' argued Askew, 'she should send a servant to get them.'

'That', responded the Queen icily, 'is an extremely pompous remark, if I may say so.'

The apparently trivial exchange spelt out some important issues. The Queen and Rupert Murdoch's man were tussling over territory, with Askew arguing that the streets were his, while Elizabeth II claimed the more subtle right for the most sought-after member of her family, when off-duty, to retain some sort of privacy while in public. Askew was also advancing the class-based justification of tabloid intrusiveness, that people living in big houses with servants were fair game. It was the right of little people to be nosy, ran this logic, since they were the source of the wealth and deference that created such privilege.

This was an explicit principle of policy for Askew's colleague, Kelvin MacKenzie, the editor of the *Sun*, who had declined to attend the Palace meeting. MacKenzie did not wish to be party to any agreement or 'understanding' that he did not intend to keep. 'Kelvin's attitude', recalls James Whitaker, 'was that he must have the total freedom to be nice to them one day, then kick them in the bollocks the next. It was actually very honest and proper, though you might not approve of what he did.' MacKenzie positively enjoyed upsetting the Palace. Raucous cheers from the back bench greeted the receipt in the *Sun*'s offices of royal writs and complaints, and, sliding from populist principle to commercialism, MacKenzie frankly acknowledged that there were sales and circulation in such a stance.

Two months later, two rival teams of British tabloid journalists—from the *Sun* and the *Daily Star*—rose before dawn in the Bahamas. They spent two and a half hours crawling through the sticky undergrowth of Eleuthera Island to capture pictures of Diana sunning herself in what she thought was total privacy, obviously pregnant and wearing a bikini. 'What a Lovely Di!' proclaimed MacKenzie's front page with glee.

When Michael Shea issued a stern statement expressing the Queen's extreme displeasure at this 'black day for British journalism', both papers declined to apologise. The *Sun* even republished the offending pictures, with a story lauding the bravery and enterprise of the sleuths who obtained them.

James Whitaker had spearheaded the *Daily Star* team. When he next met Diana, he was greeted with less disapproval than he expected.

'Actually,' the princess confided, 'I didn't mind nearly as much as the Palace said.'

'Did you make much money from the pictures?' she asked Arthur Edwards, the *Sun* photographer, with interest.

'No,' he replied, explaining he was on a regular

salary.

'Pass the Kleenex,' she replied with a grin.

The problem for Michael Shea and his royal employer was that the rebellious young princess had a subversive streak which gave her common cause with her press tormentors. She had come to enjoy their cheeky wooing. For all her tears and tantrums, an important part of Diana was delighted and flattered to be pursued into a sweet shop or to a tropical island halfway round the world. She would study the resulting photograph closely when it appeared in the newspaper next day. The British press and public had got hooked on regular doses of their radiantly beautiful princess, and Diana herself was getting equally ensnared. It was a collusive process.

'She thought she could outsmart them,' remembers a royal press officer sadly. 'She never realised they were playing a different game.'

James Whitaker had been shocked in the days of Sarah Spencer's relationship with Prince Charles to discover that Sarah had hired Dunn's, the press clippings agency, to send her every story about herself, which she lovingly collected in huge albums that recorded the story of her royal romance. Now her younger sister was scanning the papers just as avidly, and was increasingly steadying her wobbly self-esteem with the balm of popular approval. Fame was going to Diana's head. It was the curse of Uncle David. The new princess was starting to mainline on her own celebrity.

*　　　*　　　*

The Queen and her family did not yet realise that

their popular recruit was becoming a fifth column in their midst. The birth of Prince William in June 1982 provided some respite from the troubles, and there were many genuinely loving interludes in the Waleses' tempestuous relationship. The photographers lurking in the undergrowth off Eleuthera captured enchanting pictures of Charles and Diana cuddling lovingly in the surf, which the tabloid editors and their proprietors, in a sudden fit of scruple, thought 'too intimate' to publish. In truth, the couple's affection made obvious the privacy of the situation on which the cameras were intruding. 'Banging', 'blitzing', 'ripping', 'smudging', 'hosing', 'whacking'—the photographers' own words for capturing their prey made clear the fundamental aggression of their trade.

From the PR standpoint, Charles and Diana were already an accident waiting to happen. Michael Shea took to warning photographers who came in for special photo-sessions to pay no attention if the prince and princess should happen to 'blow up'. They were two demanding egos, both looking for support that neither could give the other. 'It was like working for two pop stars,' remembered one of their staff.

As Diana's bulimia continued, Charles's nerves frayed, and she retreated, spreading her resentment against her husband to include the entire royal 'firm'—though she sometimes found her mother-in-law surprisingly supportive.

When Princess Grace of Monaco's car crashed in 1982 with fatal results, Diana was determined to attend the funeral. She identified with the glamorous outsider who had made the devil's bargain and surrendered her style and beauty to a stuffy bachelor prince. In the spring of 1981 Diana's first formal evening engagement had been a poetry reading in London by the film star-turned-princess, and afterwards the two women had compared notes in the ladies' room. 'Don't worry,' Grace had sympathised sardonically in her Philadelphia drawl. 'It will get worse.'

Charles was discouraging about Diana's wish to go to Monaco. He told her to contact Philip Moore, the private secretary who had replaced Martin Charteris, and Moore, who was definitely of the old school, said 'No'. The new girl had not been in the job long enough. So Diana wrote directly to the Queen, who overruled her private secretary. In September 1982 Diana flew off to Monaco on her first solo assignment representing the entire royal family, carrying it off with an aplomb that won the Queen's quiet approval. Elizabeth II had less trouble than her son adjusting to the uncomfortable fact that this young woman who had never studied constitutional history or looked at a state paper was becoming as royal as any Windsor in the eyes of the world—and was in many respects more people-friendly.

'The Queen', says one of her closest advisers in these years, 'developed a real admiration for Diana's ability in that sort of going-out-in-public work, which had never come naturally to her.'

This feeling was picked up by a new television show, the satirical *Spitting Image*, in which grotesque puppets, the creations of the artists Peter Fluck and Roger Law, lampooned the high and mighty in the style of the great eighteenth-century caricaturists, Gillray and Rowlandson. Diana was not physically depicted in the first series, prepared in 1982 and screened the following year. The programme-makers were worried about taking on such a hugely popular figure, while the puppet-makers could not come up with a satisfactorily Diana-like doll. But the princess-superstar dominated the Windsor sketches as the brilliant and temperamental top of the cast list—the unseen diva who had locked herself in her bedroom and was declining to emerge.

'Does one want to do a jigsaw with one?' pleaded a cringing and bat-eared Prince Charles outside his wife's door, and was brusquely ordered to go away.

The Queen was also told to get lost by her daughter-in-law, and turned to the camera, oozing with admiration. 'She's so lovely,' crooned the majestic puppet, which featured huge horse-like teeth. 'So wonderful to work with, a real pro.'

Roger Law, a lifelong antimonarchist who was proud of his Fenland roots in Oliver Cromwell country, conceived his Queen puppet as a benevolent figure. The real object of his spleen was the right-wing extremism of Margaret Thatcher, for whom the puppeteer shaped Elizabeth II, by contrast, as a kindly foil—a moderate Marxist wearing a Campaign for Nuclear Disarmament badge. The Queen was even more of a victim than the rest of the country, according to *Spitting Image*, since she actually had to deal personally with the insufferable woman who happened to be Prime Minister.

Spitting Image's satire expressed a certain affection for the humanity of what was seen as an eccentric and well-meaning family, bemused by its bizarre situation and trying to do its best. Shows

423

that were advertised for their royal content got high ratings, and the highest of all went to the appearance of the Queen Mother as a saintly figure who, like Dr Dolittle, talked with the animals.

'Any tips for the three-thirty at Aintree today?' the Queen Mother was shown asking a well-informed racehorse down the telephone—and on receiving the tip, the 84-year-old headed off to the bookmakers.

'I think I'm going to have to sell one of my nice pink hats.'

The Palace old guard found such irreverence hard to take. When Michael Shea produced a copy of *Private Eye* magazine for the amusement of the private secretaries at one of the daily morning press meetings, Philip Moore seized it from him, tore it into four pieces and flung it into the wastepaper basket.

But the backhanded embrace of the satire business was reflected in opinion polls showing the highest royal approval ratings of Elizabeth II's entire reign. The early and middle 1980s saw royal popularity reach one of its historic highs. Love, marriage and pregnancy were ideal feelgood factors—and alongside the birth of the royal babies, William and Harry, in 1982 and 1984, came a good old-fashioned war. Margaret Thatcher's military expedition to recapture the Falkland Islands from Argentina in the spring of 1982 was a gunboat adventure which, unlike Suez, went spectacularly well. It contributed to a national headiness which had an additional royal component.

'Prince Andrew is a serving officer,' said a statement from Buckingham Palace on 1 April

1982, responding to suggestions that the Queen might like her second son exempted from active service, 'and there is no question in her mind that he should go.'

The presence of Andrew in the British task force as it headed into Exocet territory gave special poignancy to the Queen's words on 26 May, when she went to Northumberland to open the Kielder Dam. 'Our thoughts today are with those who are in the South Atlantic and our prayers are for their success and a safe return to their homes and loved ones.'

Victory was not bloodless: 255 Britons and 652 Argentines died in the conflict, and Andrew risked his own life. As a helicopter pilot, he was assigned the duty of dangling huge sheets of foil as a decoy to the enemy's deadly Exocet missiles, which had proved lethal in their surprise attacks on British ships. The handsome warrior prince returned with a long-stemmed rose clenched between his teeth, to be greeted by his mother on the quayside in an emblematic picture, and then promptly threw himself into a succession of red-blooded flings appropriate to a conquering hero.

The tabloids had a new hero in 'Randy Andy', and when his heart settled on Sarah Ferguson, the daughter of Prince Charles's polo manager, in 1985, it was counted no obstacle that she had a colourful 'past'. She had been living with a playboy racing driver twenty-two years older than herself when Andrew started courting her. But Charles had got the sweet-natured virgin, and it was considered acceptable for the younger brother to pick a bride more in contact with the mores of the time.

'Fergie' was a character, like her name, made in tabloid heaven, and her marriage to Andrew in July 1986 was a downmarket version of his elder brother's fairy-tale wedding of five years earlier. On the night before, the couple spiced up their version of the now-hallowed pre-wedding television interview with their own attempt at a pop video: a mawkish sequence of dancing and embracing to the hit of the moment, Jennifer Rush's 'The Power of Love'.

When the couple appeared on the Palace balcony the next day they even parodied 'the kiss' that Andrew had choreographed five years earlier. As *The Times* described it, 'The Duke broadly cupped his ear to the chanting of: "Give her a kiss then!" So he gave her a kiss; not a moth's kiss, but a smacking naval kiss like a tyre explosion, or as if he were trying to clear the drains.' The slapstick collusion between audience and performers marked yet another erosion of royal distance. Ostensibly admiring and adulatory, the crowd was actually giving the prince instructions, and he was performing to order, hamming up his response. And what of the august *Times*—owned since 1981 by Rupert Murdoch—which would once have reported such an event with clipped respect, but now injected its own note of burlesque?

Mock videos, bawdy kisses and glamorous photographs of young royals in the papers every day—all this might make the family more popular, but it also made for a dangerous familiarity. Cutting loose from traditional moorings, the new royal generation was taking the monarchy into the marketplace, consummating the long-sought marriage with celebrity culture which had started in the reign of Queen Victoria. The Latin word *celebritas* carries the democratic connotation of being touched by the masses. But it also carries connotations of the self-seeking and the notorious—of things that do not last. Celebrity is not the same as fame.

CHAPTER TWENTY-FIVE

Elizabeth Regina

If any member of the tribe ever sees inside the hut, then the whole system of the tribal chiefdom is damaged and the tribe eventually disintegrates.

David Attenborough, BBC wildlife film-maker

Early on the morning of 9 July 1982, Elizabeth II was awoken in Buckingham Palace by the sound of her bedroom door opening, and by heavy, unfamiliar footsteps that appeared to be making for her bed. She knew it was not her footman, who was out exercising the corgis at that time. So, in her most imperious voice, she said, 'It's too early yet for tea.'

The intruder, Michael Fagan, a 31-year-old unemployed labourer, paid no heed. He kept walking across the room, drew back the curtains and then sat down on Her Majesty's bed. Apparently schizophrenic, with an incoherent manner, the tousled and scruffy figure was carrying the fragment of a heavy glass ashtray with which, he later said, he was planning to slash his wrists.

'I want to know who I am,' he later explained to the police. 'She can tell me . . . I am in love with Elizabeth Regina.'

Confronted by a fixated stalker in more intimate and threatening circumstances than Queen Victoria ever experienced, Elizabeth II displayed cool presence of mind.

'I got out of bed,' she later related, 'put on my dressing gown and slippers, drew myself up to my full regal height [5 feet 4 inches], pointed to the door and said, "Get out"—and he didn't.'

In his own account of the conversation, Fagan said he told the Queen that her Palace security was 'diabolical'—and so it proved. This was the north Londoner's second dawn jaunt around the corridors of the royal headquarters, which he had entered by shinning up a drainpipe on the other side of the quadrangle. On his last visit just a week or so earlier he had opened and sampled a bottle of wine that had been sent to the Prince and Princess of Wales to mark the birth of Prince William on 21 June.

The Queen pressed her night alarm button but got no response, then had to make two calls to the Palace switchboard before a policeman eventually arrived.

'I have never heard the Queen so angry,' said a footman after Fagan had finally been escorted away. On her bed the intruder had left bloodstains.

Public interest focused on where Prince Philip had been at the time. It was a wonderful pretext for speculation on the taboo subject of the royal sleeping arrangements. It was disclosed that, facing a 6 a.m. departure for a distant official

428

engagement, the prince had slept in his own quarters. The Queen later said that it was a blessing her husband had not been there—'I knew that all hell would break loose.'

Two weeks later, in the fall-out from the mind-boggling breach of security, the Queen's personal protection officer, Commander Michael Trestrail, resigned from the Metropolitan Police after confessing to a long-term relationship with a male prostitute. Fagan, for his part, got off scot-free. He was not charged with trespass, and a jury later found him not guilty on the only charge he had had to face—'stealing' the wine that he had sampled from Prince William's gifts. For a brief season he became a mini TV celebrity.

The papers were divided as to the meaning of the tragi-comic episode. All praised the Queen's 'cool as a cucumber' reactions, comparing them to the impassive courage with which she had faced fire in the Mall the previous summer. There was concern at such a crass security lapse at a moment when the IRA was more active in London than ever—on 19 July two fatal explosions blew up uniformed troops in the capital. But the general reaction was one of disbelief. Like a number of the royal misadventures that would mark the 1980s and 1990s, you could hardly have made it up if you'd tried.

*   *   *

The shuffling amateurism which ignored the Queen's alarm button and required two calls to summon a rescue party reflected a general casualness in Buckingham Palace in the early

1980s. There was little evidence of Margaret Thatcher's bracing ethos sweeping away the cobwebs of ancient practice. Following the tradition of countless predecessors, the Lord Chamberlain of the day, the amiable 'Chips' Maclean—'a very nice boy scout', as one of his colleagues fondly remembers him—declined to communicate significant decisions, or to discuss any matter of importance, on the telephone. Everything had to be set down in writing and hand-delivered by liveried messenger.

This was to change dramatically with the arrival on 1 December 1984 of a new Lord Chamberlain, David Ogilvy, Thirteenth Earl of Airlie. Just retired from a dynamic career as a merchant banker, running the profitable firm of Schroder Wagg, Airlie managed to blend his business dynamism seamlessly with his aristocratic pedigree. His sixty-nine thousand acres in Scotland featured two elegantly ancient castles. As one of his admiring but slightly intimidated Palace colleagues put it, 'David was part Wall Street executive, part Highland chieftain'.

Most important of all, he was a very old friend of the Queen. His grandmother, Mabell Airlie, had been the confidante of Queen Mary. His younger brother, Angus Ogilvy, whose lean good looks he shared, was the husband of Princess Alexandra. Born within a month of the Queen, David Airlie had been a guest at royal shooting parties since the days of George VI; and his vivacious wife Virginia, grand-daughter of the New York financier Otto Kahn, was the first and only American lady-in-waiting to the Queen. Like her husband, she was known for cycling to her royal duties from the

Airlies' pied-à-terre beside the Chelsea Physic Garden. The hyper-qualified Thirteenth Earl recruited for the job that made him nominal head of the entire royal household was hardly the type to be a 'nominal' anything.

The position of Lord Chamberlain dates back to the mists of royal officialdom, with responsibility for everything from court ceremonial to the running of the stables or Royal Mews (which nowadays includes motor cars). Its symbol of office is a thin white staff, which its holder is required to break over the coffin of a deceased sovereign. By the late nineteenth century the position had become a political appointment which changed with every government. Viscount Sydney, the Lord Chamberlain who admitted the working men to the great St Paul's Thanksgiving of 1872, had been chosen by Gladstone.

But when Ramsay MacDonald became Britain's first Labour Prime Minister in 1924, he handed the job back to the King. MacDonald scarcely had enough MPs with the experience and qualifications to take care of the serious jobs of government, and, unsurprisingly, he found himself short on comrades with an interest in precedence and processions. In 1968, to the relief of all parties, the Lord Chamberlain's office also abandoned the controversial duty, which dated back to Shakespeare's time, of regulating and censoring London theatres. So the office that Airlie took up in 1984 was primarily concerned with ensuring that royal extravaganzas, from funerals to jubilees, kept running with their legendary style and precision. His very first task was to practise walking backwards holding his white staff—the Lord

Chamberlain's role as he precedes the Queen into state banquets and at the State Opening of Parliament.

In the six months that the new Lord Chamberlain gave himself to study his responsibilities, he found that the 'walking backwards' side of things—the ceremonial work of the Lord Chamberlain's office *per se*—called for little attention. The investitures at which people came to the Palace to receive their honours were in need of some humanising, but in general the office was running with well-oiled efficiency. What concerned Airlie were the other departments that fell within his remit as the Palace's supreme commander.

The royal household itself, employing over four hundred staff, had a ramshackle, bureaucratic style, and its maintenance department had been run for some years as a department of the Civil Service by the Ministry of the Environment. The Queen's inherited collection of paintings and art treasures, a hoard of overwhelming richness, lacked the staff or funding required by such a major national resource, while the office of the Privy Purse, the royal accounts department, struggled with inflation and short-term cash injections under the suspicious eye of the Treasury in Whitehall.

Airlie found little to criticise in the private secretary's office, which dealt efficiently with the Queen's public duties and relations with government. But it struck him that, like the other departments, it did tend to operate from one day to the next. In every department of the Palace the former merchant banker detected a general lack of integrated long-term planning—and if anyone was supposed to provide this, it had to be the Lord Chamberlain himself.

In the middle of 1985 Airlie sat down with the Queen and asked her for a job description. Was the Lord Chamberlain really in charge of every single department of the Palace, he needed to know? The Queen told him that he was. In that case, Airlie responded, he suspected there was a need for some major changes. Did he have his boss's backing for that? Once again, the answer was 'Yes'.

These were the years when businesses of all sorts were being reformed and modernised, and it seemed to Airlie that it was time for the Palace to follow suit. Drawing on his merchant banking experience, he could not help thinking along corporate lines.

'In business terms,' as he once put it to a gathering of Palace staff, 'the Lord Chamberlain is a sort of chairman of the royal company. The private secretary, who handles the day-to-day business, is really the managing director or chief executive. And the whole organisation is responsible to one shareholder, the Queen.'

With the departure of Philip Moore as private secretary in 1986 Airlie had a new chief executive in Bill Heseltine, who very much shared his appetite for reform, and the two men commissioned a management efficiency study of the Palace by Peat Marwick McLintock, the royal auditors—starting at the very top.

'Why have I got so many footmen?' was the first question supplied by the royal company's single shareholder.

Peat Marwick's 1,393-page report, completed at the end of 1986 and largely the work of Michael

Peat, a forceful young partner in the firm, contained 188 proposals for change. The Queen approved every one and Airlie set about canvassing the rest of the Palace. 'David was a great hands-on moderniser,' remembers one of his colleagues. 'He was always popping into one's office to bounce ideas off you.'

For the rest of the 1980s Buckingham Palace set about its first major administrative restructuring since the early years of Queen Victoria. In fact, Peat Marwick found that the Queen's footmen were quite efficiently employed, and the overall impact of the Airlie reforms was actually to swell the number of employees under the royal umbrella, particularly when it came to art. The Royal Collection was formed into a department in its own right.

'It gave us a whole new impetus,' remembers Sir Oliver Millar, the Surveyor of the Queen's Pictures who became the first director of the Royal Collection in 1987. 'David made us independent. That stimulated us and we became, I am sure, much more professional.'

Since the late 1980s the Royal Collection Department has hired bright young academics, mounted creative exhibitions, raised conservation to new levels, and launched social outreach programmes to match those of the most dynamic museums and art institutions in the country. The department makes a profit and has made it possible, for the first time in a century, for the Royal Collection to acquire new works.

Less visible to the public, the internal management of the royal household and palaces was also transformed. 'The overall aim', Lord

434

Airlie was reported to have said, 'was to make us more master of our own destiny. Over the years we were being sucked more and more into the Civil Service and that was not a good thing. It is the job of the household to provide a strong, independent support and bastion for the sovereign.'

Taking advantage of the Thatcher government's wish to reduce bureaucracy, the Palace took back control of its own maintenance operations from the Department of the Environment, and also started negotiating a new arrangement for the Civil List. When inflation had reached record levels in the 1970s, the Treasury had taken to paying the Palace on a year-by-year basis, a system of drip-feeding which made proper financial planning impossible.

By the end of the 1980s, Airlie was in a position to start negotiating a new, more efficient and longer-term system of royal financing by the Treasury. In 1990 he hired Michael Peat with a view to the energetic accountant taking supreme control of the Palace finances, and as the two men started to study the figures, it became clear to them both that the Queen could probably afford to pay tax without too much difficulty.

*   *   *

In the early 1980s the Right Reverend Michael Mann, the Dean of Windsor, received an official invitation to visit China. It came out of the blue, but negotiations were under way with regard to the handing back to China of the last great British colonial possession, the Crown Colony of Hong Kong, and it seemed to the Foreign Office that this invitation could somehow be connected to that process.

So it proved. The Chinese had invited Mann because they knew that, as Dean of Windsor, he was personal chaplain to the Queen. The atheist rulers of the world's largest socialist republic wanted to invite the Queen to visit, and official channels were not somehow good enough. When it came to the Queen of England, they felt they had to ask through her spiritual adviser.

Sir Geoffrey Howe, the Foreign Secretary, who accompanied the Queen and Prince Philip on their historic, first ever visit by a British head of state to mainland China in the autumn of 1986, discovered the same reverence. As he walked forward with the Queen to shake hands with Deng Xiaoping and the other Chinese leaders, the Foreign Secretary kicked himself for not giving his royal boss three or four key briefing points to push. But by the time the tour ended, Howe had realised that mass-media monarchs do not do their business in tête-à-têtes. It was the eight days of encounters with massive crowds, transfigured by the chance to see and make some contact with this famous ancient motherhead, the Queen of England, that got the important job done. The royal impact went beyond words. Months of painstaking negotiation had done the deal on Hong Kong two years earlier. The politicians had shaken hands. But what was still required to make it real was the emotional component of Her Majesty's presence.

The hundred or more British journalists who flew out to cover the most momentous tour of Elizabeth II's reign saw things more prosaically. Alan Hamilton, the wry and seasoned royal correspondent of *The Times*, was delegated as the 'pool' reporter to follow Prince Philip while he mingled with the British community in Z'ian. An Edinburgh man, Hamilton recognised the accents of a group of Edinburgh students who were living for a year in China and had spent some time chatting to the Duke, the chancellor of their university. Philip had been particularly delighted to discover this group of his own students in a foreign land, and had talked to them with special friendliness, yielding some warm and chatty comments that might fill a few paragraphs in a sidebar, human-interest story.

As Hamilton got on to the press bus to report the details he had garnered, his tabloid colleagues yawned with the special disdain they reserved for egghead broadsheet writers—until he read out one particular aside that the Duke had made to one of the students.

'If you stay here much longer,' His Royal Highness had remarked with a laugh, 'you'll go slit-eyed.'

On the press bus a roar went up from the suddenly attentive hacks. Hamilton himself had seen no special significance in the remark; he planned to report it as one jocular aside among many. His tabloid colleagues saw 'SLIT-EYED' stacked in black 120-point headlines on their front pages—a racial insult they could retail with impunity. At the next rest stop, Harry Arnold of the *Sun* commandeered the solitary working payphone and, in an extraordinary demonstration of fourth estate ingenuity, got the Chinese operator to connect him with the hall of residence where the Edinburgh students were staying. He spoke to the student whom Hamilton had interviewed and

437

confirmed that the Duke had indeed uttered the words 'slit-eyed'. And that became the sentiment for which, in the United Kingdom, one of Elizabeth II's most epoch-making state visits came to be remembered.

Next day Geoffrey Howe conferred anxiously with William Heseltine, the Queen's private secretary. They discovered, to their relief, that the Chinese authorities were less insulted than baffled by the bizarre news values of the British press. One official explained that they had their own eye joke—they would warn Chinese students going to the West not to stay away too long in case they came back 'round-eyed'.

Poached from an informal conversation, Prince Philip's remark did not come close to provoking a diplomatic incident. But, like many another royal story, it was news because the tabloids decreed it so, relishing the offence that they affected to scold.

The 'slit-eyed' débâcle illustrated how little concern an entertainment-oriented press had with serious themes. An important moment in modern British history had been demeaned by a commercial urge for sensation and simplicity. But Prince Philip did say it, and the press were right in sensing that the dukely weakness for dropping politically incorrect bricks was a token of his personal high-handedness.

'How nice to be in a country', he had remarked to the Paraguayan dictator Alfredo Stroessner in 1969, 'that is not ruled by its people.'

The episode was a reminder of how the good work of a generally impeccable queen existed in the framework of an all-too-fallible family—and fallibility was to prove a dominant theme in the

438

decade that lay ahead. Nearly ten years of royal feast, from the Silver Jubilee through the glamorous royal weddings and royal births of the mid-1980s, were to be succeeded by as many years of famine: a helter-skelter of scandal, misbehaviour and controversy that would reach its nadir in the dark days following the death of Diana in the autumn of 1997. Was it just an extraordinary run of bad luck, or did it show something deeper—what happens when a society places too much trust in royal dreams, and when royal heads are turned by that?

CHAPTER TWENTY-SIX

Royal Knockout

If a prince, an heir apparent, with all the advantages of great wealth, huge houses, many servants, constant occupation and access to every kind of advice, will not work at his marriage to save it, why should other fractious couples, harassed perhaps by poverty, poor housing and other social handicaps, even bother to try?

Paul Johnson, February 1996

The royal euphoria of the 1980s wedding-and-baby years spawned its own branch of the media business. Bookshops devoted entire sections to royal picture books, biographies and glossy magazines, and the younger royals could not resist the temptation to get in on the act. *The Old Man of*

Lochnagar, a children's bedtime story by Prince Charles, Prince Andrew's book of *Photographs, Princess Anne and Mark Phillips Talking About Horses*—scarcely a publishing season went by without some royal author chancing his or her arm, many of them making use of television to plug their products.

The new recruits were particularly assiduous. Princess Michael of Kent produced *Crowned in a Far Country*, an ambitious historical account of princesses who had married into foreign dynasties. It turned out that sections of her text had been plagiarised from other books; and there were also problems when the new Duchess of York hogged the creative glory for a volume on Queen Victoria's beloved Osborne House that had, in fact, been largely written by Benita Stoney, the niece of the Royal Librarian.

Fergie was a publishing enterprise in her own right. For the less historically inclined, she produced a series of children's books on Budgie, a talking helicopter, and on completion of their £3.5 million dream home on the edge of Windsor Great Park, she and her husband were photographed, film-star style, with their children in the opulent interior. *Hello!* magazine paid £200,000 for the rights. The press promptly dubbed the gaudy mansion—which bore a striking resemblance to the pseudo-rural style of Tesco supermarkets—'South York', after South Fork, the Ewing family ranch in the Texas TV soap opera *Dallas*.

The young royals' assiduous trading on their celebrity made it clear that they were no more talented than, and just as vain as, any other attention-hungry personality—and if one moment crystallised that perception it came in the summer of 1987. In the last week of June the most watched programme on British television was *It's a Royal Knock-Out*, a one-off variation of the rough-and-tumble *It's a Knockout* game show in which teams of celebrities and members of the public made fools of themselves playing silly games. On this occasion the younger members of the royal family joined in to raise money for charity. The ill-starred venture marked the public debut of the Queen's youngest and most indulged son, Prince Edward, whose profile had been limited to a sudden departure from the Royal Marines earlier that year.

'It was a matter of self-esteem,' recalls a courtier of the time. 'We were all solidly against the *Knockout* project, but Edward had privately plotted it so far that the Queen felt she could not say "No". After the Marines, it would have involved him in a second loss of face.'

Even then, the programme—in which Charles and Diana had firmly refused to appear—might have passed off as a cringe-making damp squib if it had not been for the behaviour of Edward afterwards. As fifty embarrassed journalists struggled to think of something polite to ask at the ensuing press conference, the 23-year-old prince began by asking them a question: 'Well, what did you think of it, then?' In the painful silence that followed, Edward stormed petulantly out of the tent. An occasion designed to demonstrate how amusing and light-hearted young royal folk could be, showed, on the contrary, that one of them at least took himself far too seriously.

The newspapers had their headline for the next

morning—'It's a Walk Out'—and the combined impression of arrogance and idiocy proved enduring. *It's a Royal Knock-Out* was a serious false step in the media progress of Elizabeth II, standing on its head the seductive artifice of the *Royal Family* film eighteen years earlier. Over-familiarity, trivialisation, banality—all the creeping sins of television were committed, and a heavy price was paid.

'It simply got out of control,' remembers a courtier who had been involved in the original *Royal Family* project. 'There was a time in the mid-1980s when it seemed that every younger member of the family was their own press officer. It just went to their heads.'

What this courtier, and virtually everyone in Buckingham Palace, kept hoping for was that Elizabeth II would take action and exercise her very well respected authority. But she did nothing. 'Confrontation,' sighs one of the extended family regretfully, 'is just not her strong point.'

The Queen had positively rejected her staff's considered advice to block Edward's *Royal Knock Out*, and she was equally hands-off with her other children and their spouses. 'The Queen', says one of her close advisers, weighing his words judiciously, 'finds the boxes rather easier to organise than the children.'

Another puts it more positively. 'The Queen is very laissez and also very fair. She believes it is a very important right that the members of her family should be allowed to shape their own destiny—and that has to include making their own mistakes, if necessary.'

Nowhere did this apply more than in the arena

442

of her children's marriages. Charles and Diana had worked quite hard at their problems in their early years together. In an attempt to placate his wife's insecurities and suspicions, Charles had jettisoned swathes of friends from his single days, including the Parker Bowleses—'right down to getting rid of his Labrador', recalls one of his old acquaintances bitterly. Diana, for her part, had made an effort to be less needy, developing more independence in her public appearances and trying not to upstage her husband. She wore low heels and tried to do more of a Prince Philip, keeping a public step behind the sensitive prince. She also gained self-confidence as she learned, with the help of the actor and film director Richard Attenborough, to speak in public.

But at moments of stress, Diana's bulimia would recur, and she would take out her tensions on her staff. Nannies, valets, even private secretaries—it soon came to be noticed that there was a high casualty rate among the staff of the Princess of Wales. These departures were the subject of a dribble of newspaper stories that were the first, veiled, public suggestion that the perfect princess might have a darker side.

'She gives her all to the public,' explained her Canadian-born press secretary, Victor Chapman, describing how, when she got home from a public engagement, Diana would collapse, totally drained. 'So she expects her staff to go that extra mile as well.'

The presence of Chapman, a beefy former American footballer, reflected the Queen's concern for her erratic daughter-in-law. The pregnant bikini pictures in the Bahamas, snatched

443

so soon after Elizabeth II had made her personal appeal to the editors at the Palace, had angered her profoundly. Chapman looked like a bodyguard, and so, with the Queen's approval, he was assigned the job of being Diana's press minder. He used his substantial physical bulk to block and even intimidate photographers, and Michael Shea, in charge of the entire press office, adopted similar tactics. The traditional Palace response had been to ignore sloppy or malicious reporting. Now Shea fought back. He embarked on a policy of proactive briefing and systematic rebuttal of stories that were deemed damagingly inaccurate.

By the mid-1980s, newspaper swooning over Diana's developing fashion interests was being tempered by criticism of the cost of her wardrobe, while her husband was being ridiculed for his developing environmental interests. In 1984 the prince had made his famous speech denouncing the inhumanity of modern architecture, a theme which was linked to his social concerns about urban planning. Stories that he talked to his plants made him seem both eccentric and out of step with his young, fashion-conscious wife. To give the couple a chance to answer back, Michael Shea hatched a domestic interview-documentary under the cosy aegis of the nation's TV uncle of the time, the newsreader Sir Alastair Burnet, which went on the air in late October 1985.

'My clothes are not my priority,' Diana declared when the carefully vetted questions turned to her wardrobe, while Charles was given the chance to defend his public outspokenness. His controversial remarks, he said, had been his attempt 'to throw a rock into a pond and watch the ripples create a certain amount of discussion'.

Diana avoided the truth about her eating habits. 'I'm never on what's called a diet,' she said. 'Maybe I'm so scrawny because I take so much exercise.'

But she lied most spectacularly when discussion turned to domestic disagreement.

'I suspect,' admitted Charles in a characteristic stab at honesty and complexity, 'that most husbands and wives find they often have arguments.'

'But we don't,' responded Diana uncompromisingly.

'Occasionally we do,' insisted a bewildered but still humorous prince.

'No, we don't,' persisted Diana.

Diana's insistence on an image of impossible perfection could, with hindsight, be seen as a telling clue to some of the problems in the marriage. But in 1985 the papers were only too delighted to accept the window-dressing at face value.

'What a smashing royal couple they are,' wrote James Whitaker in the *Daily Mirror*.

'Di and Charles are so very much in love,' enthused the *Sun*.

*   *   *

In reality, the difficulties between the heir to the throne and his wife were moving into a phase of more permanent alienation. After less than five years their marriage had accomplished its purpose in bottom-line terms: they had provided the dynasty with a couple of bright and healthy boys. Several family friends have identified the birth of

Prince Harry in September 1984 as the surprisingly early moment after which both Charles and Diana seemed to make less effort with each other. In ordinary marriages, couples often try to stick together for the sake of the children; in dynastic alliances, the opposite can be the case.

Charles's friends have blamed the breakdown on the difficulty that he had dealing with Diana's neuroses, working these up into a theory that seized on a category of behavioural symptoms that have been medically described as 'borderline personality disorder'. This has been defined as the ability to appear 'superficially intact' while experiencing 'dramatic internal chaos'. Doctors have found it a useful box to tick on medical insurance forms after seeing a patient who is not ill in any conventional sense, and whose symptoms are hard to isolate. The sufferer is said to feel panicky, despairing, inferior and dependent, while putting on a show of competence—which provides a pretty accurate description of the human condition itself.

Psychologists have argued over whether BPD is a helpful explanation of Diana's complex and challenging make-up. But if the princess reflected one abnormal behavioural syndrome, her husband reflected another—Spoiled Prince Disorder.

'I think Prince Charles really did try quite hard,' remembers one of the Queen's most senior advisers. 'But there was a sense in which he always remained a bachelor, and there is a basic selfishness about bachelors.'

Given all that Charles himself had frequently said about the lofty ideals of marriage and the importance of working hard at its difficulties, the speed with which he decided that the relationship had 'irretrievably' broken down seems very rapid. By 1987 the pattern was well established. On Sunday nights Diana would leave Highgrove with the boys, heading for London. The Highgrove staff would hear the water running upstairs and Charles would appear shortly afterwards, pink and groomed and smelling of soap and spicy shampoo, in a blazer, open-necked shirt and cravat. He would get in his car and drive the twenty minutes over to Middlewick House, the home from which Andrew Parker Bowles had that evening departed on his own way up to London to take up his military duties for the week.

Diana was later to claim, and persuaded much of the world to believe, that her husband was unfaithful with Camilla from the very start of their marriage. In fact, there is no reason to disbelieve Charles's assertion that he deliberately kept away from his old love in the early years—and there seems no way at all of deciding the big question, whether Charles or Diana was the first to be unfaithful. Either way, there can have been little difference in terms of time, for the settled intention on both sides was the same.

Certainly, by 1987 Diana was herself turning outside her marriage for love and warmth. Even as Charles was driving down to Middlewick House, his wife was developing an attachment of such closeness with her police bodyguard, Sergeant Barry Mannakee, that the detective was moved on to other duties by worried superiors. In the late 1980s the Princess of Wales deliberately set out to enjoy the romantic knockabout that she had so carefully avoided in her teenage years, indulging in a series of affairs with young men from the pool of bankers, Guards officers and wine merchants of her own generation and natural habitat. Major James Hewitt, her dashing riding instructor, would become the most famous, but there were others. One evening in 1987 a photographer snatched pictures of the princess after a party in a London mews house indulging in horseplay with David Waterhouse, a young army major. She and her detective successfully pleaded with the photographer to hand over his film, and without pictures, the resulting newspaper story made little impact. People did not want to know that the Waleses' marriage might be in trouble.

'Separate breakfasts, separate timetables, separate friends,' wrote Andrew Morton, an enterprising young journalist on the *Daily Star*, in April 1987. Studying the Court Circular, the tabloids kept a running tally of how many days the couple spent apart. It had reached thirty-seven when they met up to inspect Welsh flood damage following the freak 'Storm of the Century' of October 1987, and then went home separately, Diana to Highgrove and Charles to Balmoral.

But the doubts were swamped by the regular flow of images of the handsome young couple, who attracted immense and enthusiastic crowds wherever they went. There were spectacularly successful foreign tours every year, reported in resolutely upbeat tones supported by happy-seeming colour photographs. It has often been suggested that the Waleses' marriage fell victim to the intrusiveness of the undeferential media. In fact, for five years, from 1987 (if not earlier) until 1992, the couple conducted routine infidelity and a permanent double life that was known to the servants who made their beds and cooked the dinners, while detectives accompanied the faithless spouses on their assignations. The whole pretence was cocooned in Edwardian discretion, and when the press got wind of it, they chose to look the other way.

'Of course we heard the gossip about difficulties,' says James Whitaker. 'But intensive, full-scale adultery on both sides? It did not seem credible.'

The royal rat pack were nosy, but in a curious way they were also loyal to their readers' dreams. They enjoyed their role in the relating of the nation's comforting bedtime story.

*   *   *

While the Queen and her husband were worried by the rows and signs of disharmony they witnessed quite regularly in their eldest son's marriage, they remained oblivious to how totally the relationship had broken down. The Waleses' detectives did not pass on the details of the couple's assignations. The only evidence of scandalous royal behaviour in these years involved Princess Anne, who separated from her husband Mark Phillips in 1989. Love letters to the princess from Commander Tim Laurence, a naval officer who was serving at the time as an equerry to the Queen, were stolen and taken to a tabloid newspaper.

'Most of the household were deeply shocked,' remembers a courtier who was a friend of the quiet and serious Laurence. 'There was much talk of high treason for Tim committing adultery with the princess. I think one of the few people who weren't shocked was the Queen. She liked her equerry, and I think she took the view that if the princess found some satisfaction in her relationship with him that was not a bad thing. "I've decided," she said, "that I'm not stuffy enough for my age."'

In 1989 Elizabeth II was a youthful and vigorous sixty-three. But she was starting to feel censorious about several aspects of her daughter-in-law Diana's behaviour. 'She was very uneasy', says a courtier, 'about the way in which Diana, really from quite an early date, started manipulating the media, getting herself photographed going to the gym and that sort of thing.'

'The Queen actually had reservations at an earlier stage than most,' recalls one of her senior advisers. 'There were strange signs. In lots of ways Diana was a tremendous addition of strength to the whole show. But I think that she and the Queen both found each other difficult to deal with. And Diana behaved personally with the Queen in ways that were quite unheard of.'

The trouble centred, once again, on Balmoral, where evenings in the castle were still regulated by etiquette of Victorian formality.

'It certainly can be a penance,' admits a frequent guest. 'You see the same people at breakfast, lunch and tea. And then you have to sit with them in the evening for hours, knowing that you're going to see them at breakfast again.'

The cardinal rule for the period while guests sat talking over coffee and drinks after dinner was that no one should leave until the Queen herself made a move. But Diana soon took to ignoring this.

'She would just get up and walk out before the

Queen did,' remembers the guest. 'She simply couldn't conceal her boredom.'

The princess also took to issuing instructions about the guests with whom she would and would not sit at dinner. 'Thank goodness,' said the exasperated Elizabeth II to one of her more youthful and nimble courtiers as she juggled with a mealtime placement to accommodate her daughter-in-law's wishes, 'that you are one person that the girl is willing to sit with.'

*   *   *

Early in 1991, the journalist Andrew Morton was gathering material for a biography he was planning on the intriguing and glamorous Diana, who had now been Princess of Wales for ten years. Morton had learned his trade as James Whitaker's successor on the *Daily Star*.

'I was the sorcerer,' says Whitaker proudly. 'He was my apprentice.'

Following Diana on a hospital visit, Morton noticed that the princess seemed to know one of the doctors personally. He was James Colthurst, an old Etonian who, Morton discovered, had been one of Diana's friends in her Coleherne Court days. Colthurst and Diana had had a brief and decorous flirtation on a skiing trip and had met up again in the late 1980s, both disillusioned by their very different career paths. The princess told the doctor about her marital troubles, to which Colthurst responded in a pastoral fashion, listening sympathetically and giving her counselling, although he was not a trained psychologist. His professional interests were moving away from the high-tech medicine in which he had been trained towards homoeopathy, and this matched a changing of the tide in his personal life. 'James has a bit of a mission to save the world,' said one of his friends.

Colthurst's disenchantment with his upper-class English background matched Diana's developing view of herself as a victim of the royal system, and Colthurst gently egged her rebellion on. The young doctor helped her draft some of the speeches in which she was beginning to frame her identity as an alternative, compassionate royal. He also encouraged her adversarial view of the House of Windsor, and went along with Morton when the reporter began cultivating him as a source. The two men started meeting for games of squash.

The trigger that brought Diana to share her revelations with Morton was a series of marital squabbles over the celebration of her thirtieth birthday in July 1991. When newspapers discovered there were no plans for a celebration, speculative stories appeared suggesting that Charles was too old and stuffy, or perhaps even too mean, to give his glamorous young wife the sort of rave-up she would enjoy. These were followed by better-informed leaks, which could only have come from Charles's inner circle, that the prince had quite definitely offered his wife a grand party, but that Diana had refused.

Charles's friends were incensed by Diana's saint-like public aura, which contrasted so starkly with the tantrums and pettinesses they had witnessed in private. In 1987 Diana had memorably and bravely taken off her gloves and, though rather scared, had worn no mask or protective clothing when she

452

shook hands with an AIDS patient. This had been the beginning of the Mother Teresa persona that was to develop so potently alongside her glamorous image as a fashion icon, and Charles's friends resented the publicity this attracted. They saw it as posturing when compared to the solid but less eye-catching work Charles had been doing for more than a decade among underprivileged youth.

They were particularly upset by one story that Charles had told them—that Diana had set upon him one night without warning, and started boxing his ears while he knelt by his bed, as he did every night, saying his prayers. Diana came to hear of dinner-party gossip in which Charles's friends called her 'the mad cow'—a phrase given contemporary currency by the recently discovered cattle disease, bovine spongiform encephalopathy. Her revenge was swift and dreadful.

The turning point in the history of the modern British monarchy occurred in a transport café in North Ruislip in the summer of 1991. Over bacon and eggs, James Colthurst poured out to Andrew Morton Diana's catalogue of marital grievance and proposed that this should form the basis of a book, which Morton would write with the covert assistance of the princess, alongside the on-the-record testimony of her family and friends, whom Diana would authorise to speak.

The mechanism was elaborate and deliberately deceptive. Diana and Colthurst would have long sessions round the tape-recorder and Colthurst would take the resulting tapes to Morton. The author would then send back questions and requests for clarification that Colthurst would explore at the next session.

Colthurst's role as intermediary gave Diana deniability. When questioned about Morton, she would be able to say, 'I never met the man.' The possibility that the Princess of Wales herself would kiss and tell for publication—exposing such a concentrated welter of painful and intimate details—was so extraordinary that many refused to believe it. Only after Diana's death, when Morton published his transcripts of the tapes, did people realise the full extent of her betrayal. *Diana: Her True Story* was not the biography that people assumed. It was effectively the princess's own autobiography and life testament.

The impact when the book appeared, first serialised in the *Sunday Times* on 7 June 1992, was searing enough. No detail was spared. As related through the testimony of her friends, horrified readers learned how, on her very first Christmas at Sandringham, following a row with Charles, Diana had felt so desperate she had thrown herself down the stairs, apparently in an attempt at suicide. She was pregnant with William at the time. There had been attempts at self-mutilation when she had cut herself with a penknife. A picture was painted of a royal family who were at best judgemental and disapproving, and at worst cold and indifferent, towards the solitude and despair of their beautiful new recruit. The most damning accusations of all related to Charles's long-term infidelity with Camilla.

As an account of the once-idealised home life of the Windsors, Morton's story seemed downright incredible. It also constituted the most extraordinary intrusion into any personal relationship, let alone a royal marriage. Reflecting the national shock, and referring not only to the *Sunday Times* but to the flood of competing stories that rival newspapers had run as 'spoilers', Lord McGregor, the chairman of the Press Complaints Commission, condemned the 'odious exhibition of journalists dabbling their fingers in the stuff of other people's souls'.

Before releasing his statement on Monday, 8 June, McGregor checked with Robert Fellowes, who felt that he should check in turn with Diana.

'Are you quite sure, Diana,' her brother-in-law asked, carefully explaining the strong statement that the Press Complaints chairman was about to make, 'that we are not going to find your fingerprints on this material—that it can't all be traced back to you?'

The conversation took place on an open 'squawk box' telephone, and the answer came back loud and clear.

'Certainly not. I had nothing to do with it.'

Two days later tabloid photographers got a call to go to the Fulham home of Carolyn Bartholomew (née Pride), one of Diana's Coleherne Court flatmates, who had been a source much quoted by Morton. When Kenny Lennox of the *Daily Star* arrived, Diana's detective was already on the pavement.

'Can you get your photograph from there?' the detective asked.

Shortly afterwards Diana emerged from the front door with her friend and embraced her warmly and slowly, while Carolyn's husband and young son gazed in wonder at the photographic posse who had mysteriously appeared in their street to record the occasion. No royal warrant 'By

455

Appointment' could have conveyed a clearer message. By publicly endorsing the person who was Morton's main quoted source, Diana made clear that she had effectively invaded her own privacy.

When the photograph of his sister-in-law's meaning-laden embrace appeared on the front of every newspaper next day, Fellowes felt he had no choice but to offer his resignation immediately to the Queen. He, who should have known better, had been deceived. Elizabeth II absolutely refused to accept it. She trusted Fellowes completely, and she found his role as a family go-between very useful.

Within days of Morton's first instalment, the realisation had dawned on the royal family that they all had been deceived.

'I could hear my wife talking,' said Prince Charles, 'as I read those words in the paper.'

The middle of the month saw Royal Ascot, the June race meeting which brought the entire clan together for the traditional week-long house party at Windsor Castle.

'The atmosphere was dreadful,' remembers one of the guests. 'Absolutely no one in the family was speaking to Diana. They were blanking her completely. She curled up at the back of the royal box in floods of tears.'

Without any knowledge of how the details in the book had been co-ordinated, the Queen and her husband nevertheless felt instinctively that they were victims of some unprecedented betrayal. But with Diana flatly rejecting everyone's suspicions, it was difficult to see what they could say, short of calling her a liar. 'If anything, they tried not to side with Charles against Diana,' says a friend. 'They were very conscious that, in a sense, she did not have a family, and that they had to try to supply her with that.'

Personally distraught at the public and private catastrophe she was witnessing, the Queen fell back on the therapy her husband described as her 'dog mechanism'. She would take out her corgis for long walks, bring them home, wash them, then take them out all over again. She was poignantly powerless in her theoretically all-powerful position. Not for the first time, she found herself playing the constitutional monarch inside her own house, trying to stay above the fray and leaving it to her husband to express their joint feelings in his name. In the course of the next few weeks, Prince Philip despatched no fewer than four of his word-processed homilies to Diana, trying to mend the painfully widening breach. The Duke drew on his own experience as a young outsider who had had dust-ups with the stuffiness and constrictions of the Palace, encouraging his daughter-in-law to take the longer view and assuring her of his fundamental support. He also tried to emphasise how both he and the Queen wanted to give her all the help they could.

'They were absolutely splendid letters,' says someone who read the correspondence, 'and in every reply she thanked him in a big way. She said in one response that she was really "touched" by all the trouble he was taking.'

But Prince Philip can sound wounding when he thinks he is being kind, and the effect of the letter-writing was to push forward the logic of the situation. The Duke's sharp-edged thinking inescapably homed in on the deeply serious issues that were involved in what Diana had enabled

Morton to do. 'Either she had had no conception of what she was getting into, or else she wanted to bring the marriage to an end,' says a courtier who had always kept a fatherly eye on the princess. 'I still have a hard time deciding which of those two it might be. I don't think she could have answered that herself.'

Whatever Diana's intentions when she first linked up with Andrew Morton, her father-in-law's computer missives made clear what the consequences might be. Communications from the man whom Diana knew to be the firm's boss in family matters conveyed a sobering message. She was playing for higher stakes than she could have realised when she and James Colthurst started plotting the deception that had then seemed so clever. Diana contacted a lawyer, and her replies to Prince Philip were carefully drafted in formal terms. In effect, the separation negotiations had begun.

'Why do you write all those letters?' asked two of Philip's very oldest friends. 'Wouldn't it be much better if you actually talked to her?'

'It just makes her upset,' explained the Duke, and he recounted an extraordinary story. Before the Morton book was published, he and Elizabeth *had* tried talking to Diana, he said—and to Charles as well. For a long time the parents had sought not to interfere, but as they saw things getting worse and worse, they felt they had no choice but to intervene. They had met for a summit meeting, an attempt at self-help family therapy, at which the Queen and her husband, as an older couple, tried to explain how they understood the problems that marriages go through, and how they were both just desperate to help.

'Can you tell us what's the matter, Diana?' asked Philip, at which his daughter-in-law collapsed in tears. The princess stayed sobbing on her own, refusing all comfort and uttering nothing coherent.

'Well, Charles,' enquired the Queen rather desperately, turning to her son, who was smouldering on the opposite side of the room. 'Can you explain to us?'

'What?' responded the prince. 'And read it all in the newspapers tomorrow? No thank you.'

And that was the end of the royal family therapy session.

*   *   *

Nineteen ninety-two marked the fortieth anniversary of Elizabeth II's accession—and at what should have been a moment of serene consolidation, everything was disintegrating around her. In January embarrassing photographs of the Duchess of York with Steve Wyatt, an American playboy, had been published, leading to the legal separation of the Yorks in March. Anne's separation from Mark Phillips was finalised when the couple divorced in April. May saw Fergie packing up and leaving 'South York' with her daughters, with whom she turned up as members of the general public at the fateful Ascot race meeting that followed the Morton disclosures. Photographers recorded the bizarre spectacle of the separated duchess standing at the rail among the crowd, encouraging her daughters to wave to Granny as she rode by in the royal carriage procession.

459

July provided a brief respite. People joked about suffering from royal scandal deprivation—until August brought a double dose. First James Whitaker's binoculars lighted on the topless Fergie sunbathing beside a pool in the South of France with John Bryan, an American whom she had described as her 'financial adviser', kneeling at her feet, apparently sucking her toes in a sensuous fashion. The immense boost in sales—nearly two million extra copies—that this story and its accompanying photographs earned for the *Daily Mirror*, prompted its rival the *Sun* to publish the transcript of a tape that it had been keeping in its safe for some time. Recorded on New Year's Eve 1989, it captured a mobile telephone conversation between Diana and a young car salesman, James Gilbey, of the Gilbey gin family, who referred to her affectionately as 'Squidge' or 'Squidgy'. The conversation implied some sort of sexual relationship between Diana and Gilbey, and left no room for doubt about the ill-feeling between the princess and her in-laws.

'I was very bad at lunch and I nearly starting blubbing,' said Diana, describing mealtimes at Sandringham, where she was staying at the time of the phone interception. 'I just felt really sad and empty and thought, "Bloody hell, after all I've done for this fucking family."'

The *Sun* refused to say how it came by the tape that became instantly notorious as 'Squidgygate'. There was talk of 'dirty tricks' by the official surveillance services. In fact, in the days before widespread digital technology, it was a common hobby of radio hams—high-tech and unregulated versions of Mass-Obs snoopers—to intercept

460

mobile phone conversations for their private pleasure. In the small hours of the morning a high proportion of such chats were about sex.

That summer a Chester reader of the *Daily Mirror* was playing one of the conversations that he regularly captured for the lunchtime amusement of his workmates when he realised the sensational identity of the couple exchanging intimacies. Following the furore over Squidgygate, he also realised that there must be money in it—and early in 1993 the *Mirror* duly published the heir to the throne's private and not very regal take on life and love.

'Your great achievement is to love me,' said Charles.

'I'd suffer anything for you,' responded Camilla, clearly accepting her prince's vanity as fully justified. 'That's love. It's the strength of love.'

The tender appeal of this devotion was mitigated by a long conversation in which the couple canvassed the names of famous and largely titled friends who were willing to provide safe houses where they could conduct their next illicit coupling—and by Prince Charles's confession to an extraordinary sexual fantasy. Drawing on his interest in Buddhism and reincarnation, he wondered about his next life, and expressed the thought that this might be as 'God forbid, a Tampax' that would help him to achieve his great ambition to 'just live inside your trousers'.

To generate extra revenue, the newspaper published a special telephone number enabling callers to listen to the tape for themselves. The *Sun* had done the same with 'Squidgygate'. The national weakness for royal voyeurism entered a dimension at which *Spitting Image* and its scabrous historical predecessors like Rowlandson could never have guessed. Paying an extra toll-rate, as for phone sex, it was possible for the lowliest to eavesdrop on the bedroom conversation of the mighty. People's monarchy—people's property.

Robes and dignity cast aside, these fallible icons with their 'ums' and 'fucks' and their whingeing fantasies sounded silly and confused. But there was something oddly brave in their obstinate affections. It suggested there might one day be some more honest and vulnerable way in which royal people might come to be viewed—as struggling human beings rather than as spurious 'good examples'. It also suggested that the wheel of media exposure and disclosure might finally have spun to a point where many people would really rather not know the details any more.

CHAPTER TWENTY-SEVEN

Annus horribilis

So much has happy family life become identified with the British Royal Family that it is doubtful whether a sovereign could sustain their sovereignty were this shattered.

Dorothy Laird, *How the Queen Reigns*, 1959

Standing in the shadows of the dark afternoon of Friday, 20 November 1992, Elizabeth II watched smoke billow through the roof of Windsor Castle.

The fire had been started by a spotlight that ignited a curtain, and by the time the alarm was raised, flames had leapt up into the high roof void and seized control of the north-east corner of the castle. Prompt action by Prince Andrew, who organised a naval-style rescue operation, got all but one important painting out of harm's way, but the damage to the building was extensive. Nine state apartments and a hundred other rooms were destroyed or severely scarred. As night fell, an ominous red glow silhouetted the gutted towers against the skyline.

Television cameras caught the small, sad figure of the Queen in rain-hood, mac and wellington boots as she contemplated the ruin of her childhood home. Her distress and bewilderment were unconcealed.

'She is devastated,' said Andrew in an impromptu press conference.

Never had Elizabeth II's private feelings escaped so nakedly into public display. According to some reports, she was crying. People's sympathy went out to the small, crumpled figure, and the symbolism was not lost on anyone. The graphic destruction of the ancient stronghold after which the dynasty was named reverberated eerily with the catalogue of royal disasters of the previous months.

Believing he was reflecting the national mood, the Tory Heritage Secretary Peter Brooke announced that, since the castle was uninsured, the government would pick up the repair bill, estimated at between £20 million and £40 million. But he had miscalculated. The immediate response was of outrage—a popular revolt of astonishing unanimity and power. While people might feel sorry for the Queen as a person, the misadventures of her children in the previous months had left even her most loyal supporters embarrassed and angry.

'Poor old Brooke,' recalls a courtier. 'There's scarcely a more important historic building in Britain. But to say that in 1992 . . . It really got the national goat.'

At a time of deepening economic recession, disaffection mingled with financial grievance. The previous year, a painstaking researcher, Phillip Hall, had helped produce an impressive TV programme, later turned into a book, showing how many modern monarchs had paid tax before the present reign. The royal tax immunity was *not* a time-hallowed tradition, it seemed, and in the resulting discussion of Hall's findings, the majority of commentators, including some traditional monarchists, felt it was time for the Queen to give way.

In this context, the Heritage Secretary's willingness to shell out public funds seemed a spectacular misjudgement. Normally loyal newspapers, callers to radio phone-in programmes and the other entrails of whatever constitutes the national mood were unanimous. 'While the castle stands, it is theirs,' wrote Janet Daley in *The Times*. 'But when it burns down, it is ours.' Royal wealth, royal privilege, royal misbehaviour—suddenly these were grievances that people felt personally, particularly if they were householders who struggled dutifully to pay their own insurance premiums. Something in the national psyche snapped.

It was a contrite Elizabeth II who addressed this

464

general mood just two days later. By chance she was scheduled to speak in the City of London at a Guildhall luncheon organised to celebrate her fortieth year on the throne, and she acknowledged that there seemed remarkably little to celebrate.

'Nineteen ninety-two is not a year I shall look back on with undiluted pleasure,' she said, in a thin and shaky voice that came from a cold hoarsened by a weekend of breathing in the acrid smoke of Windsor. You could hear the fumes scratching round her vocal cords. Worried that her voice might not make it through the polite conversation over lunch, she had asked that her speech be switched from the end to the start of the occasion.

'In the words of one of my more sympathetic correspondents,' she said, 'it has turned out to be an *annus horribilis.*'

She did not look up for the laugh.

'One's Bum Year' was the *Sun*'s earthy gloss next day on the royal wordplay with *annus mirabilis*. She had had to use Latin to do it, but for the first time in forty years Elizabeth II had given public voice to some genuine pain and vulnerability.

She also addressed the current national issue—a tarnished crown. The Queen and her family were custodians of the nation's most cherished dignity, and many in the nation felt that her family had let that dignity down. Her audience was the great of the land—the Prime Minister and the Leader of the Opposition, London's Lord Mayor and City worthies—and she rose above platitude to present them with a solid policy statement in the sphere that was her personal responsibility.

'No institution,' she declared, 'City, monarchy, whatever—should expect to be free from the scrutiny of those who give it their loyalty and support, not to mention those who don't.'

This reference to antimonarchists was the closest a royal speech had ever come to acknowledging the dread concept of republicanism; and Elizabeth II took another historic step. While never enunciating anything so crude as royal infallibility, all royal statements are traditionally framed as if handed down from on high. In 1917 worried courtiers had transformed the royal house's name and style without acknowledging that they were responding to 'Unrest in the Country'. Seventy-five years later came the public admission that the real motor of royal evolution was what came up from below.

'This sort of questioning,' conceded the Queen, 'can also act, and so it should do, as an effective agent of change.'

The momentous eating of humble pie had been drafted in the knowledge of impending action. Two days later, on Thursday, 26 November 1992, John Major announced in the Commons that the Queen and Prince of Wales would pay tax on their private income, starting the following year.

The royal tax exemption had traditionally been justified inside the Palace on two grounds: first, that it was a hallowed and ancient right deriving from the doctrine that the crown could not tax itself; and second, that the Queen could not afford to pay tax in any case.

The second argument had been removed by the reforms of Lord Airlie and Michael Peat. Having put the household's affairs in order, in 1990 they had negotiated a new ten-year arrangement for the Civil List—the Palace's last dealing with Margaret

Thatcher, who was replaced as Prime Minister by John Major that November. The guaranteed payments to 2000 (since extended to 2010) had placed the royal finances on a steady long-term footing. When it came to the trickier issue of ancient precedents, the self-inflicted wounds of the *annus horribilis* and the widely accepted findings of Phillip Hall persuaded Robert Fellowes that the time had come to throw in the towel. Tax would have to be paid. Arguments over money were never good news for the monarchy, and in 1992 the monarchy needed bad news like a hole in the head.

When the Queen came down from Sandringham at the beginning of the year, Fellowes had presented her with his recommendation that the time had come for her to start paying income tax. Knowing her attitude in the past, he had his arguments marshalled ready for a battle.

'Robert was quite apprehensive,' remembers one of his colleagues.

But the Queen yielded the point after the shortest of conversations. Confronted with the double audit of national opinion and of her own finances, Elizabeth II took 'just a matter of minutes' to agree to a change that had once seemed impossible. 'Fine, let's go,' ran one account of her reaction. 'Stop mucking around.'

'The Queen is much more willing to listen to the arguments for change than people give her credit for,' says one of her long-serving staff. 'I don't know any single subject which is taboo to her. There was nothing I could not discuss with her. She may not have agreed with me. But it was never "That's a no-no." On the tax thing she was actually ahead of her Prime Minister who, at that time, would fervently have advised against it.'

'The ground had been prepared quite carefully,' says another official. 'I think Airlie had had more than a few words with Prince Philip. When it comes to getting the big decisions past her, you have got to get the Duke on side.'

Early in 1992 Fellowes and Airlie took the proposal to the Treasury, and had the pleasure of shocking the mandarins with a reform they had not contemplated.

'John Major's people were not at all keen,' recalls one of the Palace team. 'They said, "The public will think we've gone republican."'

The satisfaction of being ahead of the game was spoilt by the Windsor fire and the outcry it prompted, but Fellowes decided to make the best of a bad job. The announcement that the Queen would be paying tax on her own initiative had been scheduled for the spring of 1993, but the private secretary now decided that the concession should be made immediately. 'I don't see any point in soaking up this flak for another three months,' Fellowes told the Cabinet Secretary, Sir Robin Butler. The Queen and the Prime Minister both agreed. John Major's Commons announcement came less than a week after the fire.

The reforms went beyond taxation. Government financing would be ended for all but the Queen herself, her husband and her mother. Princess Anne, Prince Andrew, Prince Edward and Princess Margaret would remain on the Civil List—literally a list enshrined in an Act of Parliament—but the Queen would now reimburse the government for these payments from her personal resources. This saving of £900,000 a year addressed media criticism of 'royal hangers-on', but it was a muddled compromise that smelled a little of panic. Even the severest critics did not class the hard-working Princess Anne as a hanger-on. Nor was it clear why popular but low-key cousins like Princess Alexandra, the Kents and the Gloucesters, whose public and charity work the Queen was already underwriting, should not have their staff and expenses supported from public funds. In effect, it was extra penance. Devoting some of her private money to the financing of public duties lent an element of personal deprivation to the Queen's *mea culpa*.

She received little thanks for it. Critics of the monarchy were now speaking and writing with a vehemence not seen since Queen Victoria's nadir in the 1860s. Early in 1993 *The Times* organised a major conference on the future of the monarchy in conjunction with Charter 88, a left-of-centre reform group which included committed republicans. The playwright David Hare boldly argued that the tabloid press had been acting as powerful agents for reform. 'Newspapers, led by the Murdoch group,' he said, 'have begun the project of putting the Royal Family in such a state of tension that their lives will become unliveable . . . We shall mock them till they wish they had never been born.'

The media response to the royal tax reform bore out Hare's words. Elizabeth II had agreed to pay tax on her personal income, but she had negotiated an exemption from inheritance tax on what she left to the next sovereign. While her estate would pay duty on bequests to children who did not succeed, and on bequests to anyone else, her successor on

469

the throne would receive whatever she bequeathed to him tax-free. The main purpose of this provision was to ensure that the estates of Sandringham and Balmoral, along with the core royal fortune, remained attached to the crown. But both the *Guardian* and the *Daily Mirror* were offended by the deal. 'HM the Tax Dodger' ran the *Daily Mirror*'s first-page headline, alongside a caricature of the Queen as a grasping miser.

The precise size of the private royal fortune also remained a grievance. At an unprecedented press conference David Airlie took questions on all aspects of the royal finances. He asserted that newspaper estimates of a £100 million personal fortune were 'greatly overstated', and the diligent researchers of Sunday newspaper 'rich lists' were to confirm the truth of this in the years that followed. The *Sunday Times* Rich List for 2001 did not even rank the Queen among the country's hundred wealthiest people. After stringent research, the paper ranked the Queen's wealth at no. 105=, a ranking she shared with the Duke of Devonshire, the former Conservative minister Michael Heseltine, and Richard Desmond, the pornography publisher who had recently purchased the Express newspaper group. Her private fortune, which by 2001 was estimated at £300 million, was comfortably outranked by scores of unknown entrepreneurs and by every major media tycoon, along with the composer Lord [Andrew] Lloyd Webber (£420 million, no. 69=) and the ex-Beatle Sir Paul McCartney (£713 million, no. 36).

But the antimonarchist view was that, whatever the size of the fortune, it was objectionable. Rulers in countries like Iran, Indonesia and the

Philippines who had built up private fortunes from their public positions were deemed in the West to be corrupt. Royal critics could not see the intrinsic difference between the wealth of the Queen and that of the Shah or Imelda Marcos.

This was rough company. There was a clear and ethical distinction between the pocketing of bribes in the present and the pocketing of savings in previous generations. But in the early 1990s few people were in the mood to hear it.

*   *   *

There was one last painful twist to the annus horribilis. Since the rending summer rows over the Morton book, relations between the Prince and Princess of Wales had sunk to new lows. That autumn the Queen had intervened to insist that Diana accompany her husband on the couple's forthcoming visit to South Korea. It was a matter of public duty, and Elizabeth II hoped against hope that some reconciliation might ensue. But the tour proved a disaster, with the Waleses unable to hide their mutual despair and antipathy from the cameras. The unforgiving tabloids put their finger on it, nicknaming the couple 'the Glums'.

On Wednesday, 25 November 1992, the day after the Queen's Guildhall speech, Charles and Diana met at Kensington Palace and agreed, on Charles's insistence, that they should formally separate. Lawyers were contacted, letters were exchanged, and the sad news was conveyed to the Queen and to the Prime Minister.

Proud of his negotiating skills, and hoping doggedly for some change of heart, John Major requested separate last-minute meetings with both the prince and princess, but to no avail. On 9 December he rose in a crowded but silent House of Commons officially to announce the separation.

The oddest part of his announcement was the assertion that, despite being legally separated, there was 'no reason why the Princess of Wales should not be crowned Queen in due course'. Legalistically, this reflected the constitutional position. But it was not what the monarchy had come to mean to most people. There was little function in crowning a king and queen who had made themselves internationally famous for hating each other. Major had read out the far-fetched assertion to his assembled ministers that morning, and no one had questioned it—demonstrating how even a hardened Prime Minister and his Cabinet found it difficult to accept that Diana would never be Queen.

In this novel situation, with no precedent to go by, Elizabeth II displayed her talent for compromise. Charles and Diana were not separating, at that point, as a first step to divorce. Diana was quite adamant that she wished to remain Princess of Wales, and, as mother of the future king, she was in a different position from Mark Phillips and Sarah Ferguson, for whom marital breakdown had meant the end of any direct royal role. The key ingredient in Diana's private conversations with John Major had been the Prime Minister's agreement that she would remain an established public figure in her own right, and the Queen went along with this.

Charles saw things differently. In the separation negotiations, his office argued that Diana's use of the Queen's Flight and the royal train should be curtailed. According to one aide, the prince 'took the attitude "She's completely off her rocker and has to be written out of the script." ' Charles's team tried to downgrade Diana's protocol, and argued that her staff should no longer work alongside his in St James's Palace.

' "You're in or you're out"—that was Charles's view,' remembers one of Diana's staff. 'His people pushed very hard. But the Queen wasn't having it. She insisted that Diana should have her dignity and rights.'

Elizabeth II accepted the novel prospect of a semi-independent Princess of Wales, and she tried to make it work. It was decided, against Charles's wishes, that Diana's private secretary, Patrick Jephson, should continue to work out of the Waleses' offices in St James's Palace, while Geoffrey Crawford, the Queen's deputy press secretary, would continue to look after the princess from Buckingham Palace. Diana would be encouraged to develop her own public life under the royal umbrella, and could undertake visits abroad, albeit in an 'official' capacity rather than as a personal representative of the Queen.

The Palace was well aware of the dangers of Diana, a proven loose cannon, feeling excluded and brooding on her own out at Kensington. 'After the separation,' recalls one of the Buckingham Palace press staff, 'we made it a policy to phone her every day, and to get in touch any time there was even the smallest problem, so she felt we were keeping her in the picture. If she didn't hear your voice for a day or two, the paranoia kicked in.' The idea was to keep the separated princess firmly bound in as part of the royal team. Jephson and Crawford liaised continually with Robert Fellowes and the Queen's other staff. They arranged some highly successful foreign trips for Diana, and helped shape a domestic schedule that combined her personal concerns with the greater royal programme.

The Queen's cautious 'live and let live' instincts were well suited to picking up the pieces from apparent catastrophe and pragmatically shaping something new. In the aftermath of her sister Margaret's separation in 1976 she had taken a lead in ensuring that Lord Snowdon was still regarded as a respected member of the extended family. It helped the children, and it avoided the awful precedent of the bitter Duke and Duchess of Windsor schism.

But the Queen had not reckoned with her eldest son. In the summer of 1992, before the Andrew Morton revelations, Prince Charles had authorised the writer and broadcaster Jonathan Dimbleby, younger son of Richard, the 'gold microphone in waiting', to start work on an ambitious double project. Dimbleby would produce a television documentary and an authorised biography to mark the twenty-fifth anniversary of Charles's investiture as Prince of Wales in July 1994.

The original intention was to focus on the prince's serious and worthy work in the inner cities, along with his other environmental, social and spiritual concerns. 'There's a very nice film there that never got shown,' recalls someone who worked on the project in the early days. But by the end of the *annus horribilis* it was clear to Dimbleby, as a prominent and reputable journalist, that he could not possibly ignore the national issue of the moment. He convinced the prince's private secretary, Richard Aylard, that both book and film must also present Charles's explanation of his disastrous marriage, and the two men persuaded Charles to go along with this.

From that moment, Dimbleby's combined book and film effectively became an open and authorised imitation of Diana's collaboration with Andrew Morton—another stage in the process by which the ancient tradition of royal reserve was converted into royal exhibitionism.

Dimbleby did not need to put his foot in the door. He was an invited guest at the table, with a contract giving him 'sole discretion about the contents' of his double project, tempered only by an agreement 'to take into account any comments made by HRH with respect to factual inaccuracies'. Provided he was an accurate observer, in other words, Dimbleby was free to reveal whatever he discovered.

One reading of the prince's motives is that he was behaving honourably and openly in allowing Dimbleby to take his inventory and display it to the world. But his staff undoubtedly saw the film and book as a propaganda effort, a double-barrelled blast to present their man's side of the story. They expected favourable treatment by Dimbleby in return for the special access being granted—and Charles's separated wife had no doubt about what the sudden appearance of the cameras and microphones portended.

'The next time they're filming,' Diana joked, 'I'll make a grand entrance. I'll poke my head round the door and say, "Hope you're going to let *me* get a word in!"'

Buckingham Palace viewed the enterprise with foreboding.

'Charles's people informed us about the project at the very beginning, when it was in its "Twenty-five Years of a Goodly Prince" mode,' recalls a member of the press office. 'But once it had got going, it was funny how the lines went quiet.'

The foreboding was justified. On the evening of 29 June 1994 fourteen million viewers in Britain sat down to watch the Prince of Wales confessing to adultery.

'Did you', asked Dimbleby, 'try to be faithful and honourable to your wife when you took on the vow of marriage?'

'Yes,' said Charles '—until it became irretrievably broken down, us both having tried.'

Charles described Camilla as 'a friend for a very long time', and the following day Jonathan Dimbleby confirmed that the infidelity to which the prince had confessed was indeed with Mrs Parker Bowles.

Coming from his own mouth, Charles's admission shattered one of the fundamental underpinnings of the monarchical edifice, the subconscious belief that royal people, like one's parents, do not actually do things like that. At a stroke a million maiden aunts were robbed of their comforting illusion that royal folk adhered by their nature to a higher standard, and that the lurid tales of royal misconduct, and even the Camillagate tape, had been 'all got up by the papers'.

'The boy was off his head,' growls a canny, long-serving confidant of both the Queen and the Queen Mother.

The TV documentary achieved precisely the opposite effect from that intended. Charles's disclosures actually seemed to corroborate the main thrust of Diana's story, that the dream marriage had been a sham, and they quite nullified the betrayal which had been the weakest plank of her platform. Diana's disloyalty could at least be justified by her youth and by her sense of isolation. Here was Charles deploying the staff and full resources of his office publicly to embarrass his wife and children—not to mention his mistress and her own family. Following the public announcement of his cuckolding by the man he had courteously continued to treat as his friend, the hitherto patient Colonel Andrew Parker Bowles sued for divorce.

But the sting for Elizabeth II came in the 620-page book about Charles which Dimbleby published later that year. The prince had given his biographer unprecedented access to his diaries and letters—material usually made available only for official royal biographies, published after the subject's death. Without consulting his mother, he had also allowed Dimbleby to look at a number of official documents, and when the Queen discovered this in September 1994 she exploded, insisting that the papers be returned immediately. When Charles went to Scotland that autumn, he judiciously limited his visit to his traditional stay with his grandmother at Birkhall, avoiding Balmoral. 'He'll only be coming here for one day,' remarked the Queen—and sure enough, her son just turned up for the ghillies' ball, allowing himself no time to talk to his mother.

Elizabeth II and her son were finding it as

difficult as ever to communicate—and in November 1994, Dimbleby's book, meticulously checked and confirmed by the prince for its accuracy, provided chapter and verse of the difficulties of their relationship in painful fashion. Charles's mother was portrayed as 'detached', his father as 'inexplicably harsh', and both parents as 'unable or unwilling' to offer their son 'the affection and appreciation' he required. Diana's account of her unhappy childhood, via Andrew Morton, had done full justice to its miseries, while conveying a touchingly warm forgiveness for both her father and mother. Prince Charles, via Jonathan Dimbleby, displayed considerably less compassion.

'This was a man of nearly fifty talking,' comments a scornful Palace official. 'It was like the chairman of ICI saying that the company was in trouble because of Mummy and Daddy.'

It was typical of the Queen that she should betray no sign of her feelings at being publicly stigmatised as a bad mother. But Anne, Andrew and Edward were outraged by Charles's behaviour, and told him so directly. The prince's need to be congratulated for his good works also earned his family's scorn. Anne's record of creative public service was in some ways more solid and consistent than Charles's, and both children were following in the footsteps of a formidably energetic father, who had blazed the original trail when it came to youth development and the environment. 'Prince Philip has kept slogging at all sorts of important projects for decades,' says one of his relatives, 'and he has never felt the need for a pat on the back.'

Both the purpose and the substance of the

Dimbleby project defined the country's next king as a whinger—just as insecure as his maligned wife in his need both to justify and to define himself through the media.

'I now remember', says an eminent former Cabinet minister, 'a curious thing that would happen on the yacht. Charles and Anne were not much more than teenagers at the time, and every morning at breakfast they would tear open the newspapers, looking for stories about themselves.'

Princess Anne had moved on. But there clearly remained a question mark over her brother.

*   *   *

By the end of 1994 debate had displaced disclosure in the nation's discussion of the royal family. After Dimbleby, Morton and the intercepted phone calls there was little more to reveal, and public opinion divided in a sort of civil war. 'Charles versus Diana' split the country like Cavalier against Roundhead. The issues that people were debating—fidelity, what constitutes reasonable behaviour in a partner, 'thinking about the children', whether it was right to wash dirty linen in public—were all, of course, the dilemmas which many faced in their own daily lives.

The prevailing sentiment was of collective disappointment, a feeling of having been let down. The 'dysfunctional' royal family became a platitude of newspaper analysis in these years, providing the posh press with their own clever and particularly merciless channel for invading royal privacy. The telephoto lens had its physical limits. Psychological speculation could take you anywhere—and

Charles's authorised biography provided a treasure trove of raw material.

But the greatest problem with the prince's self-justifying memoir was that, far from ending the battle, it reopened the campaigning with fresh bitterness.

'I'll get my own back on him,' Diana vowed to her staff with real relish. 'Just you wait and see. I will get my revenge.'

CHAPTER TWENTY-EIGHT

Safety Zone

Ordinary people are animals in the jungle. Royal people are animals in the zoo.

Margot Asquith, Memoirs

While Britain worked itself into a lather in October 1994 over Prince Charles's confessions—serialised, like his wife's collaboration with Andrew Morton, in Rupert Murdoch's *Sunday Times*—Elizabeth II got on with her job. The Queen was making her first ever state visit to Russia. It had been a matter of Windsor principle not to visit the Soviet Union while it was controlled by the successors of the Bolshevik regime that had murdered the Romanovs. But Boris Yeltsin was Russia's first ever ruler to be chosen by democratic election, marking a fresh start. When the Queen emerged into the sunlight on the steps of the Assumption Cathedral inside the Kremlin on 18 October the church bells that had been silenced through the long decades of communist rule pealed out for the first time for a visiting head of state.

Yeltsin and Elizabeth II had not met before, so at the heart of the state visit lay a potentially awkward blind date. The Queen broke the ice with a personal gift inspired by the Foreign Office discovery that the President's influential wife Naina loved gardening: a delicate crystal set of drawers containing seeds specially harvested from the gardens of Buckingham Palace.

'Oh, Borya,' exclaimed the delighted Naina Yeltsin. 'We can have our own Queen's garden out at the dacha!'

The Yeltsins returned the compliment with an album of rare Romanov letters, documents and family photographs, over which two royal heads pored delightedly. Prince Philip took great pleasure in pointing out his numerous Tsarist relatives to his wife.

Like Britain's prime ministers in their weekly royal audiences, Boris Yeltsin rapidly discovered the comfort of speaking in absolute confidence to someone who would not twist or leak his remarks and who would listen in sympathy. To his great pleasure, Elizabeth II was a safe zone. She was well used to offering solace to beleaguered politicians, and Yeltsin poured out his heart to her, explaining the problems of corruption and violence in the new Russia, and how difficult it was proving to establish decent government in the ruins of the old regime.

'Yes,' said the Queen as she listened supportively. 'You know, democracy takes a long time.'

Like many of the Queen's foreign trips since

1970, the momentous visit was filmed for inclusion in her Christmas broadcast by the old *Royal Family* team of Philip Bonham Carter and Peter Edwards. Bonham Carter operated the camera, while Edwards picked up the sound transmitted from the lightweight, high-powered radio microphone concealed in Her Majesty's posy of flowers. Edwards had ordered the blooms prior to his arrival in Moscow, and was surprised when they were delivered in a large black car by two official-looking women who proved to be knowledgeable about a great deal more than flower arranging. 'Is this transmission diversity system on VHF or UHF?' enquired one of the agents in perfect English. The 'florists' watched Edwards make up his electronic posy, and left deeply impressed by Her Majesty's state-of-the-art bugging techniques.

The following spring found Elizabeth II marking another hinge moment, this time in South Africa, where Nelson Mandela had been elected president in April 1994 in the country's first ever fully democratic, non-racial election. The white supremacist regime had stalked out of the Commonwealth in 1961 to avoid being expelled, and the ending of apartheid owed not a little to the Commonwealth staunchness in which the Queen had played a part.

In her forty-three years as Queen some of the warmest relationships of this shy, restrained woman had been with larger-than-life black African leaders. She was closer, in some ways, to ex-freedom fighters like Kenneth Kaunda, Jomo Kenyatta and even Kwame Nkrumah than she was to her middle-class Anglo-Saxon prime ministers. Maybe it was something to do with the regality with which Africa's twentieth-century chieftains embodied their new nations, and the unembarrassed naturalness with which they approached the totem of another tribe.

Elizabeth II had first met Mandela in 1991, shortly after his release from prison, when he was representing the African National Congress as an observer at the Commonwealth Conference in Zambia. At that date South Africa had not yet been readmitted to the Commonwealth, so Mandela had no status at the final banquet for the heads of government. But his Zimbabwean minders took him along just the same, and there was a very British scene as the Queen graciously greeted the unwitting gatecrasher while the table placings were hurriedly rearranged behind his back. Afterwards Elizabeth II made a point of talking to the ultimate freedom fighter, and the rapport was immediate.

'She's got a lot in common with him,' remarked one of her staff. 'You see, they've both spent a lot of time in prison.'

Mandela had been born into a tribal royal family, and on her March 1995 visit he summoned his country's chieftains to meet Elizabeth II. There were no fewer than thirteen South African kings at the state banquet in her honour in Cape Town. The President himself, in his genial old age and with his iconic status, had something of the constitutional monarch about him—floating serenely above criticism, his faults and unpopular decisions blamed on his underlings. When he started his letters to the Queen 'Dear Elizabeth', she did not take offence at his directness and simplicity. 'Family atmosphere' was the phrase independently coined by both white and non-white guests at the Britannia dinner that the Queen organised at the end of the visit, and on getting home she remarked several times on how much she had enjoyed Mandela's company. She also noted and appreciated his thoughtfulness in delaying his divorce proceedings from his second wife Winnie to avoid embarrassing headlines during the visit.

It was in South Africa in 1947 that the Queen, as Princess Elizabeth, had made her important coming-of-age vow, and the memory of those early years was conjured up later in the summer of 1995 with the commemorations of the fiftieth anniversaries of VE (Victory in Europe) and VJ (Victory in Japan) days. There had been some anxiety that the crowds might not turn out, and the organisers laid contingency plans to move the soldiers and bands outside the Palace railings to march and perform where the people should have been. In the event, there was more than enough fond nostalgia to fill Edward VII's amphitheatre in traditional style. Tens of thousands cheered the Queen, the Queen Mother and Princess Margaret on Saturday, 6 May 1995, standing on the balcony where they had stood half a century earlier for VE day.

Three and a half months later, on Saturday, 19 August, the VJ day celebrations were marked by Prince Philip wearing the Burma Star beret, saluting, eyes left, to the Queen as he led the veterans of the Far East down the Mall. But there was a logistical problem the following night. The Balmoral break had started, and the Queen, in her very literal way, did not think it would be genuine to wave from the balcony of a palace where she was not in residence. While in London, the royal family was staying on the royal yacht Britannia, moored beside Tower Bridge.

'The Queen', explains one of her staff, 'has an instinctive suspicion of anything contrived.'

In the end, Her Majesty was persuaded to pretend that she was home for this special occasion. It was important that the sometimes neglected survivors of the Japanese campaigns should have a full-scale commemoration—including a balcony appearance—to match that of the European veterans. But her regal instincts revived when an over-officious producer tried to hurry the family out on to the balcony to fit inside the BBC's scheduled time-slot. Elizabeth II declined to be hurried, and the seconds ticked down to the deadline.

'You'd better speak to Prince Philip,' Prince Edward told the frantic producer with a shrug. 'He's the only one she listens to.'

Her face set in an obstinate cast, the Queen was not for moving. She declined to be shooed outside at the bidding of a media stopwatch. In the end she went in her own time, followed by the family, just as the cheers were reaching a crescendo. VJ day itself, half a century earlier, had been one of the rare moments in her life when she had not paraded to order, but had wandered off into the crowds as her own timetable and fancy led.

*   *   *

By the middle of the 1990s, the royal rat pack had been swelled by some aggressive new rodents. For all their intrusiveness, James Whitaker, Arthur

Edwards and the rest of the old guard operated with courtesy and deference. Officially accredited to royal tours, they wore badges, obeyed the pooled access conventions, and derived the bulk of their stories and pictures from officially sanctioned photo-opportunities. After nearly two decades on the job, they had matured into solid and senior citizens, full-time employees with generous holiday pay and pension schemes.

But the explosion of the market for celebrity pictures all over the world had stimulated the growth of a new, lean and hungry style of freelancer, who sold his pictures to the highest bidder—which might be a British newspaper if its own man did not get the shot. The *Mirror*'s sensational photographs of Fergie having her toes sucked were the product of a guerrilla operation by an organised gang of French freelancers, who made some £50,000 from the *Mirror* and nearly £1.5 million from the syndication fees around the world.

Mark Saunders, one of the new breed, later recalled the price list, which started at £1,500 to £2,000 for a 'routine set' of Diana shopping.

'Swimming-costume stuff was picking up £10,000—£10,000 for a set of pictures—and then remember you will be selling that abroad as well, so you'd be picking up money on the foreign rights . . . I look at my sales reports sometimes from those days and there are some countries there I didn't even know existed.'

Jayne Fincher, a well-respected photographer and one of the very few women on the royal run, was horrified by the tactics of the new bovver boys—'right up close in front', she later remembered of how they swarmed around Diana, 'so she couldn't walk one step'. It was 'physically oppressive', in Fincher's opinion—'like being hunted in a pack. And they would be verbally aggressive to her. They would say, "Take your clothes off because we need to earn some money." They'd use foul language at her and be completely abusive and horrible.'

Delighting in provoking Diana into breaking down or into angry shots that would fetch more money, the new paparazzi called her 'the loon', and proudly called their own commerce 'looning'. Getting cosy with the press had not earned the princess the respect of this piratical and cynical bunch of men. They saw her as a commodity, and they despised her for it.

Diana's response to the challenge was to take them on single-handed. Semi-detached from the royal orbit and still locked in her image battle with her husband, she wanted to prove she could cope on her own. The freelancers stationed themselves round the entrance to Kensington Palace, with motorbikes and fast cars, working in pairs. They would set off in open pursuit when they saw the princess, and there was a sense in which Diana encouraged the chase. Though she was entitled to a royal protection officer, she would sometimes steal out of the Palace without telling him, to drive off on her own, pitting her nerve and driving skills against the pack.

'There were several occasions', remembers one of her staff, 'when she was with her protection officer, and she just jumped out of the car and gave him the slip. That led to a formal showdown with the police. They said they could not protect her unless she stayed with them, and she said she would rather do without. So that was why she often had no royal bodyguard in the last stages of her life. She could have had the protection officers any time she wanted. She had only to say. But she often went without them because that was her choice.'

In one of her chases in the summer of 1994, Diana at first successfully eluded her pursuers, but they kept on cruising and eventually spotted her distinctive Audi convertible parked, but empty, a mile or so away in Paddington. The paparazzi waited, cameras ready, and suddenly saw her, in another car, talking intensely to a handsome, tousle-haired young man. This looked like a story worth hundreds of thousands—the princess caught secretly meeting with her latest lover—until the car door opened and the young man got out. It was Richard Kay, royal correspondent of the *Daily Mail*.

Four years older than the princess, the 37-year-old Kay combined charm and discretion with a platform in Britain's most successful heartland newspaper, less stuffy than a broadsheet, but more loyal than a red-top like the *Sun*. The newspaper that had been started a century earlier for office boys was now the tabloid of choice for Britain's *Sex and the City set*—the staple breakfast reading of Diana and her girlfriends.

For more than a year Diana had been using Kay as a conduit for her most sensational stories. Kay's uncannily well-informed reports on the princess's single life displayed all the touches of humour, malice and paranoia that were the authentic Diana, and they were backed up with confident quotations that were sourced to a close 'friend'. Now the world knew just how close the 'friend' was—confirming

488

Palace suspicions, as one courtier put it, that Kay's reports in the *Daily Mail* were 'Diana's own dead-letter drop'. Queen Elizabeth II might decline to appear on her balcony to the media's timing, but the Princess of Wales was happy to go and sit in their cars in the back streets of Paddington.

After the wicked Mr Whitaker and Andrew Morton, the sorcerer's apprentice, Diana had achieved the ultimate in media-savviness—her own press officer and news agency combined. She could phone Richard Kay with a story at teatime and see her words reproduced in two and a half million copies next day. Rival newspapers anxiously scanned the *Daily Mail*'s earliest, late-night edition to see if there was a Diana story they must run with themselves the next day. The *Mail* took to delaying its Kay exclusives to later editions to foil its competitors, while Kay himself had a knack of including contrary and even critical material about Diana in his pieces to preserve his independence.

But it was the princess's affliction that she never had quite enough. The curse of daily image management is that one day always leads to another—and Charles's double Dimbleby project continued to rankle. Diana had had her book. But Charles had had a book and a TV programme. So when, in the summer of 1995, her brother Charles Spencer introduced her to Martin Bashir, a young television reporter working for the BBC news programme *Panorama*, Diana saw the means to accomplish her revenge.

On 5 November 1995, after her staff had gone home, she opened the door of Kensington Palace to the *Panorama* crew, and spent three hours filming and refilming her carefully prepared answers to the questions that she had pre-arranged with Bashir. 'She was behaving', remembered one of the crew, 'like she was an extra producer.'

The resulting fifty-five minutes of compulsive television on 20 November was watched by twenty-three million viewers in Britain, the BBC's highest rating ever, and by millions more around the world. In America, NBC paid $642,000 for Barbara Walters to rebroadcast the interview on 20:20.

Diana looked fragile and under pressure, heavily made-up with bright blue- and black-rimmed eyes. Her rare attempts at humour were sardonic and obviously rehearsed.

'There were three of us in this marriage, so it got pretty crowded,' was her edgy attempt to make light of the Camilla situation, while keeping it firmly to the fore.

Confronted with the issue of her own infidelity, she carefully avoided the suggestion of 'adultery', with its Old Testament and divorce court grimness, and tiptoed deftly into the meadow of romance.

'Yes, I loved him,' she said of James Hewitt. 'I adored him . . . and he let me down.'

Twenty-three million hearts went out to her—particularly among her already overflowing constituency of women who knew a man who had done them wrong. But the thrust that betrayed both the enormity and the poverty of the princess's celebrity-defined ambitions was the dream that she famously disclosed, to be 'a queen of people's hearts'. Not for Diana the hard-working grind of being an ordinary, constitutional queen, sticking by the rules and plodding through the boring chores. She wished to flit for ever through the miasma of superstardom, known for her well-knownness, darting from fashion to compassion and back again—a queen as defined by her own fancy and by the circulation figures of *Hello!* magazine.

Unsurprisingly, the real Queen was not impressed. Overcoming her natural inclinations, Elizabeth II had yielded to pragmatism, with a dash of Christian forgiveness, to let bygones be bygones over Diana's role in the Andrew Morton disclosures. Diana's recently exposed collaboration with Richard Kay could also be excused as a magnified version of the leaking in which Charles's endlessly indiscreet friends indulged. But this time the princess's betrayal, both in the secretive arrangements for and in the directly critical content of her *Panorama* interview, was inescapable. At one point Diana had even questioned the fitness of Charles to be King.

'My wish', she declared, in a fine example of her many-layered style of attack, 'is that my husband finds peace of mind, and from that follow other things.'

Elizabeth II acted at last. The previous December had seen the second anniversary of the couple's separation, the moment when the law permitted a simple no-fault divorce. Princess Margaret, who had divorced promptly on her two-year deadline, felt strongly that Charles should do the same.

'Do it straight away,' she had told her nephew, and seeing his eyes glaze over at advice he had clearly heard before, she kicked him sharply on the knee.

'What's that for?' he asked.

'Shape up,' she said.

Robert Fellowes felt there was no alternative to

divorce—and so, more crucially, did the Duke of Edinburgh. According to the journalist Paul Johnson, even John Major added his view that the Waleses' bickering had gone so far it was damaging British prestige abroad. Three weeks after the *Panorama* broadcast, on 12 December 1995, Elizabeth II formally notified her Prime Minister that she would be writing to her son and daughter-in-law, requesting that they agree to an 'early divorce . . . in the best interests of the country'.

The letters, measured but firm, went out to the couple. Divorce negotiations were begun—and shortly afterwards Her Majesty brought an end to another special relationship. Since 1932 every royal Christmas broadcast, on radio or television, had been handled by the BBC, whose modern bosses had elbowed aside the attempts of ITV to get in on the act by stressing their traditions of loyalty. When it came to the *Panorama* interview, however, this loyalty had taken the form of the Corporation conspiring with the princess to conceal all news of the project from the Palace until just half an hour before the rest of the world was told. The connivance had included the Director-General himself.

For some time the Palace press office had been considering inviting ITV to freshen up the Christmas broadcast, and this seemed the moment. The BBC's monopoly was ended.

*   *   *

On 28 August 1996, the marriage of the Prince and Princess of Wales was officially dissolved. It was the fourth major royal divorce of Elizabeth II's reign.

The terms included a confidentiality agreement which Diana broke immediately by leaking the separation details to the press: a lump sum of £15 million for the princess, most of it out of the Queen's pocket on her son's behalf; joint custody of the children; and accommodation for Diana in Kensington Palace.

The most controversial element was Diana's new title and status. She would be known as Diana, Princess of Wales—so, if Charles were to marry again, his new wife would be known as The Princess of Wales—and she was no longer a Royal Highness. For the rest of her life she would be as HRH-less as Wallis Simpson.

Diana herself had proposed that she should surrender her HRH in a meeting with the Queen on 15 February 1996, before the formal divorce negotiations had begun. It was a get-together that the Queen had suggested. Hoping to mitigate the now rancorous ill-feeling between the spouses, Elizabeth II thought it might diffuse the situation if she met her daughter-in-law to discuss face-to-face the issues, like royal status, that were hers, and not Charles's, to decide.

Diana later explained to friends that she thought the Queen would wish her to give up her HRH. At this opening stage, the mood of the princess, always ambivalent about her royalness, seems to have been that she wanted to walk before she was pushed. 'I think,' says a courtier, 'there was great relief all round that Diana had made the offer.'

But when Diana had met Charles two weeks later at the end of February, and, in her now established fashion, rushed out her own version of those discussions, there was no mention of her having offered to surrender her HRH. In fact, wrote Richard Kay, 'The Princess wanted to remain HRH the Princess of Wales, but the other side refused and that had been the sticking point for the last two weeks.'

It was a very serious mistake. Up to this point it had been possible for Elizabeth II to give Diana the benefit of the doubt over the inconsistencies of her behaviour—and she had done so. But the question of HRH status was something that she had discussed face-to-face with Diana, while her deputy private secretary, Robin Janvrin, took notes, and it was Diana who had volunteered to surrender the dignity. Here was explicit, incontrovertible evidence of the girl's dizzying unreliability. She was trying to present the Queen as the baddie, and was getting the *Daily Mail* to present this falsehood as the truth. The Queen instructed her press secretary, Charles Anson, to issue an unprecedentedly specific denial.

'The decision to drop the title is the Princess's and the Princess's alone,' said Anson. 'It is wrong [to say] that the Queen or the Prince asked her. I am saying categorically that is not true.'

The press secretary made sure that every newspaper got the message.

'The Palace does not say something specific on a point like this,' he told the *Daily Express*, 'unless we are absolutely sure of our facts.'

Palace-speak could not get closer to the Queen calling her daughter-in-law a liar. It was the moment when Diana truly became a royal outsider.

*   *   *

494

The surrender of Diana's HRH dominated the immediate newspaper verdict on the divorce settlement.

'Her Royal Humiliation', said the *Daily Mail*. 'The Final Betrayal', pronounced the *Daily Mirror* beside a photograph that showed Diana looking drained—'the face of a woman utterly destroyed'.

But perspectives shifted twenty-four hours later when it was announced that Diana was giving up her links with nearly a hundred of her charities. She was maintaining her formal connections with just six. So abrupt was the decision that some of the charities only learned they had been abandoned from the press.

'We had all argued with her hard about that for some time,' remembers one of her staff. 'A lot of her charities were no work at all. They were perfectly happy just to have her name on the letterhead. But she just wouldn't listen.'

Diana had always been a mixture of self-indulgence and idealism, reflecting her own personal turmoil. But as she cast loose from her royal moorings, the contradictions became more obvious to the outside world.

In the summer of 1994 a glimpse of her obsessiveness had been revealed when stories surfaced of her pursuit of Oliver Hoare, a handsome, cultured and unmistakably married dealer in Islamic art. The Hoare home had been the victim of hundreds of mysterious phone calls, and Hoare's wife insisted the police be called in to track the identity of the caller, who would ring 'five or six times on a quiet day'—then say nothing when the phone was picked up. The police traced the calls to four numbers: three inside Kensington

Palace and Diana's own mobile phone. Diana later confessed to Joseph Sanders, her financial adviser, that she had even gone to public payphones to call Hoare, wearing disguises and putting on gloves so she left no fingerprints.

Her staff were to report being the victims of similar bizarre harassment, when the princess left disturbing messages on their answering machines. 'The boss knows about your disloyalty and your affair,' read an anonymous message in January 1996 on the pager of her private secretary Patrick Jephson, who took the hint that his resignation was required.

The other side of this desperation was Diana's visionary altruism. The hectic period between her divorce at the end of August 1996 and her death just twelve months and three days later was marked by the crusade in which she arguably helped accomplish the most widespread human good of all. Through her visits to Angola and Bosnia to draw attention to the human suffering caused by land mines, she inspired worldwide concern on the issue and helped secure, posthumously, an international agreement to ban the devices.

'In that last year of her life,' says someone who crossed swords with her more than most, 'I felt that her life was coming back into some sort of order. The land mine campaign was a truly genuine passion of hers—and when she focused on something, she was just formidable.' Helping others provided Diana with some exorcism from her own demons. She was able to hand out the unconditional affection that she so much wanted to receive.

June 1997 found the princess in New York

auctioning her dresses to raise $3.26 million, most of which went to the AIDS Crisis Trust—an imaginative gesture for which she gave the credit to William, her elder son. But Diana had no previous affiliation with this glitzy American charity. Her formal AIDS patronage, one of the six affiliations she had kept, was with Britain's more sober National AIDS Trust, which in June 1997 was nearly bankrupt. 'If you are a patron,' says Michael Adler, chairman of the National AIDS Trust, in carefully measured words, 'you have responsibilities that go with patronage that you must fulfil.' The American AIDS Crisis Trust raised its funds primarily through film premières and celebrity-studded social occasions. So even in her good works lurked Diana's other strand—the lure of fame and fun without consequence, which found the princess in the summer of 1997 taking her sons on holiday in the South of France with the controversial owner of the Harrods department store, Mohammed Fayed.

Diana had had occasional contacts with Fayed on London's champagne charity circuit, but it was after her divorce that she found they had something deeper in common. Fayed had been denied a British passport on grounds of government doubts over his business practices in acquiring Harrods, and he had cultivated his image as a persecuted outsider, taking pleasure in being an irritant to the establishment. One *enfant terrible* had found another. On previous occasions Diana had turned down Fayed's offers of favours and hospitality, but when they met at a ballet gala in June 1997, she accepted his invitation to take her sons for a summer holiday with his family at their villa in St Tropez.

One attraction of the holiday was the chance to enter the rich man's world of private jets, chauffeured limousines and walkie-talkie-linked bodyguards that mimicked the cocoon of royal life. The break also provided an escape from the latest of the princess's ill-starred love affairs—her bid to marry the modest and reclusive Pakistani heart surgeon Hasnat Khan.

Khan worked at London's Royal Brompton Hospital, and he was deeply serious about his medical career. It was another of the miscalculations of the most photographed woman in the world to fall in love with a man who, in his family's words, felt 'terrorised' by media attention. The twenty-month relationship ended with a row over Diana's games with the press, which Khan had insisted be kept out of their romance. The heart surgeon accused Diana of leaking a story about a visit she had made to his family in Pakistan, and though she denied it, Khan apparently decided he had had enough. As she packed to leave for her holiday, Diana 'was sobbing her heart out', according to her hairstylist Nathalie Simmons— who, like Diana's astrologer, psychic, acupuncturist and virtually every other soldier in her regiment of New Age carers, would later sell her story to the newspapers.

Within a day of Diana's arrival on Friday, 11 July, the Fayed compound in St Tropez was surrounded with boats filled with long-lens paparazzi, who recorded the princess's jet-skiing with her sons, swimming and diving in an elegant leopard-print bathing costume. It was no accident, it seemed to Arthur Edwards, that she posed most extravagantly on 17 July so her picture was sure to dominate the front pages next morning—the day Charles was organising a fiftieth birthday party for Camilla. 'She was happy to be seen,' said Piers Morgan, editor of the *Daily Mirror.* 'I offered to pull out of St Tropez after two days, and her office said, "That won't be necessary." After that she did daily photo-calls.'

Just ten days had passed since the publication of Sir Gordon Downey's official report into the parliamentary 'cash for questions' scandal, in which Mohammed Fayed had confessed to bribing Conservative MPs with 'used notes in brown paper envelopes'. Though Fayed's misdeeds had helped expose and end a shamefully corrupt practice whereby MPs sold their right to ask questions of government ministers in Parliament, it deepened his reputation as a dubious character. For Diana to pose on his jet-ski with her son William, the heir to the throne, was a subversive interpretation of royal behaviour.

Back in London, the royal family and their staff were horrified. Outside the press office in Buckingham Palace, the newspapers of the day are laid out on a dark mahogany table, and Robert Fellowes was seen to wince as he walked past front page after front page, each displaying his sister-in-law in her bathing suit. One set showed Diana embracing the portly figure of her host, Mohammed Fayed, provoking the *Sunday Mirror* to complain at 'Di's Freebie', while the *News of the World* wondered at the public favour that the princess was bestowing on the 'Sleaze Row Tycoon'.

It seemed scarcely credible. Even the *Daily*

Sport, whose sales were based on transferring Page Three girls to page 1, and normally featured bare breasts on its cover, found that the princess filled the slot. Down the Mall, in Clarence House, the Queen Mother banned newspapers altogether.

But there was more to come. Halfway through the holiday, the family party was joined by Fayed's 42-year-old son, Dodi. Soft-voiced, darkly handsome and very eager to please, Dodi was classic material for a holiday romance. When Diana got home to Kensington Palace she found her apartment filled with pink roses and an $11,000 gold Cartier Panther watch.

Five days later she joined Dodi in Paris for a secret weekend, staying at his father's lovingly restored Ritz Hotel. On Saturday afternoon, Dodi took her to another of his father's restoration projects, the villa where the exiled Duke and Duchess of Windsor had stayed in the Bois de Boulogne. Fayed was selling the contents of the villa through Sotheby's, but there remained just a few of the paintings, furniture and initialled knick-knacks that had provided consolation to another royal outcast for a lifetime in exile.

The world did not yet know of Diana's latest romance, but she put that to rights once August had started. Her sons went up to Balmoral to join their father and the rest of the royal family; Diana returned to the Mediterranean for a six-day cruise, now alone with Dodi on his father's yacht, the *Jonikal.*

A few days later, the paparazzo Jason Fraser received a call telling him where Diana could be located in very interesting company. Fraser's Italian business partner, Mario Brenna, made his way there, and from a small yacht which took him as close as ten yards from the *Jonikal* he ran off a series of shots of Dodi and Diana swimming, sunbathing and kissing. Fraser and Brenna made more than $2 million from selling their pictures, which first appeared in the London tabloids on Thursday, 7 August.

As usual, Richard Kay supplied the authorised commentary. 'The Princess herself,' he wrote of Diana and Dodi, 'was yesterday astonishingly relaxed over the revelation of their closeness and the prospect of intimate photographs . . . She's sick of all the cloak-and-dagger stuff. Why shouldn't she have a man in her life and for people to know about it?'

In the view of many of her friends, Diana's apparent cry of liberty was actually a message aimed at Hasnat Khan, her personal complaint at the year and a half of cloak-and-dagger courting that she had had to go through with him. Having learnt how to use the press as a weapon against the royal family, Diana was now using it in the machinations of her personal love life.

The very next day the messages she was conveying were suddenly regal and caring again, as she was photographed in the minefields of Bosnia, bringing comfort to the victims of land mines. She had scheduled the visit several months earlier, and in arranging the details had insisted that she should not just shake hands and move on; she wanted to spend a full thirty minutes with each young land-mine victim, she said, so that she could listen properly to all of their stories. At some point during each of these moving encounters, remembered William Deedes, the 83-year-old journalist who accompanied her, 'she would stretch out a hand or both hands and touch this person on the arm or face. I found some of the tales we had to hear almost unendurable. Yet I never saw her lose this calm, which plainly had a most soothing effect.' Here was the other Diana, the angel of mercy, whose healing and uplifting charisma contrasted so strongly with the trivial celebrity games and feuds she pursued.

These were the contradictions that had made her life so difficult to understand—and which remained tragically unresolved when she died in Paris in the small hours of 31 August 1997, trying to outwit the paparazzi whom she had spent her last weeks both enticing and attempting to escape.

The couple had been due to fly straight back from Sardinia to London after another yacht cruise, but Diana was worried about the mass of photographers who would be waiting for her in London. So she adopted Dodi's suggestion of one last night in Paris. Cornered in the Ritz, the Fayeds' royal cocoon of limousines and bodyguards produced a driver with nearly three times the legal amount of alcohol in his blood, and a cunning scheme to drive at high speed through a tunnel beside the River Seine. The intention was to escape the pressure of what proved to be the media's last and lethal exercise in 'looning'.

*   *   *

The first reports of the accident said that Dodi had been killed in the crash, but optimistically suggested that Diana might have escaped comparatively unscathed. Princesses do not exist to die mangled in cars. The conspiracy theories about her death that flourish to this day display the same refusal to acknowledge that while famous people, like royal people, may try to live by different rules from the rest of us, they can be killed, like anyone else, if they fail to fasten their seatbelts.

The news of her death reached London at 4.41 a.m., and soon after dawn the first bouquets of flowers were being laid outside the palaces, many of them by her gay constituency as they emerged from their clubs. People were weeping openly, as if a member of their own family had died. By lunchtime there were already nearly a thousand bouquets outside Kensington Palace, and Matthew Engel, the Guardian writer, found photographers being shouted at and jostled by angry mourners as they tried to take photographs of the flowers.

Helen Fielding, author of the best-selling novel *Bridget Jones's Diary*, read the news as she picked up the Sunday papers from her doormat, and was inspired to sit down and compose a special, one-off entry to her mixed-up heroine's diary that captured the general sense of disbelief. 'Am going to put on telly, and they will say it has been a mistake, and she is back. Then we will see her coming out of the Harbour Club with all the photographers asking her what it was like . . . Really, she was the patron saint of Singleton women.'

Helen Fielding went through the experiences of many Londoners that Sunday, calling friends in horrified incredulity, buying tributes at her local petrol station, then going to lay them among the mounting pile of flowers in Kensington Gardens. Studying the messages on the bouquets, Fielding was especially moved by one, in wobbly old lady's handwriting, which she committed to memory. She went home to write it down as a postscript to Bridget's diary entry for 31 August 1997, summing up what Diana had come to mean to her fictitious heroine, to herself, and to many millions of others: 'When I was in trouble you cared about me, when I was in danger you tried to stop it, when I was sick you visited me, when people ran away you took my hand. Whatever you did for the poorest and smallest people I felt as if you did for me.'

The *Independent*, which published Bridget's loving tribute a few days later, was the one British newspaper which had consistently shunned the media hysteria surrounding Diana. Founded in 1986 by a group of journalists—a number of them Murdoch refugees—who aspired to create a serious broadsheet that was worthy of its idealistic name, the paper had made a deliberate policy of not running royal stories. But death changed many things about Diana. 'Her death', reflected the *Independent* in a thoughtful editorial, 'ought to start a much-needed debate about the structure and appetites for this global industry of images and words which the public both adores and loathes . . . [The princess] was sucked up by forces which, tide-like, came to overwhelm her. Like some heroine of old, she thought she could tame the beasts—and was wrong. Some accidents have a force that feels like Fate.'

CHAPTER TWENTY-NINE

Bridge Procedures

I admired and respected her for her energy
and commitment to others and especially for
her devotion to her two boys.

Queen Elizabeth II, Friday, 5 September 1997

Sir Robin Janvrin was woken shortly before one
o'clock in the morning by a phone call from the
British ambassador in Paris. There was news of a
car crash involving Dodi Fayed and the Princess of
Wales. The deputy private secretary was on duty at
Balmoral in his house on the estate, and he called
the big house to talk to the Queen and Prince
Charles in their rooms. Then he threw on some
clothes and went up to confer.

Sir Guy Acland, the Deputy Master of the
Household, was sleeping in his bedroom across the
corridor from the private secretary's office. He was
woken by the sound of conversation and went out
to discover Janvrin, in rough shirt and trousers,
talking intently on the telephone to Paris.

Within minutes the phone calls were coming and
going. Robert Fellowes was on the phone from
Norfolk, where his distraught wife Jane was
desperate to find out how her sister was. Radios
and televisions went on around the castle as people
woke up to the unfolding drama, which was now
centring on the hospital Pitié Salpetrière, where
French doctors were fighting against the odds to

save the princess's life.

The news that Diana had died came through from the embassy just before 4 a.m. Still in dressing gowns and slippers, the Queen and Prince of Wales called Janvrin and Acland to a hurried meeting in Prince Charles's sitting room. The prince was desolate and got straight on the phone to his deputy private secretary, Mark Bolland, who was in London and in touch with the press.

'They're all going to blame me, aren't they?' he asked, in a state of some panic. 'What do I do? What does this mean?'

The prince suffered an emotional collapse, though, according to his private secretary, Stephen Lamport, he made no mention of Diana in his distress.

'They're all going to blame me,' he repeated. 'The world's going to go completely mad.'

His mother and father were more practical, conferring with Janvrin and Fellowes to pass on the sad news and their condolences to Diana's mother, brother and sisters, and to work out what would happen next.

'The family went into action, operating at their very, very best,' remembers one of those at the centre of the logistics which started at that moment. 'Later in the week there was all the business of the flag. We got out of touch, and it's no use pretending we didn't. But that Sunday morning, sitting in Balmoral, the Queen and Prince Philip did foresee the public shock and distress, because they actually felt the same. Everyone was just devastated. It was a terrible tragedy, and they wanted to do the best for the person who, underneath, I believe, they all loved.'

Lieutenant-Colonel Malcolm Ross, the brisk and quizzical former Guards officer who was comptroller of the Lord Chamberlain's office, was authorised to set in motion Operation Overlord. This long-planned, but never previously used set of procedures had been worked out by the police, the military and the Lord Chamberlain's Office, to bring back a royal body from abroad.

'Someone has got to fly to Paris and bring back the princess,' Robin Janvrin told the Queen, Prince Philip and their son. Prince Charles was the obvious candidate for the job.

The Queen's very first reaction to her daughter-in-law's death had been to think of her two grandsons. 'We must get the radios out of their rooms,' she said to Charles. There was also a television in the nursery. Mother and son discussed whether to wake William and Harry with the news. Their grandmother felt strongly that they should be left to sleep so they could face what would be the most difficult day of their lives after a decent night's rest.

One of the problems about the boys' reactions was that they had been even more embarrassed than the rest of the family by Diana's cavortings during the previous month. Though pressurised by the princess to send thank-you letters to Mohammed Fayed, the two princes had experienced their last period of time with their mother, under the aegis of the loud and over-familiar Harrods proprietor, as 'creepy'. William, just fifteen, had been particularly embarrassed by his mother's romance with Dodi, and he had had at least one fierce row with her about it over the telephone.

507

At 7.15 a.m. a more composed but still red-eyed Prince Charles went to his sons' rooms to wake them. Trying to help William and Harry come to terms with the dreadful news, he slowly went through what was likely to happen in the coming day. He explained that he would be going to Paris that afternoon to bring back Mummy's body. The two of them would be staying with their grandparents and the rest of the family in Balmoral. Church was scheduled, as usual, for 11.30 a.m. and he was planning to go. Would they like to go with him, he asked? He suggested that church would be a comfort.

William said yes. He would like to go, he said—so he could 'talk to Mummy'.

By eight o'clock the plans for Operation Overlord were getting under way. An RAF Hercules was designated to set off from Brize Norton in Oxfordshire, with a royal coffin and team of undertakers to embalm and handle the corpse. Paul Burrell, Diana's butler, was also heading for Paris with the clothes in which the princess's body would be dressed. Diana's sisters, Jane and Sarah, were preparing to travel to RAF Wittering in Rutland to await the plane which would take them up to Aberdeen, where Prince Charles would join them for the sad flight to Paris. Operation Overlord envisioned that the body would be brought back to lie, for the time being, in the Chapel Royal in St James's Palace.

The Spencers were the crucial factor in what would happen after that. The logic of the

508

procedures set in train by the Lord Chamberlain's office was that Diana's funeral would be organised with full royal pomp and ceremony. But that was precisely what the most vocal and influential members of her own family did not want.

Phoning from South Africa, Diana's brother Charles, who had been Earl Spencer for five years, made clear his feeling that his sister's funeral should be a private affair for just the close family at the ancestral home of Althorp. A public memorial service could come a month or so later, in the traditional style of aristocratic mourning. The young earl had once spoken to his sister about what she would like to happen in the event of her death, and she had told him that she would like her memorial service to be centred around a performance of Verdi's Requiem.

Diana's mother, Frances Shand-Kydd, was actually not on speaking terms with the princess at the time of her death. Diana had been incensed at remarks her mother had made in a series of articles she sold to *Hello!* magazine that summer. But Mrs Shand-Kydd shared her son's determination that the House of Windsor should not reclaim their girl in death. Both Spencers felt that Diana had been wickedly ill-used by Prince Charles, and that the princess had received precious little back-up from the rest of the royal family in the course of her unhappy marriage. Charles Spencer, who was closest of all the family to Diana in age and outlook, had been a prime collaborator in the Andrew Morton project, and had later introduced Diana to Martin Bashir of *Panorama*. Her sisters, Sarah and Jane, went along with the family line, and in the welter of confusion and emotion it fell to

Jane's husband, Robert Fellowes, to speak at length to both his mother-in-law and brother-in-law in the small hours of the morning.

When Fellowes conveyed the Spencer sentiments to the Queen, her first reaction was to accept them. For Diana's mother and brother to take charge of the princess's funeral seemed a natural, family way to go, and it solved the protocol problems of Diana's divorced and detached royal status. How should a royal family mourn a downgraded ex-HRH? In any ordinary family, no one would expect the cut-off mother-in-law to step in and organise an ex-wife's funeral service; she would be praised just for slipping into a pew at the back. So if the Spencers actively wanted to take charge, it suited the Queen very well not to stand in their way. It was agreed that the Princess of Wales would be taken with full royal honours to the Chapel Royal in St James's Palace, and that the Spencer family would take over after that.

That Sunday morning Geoffrey Crawford, the Queen's press secretary, who was visiting his family in Australia, rang Robert Fellowes to say he was flying back to London immediately. There was no need to rush, replied the private secretary. The plan was for a private family funeral. Crawford would not be needed until the Palace started helping with the full-scale public memorial service that would be planned some time after that.

*   *   *

Tony Blair, the recently elected New Labour Prime Minister, had also been up since the small hours, talking to the Foreign Office and discussing the ramifications of the princess's death in a series of telephone calls with his kitchen cabinet of close advisers.

'This is going to be absolutely enormous,' he said to Alastair Campbell, his press spokesman, 'probably bigger than any of us can imagine.'

Blair was in his Sedgefield constituency in County Durham, Campbell at his home in London. Shortly after eight o'clock, the Prime Minister made another call to Balmoral to enquire if the Queen was planning to talk to the nation. Elizabeth II said she would be going to church as usual, but that she had no plans to add to the statement of regret that she and Prince Charles had already issued. Blair replied that, in that event, he felt that he should make some sort of public tribute to the princess. It was the new Prime Minister's uncanny instinct for the popular mood that had helped get him elected four months earlier with an historic majority, and he had no doubt that something needed to be said.

Over the phone, Blair and Campbell roughed out the remarks that the Prime Minister would deliver as he paused to speak to cameras on his way to church in the village of Trimdon that morning, just before 11 a.m.

'We are today a nation in a state of shock, in mourning, in grief that is so deeply painful for us,' said the Prime Minister. 'We know how difficult things were for her from time to time . . . But people everywhere, not just here in Britain, kept faith with Princess Diana. They liked her, they loved her, they regarded her as one of the people. She was the People's Princess, and that is how she will stay, how she will remain in our hearts and our memories for ever.'

'People's Princess' was not Tony Blair's phrase, nor Alastair Campbell's. The author Anthony Holden had used it as a chapter title in his 1993 book *The Tarnished Crown*, and Julie Burchill, Diana's vociferous feminist champion, had deployed it in her columns. In 1984 it had been the title of a book by S. W. Jackman on Queen Mary's crowd-pleasing mother, Princess Mary, Duchess of Teck. But in September 1997, 'People's Princess' captured the moment. Blair's elegiac tribute has been described as his Falklands. As Margaret Thatcher made herself more-than-just-a-political-leader by her decision to recapture the South Atlantic islands after their invasion by Argentina in 1982, so in 1997, after just four months in power, Blair found the words that expressed what most of the country was feeling at that moment.

*   *   *

While the royal family may have been feeling Britain's grief about Diana, they failed to reveal much evidence of it as they drove to the little stone parish church of Crathie at 11.30 a.m. on Sunday 31 August. Indeed, they concealed their feelings with such grim success that all of them—from the normally outgoing Queen Mother down to the two princes, William and Harry—might have been taken for wooden and uncaring. This impression was heightened by the service itself, which contained special prayers for the Prince of Wales and his sons, but which made no mention at all of Diana. Afterwards, the clan got in their cars and drove back undemonstratively to Balmoral. Not a

512

public tear was shed. It was the Aberfan syndrome. Elizabeth II's dislike of disclosing emotion, along with her mistrust of crowd-pleasing, Diana-style gestures, froze the whole family in an appearance of apparent—and rather appalling—indifference.

'No Mention of Accident' ran the *Times* headline reproachfully next morning, alongside photographs of the family. Black ties apart, one studied the pictures in vain for some obvious sign on the royal faces that a family catastrophe had just occurred.

The raw emotion of Diana's brother Charles was far more in keeping with the general mood. Emerging from his house in Cape Town, the young earl delivered a fiery message.

'I always believed the press would kill her in the end,' he said with feeling. 'But not even I could imagine that they would take a direct hand in her death, as seems to be the case. It would appear that every proprietor and editor of every publication that has paid for intrusive and exploitative photographs of her, encouraging greedy and ruthless individuals to risk everything in pursuit of Diana's image, has blood on his hands today.'

*   *   *

The Palace press office had been on duty since dawn. Dickie Arbiter, the former radio journalist who was in charge of TV and press facilities, was co-ordinating the media aspects of Operation Overlord. After several hours on the phone, he drove out to Northolt, the military airport in north-west London where the prince's plane was due to arrive from Paris at the end of the afternoon with

Diana's coffin. Arbiter summoned the reporters, photographers and cameramen for a briefing in the hangar. An ice-skating champion of particularly upright posture, the press officer made an impressive figure as he stood atop a tall stepladder in his immaculate suit, collar and tie.

'The world will be looking at us,' he said with a sternness worthy of Commander Colville. 'So let us all behave with dignity. We don't want the noise of motor-winds, so it'll be only single-shutter shots—and no long boom mikes intruding. Let us give the princess a welcome home to be proud of.'

Only hours after the reports that cameramen had chased Diana to her death, the rat pack nodded meekly and silently.

'There was a deep sense of shame,' Arbiter remembers.

Meanwhile, across the tarmac, in the VIP lounge, the Prime Minister was talking with the Lord Chamberlain, as they awaited the arrival of Prince Charles and the funeral party.

'This is going to be pretty tricky,' Airlie said to Blair.

By now it was nearly evening, and it was already clear to both the Lord Chamberlain and the Prime Minister that the Spencers' wish for a private family funeral was not going to work. The television channels had been running open-ended coverage of Diana's death all day. Newspapers had brought out special editions. The crowds of mourners outside both Buckingham and Kensington Palace were growing. At town halls around the country people were creating local shrines for flowers, and gathering in churches for instantly organised sessions of prayer. The Prime

Minister's eulogy that morning had helped stamp this tide of emotion with national significance— with a sense of national entitlement, even. Diana's embrace with celebrity culture had lent the culture rights over her that her own family did not possess. She had become much more than a Spencer. She had made herself everyone's—and that meant the Spencers could not have what they wanted.

Some time that evening the difficult call was made to Mrs Shand-Kydd, the princess's mother, in Scotland. 'She was persuaded, unhappily, to go with us,' remembers a Palace official.

A call also went to the Dean of Westminster, asking him to clear the Abbey schedule for a full-scale royal funeral.

'We're going to need your help,' said Airlie to Tony Blair, 'in how we handle all this.'

The Prime Minister called over Alastair Campbell, and the three men conferred.

'Look,' said Airlie to the spin doctor, 'I think it would be helpful if you could come over to the Palace tomorrow.'

*   *   *

The plans for royal funerals are codenamed after bridges—Tay Bridge for the Queen Mother, Forth Bridge for Prince Philip, London Bridge for the Queen. Each codename indicates a set of procedures over as many as nine days, from D (the day of the death) to D + 9 (the day of the funeral and burial). The details of lyings-in-state and processions are drawn up in the Palace by the Lord Chamberlain's office, then checked with the wishes of the royal individual concerned. Arranging your own decorous and memorable exit is your last duty as a royal—Lord Mountbatten slaved long hours over the choreography of his funeral—and 'bridge procedures' are regularly rehearsed by the regiments involved. For a quarter of a century it has been a favourite prank of young Guards officers to phone their colleagues who are on skiing holidays and leave the message 'Tay Bridge' with the hotel desk.

In September 1997 there was no 'bridge procedure' for a young Princess of Wales, let alone one who was divorced, semi-detached from the royal family and disqualified by the strictest codes of protocol from the dignities of a formal state occasion. So that Sunday evening, David Airlie went straight back from Northolt Airport to the Palace to start devising a ceremony from scratch. His office had already dealt with one knotty problem. As royal officials had wrestled that morning with the details of returning the princess's body to Britain, they had come up against the legal requirement that her corpse be the subject of an official post-mortem—which meant taking the body to a morgue.

'That seems a great pity,' said Robert Fellowes when he heard the news. 'But if that's what the law says . . .'

Malcolm Ross conferred on the phone with Dr Richard Burton, the royal coroner. There was absolutely no way around the law—and in later months when Mohammed Fayed launched his headline-grabbing conspiracy theories, taking advantage of court privilege actually to accuse Prince Philip of masterminding the accident in Paris, the Palace was very grateful that proper legal procedures had been followed. Between Northolt Airport and St James's Palace, the police escort discreetly guided Diana's hearse to Dr Burton's mortuary in Fulham. There the coroner carried out the full examination, completed all the paperwork, and sent the hearse on its way without the morbid and levelling formalities becoming an issue. On the evening of the day she died, the coffin of Diana, Princess of Wales, surrounded by tall candles and covered in white flowers, lay in full dignity on a catafalque in the centre of the wood-panelled Chapel Royal in St James's.

Meanwhile, down the Mall in Buckingham Palace, the lights burned late as Malcolm Ross and David Airlie pulled the decorators' dustsheets off their desks, and, with Ross's no. 2, Lieutenant-Colonel Anthony Mather, got down to work on the details of a ceremony that had to be right.

Starting from first principles, the primary question was: hearse or gun-carriage?

'The trouble with a hearse,' says one official, 'is that there is a sheet of glass between you and the coffin. So you're not in touch with it at all. The gun-carriage is perfect and the gun-carriage is high—eight feet high, so everybody can see it.'

The problem with a gun carriage was that it would lend an over-military flavour to the occasion. The Lord Chamberlain and his men were joined by Penny Russell-Smith, Geoff Crawford's deputy press secretary, a matter-of-fact young blonde with spiky, punk-style hair, who had been fielding questions from the media since dawn.

'If we're starting with a blank slate,' she said, 'we should play down the military.'

Russell-Smith was very conscious of the pacifist

stance Diana had taken in her final months, and from the deputy press secretary's intervention, late that night in the deserted Palace, came the epiphany. Instead of soldiers and marching bandsmen, Diana's coffin would be accompanied by a procession of the workers and beneficiaries of her charities: the people with AIDS, battered wives, street-dwellers and anti-landmine campaigners who made up the princess's constituency of the dispossessed. It was in the tradition of the Lord Chamberlain inviting the people's representatives to join the celebration of the Prince of Wales's escape from typhoid in 1872, but in 1997 Lord Airlie's officials were thinking more personally.

'We just wanted her to have company,' says one of them.

Airlie and Ross were working in their offices on separate floors, meeting every hour on the hour, and by three o'clock in the morning they had roughed out a complete blueprint for the funeral. Ross stepped out through the Palace gates to snatch a little rest in his apartment at St James's, and discovered tangible evidence of the new world to which the funeral ceremony must speak: seven or eight hundred young people sitting quietly on the pavement outside the railings, their faces lit by flickering candles as they meditated in front of the flowers.

David Airlie went home to bed and got up early next morning to write down everything that he and Ross had agreed. The Lord Chamberlain phoned Balmoral soon after eight o'clock to ask Robin Janvrin to go through all the details with the Queen, and by nine he had the answer back. It

518

would have to be cleared with the Spencers, but so far as the royal family was concerned, everything that he and Ross were proposing was just fine. The Queen particularly liked the idea of the charities walking behind the coffin.

*   *   *

From ten o'clock on Monday, 1 September 1997, D + 1, the day following the death of the princess, the arrangements for Diana's funeral were monitored and managed from the high-ceilinged Chinese Dining Room on the front, right-hand side of Buckingham Palace. Looking down on to the outside courtyard and the Victoria Memorial, with a long table down the middle, it is one of the Palace's main conference rooms, and it is only occasionally dined in. The 'Chinese' refers to the extraordinary wall panels, all dragons and pagodas, and the lacquered furniture salvaged in the early nineteenth century from George IV's seaside folly, the Brighton Pavilion.

In these oriental surroundings Lord Airlie had assembled representatives of all the official bodies likely to be involved in the staging of the princess's funeral. The police and the military were there, as well as Palace officials from both the press office and the Lord Chamberlain's office. Prince Charles was represented by his staff in London; Diana by Michael Gibbins, who ran her office in her final months. Alongside Airlie the two heavy hitters were Sir Robert Fellowes, now back from Norfolk, and Alastair Campbell from Downing Street. Sitting in the middle of the table was an open speaker-phone that relayed all the proceedings, and also got the feedback, from Robin Janvrin in Balmoral.

'This has got to be something that brings old and new together,' said the Lord Chamberlain.

Airlie's ambition had been put to the test only minutes before the meeting started, when the police had called him to enquire about the next day's arrangements for the Changing of the Guard. 'There are a whole lot of flowers outside the main gates,' the police told him, 'and the guards will need to go through it. What are we to do about the flowers?'

'Leave the flowers,' said Airlie. 'The guards can march through the North Gate.'

Alastair Campbell had arrived for his first major Palace meeting expecting to sit down with pompous stuffed shirts, and found himself dealing with sophisticated and remarkably sensitive showmen.

'They encouraged ideas,' he remembers. 'They encouraged creative thinking and even risk-taking.' Campbell had orders from Downing Street not to appear to be either rescuing the royal family or giving it instructions, but as he walked into the Palace that morning, he had been recognised by an old Fleet Street colleague in the crowd. Calling in a favour, Campbell swore him to silence—and when the press became aware of the committee meetings during the week, the official spokesman stayed in his office, and sent along the less recognisable Anji Hunter, Blair's longest-serving confidante and aide, in his stead.

There was something of Churchill's wartime bunker about this hastily assembled group of specialists who had never worked together before. As the week went by, their formal task of organising a funeral developed into an exercise in national crisis management. The police were already worried by the surprising numbers of mourners who were flooding into the capital. Once people had laid their flowers, they were looking for something else they could do, and one of the committee suggested the opening of condolence books that people could visit and sign.

Condolence books were something new for Britain. No royal funeral had featured them before. It was out of the question that the coffin should lie in public state with weeping mourners passing by. That was an honour reserved for monarchs—and for Diana it would have been pure Evita Perón. But the condolence books were a dignified compromise, and if the Palace did not act quickly, the idea would certainly be hijacked by the tabloids—'Your Chance to Sign the *Sun* Book of Condolence to the People's Princess'. Mohammed Fayed had already put pictures of Diana and Dodi in the windows of Harrods, and was turning the ground floor of the department store into a shrine.

Radio and television broadcasts gave out news of the condolence books that Monday afternoon, and people started queuing immediately.

The date of the funeral was the other big decision that had to be made at once. The standard, nine-day funeral timetable of the Lord Chamberlain's office would mean a ceremony the following Tuesday. But Downing Street did not want to delay important Northern Ireland legislation that was coming up in the Commons, and it seemed to the Prime Minister that a Saturday ceremony would involve minimum disruption of the nation's work. Nine days' preparation would have to be condensed into six.

*   *   *

On D + 2, Tuesday, 2 September 1997, the Lord Chamberlain drafted in reinforcements. London's top cop, Sir Paul Condon, Commissioner of the Metropolitan Police, and Major-General Evelyn Webb-Carter, General Officer Commanding London District, the senior army officer in the capital, joined the ten o'clock committee.

'We realised', says a court official, 'that we had to get instant answers on the big and complicated questions. We didn't have time to have messages passed up the chain and back again.'

Paul Condon had already been briefing his police on London's pilgrimage mood. From Sunday, officers had been instructed to offer maximum help to mourners in the laying of their flowers. Every evening from 1 to 5 September, between 6 and 7 p.m., the Metropolitan Police Commissioner put on his uniform and walked out with his personal protection officer into the crowds. His route went from Scotland Yard to St James's Palace and down the Mall, and as he walked he stopped to chat to the mingled mass of humanity who had taken occupation of London's ceremonial area since Sunday night. The rules and regulations prohibiting rough sleeping in the royal parks had been quietly abandoned. 'It was clear from the Monday onwards that some people were reacting quite irrationally,' Condon remembers. 'I met people who had brought their children with no thought of where they were going to stay that night.'

The Metropolitan Police know to a few thousand how many people can be accommodated in the amphitheatre in front of Buckingham Palace (20,000), or along the length of the Mall, five or six deep (85,000), and they were already worried that these areas, and the entire processional route, would be swamped on Saturday. It seemed possible that as many as three million people could come out on to the streets of London to get their last glimpse of Diana.

Dickie Arbiter suggested that huge video screens in Hyde Park, pop-concert-style, might siphon away some of the influx, and David Airlie asked Condon if the police could look into extending the funeral route by running it around Trafalgar Square. Meanwhile, to deal with the immediate pressure of people, it was decided to increase the number of condolence books from four to fourteen. The following day the fourteen were increased to thirty-four.

*   *   *

At Westminster Abbey, the Dean, Dr Wesley Carr, was holding his funeral meetings at 4.30 p.m. each day. In the absence of any pre-planned ceremony, the Dean's task was not so different from that of any vicar arranging a parish funeral. He took the basic Church of England form of service, then filled it out with the requests and preferences of the family.

'We obviously wanted a funeral', he recalls, 'in which, through the media, everyone could participate.'

But Dr Carr declined to be trendy. He chose

readings from the Authorised Version of the Bible, all 'thees' and 'thous', in keeping with the Abbey's time-honoured character, and, working by fax with the Archbishop of Canterbury, with whom he would be sharing the conducting of the service, he composed prayers that had a traditional ring. The Dean refused on principle to use the phrase 'People's Princess'—'I don't think that she belonged to the people'—and the Bidding he composed to open the service contained a mild corrective to one of the features of the week. Television and radio shows had been overflowing with people talking about the dead princess as if she had been their closest friend.

'We are gathered here in Westminster Abbey to give thanks for the life of Diana, Princess of Wales; to commend her soul to almighty God and to seek his comfort for all who mourn . . . Although a princess, she was someone for whom, from afar, we dared to feel affection.'

The royal family left the Spencers to make all the choices. Charles Spencer had not been pleased to get back from South Africa and discover that his sister's funeral had been hijacked into a royal occasion, and he was particularly unhappy with Prince Charles's wish that his sons, William and Harry, should walk behind the coffin through the streets. This was in the royal tradition, but the earl felt quite certain Diana would have been horrified at the idea of her sons having to go through such an ordeal. He told his former brother-in-law as much and argued angrily with him in a series of phone calls which were the most unpleasant private aspect of the week. One call ended with the earl slamming the phone down on the prince.

When it came to the service, the earl and his family asked if the Abbey could select an extract from Verdi's Requiem to reflect Diana's wishes, and the hymns were also her favourites. 'I vow to thee my country' was the patriotic hymn she had requested at her wedding. 'Make me a channel of your peace' was a translation of words by St Francis of Assisi—for which Martin Neary, the Abbey's organist and master of choristers, composed a new arrangement and descant overnight.

The service's memorable musical elements were coordinated by Neary, who felt that for all the traditional beauty of Anglican church music, something extra must 'cross the barriers' to the worldwide audience that was expected to be watching the service. So he made contact with Elton John, and in a series of conversations the organist and the pop star worked out the idea of creating a new Diana-version of 'Candle in the Wind'. This elegy that Elton John and his lyricist Bernie Taupin had composed to Marilyn Monroe in 1973, was the prototype pop anthem to a fragile woman destroyed by her fame.

The funeral's other great musical coup was also customised for the occasion. Neary has suggested the cortège should leave the Abbey to the strains of the contemporary composer John Tavener's evocative 'Song for Athene', in which lines of Shakespeare and Greek Orthodox liturgy are set to soaring choral harmonies inspired by the Orthodox mass. The Abbey choir of twenty-four boys and sixteen adult lay vicars had recently recorded the piece. 'It was in the blood,' says Neary.

The drawback of the anthem was that, having reached the climax of a loud Alleluia, the music then tailed away into a low murmur, and the Dean felt that this was too quiet. He wanted the funeral to end with Alleluias of affirmation. So Neary secured Tavener's agreement to cut these final phrases, so that Diana's recessional could end, literally, on a high note.

In Buckingham Palace on Wednesday, 3 September, D + 3, Lord Airlie's committee was still pondering the length of the funeral route. The police reported that it was not possible to extend the procession around Trafalgar Square, as the Lord Chamberlain had suggested the previous day. Such a route would create unacceptable crowding and safety problems, and would also mean that the several hundred people of very different ages and capacities who were walking behind the coffin would need the stamina for a longer march.

Michael Gibbins, Diana's final aide, a quiet accountant whose meekness had enabled him to survive the hazards of serving the volatile princess, tentatively made a suggestion. Might not the coffin start its journey from the princess's home in Kensington Palace on the far west side of Hyde Park? Dickie Arbiter and Anthony Mather were despatched that afternoon to investigate, with officers of the King's Troop, whose horses would pull the coffin, alongside the Welsh Guards who would be marching as pall-bearers. The scouting party worked out a route with the police, and by teatime the problem was solved. The walkers would still only process from St James's to the Abbey; but the coffin itself would previously have travelled past nearly two miles of crowds—with most of the route extension running along the wide South Carriage Drive of Hyde Park, where the giant video screens were being set up.

Elton John, condolence books, video screens, an extended route—the courtiers and ecclesiastics in London were coming up with ideas to match every new circumstance. As the proposals went up to Balmoral, they were all greeted with approval, and the idea of quickly getting a Union Jack fluttering at half-mast over the Palace, also mooted on Wednesday, was in the spirit of the other changes. It was scarcely out of scale with the innovations being worked out that week. The idea had first been mentioned, almost in passing, at the beginning of a long think-piece that morning on an inside page of the *Sun*. But when, at Alastair Campbell's prompting, Robert Fellowes sent the flag suggestion north of the border, the reaction was totally different.

The *Sun* had concluded its piece that morning with a call to throw out 'the old guard' at Buckingham Palace. 'There will be no revolution of royal thinking,' argued the paper, 'while the same old advisors, from such stuffy, privileged backgrounds, have sole access to the Monarch's ear.'

But the newspaper was wrong. The problem was not the advisers. It was the monarch herself. While her 'stuffy' courtiers were reacting with vigour and creativity, happily jumping somersaults in their responses to this challenging moment in the life of her country, Elizabeth II was in a different time zone—a state of mind that a former member of her staff calls 'Balmoral time'.

'When the Queen was at Buckingham Palace or at Windsor,' he recalls, 'she was psychologically much more prepared to get involved in something unexpected. But her time relaxing in Scotland was so precious to her that she was not thrilled when Prime Ministers or Privy Councils or something interrupted "her Balmoral". She did it, but she didn't like it. At Balmoral it required much more effort on her part to do anything.'

The sense of being in a different world was emphasised by the fact that the royal family wore different clothes at Balmoral. They had their own special kilt, the grey Balmoral tartan. One of the jarring notes in the images of the clan going to church on the morning of Diana's death had been that the men of the family, with the exception of young Prince Harry in a dark blazer, were all wearing light-coloured tweed jackets.

There was a sense in which the Queen was deliberately encouraging this mood of detachment for the sake of her grandsons, but it militated against her paying full heed to the counsel of her advisers, who were more in touch with events. Her deputy private secretary, Robin Janvrin, a laid-back former diplomat with a naval background, was on the Scottish end of the line that relayed the discussions in the Chinese Dining Room.

'Robin had a tough job up there,' remembers one of the members of the London team. 'We were all coming in off the street, as it were, with our feeling of what was happening out on the ground. Then he had to walk down the corridor, a delegation of one, and convince the family—the Queen, Prince Philip, Prince Charles—all gathered in the sitting room, that there was a crisis and they couldn't just look at it in the traditional family way. Robin's a diplomat, a conciliator, and then he was still relatively junior. It was very easy for Prince

Philip to overrule him—"What's all the fuss about? It will calm down." '

Robert Fellowes did his best to back up his Number Two down the line from London.

'I love Robert—he's incredibly brave,' says one of his former colleagues. 'If he believes in something, he'll go right over the top fighting for it, whatever the cost.'

The cost for Robert Fellowes, and for a number of other senior courtiers, was several episodes of deeply wounding confrontation with the Queen. Equally hurtful disagreements occurred with Prince Philip, who was as resolute as his wife that the sanctity of the Palace flagpole was not going to be violated for Diana. By the end of D + 3— Wednesday, 3 September 1997—the advice being given by the senior royal staff was unanimous. There must be some compromise over the flag. But the Queen and her husband were unmovable, and when the memory of those hours and what was said at Balmoral comes up nowadays, those who were involved go silent and refuse to describe what transpired. It is as if they had seen a side of Elizabeth II that they would rather forget.

'A lot of people,' recalls one of them, 'were heavily scarred by it.'

CHAPTER THIRTY

Clapping in the Abbey

May those who died rest in peace, and may we, each and every one of us, thank God for someone who made many, many people happy.

Queen Elizabeth II, Friday, 5 September 1997

Shortly after Prince Philip arrived home from his controversial long southern voyage on *Britannia* in the winter of 1956–7, he got out his paints and easel to attempt a portrait of his wife—'Her Majesty the Queen at Breakfast'. It is a tender portrayal, impressionistic in style, with brushstrokes that are charmingly soft and fuzzy. Young and fresh in a lightly patterned day dress, the Queen sits alone, with a rack of toast and butter and a tasty-looking pot of marmalade beside her on a dazzling, starched white tablecloth. But Her Majesty seems unconcerned with her breakfast and the grand surroundings of classical oil paintings and polished Regency side tables. Her head is bowed while she studies a newspaper— which is unmistakably, to judge from the size of it, a tabloid.

Thus we may imagine Queen Elizabeth II sitting down to her toast and marmalade in Balmoral on the morning of Thursday, 4 September 1997—D + 4—contemplating the chorus of disapproval from Britain's tabloid editors as they deplored her refusal to fly a flag over Buckingham Palace. Far into the territory of disrespect, and teetering on the edge of mutiny, they addressed themselves to Elizabeth II personally. It was like October 1952, at the very beginning of her reign, when the young Queen had refused to let her crowning be televised, and the newspapers had protested. She was forced to surrender then, and now she surrendered again.

'What the papers said that morning obviously influenced her thinking,' says one of her staff, reluctant to give too much credit to the hated red-tops. The broadsheets were less strident than the tabloids, but the verdict was unanimous. It was the nation's message of the day, and the tone of the editorials was sharpened by some particularly unflattering photographs. The picture editors had rifled their archives for images of Elizabeth II at her grimmest, grumpiest and most double-chinned—the last sort of picture of herself that any woman would care to contemplate over breakfast. 'Crowds', ran a typical caption in the *Express* below a sour-faced image, 'say she has failed to appreciate the mood of the nation.'

Down in London, Geoffrey Crawford had just arrived back from Australia and went straight from Heathrow Airport to the Palace. There he sat down with Robert Fellowes to study the depressing and critical tone of the morning's press. The message was inescapable. The Queen must give way on the flag issue, and must also alter her travel arrangements in order to arrive in London earlier—which meant tomorrow. She would have to make some overt statement that put royal feelings about Diana into words—and perhaps it would be as well if her press secretary also spoke out directly in the interim. Before nine o'clock, Fellowes and Crawford got on the line to Janvrin in Balmoral to discuss the new strategy further, and Janvrin said he would go through everything with the Queen.

At ten o'clock the private secretary and press secretary went along to Lord Airlie's committee in the Chinese Dining Room. Through the windows come the smell of the flowers against the railings—part fragrant, but now also part rotten and putrified—and the two courtiers reported on the gist of their conversations with Janvrin, who was, by now, on the squawk box so he could participate in the meeting from Balmoral.

Everyone had read the newspapers and felt that something had to be done.

'The thing about ceremonial,' remembers one of the committee, 'is that it has got to be relevant. Relevant is the key word. You must be in touch with what is going on, and if that does mean overturning history and tradition, too bad. It is right.'

But the function of the Lord Chamberlain's committee was largely administrative—concerned with such matters as the siting of cameras, crowd safety, and all the details that flowed from the previous day's decision to extend the route. It was not until the meeting had broken up and Crawford and Fellowes were back in the private secretary's office that the crucial issues were finally resolved. The two men in London got on the intercom again to Janvrin in Balmoral, and this time the deputy private secretary was joined by the Queen. In the next forty-five minutes, the three courtiers and Elizabeth II worked out an entirely new sequence of royal events to be followed in the forty-eight hours that remained until Diana's funeral. The previous day's arguments over the flagpole were quite ignored.

'The Queen is a professional,' says one of her staff. 'She has the ability to move on—and she does so in a very healthy and wholehearted fashion.'

Elizabeth II's battling of the previous day had been on behalf of the timelessness that she had always felt to be at the heart of the monarchy. Now she bent to a principle that was equally timeless and central to her role: the ultimate accountability that she owed as head of a democratic state to her inaptly named subjects.

'If you were starting from scratch you would never invent a monarchy,' says one of the shapers of that week's events. 'So in that sense, the monarchy cannot be described as the creation of the people. It has its own existence and its own values, and one of the Queen's jobs is to defend those values. On the other hand, a monarchy which ignores the people has no function and cannot survive.'

The Queen would give her people the expression of royal emotion that their newspapers had so eloquently requested. The unfeeling impression created by the drive to church the previous Sunday would be rectified by another service that was hastily arranged in Crathie that very evening. In this rerun Diana's name would be mentioned by the pastor, and afterwards the royal family would get out of their cars and look at the floral tributes which had been laid outside Balmoral's gates. The arrival of the family in London would be moved to Friday afternoon so the same thing could happen outside the London palaces—and that was when the Queen would broadcast to the nation.

Someone voiced concerns about the security aspects of the royal family suddenly being brought into contact with an unhappy public, which, if the tabloids could be believed, was angry enough to string them from the nearest lamp-posts. Newspapers were reporting that the messages on some of the bouquets being laid outside the palaces were starting to take on a hostile tone.

'Your Majesty, Please Look and Learn,' read one message reproduced in *The Times*. 'Wills and Harry,' read another, 'live your life like her, not the others'—'her' evidently being Diana, not the Queen.

It was decided that Princes Edward and Andrew should be the stalking horses. There had been a stream of Palace staff and relatives going to the Chapel Royal to pay their respects to the princess; Princess Alexandra, the Kents and the Gloucesters had all made private visits. Edward had already been to the chapel that morning, privately. Now he and Andrew must go publicly. Both young men were in London. They were ideally placed to make an overt gesture—and they could test, in the process, whether it would be safe for the rest of the family to risk the crowds next day.

The meeting broke up, and the courtiers went off to start arranging the details. The royal train trip was cancelled. Two RAF planes were commissioned to bring the family down from Scotland the following afternoon half an hour apart—one plane was not enough for the job, since security regulations forbade sovereign and heir from travelling in the same aircraft. With the Queen's private apartments in Buckingham Palace still closed down for the holidays, a set of rooms for official visitors, the Belgian Suite, was dusted down, so Elizabeth II and her husband would be guests in their own home. Geoff Crawford made his statement to the press, and the Princes Andrew and Edward ventured out into the Mall in their role as cannon fodder. They were greeted unfailingly by sympathetic smiles and handshakes.

Meanwhile the preparations for Saturday continued. That night saw a group of cavalrymen, soldiers and mounted policemen moving together with timed deliberation along South Carriage Drive in Hyde Park. It was the gun-carriage party carrying out their final rehearsals. They travelled the whole route, the mounted policemen checking their progress with stop-watches against designated lamp-posts and landmarks, to make sure that they would reach the Abbey in precisely one hour and forty-seven minutes.

*   *   *

The decision that the Queen and her husband would stop and get out of their car when they arrived home at Buckingham Palace on Friday, 5 September 1997, the afternoon before Diana's funeral, reflected a new royal awareness of the importance of how things looked. Robert Fellowes, Robin Janvrin and Geoffrey Crawford had tried to visualise the scenario in advance. It would clearly be a disaster if the royal limousine swept imperiously through the Palace gates, ignoring the piled-up tributes of the people. What would any ordinary couple do if they got back from holiday to find their home barricaded shoulder-high by flowers? So the car drew to a halt and the Queen got out with her husband to inspect the cellophane-wrapped bundles by which the Palace railings had been engulfed and oddly softened.

All apparently friendly and informal pavement-level contacts between royals and populace are treated by the police as high security alerts. The Royal Protection Squad have photographs of fixated royal watchers. They refer to these sub-stalkers as 'cat-stranglers' on the theory that, though weird, they probably do not constitute threats to human life. But that is not a theory on which a 100 per cent protection policy can be based. 'They only need to get lucky once,' is one of the principles of police protection; so each royal operation is preceded by a briefing at which the photographs get checked through carefully. It is the job of every officer, in uniform or plain clothes, to look out for suspects and track their movements—and the Queen's arrival back in London on the afternoon of Friday, 5 September provided a moment of special anxiety. Would the waiting crowds boo, or angrily pelt the royal couple with flowers? Extra plain-clothes police had been drafted the length of the planned 'walkabout', briefed to close around the Queen in case of trouble and bundle her back into the car.

As Elizabeth II, dressed in black, walked down the line of mourners, an 11-year-old girl handed her five red roses.

'Would you like me to place them for you?' asked the Queen.

'No, Your Majesty,' replied the girl. 'They are

for you.'

'You could hear the crowd begin to clap,' remembers an aide. 'I remember thinking, "Gosh, it's all right."'

*   *   *

That Friday night, an hour or so after Elizabeth II's historic and mood-altering live broadcast into the six o'clock news, Nick Edmett, a chauffeur from Blackheath, brought his 5-year-old daughter Lois up to lay her flowers outside the Palace. They had just laid the bouquet at the edge of the pile that now sprawled fifty yards away from the railings, when they saw an eerie flashing of lights moving along the Mall. The darkness was lit up by a quivering blue-white radiance: the flashes of a thousand cameras that were trained on a large black car driving out of St James's Palace. It was the hearse carrying Diana's coffin from the Chapel Royal to Kensington Palace, where it would lie through the night before the funeral next morning.

'The light followed her,' remembers Edmett, 'like travelling lightning. It was so ironic—all those camera flash bulbs. I thought, "That was what killed her."'

The chauffeur watched the hearse turn right at the Palace and drive up Constitution Hill, the vivid lightstorm flickering along the cathedral-like vaulting of the trees as it went. The police officers monitoring the coffin's progress had similar emotions as they sensed the reverence rippling through the crowd. They felt they were tracking a source of energy moving from one part of London to another.

Meanwhile, inside Buckingham Palace the family was gathering for dinner. In the course of the afternoon everyone had been to pay their respects to the princess's coffin before it left the Chapel Royal. Prince Charles had taken his sons, and later the Queen and Prince Philip went along. The chapel seating is in collegiate style, the pews all facing towards the central aisle where the coffin was standing, and the royal couple knelt down in front of the coffin, heads bowed, eyes closed.

Over dinner, talk turned to the ceremony next day. It still was not resolved exactly who was going to walk behind the gun-carriage. Charles Spencer had continued to have arguments with both Prince Charles and his brother-in-law Robert Fellowes over whether or not William and Harry should walk—and the boys themselves had changed their minds several times. The Lord Chamberlain's office had foreseen two, three, maybe four mourners walking in the first rank behind the coffin, on the assumption that Prince Charles and Lord Spencer would definitely walk, accompanied by neither, either or both of the young princes. William was particularly reluctant. He shied away from the ill-feeling between his father and his uncle, and it was only in these last-minute discussions over dinner that Prince Philip—who had never been scheduled to walk—resolved the problem.

'If I walk,' he asked his grandson, 'will you walk with me?'

*   *   *

Next morning the five were waiting outside St

James's Palace, ready to set off side by side, with Diana's 'regiment' of nearly five hundred charity workers waiting behind them. Spick and span and dressed in their Sunday best, the much-publicised posse of the compassionate and the underprivileged were somehow too smart for their democratic billing, and the TV coverage of the procession virtually ignored them. The compelling image of the day was of the four princes and the earl who walked behind the coffin. The cameras were drawn inevitably and inexorably to the young faces of William and Harry—and to their wreath on the front of the coffin, a small ring of white roses, bearing the inscription 'Mummy'.

Two hundred yards away, outside the railings of Buckingham Palace, the Queen, her sister and the rest of the family were also standing at street level on the pavement. It was another last-minute addition to the ceremonial.

'Good heavens!' Robin Janvrin had exclaimed the night before. 'The coffin will be coming down Constitution Hill, right past the Palace. How will it look if it just sails past an empty building?'

For the family to look down from the balcony would give quite the wrong message; so, at the Queen's suggestion, they all walked out through the gates to stand among the flowers. As the gun-carriage and its escort came past the Palace, Elizabeth II slowly and deliberately bowed her head. Monarchs have bowed their heads at funerals, but never in the street at a passing coffin.

There had been crying and wailing when the coffin first left Kensington Palace at 9.08 a.m., but most people now stood in silence, listening to the slow march of the Guardsmen, and the regular boom of cannon fire from the artillery lined up in the park. From ten o'clock the tenor bell high in the towers of Westminster Abbey started tolling every minute, sounding ever louder to the walkers in the cortège as they got closer to the church. To maintain the silence, all aircraft flights over central London had been rerouted.

Inside the Abbey, the waiting congregation watched the procession getting nearer on the television screens that were scattered around the church. With the giant video screens in the park and the TV monitors inside the Abbey all displaying the pooled BBC, ITV and SkyTV coverage, a novel electronic cohesion had been created between the inside and outside dimensions of the ceremony. Everyone in London that day was both a participant and a viewer. The Abbey marshals asked the Dean whether they should close the huge double doors of the church once the service started, and the Dean said to leave them open. It would be good, he felt, if the onlookers near the doors could have some connection with what was going on inside.

After its two-and-a-half-mile journey, the coffin entered the Abbey on the shoulders of the Welsh Guardsmen's bearer party with spine-tingling punctuality, as the bell above them tolled the first strokes of eleven. The fear had been that old-fashioned protocol could not soar as the occasion required. But it was old-fashioned tradition and discipline—a ceremonial version of Robert Fellowes' 'bloody good manners'—that actually made it possible for emotion to take wing.

The most difficult aspect of the preparations for the Lord Chamberlain's office had been tracking down the great diversity of the princess's extended family in the worlds of charity and showbusiness, and the effort had left no time for a seating plan to be arranged. So it was first come, first seated. There were reserved places for the immediate family, a few VIPs and the press, but otherwise, uniquely for a royal occasion, most of the congregation sat as chance fell, Hollywood film stars beside hospice workers.

' "If I should die and leave you here awhile," ' read Diana's sister Sarah, ' "be not like others sore undone who keep long vigils by the silent dust and weep. For my sake, turn again to life and smile." '

The two sisters' untheatrical delivery of their brief tributes contrasted with the over-elaborate Bible reading of the Prime Minister who, unlike the previous Sunday, had had far too long to rehearse his words. The prospect of Elton John rehashing his ballad to Marilyn Monroe seemed destined for a particularly grating clash with the dignity of Edward the Confessor's Abbey. But it proved an inspired reinvention, to match several others that day.

Then came her brother's avenging speech. Pursuing the theme that he had struck on the morning of her death, Lord Spencer had banned all tabloid representatives from the Abbey. If the Palace had tried it, the outcry would have been impossible. But thanks to the anger of a ninth earl, the reporters and editors were excluded from the supreme moment of the era they had done so much to create.

'Of all the ironies about Diana,' said her brother, 'perhaps the greatest was this—a girl given the name of the ancient goddess of hunting was, in the end, the most hunted person of the modern age.'

He recalled their train journeys together as children, shuttling, confused, between their divorced parents' separate homes. Cleverly, he claimed for her a higher title than saint. She was 'human', he said. And he shrewdly drew attention to her 'deep feeling of unworthiness' that had spoken so eloquently to her vast 'constituency of the rejected'.

It was a profoundly fraternal speech, saying all that a sister could want her brother to say. Long before Diana's death, the earl had clearly reflected hard on his extraordinary sibling and what her remarkable life meant. He captured her meaning. Some later suggested that such a coruscating diatribe must have been drafted or polished by some professional wordsmith. But they forgot that Charles Spencer had not always been an earl. Before inheriting his title, he had worked for six years as a reporter and presenter for NBC's Today show on US television. Technically his speech was a progression of heartfelt soundbites, whose connecting argument achieved lift-off through their passion.

The earl's pledge to his nephews William and Harry, that their 'blood family', the Spencers, would keep their souls singing so that they were not 'immersed by duty and tradition', reflected the battles that the earl had been fighting all week with the Windsors—and in particular with Prince Charles. In the emotion of the Abbey, the royal family did not take in the full import of what he said. It was not until they got home and watched the replay on the video that they latched on to the fact they had been eloquently insulted to their faces, and in front of a worldwide audience approaching two billion. Lord Spencer himself has always insisted he meant no disrespect. His sister would have said much worse. But his very anger gave voice to the conflict that had boiled so close to the surface that week, bringing it to the heart of the proceedings, and also releasing it in a torrent of applause.

It started with the crowds watching on the big screens in the park. Down Constitution Hill and along the Mall it swept, some of it transmitted physically, the bulk of it moving through the electronics of people's radios and the TV screens, until it reached the Abbey and scudded inside through the huge, open, wooden double doors.

'I thought it was raining,' remembers the Dean, Dr Wesley Carr, who was standing at the other end of the church. 'Then I looked out at the sky and saw it was blue.' The applause invaded the Abbey itself, rolling up the nave. People are not supposed to clap at funerals, but this congregation did. Eye witnesses remember Diana's two sons both joining in the applause. But Elizabeth II and her husband did not clap.

*   *   *

The final homage was the most unexpected. The coffin was driven north on its 77-mile trip to the Spencer home in Northamptonshire in a conventional, glass-sided hearse, escorted by police outriders. Up through St John's Wood it travelled, making the transition from the grand ceremonial avenues of central London to the suburban streets of Finchley, Cricklewood and Hendon—the dreary

543

commuter route followed by lorries and delivery vans heading for the M1. All along the way the streets were as packed with spectators as Whitehall had been; and, as the coffin drove by, people started to throw flowers at it.

'What's going on?' asked the police officer overseeing the operation from the video control room in Scotland Yard, linked to his outriders by the headphones and microphones in their helmets. Were these flying flowers dangerous, he wanted to know? After thirty seconds it was clear that they posed no threat to security—or to the dignity of the occasion. In fact, the flying bouquets added a spontaneous final flourish to the folk tributes of the week. Unprompted by any previous suggestion in the media, people had come with their flowers evidently intending this gesture, never seen before in Britain. By the time the hearse had reached the motorway, there were so many flowers piling up from the bonnet on to the windscreen that the driver had to halt, get out and lift them off, laying them with reverence by the side of the road.

The only police intervention came when the hearse had speeded up and was travelling northwards out of London. As it entered the territory of a neighbouring police authority, a local squad car came up behind to join the back of the procession, its blue lights flashing stridently. Consternation reigned in the Scotland Yard video room.

'The Commissioner's compliments,' cracked out the order over the radio. 'And get those lights off!'

'Other countries might need flashing lights,' explains a police officer. 'But there are some things we do differently in Britain.'

544

The sort of thing we under-do so well.

As the gates of Althorp closed behind the hearse and its escorts, the car drew to a halt in the farm buildings where the Royal Standard would be replaced by the Spencer standard for the family burial—and refused to restart. But the burial ceremony was not delayed. The Lord Chamberlain's office had another, empty, duplicate hearse quietly travelling north with its own police escort on the A1, a parallel route. A quick radio message got the back-up team to Althorp within twelve minutes.

*   *   *

Britain's reaction to the death of Diana, Princess of Wales was diagnosed at the time as a very modern sort of nervous breakdown. But one day of immaculately executed ritual, broadcast with taste and style, triumphantly resolved the crisis and left most people feeling better. A gun-carriage rolling slowly, stiffly uniformed military backbones, young princes marching with solemnity—the remedies for the national trauma proved to be essentially traditional and royal.

CHAPTER THIRTY-ONE

Bagshot for Eddie

I for one believe that there are lessons to be drawn from her life and from the extraordinary and moving reaction to her death.

Queen Elizabeth II, 5 September 1997

The Queen was shaken to the core by the experience of being pilloried by the newspapers, then getting back to London to find the familiar vista of her palace swamped by the flood of tributes to Diana.

'She was overwhelmed,' as one of her staff put it, 'like a stunned fish.'

But the success of her broadcast on the eve of the funeral also gave her a justifiable sense of achievement. Elizabeth II had been challenged by events, and she had changed them. She had been proved wrong about the flag, but it could be argued that her senior staff had been vindicated, and that the entire royal machine had reacted with some skill to the challenges of the funeral week.

'After the broadcast,' says one of her advisers, 'we found it easier to convince her about doing things. She listened to us more, and was just a little more prepared to take risks.'

When the Queen had visited a school before Diana's death, she would stand in the doorway, listening to the teacher. Now she was prepared to go and sit inside among the children—and even, in the case of one French-language class, to show off a little of her immaculate French. In an Australian outback school, she took questions from the class, cheerfully admitting she had no idea how many rooms there were in Buckingham Palace.

On foreign tours she would be briefed by her press staff about the message they had planned to convey from that day's engagement.

'No stunts, please,' she would warn. 'I am not a politician.'

Diana's shadow hovered over such conversations, but the princess's name was never mentioned, either as an example to follow or one to avoid. The one public figure to whom it was felt permissible to allude, albeit indirectly, was Mrs Thatcher, whose eagerness to be seen early at the scene of national disasters had earned her a faintly ridiculous reputation during the 1980s. Whenever 'ambulance chasing' was mentioned at the Palace, everyone knew who was being referred to.

The press noted the measured informality of the new style—a walkabout outside McDonald's, tea in a Glasgow housing association bungalow, even signing 'Elizabeth R' on a football for children in Malaysia. This apparently small gesture was a major departure for someone whose habit is not to give 'autographs' and the new style itself sometimes became the story. In the autumn of 1998, the Queen expressed mild annoyance when her 'new informality' was the theme of reports about a successful walkabout that she had carried out in a street market beside the water in Brunei.

'Don't they realise I've done it before?' she asked, looking at the press digest next day. 'I've done everything before.'

'She would often chat informally to people and have tea in their houses,' remembers a senior courtier from the 1980s. 'But the press found it too boring to report. They were following Diana.'

To make clear her endorsement of the late princess's philanthropic dimension, the Queen took over the patronage of some of her major charities, and Diana was also assigned a 'hot button' of honour at the head of the highly successful royal family website. Going on-line early in 1997, www.royal.gov.uk pre-dated the death of the princess by six months, and was a modernisation in which the seventy-year-old monarch took particular pride. Though not herself a web-person, she has enthusiastically embraced such contemporary high-tech indulgences as the mobile phone and afternoon horse-racing on television.

Through most of the 1980s and 1990s, royal press secretaries had regular lunch dates with Professor Robert Worcester, the egghead creator of MORI, Britain's leading opinion pollsters. For the price of lunch, the courtiers got an expert briefing on the latest sampling data on the monarchy, along with satisfaction ratings on individual members of the family. The prospect of the Palace coughing up for Worcester's expensive polling services seemed remote—but hiring MORI was one of the Palace's first actions in the aftermath of September 1997, along with the recruiting of a new super-spin-doctor figure, a 'director of communications' whose mission, Alastair Campbell-style, was to get the entire royal machine 'on message'.

The first occupant of this post was Simon Lewis,

the smooth, 39-year-old PR director of British Gas, which generously agreed to second him to the Queen and keep his salary topped up at its impressive level of £230,000 a year. This made Lewis by far the highest-paid employee in the Palace, earning twice as much as the Queen's private secretary (or, indeed, the Prime Minister). In 1998 only Michael Peat, the financial controller, received more than £100,000 a year, and when the details of Lewis's recompense became known, the envy was painful to behold. 'Meter Man' was the nickname coined by Prince Philip for the gas company employee, and this was seized on gleefully in the corridors. Lewis and his successor Simon Walker, seconded from British Airways, spent much of their time analysing the results of MORI's polls and focus groups—only to have their confidential findings hijacked and leaked by Prince Charles's minders in St James's Palace, anxious for data to boost their boss's image. Buckingham Palace has found spinning to be a double-edged sword.

'I would not say,' remarks one of the Queen's senior officials, a mite huffily, 'that focus groups are currently a growth industry around here. It's been interesting to see what they can yield.'

The process of placing a very traditional monarch in closer contact with an ever more casual and in-your-face world has also had its setbacks. 'Who are you?' asked a cheeky little boy in an Australian classroom when the lady in the hat did not stop at his classroom door but invaded his territory. Stunned by the one question that, in three-quarters of a century, no one had ever asked her, the Queen was literally dumbfounded. Her smile froze, and after a pause in which you could almost hear the alternatives churning round in her head, she chose to move on in enigmatic silence.

She is usually better served by her dry and slightly mordant sense of humour. At a recent Buckingham Palace garden party she was chatting happily to a youthful couple when the girl's mobile telephone rang, to the young woman's agonised embarrassment.

'You'd better answer that,' said the Queen, without blinking. 'It might be someone important.'

* * *

Soon after his appointment as royal communications supremo in 1998, Simon Lewis found himself in St James's Palace for a meeting with Prince Charles. As Lewis departed, the Queen's deputy private secretary, Sir Robin Janvrin, arrived for a meeting with the Prince's staff, and Lewis walked back up the Mall meditating happily on the harmony of purpose this reflected between the two palaces. Little did he know what was transpiring at that moment between Janvrin and Stephen Lamport, Prince Charles's private secretary.

'We have Mrs Parker Bowles here,' said Lamport casually, 'and the Prince of Wales wondered if you would like to come up for a drink with her?'

'Certainly not,' responded the startled Janvrin, springing out of his chair. He could not possibly meet Mrs Parker Bowles without the express permission of the Queen—and so Sir Robin, soon to succeed Robert Fellowes as the Queen's principal confidential adviser, beat a hasty retreat back to Buckingham Palace.

The controversial status of Camilla Parker Bowles remains a prickly area in the already complicated relationship between Prince Charles and his mother, and the situation has been exacerbated by Palace geography. Until the reforms of Lord Airlie and Michael Peat in the 1980s, most of the Lord Chamberlain's staff worked in St James's Palace, which lies some two hundred yards down the Mall from Buckingham Palace in a sprawl of buildings that includes the Queen Mother's magnificent cream stucco residence of Clarence House. This reflected the ancient status of St James's Palace as the working headquarters of the monarchy. To this day the heralds proclaim the accession of a new sovereign from the balcony of St James's, not from Buckingham Palace, and foreign ambassadors are accredited to the 'Court of St James'. But both Airlie and Peat felt it was logical for the Lord Chamberlain's staff to work under the same roof as the Queen, and this coincided with Prince Charles's wish to escape from Buckingham Palace and to set up a base of his own. The swap was completed by 1988, and almost immediately the battle of the palaces began—'BP', to use Palace shorthand, versus 'SJP'.

'All the important business of the day gets decided at the early morning meetings of the private secretaries and the press secretaries,' remembers a courtier from those times. 'But that started to dwindle after Charles and Diana moved out. We tried linking up with their people by intercom, but that didn't work well.'

551

The troubles between Charles and Diana widened the gap. Prince Charles's staff felt that the princess ran crying to her brother-in-law Robert Fellowes to gain the Queen's ear, while the Dimbleby project, with its overt criticism of the Queen by her son, intensified the rift. After the Waleses' divorce in 1996 and Diana's death a year later, it was Charles's insistence on establishing a public role in his life for Camilla that kept the two royal households at loggerheads—and, at the time of writing, the battle rages more fiercely than ever.

For Prince Charles, Camilla is a 'non-negotiable' issue. For his mother, the position is more complicated. As a committed Christian and Supreme Governor of the Church of England, Elizabeth II remains painfully aware that, while the church has liberalised its attitude towards the remarriage of divorcees, it still declines to bless the union of couples whose adultery was a factor in the breakdown of their original marriages. That is the theological version of Diana's famous 'three in the marriage' complaint, and the generally held belief that Diana was done serious wrong by the prince and his mistress continues to blight Camilla in the eyes of the general public.

Since 1997, when polls showed severe hostility to the relationship, opinion has swung round to Charles and Camilla to a remarkable degree. In June 2000, a MORI survey revealed clear approval of the couple marrying—with 'Get married' agreed by 44 per cent, 'Continue outside marriage' by 31 per cent and 'Neither/Don't knows' numbering 25 per cent. But when these same respondents were asked whether Camilla should become Charles's full-scale, crowned 'Queen at his side', the responses were a strong 71 per cent 'No' to only 24 per cent 'Yes', with the 'Don't knows' down to 5 per cent. These figures would seem to show that, while being reluctant to deny the couple some form of personal contentment, Britain is no happier than it was in 1936 at the prospect of an adulterous royal mistress becoming an official national figurehead.

This is the challenge facing the most colourful, significant and influential courtier in royal service today—in either St James's or Buckingham Palace. In 1996 Prince Charles selected Mark Bolland, aged thirty, to take charge of his press relations, rehabilitate his image and to secure public acceptance of Camilla as his consort at his side. Bolland was actually proposed for the job by Camilla's divorce lawyer, Hilary Browne-Wilkinson, a member of the board of the Press Complaints Commission, whose director Bolland then was.

Of Canadian birth, educated at a Middlesbrough comprehensive school and York University, Mark William Bolland is young, gifted and extremely good company, with a fondness for champagne and lunch at the Caprice. He networks brilliantly, counting Labour spinmeister Peter Mandelson, the packager of New Labour, among his friends. Bolland's partner, Guy Black, is his successor as director of the Press Complaints Commission, prompting the royal rat pack to joke that when SJP takes a complaint to the PCC, it is essentially a domestic matter. Black and Bolland share a converted warehouse apartment in fashionable Clerkenwell, and have been hailed by the *Observer* as 'the most successful power couple in Britain'.

Arriving at St James's Palace in the wake of the

Dimbleby débâcle, Bolland took on the brief of making up the forty-point drop in public confidence that Prince Charles suffered between 1991 and 1997. It was one of the biggest declines ever measured by MORI, far outstripping the ups and downs of poll ratings for the monarchy in general. But in the view of Buckingham Palace, where teeth gnash at the mention of Bolland's name, the spin doctor's efforts to improve the prince's ratings have often been at the expense of the monarchy and royal family as a whole—and of the Queen in particular.

Within months of joining SJP, the death of Diana offered Bolland a dramatic opportunity of image-improvement for his employer. In the days leading up to the funeral, Bolland-inspired newspaper stories gave Prince Charles the credit for such initiatives as the lengthening of the funeral route, which had actually been the idea of Diana's aide, Michael Gibbins, Dickie Arbiter's suggestion of the video screens in the park and virtually every innovative proposal that came out of Lord Airlie's committee. After each morning meeting in the Chinese Dining Room, Stephen Lamport brought the news back to Bolland in St James's Palace. While the Buckingham Palace press corps stuck to officially agreed statements, Bolland slipped his press contacts appetising details which made it seem as if Prince Charles were the vital and busy force in all the funeral preparations.

In a subsequent book by Penny Junor, Bolland went still further, planting the idea that Charles was behind the bringing home of Diana's body with royal honours. The book even suggested that Charles should be credited with the entire concept of 'a full royal funeral at Westminster Abbey'—and that he had to fight his mother to achieve this.

Buckingham Palace does not recall it that way at all.

'Charles was like a wet weekend at Balmoral,' recalls one of the Queen's staff. 'He was pole-axed by guilt, and any suggestion that he was taking charge is ridiculous.'

Spin-doctoring aside, much of Bolland's power derives from his ability to boost the spirits of his frequently discouraged employer. A lively wit and raconteur, Bolland, whose official rank is deputy private secretary, cheers and chivvies both Charles and Camilla with his amusing phone calls, feeding them the royal jelly of inside-track gossip as cleverly as he woos the press. Utterly loyal and ruthless on his master's behalf, he is a courtier in an ancient tradition—but he has also shown himself reckless.

In November 1998, the Queen was horrified to read that in the course of briefing the makers of a forthcoming television documentary on Prince Charles, a St James's Palace aide (alleged in the press to be Bolland) had asserted that the prince would be 'privately delighted' if his mother were to abdicate. Furious, Elizabeth II tracked her son down in Bulgaria by telephone to discover that the prince knew nothing about it. Charles apologised abjectly to his mother; but Bolland kept his job— and went on leaking. Subsequent stories from St James's Palace disclosed the prince's opinion that his nieces, Fergie's daughters, the little princesses Beatrice and Eugenie, should be deprived of their HRH titles as part of a royal slimming-down exercise, and that their easy-going, golf-loving father, Prince Andrew, did not have the commitment required for his post-naval career as a booster of British trade initiatives overseas.

It is a common Bolland tactic to hype Prince Charles by making sure the press gets to hear every delicious detail about the follies of his siblings. In October 2001 he had a field day when Prince William enrolled at St Andrew's University, and the only TV crew to ignore the gentlemen's agreement, brokered by Guy Black and the PCC, to respect William's privacy, came from Ardent Productions, the hapless TV company owned by Prince Edward. It was not, perhaps, surprising that Bolland should let it be known that Prince Charles was 'incandescent' with rage and was refusing to take his brother's phone calls, but the aide rubbed salt in the wound. When Prince Edward was invited to a reconciliation at St James's Palace, the younger brother and his wife decided to walk to the meeting, and injudiciously remarked on their arrival that they had come through the park 'to give pleasure to the people'. Somehow, this revealing comment found its way into the press.

Bolland's formidable media power is enhanced by the fact that his office controls access to the hottest royal properties of all—the young princes, William and Harry. There is massive national and international media interest in every detail of these young men's lives, and the chosen outlet for many of Bolland's choicest stories about them and their father is Richard Kay of the *Daily Mail*—an irony that Diana would doubtless appreciate.

The greater irony is that Prince Charles has now become as image-manipulative as Diana was, stepping into his ex-wife's shoes as the royal leaker and press manipulator *par excellence.* Paradoxically, the prince himself no longer reads the papers. At some stage in the course of his battles with Diana he gave up reading them on principle, delegating press monitoring entirely to his staff. So Britain's national agenda of royal press coverage is now largely set by his deputy private secretary, Mark Bolland—the most exotic flowering yet on the convoluted creeper of royal revelation that stretches back via Jonathan Dimbleby, Andrew Morton and James Whitaker to 'Crawfie', Lady Cynthia Asquith and George Morton Smith, the Finchley registrar who would steal time from his recording of local births, deaths and marriages to distribute occasional, decorous details about the home life of Queen Victoria.

*   *   *

By December 2000 Mark Bolland had pulled Prince Charles's MORI approval rating up from its trough of – 45 in December 1994 to a comparatively respectable – 12, which was better than Diana was achieving during the controversial days of her separated life. This compared to + 29 for the Queen Mother, + 27 for the Queen and + 24 for Charles's sister Princess Anne, who consistently scores higher approval ratings than her brother without the help of any spin doctor.

But there was one corner of the globe where the prince's reputation was not redeemed and where his marital misadventures appeared to have done long-term damage to the monarchy. In the 1990s, campaigners for a republic in Australia found that the most potent words they could utter were 'King

Charles III'.

'Few Australians', declared the former Prime Minister, Gough Whitlam, 'would believe he has the personal qualities required by an Australian head of state.' Whitlam himself, the victim of dismissal by the Governor General in 1975, had done much for Australia's republican movement. But it was the catalogue of royal indignities revolving around the breakdown of the Waleses' marriage in the early 1990s which gave the final push to Australian antimonarchist sentiment that dated back to the reign of Victoria. In February 1998 a constitutional convention was held to thrash out a system for choosing a republican head of state, and this led to a referendum on the eve of the millennium, on 6 November 1999.

To the surprise of many, the vote went in favour of the monarchy.

'What's the matter with these people?' exclaimed Prince Philip. 'Can't they see what's good for them?'

'Well,' responded his wife, 'they couldn't agree on the model.'

By 'model' the Queen was referring to the proposal that had come out of the constitutional convention. This had been placed on the referendum ballot form by Australia's monarchist Prime Minister, John Howard. Polls showed that a simple question requiring a Yes or No on the future of the monarchy would result in a massive 80–90 per cent vote in favour of an Australian republic. But Howard made voters choose between the monarchy and the constitutional 'model' selected by the convention whereby the new, non-royal head of state would not be elected directly, but would be selected by members of Parliament sitting in Canberra. Considering this model to be as elitist and politician-ridden as the existing system, many root-and-branch republicans voted 'No' in the referendum, thus saving the monarchy for the time being.

Some British newspapers hailed the result as a 'victory' for Elizabeth II, but she did not see it that way. She understood that a majority of Australians wanted a republic, although they could not agree on its form, and her reaction to the vote was distinctly non-triumphalist. 'For some while,' ran her official statement of response to the referendum vote in November 1999, 'it has been clear that many Australians wanted constitutional change. Much of the debate has been about what that change should be.' De-officialised, her words acknowledged that the vote had been on the wrong model—'wrong' from her point of view because it continued to embroil her own status in controversy and left the crown in limbo. 'She would much rather visit Australia as a generally beloved Queen of Britain and head of the Commonwealth,' explains a former member of her staff, 'than be an object of controversy.'

Elizabeth II travelled to Australia in March 2000 for what might have been anticipated, before the vote, to be an emotional tour of farewell as head of state, and when she arrived she maintained her resolutely non-partisan mode. She was welcomed in Sydney at a ceremonial lunch where the speech-making was led off by the republican-voting premier of New South Wales, Bob Carr, followed by a rather smug John Howard.

'I was quite worried,' confessed the Queen

afterwards. 'After all that, I couldn't imagine there was anything left for me to say.'

In fact, she made a speech of widely praised wisdom and grace.

'I have always made it clear,' she said, 'that the future of the monarchy in Australia is an issue for you, the Australian people, and you alone to decide by democratic and constitutional means. It should not be otherwise.'

'That was her way of putting it right up the bloody monarchists,' says one of her fans, the former Prime Minister, Bob Hawke. In common with Gough Whitlam and every other antimonarchist Australian politician who has dealt with her, Hawke makes a clear distinction between the system, which he wants to scrap, and the Queen herself, whose wisdom, discretion, and hard work he greatly admires. 'She was saying to everyone in Australia—"You silly bastards, why don't you get on with it?"'

That is certainly putting it more strongly than Her Majesty would, but it may not be far from her personal sentiments. The day after her speech, the Queen gave a media reception at Admiralty House in Sydney and was asked afterwards to which group she had most enjoyed talking. 'The republicans,' she replied with a smile.

The turn-around victory of John Howard in the election of November 2001 has placed the republican issue on the back-burner in Australia for five more years at least. But it has not solved Elizabeth II's dilemma. Not for the first time in Australian politics, she is a hostage to events beyond her control. An Australian Prime Minister who says he favours the monarchy is presiding over an electorate which says it wants some sort of republic, but cannot decide on the shape it should take. So Her Majesty remains in limbo.

In 1992, Britain's best-selling book of the *annus horribilis* was Sue Townsend's disarming fable *The Queen and I*, which envisioned a republican victory in a British general election and the royal family being sent to live on a Midlands council estate. In the novel the Queen herself, like Princess Anne, copes resourcefully with this fall from grace—the men of the family go completely to pieces—and Sue Townsend captures the practical essence of the royal character.

The thoroughly pragmatic Elizabeth II finds it less difficult than people might imagine to accept the possibility of not being Queen, and she has a longstanding response to the prospect of a Republic of Great Britain: 'We'll go quietly.'

*   *   *

The Way Ahead Group was set up at Lord Airlie's suggestion in the early 1990s to ensure that the sincerity of the Queen's 'We'll go quietly' joke would never be put to the test. Prompted by the disasters of the *annus horribilis*, it was the modern equivalent of 'Unrest in the Country'—a task force to ensure the monarchy's survival and to help reshape its work for the challenges of the new millennium. Every six months the Queen, her husband and four children sit down with their senior advisers to work out their strategy for the next six months and beyond.

Much of the meeting involves the co-ordinating of future engagements. 'In the days before the Way

Ahead,' remembers a courtier, 'it was done through the private secretaries, and every so often the press office or the royal flight department would discover that Princess Anne and the Queen were both scheduled to go to Yorkshire on the same day.' The planning goes beyond locations to highlight priorities in terms of social themes deemed worthy of encouragement: housing associations were moved up the list in the early 1990s to acknowledge this initiative in low-cost inner-city home-building. In royal terms, Way Ahead decisions range from authorising the ongoing management restructurings of the ever-diligent Michael Peat to modernising the protocol of the Buckingham Palace flag. When the Queen is away and no Royal Standard flies, a Union Jack now flutters over the Palace—at full mast or half-mast, depending on the circumstances: a small but salutary reminder of Diana and of the week when the absence of a flag brought the country close to revolt.

A Way Ahead change that will one day find its way to Parliament is an alteration in the rules of succession so that, in the future, males will no longer have precedence over females. When this comes to pass, the order of royal succession will simply be a matter of who is born first—though wags have suggested that after centuries of male heirs having priority there should be a few generations of positive discrimination for the girls. To judge from the historical record since the first Elizabeth, women have done rather better by the monarchy than men.

How to downsize the royal family is one of the group's perennial headaches.

'The problem with all the HRHs,' says a royal official who has advocated restricting the troublesome title of Royal Highness to the immediate children of the sovereign and the heir to the throne, 'is that immediately you are called HRH, you are given police protection. You come to expect top security coverage, back-up cars, motorcycle escorts, the lot. The Queen was driving back from Windsor one Monday when she got stuck in the traffic coming through Hyde Park. She was sitting there quietly in the traffic jam, when suddenly there was a screaming of sirens and a Rolls-Royce with motorcycle escorts came speeding past her on the wrong side of the road. She looked out, and there was Princess Michael of Kent.'

HRH Princess Michael, a second cousin-in-law who is married to Prince Michael, the younger son of George VI's brother, the Duke of Kent, has come to embody, in the Queen's eyes, all the drawbacks of an over-extended royal family. For the Queen, one silver lining of the Windsor fire was that she no longer had to invite 'Princess Pushy', as the family called her, for Christmas any more. The character of the junior princess was captured by an interview in which she alluded to the possibility of her becoming Queen 'if there were a plague' and everyone died in the family. She had more royal blood, she explained, than any Windsor import since Prince Philip.

'You know,' said the Queen apprehensively as someone wished her a happy festive season in the pre-fire days, 'there are going to be thirty-six of us for Christmas.'

Shifting the festivities to Sandringham was the perfect excuse to restrict hospitality to the

563

immediate family. The move had been made in the late 1980s when rewiring work started at Windsor, and after the fire the Queen restored Christmas permanently to the Norfolk home where her childhood Christmases had been spent.

Downsizing the public profile of her clan remained an ongoing project. 'There are just too many of us,' she remarked briskly one June afternoon in the 1990s, watching her assembled cousins and second cousins jostling out on to the balcony after her Birthday Parade.

The issue has arisen closer to home with the controversy surrounding the roles of her younger sons, Prince Andrew and, more particularly, Prince Edward. Prince Philip declared after the birth of Prince Charles and Princess Anne that the world did not need any more royals, and the adverse publicity provoked by the attempts of Prince Edward and his wife Sophie to earn a living has fully vindicated his apprehension. 'The problem with Edward,' says a former courtier, 'is that he knows everything about everything, and his wife has picked up the habit from him.'

In June 1999, the last royal wedding of the century seemed finally to have brought into the family a level-headed, hard-working girl who would be a safe pair of hands. In fact, Sophie Rhys-Jones, ennobled on her marriage as Sophie, Countess of Wessex, provoked trouble to rival Diana and Fergie when, within two years, she solicited business for her public relations company from a prosperous-seeming Arab sheikh, who was actually a journalist working for Rupert Murdoch's *News of the World*.

The fake sheikh was already notorious in the media world for a series of highly publicised stings that resulted in prosecutions for a wide variety of crimes. But Sophie's suspicions were not aroused. She cheerfully made fun of the Prime Minister—'we call him President Blair'—as well as his wife, and launched into a scathing denunciation of the government's latest budget. Describing Prince Charles and Camilla as 'number one on the unpopular people list', she revealed there was no chance of the couple getting married until after the death of the 'old lady', by whom she meant the Queen Mother. Even more seriously in terms of both her royal and professional status, she also made plain that, while she might publicly claim otherwise, her PR business could offer royal connections and prestige to her client's accounts. 'That', she explained, 'is an unspoken benefit.'

When she discovered the truth about the sting, the countess was advised by the Palace to buy off the *News of the World* with a personal interview. Getting rather too personal, she told the paper that 'my Edward is not gay', and went on to reveal how, if she and her husband proved infertile, they might resort to in-vitro fertilisation techniques. The countess's interest in this area seems to have been linked to a fertility clinic that she had recently signed as a client.

The scandal was compounded by the continuing embarrassments of her husband's TV production company, which had registered a loss since its creation, and was surviving only by making films on royal subjects, for which Edward's family connections, as he himself boasted, gave him an inside track.

To many royal officials, it seemed that the indulgence of both the Queen and Prince Philip towards their youngest child and his wife lay at the heart of the problem.

'When they got engaged,' remembers a courtier, 'they wanted to live in this vast Victorian pile at Bagshot Park, which, apart from being a monstrosity, cost a fortune to maintain. There were all sorts of problems about government money being needed to restore it, and we made clear to the Queen we thought it a bad idea for Edward and Sophie to live there, and that they should find somewhere more modest. It was so obvious after all the bad publicity over "South York" [Sunninghill Park, Fergie and Andrew's home], and the Queen seemed to agree. But then she came back after a weekend with the family. Hey presto, it was "Bagshot for Eddie".'

Edward's unique combination of arrogance and incompetence, stretching from his Royal Knock-Out performance of 1987 to his TV company's invasion of his nephew's privacy in 2001, illustrates the drawback of monarchy's reliance on the lottery of birth. His parents' indulgence of his foibles emphasises how easily and fallibly human beings make human mistakes. When asked how long he thought the British monarchy would last, Lord Mountbatten would grow reverential, as if about to say, 'As long as the white cliffs of Dover'—then would, in fact, reply, 'Only as long as there are good people doing the job.'

But the lottery of birth that produced the over-vilified Edward has also thrown up the already dangerously idolised Prince William. With his haunting echoes of his mother's looks and style, the tall and handsome young prince appears to offer reassurance, with his brother Prince Harry, that some good may have come from the ghastly marriage into which the culture enticed his parents. William's shyness and apparent lack of pretension appear to suggest that something of Diana lives on—though appearances can be misleading. It is not generally appreciated how both young princes were distancing themselves from their mother before her death—and not only over the embarrassment of Dodi.

'There was only so much fun in going with her for a Big Mac on Kensington High Street and getting pestered by the paps,' remembers one of their mother's staff. 'They were much happier going to Sandringham or Balmoral with their father and getting muddy on their scramble bikes.'

The hope expressed by their uncle in his funeral oration has not come to pass. For William and Harry, their 'blood' family is definitely Windsor, not Spencer. They have seen little of their uncle who had such furious rows with their father in the days following their mother's death, and both boys are particularly close to their grandfather, Prince Philip, himself the product of a broken home. In January 1999, William chose to stay at Sandringham and go shooting with Prince Philip rather than accompany his father on his winter skiing holiday to Klosters, where he would have to run the gauntlet of the photographers hanging round the slopes. The future King grew up witnessing Diana's love–hate relationship with the media at first hand, and will live his entire life with the conviction that the press killed his mother.

Barring accidents, he will also live the best years of his adult life waiting to succeed his grandmother and father. When he finally becomes King William V, he will be anything but a teenage dreamboat. The immense expectations that Britain currently places on William are a cruel burden, and they may well prove unattainable. But they also suggest a widespread popular hope that the magic of monarchy may, through him, find some way of surviving into the future.

CHAPTER THIRTY-TWO

September Again

It is a complete misconception to imagine that the monarchy exists in the interests of the monarch. It doesn't. It exists in the interests of the people. If at any time any nation decides that the system is unacceptable, then it is up to them to change it.

Prince Philip, Duke of Edinburgh, speaking in Canada in 1969

On 11 September 2001 the Queen stared at her television like the rest of the world, not sure if what she was seeing could be real. She watched the hijacked airliners fly without wavering into the twin towers of New York's World Trade Center, she later said, in 'total shock' and 'growing disbelief'.

It was four years and just a few days since people around the globe had been stirred to instant grief by the unexpected tragedy of Diana's death—and now, as then, Elizabeth II was on holiday at Balmoral. In 1997 she had almost failed to match the moment. But the great lesson of those September days had been learned. Phone calls started immediately between London and Balmoral. Within two hours of the twin towers being hit, a personal message of sympathy had gone to President Bush, and the Queen's return to London for a service in St Paul's was being planned.

'These days,' says a recently retired courtier, 'everyone is really on their toes.'

The eleventh of September was also the day that Lord Carnarvon died. The Queen's old friend Porchey, her racing manager, collapsed with a sudden heart attack, aged seventy-seven. He had been discussing horses with her that week. Part of her life died with him—one of the nicest parts. Henry Carnarvon was the only person, Princess Anne once said, who could always be sure of being put through to her mother on the phone at any time without question.

Talking to Porchey always lifted her spirits. 'He had the horse news,' says a friend, 'and that was the news she really wanted to hear.'

Porchey was the Queen's hotline to the stables—which mares were in foal, the young stock that looked promising, any new race entries that her trainers might be planning. He would ring her on his mobile from the sales when he was buying on her behalf, holding the phone up in the air so she could hear the bidding. He was her companion at every race meeting, and if there was no racing, it was in the afternoons that he would call for a chat, often for half an hour at a time. They shared a business and a passion, spending hours poring over pedigrees, working out promising combinations of stallions and mares. They may not have produced Prince Andrew together, but they did produce countless racehorses and over fifty years of memories and very happy afternoons—all suddenly ended on 11 September 2001.

Personal and public mingled strangely. America's new ambassador to London—an old Texas buddy of the George Bushes, father and son—was the Queen's best American friend, Will Farish, the Texan racehorse owner and breeder on whose Kentucky horse farm she had stayed on her unofficial visits across the Atlantic to inspect bloodstock in the States. She would go round the studs of the bluegrass country with Farish, admiring the world-class stallions and arranging matings, immersed in the consuming pleasures of horse stuff. These little-publicised trips were the closest that Elizabeth II ever got to a foreign holiday. It was Porchey who had introduced her to Farish.

Down in London in the Lord Chamberlain's office, Malcolm Ross looked at the calendar. With the ending of summer, the Changing of the Guard had been switched to its off-season every-other-day schedule, and the next Changing would be on Thursday. A two-minute silence was the obvious way to mark Britain's sympathy—but how to signal its beginning and end? Talking on the phone to the Queen in Balmoral, Ross worked out that the Guard would play the American national anthem to start with, and would end with 'God Save the Queen'.

'The Star-Spangled Banner' was not in the repertory of the Coldstream Guards, but they had twenty-four hours to learn it, and Ross suggested that they should play American music as they marched down the Mall towards the Palace. The bandmaster came up with a selection of marches by John Philip Sousa, which some British hearers thought too jolly for the occasion. But the familiar melodies struck a moving note with the many Americans among the 6,000-strong crowd. The news of the tribute had been put out on radio and television, and taxi drivers had spread the word. People had heard about the silence, but they had not expected the music and the anthems. Spectators sobbed openly as the British Guards played the American tune. In a world that had proved tragically to have no frontiers, the Palace courtyard embraced international emotions.

Next day the tears were at St Paul's, at the service of remembrance for which the Queen had flown down from Balmoral. Farish was there, with 2,700 Americans, as well as British relatives of those lost in the New York catastrophe. Prince Philip read from St Paul's letter to the Romans—'If God be for us, who can be against us?' As the great organ struck up the Battle Hymn of the Republic, which she had last sung at the funeral of the half-American Winston Churchill thirty-six years earlier, the Queen was clearly struggling with her emotions. She bit hard on her lower lip and as she came out of the cathedral, there were tears in her eyes—tears for Porchey, tears for America: bitter days, empty afternoons.

*   *   *

As Queen Elizabeth II gets older, she is getting more relaxed. 'Come on, *two* kisses,' she said fondly to an old friend who greeted her with a single peck on the cheek at her Golden Wedding party in November 1997. She is allowing herself to smile more, and also allowing herself to be sad. In the circumstances of Britain's last half-century she has done better as Queen than might have been expected, losing power but retaining affection and respect. Maintaining her Commonwealth family of nations has been a genuine triumph against the odds. Who would have foreseen a peacefully elected black South African president riding down the Mall with Elizabeth II at his side before the twentieth century was out?

Her hopes for her own family have not been so blessed. It has been her philosophy to let them make their own mistakes, and that they have certainly done. When historians look back on her reign they may say that the fragmenting family of Elizabeth II has reflected the general trends of her times, in the same way that Victoria's extended clan and George VI's neat little nuclear family reflected theirs. But it has been painful to live through, and it raises the question as to what role is played by a royal family that is as fallible as anyone else's.

For the media, the answer is simple. Britain's celebrity family by appointment provides an endless source of material—and hence revenue—with royal weaknesses and misfortunes delivering many of the most profitable stories. In December 2001 the truth of George Bernard Shaw's 1887 quip about the Queen's bonnet and Bulgaria was borne out yet again when the unlucky Sophie Wessex's ectopic pregnancy and loss of her first baby wiped news of the Taliban's final surrender in Kandahar from several front pages. A mid-market British newspaper reader might understand intellectually why Afganistan matters, but that cannot hold a candle to a story that touches the heart. People want and need to exercise their feelings, and the Windsors offer a brisk and reassuring walk through the woods—the enjoyable, if vicarious sensation of sharing the ups and downs of life with familiar friends. The intense national debate that followed the disclosure, early in 2002, of the 16-year-old Prince Harry's experiments with drugs and alcohol was a therapeutic exercise for a society that has some difficulty talking about intimate and painful things.

Elizabeth II, however, sees her monarchy as serving a higher purpose than fodder for the national soap opera. She remains a believer in the old-fashioned idea of setting a positive example. Solemn moments like the 14 September service in St Paul's or the annual Remembrance Day tributes in November are closer to her quiet, stringent vision of a crown which exalts the duty and service that hold a free community together. Asked in 1992 which of the many different aspects of her job she considered most important, she replied 'investitures'—the twenty-five or so ceremonies each year at which three thousand or more of her citizens (each with three guests) come to the Palace to receive the ribbons, medals and, in some case, knighthoods that they have been awarded in the twice-yearly honours list. This is where brave soldiers, sailors, police and airmen get their medals, while many civilians and voluntary workers are decorated with the awards of the Order of the British Empire which her grandfather, George V, inaugurated in the dark days of 1917 on Glasgow

Rangers football pitch.

Elizabeth II prepares thoroughly to meet her heroes. On the previous weekend, she goes away with a briefing list containing several paragraphs on each of the individuals who are due to be honoured. She reads it thoroughly to find out precisely what each district nurse or charity volunteer has done to earn their OBE, CBE or MBE and she picks out a few key words for each person. This list is given to her equerry, who then whispers the words into her ear as each recipient approaches the gold and crimson dais in the Palace Ballroom. The whispered words prompt a personal question that the Queen has prepared for you, and if you give her an intelligent answer, she will ask you another. If you offer a vacant stare, or talk nonsense, she will put you out of your misery with a brisk smile of farewell.

'It was lovely,' recipients regularly say to court officials. 'We chatted for several minutes.' In fact, Elizabeth II processes her investiture presentations and medal-pinning at the rate of five recipients per two minutes—up to 130 people in an hour and ten minutes.

Nationally, she meets her people's elected head of government every Tuesday. Her evening audience with the Prime Minister is an occasion whose symbolism became appreciated in the Thatcher years, when people derived comfort from the knowledge that the Iron Lady had to bow her head every week to someone. Some of Tony Blair's critics now feel the same about him, but the New Labour Prime Minister has found his weekly royal audience one of the more agreeable surprises in his round of duties.

'It's the one regular thing he does,' says Alastair Campbell, 'that he really looks forward to. After a while, everything in the diary can become a bit of a chore, but it's the one fixture where you never hear him saying, "Oh God . . ." You just never ever hear it, and if he's travelling, he makes a point of phoning. There's real feeling developed there, both of them very prominent figures, him with the massive problems he's always wrestling with, her with her massive experience, and both of them able to talk to each other in absolute confidence.'

The weekly audience is the only meeting from which Blair does not emerge to brief his press spokesman on what he said and what was said to him. Campbell admits he has 'not a clue' about what the Queen and Prime Minister say to each other. It remains their secret—though one slight slip does suggest where the balance of authority has come to rest. Early in 2001 the Downing Street briefing room heard how the Prime Minister had been talking to the Queen in audience about 'the Golden Jubilee', to receive some gentle correction.

'*My* Golden Jubilee', the Queen reminded her Prime Minister.

*   *   *

The Jubilee year did not start well. Princess Margaret died on 9 February, just three days after the fiftieth anniversary of George VI's death. The princess had been ailing following a succession of small strokes, but her final collapse came as a cruel shock to her sister and still more to the Queen Mother. The royal matriarch had reached the age of 101, but had herself been weakened by respiratory infections over the Christmas holiday at Sandringham.

'Four to six weeks,' remarked a royal doctor thoughtfully, calculating the time when grief would most sharply strike an elderly widow who had faced the ordeal of burying her own child.

In the event the Queen Mother lasted seven weeks, but on 30 March 2002, a bright Easter Saturday when the daffodils were glowing outside Royal Lodge, she woke with breathing difficulties, which made it clear to the doctors that she could not last long. The Queen was riding in the woods near by when she got the news, and she went straight to see her mother in the bedroom looking out on the gardens where she had played with Margaret all those years ago, two dutiful daughters brushing and dusting the Little Welsh House. Lilibet was holding her mother's hand when she died.

The death of the Queen Mother was generally hailed as the end of an era, not least because, as a matter of considered policy, the BBC instructed Peter Sissons, the presenter entrusted with breaking the news to the nation, not to wear a black tie. But the public dismay at that decision, and the general mourning for the Queen Mother, suggested that the country's sense of tradition had deeper roots. An emotional broadcast by Prince Charles in which he seemed close to tears as he talked of his 'most magical grandmother' elicited widespread sympathy.

The prince had made a similar broadcast in February when he paid tribute to Margaret, to whom he had never been particularly close. At his mother's request he had dwelt on his aunt's great

576

'vitality'. Mother and son had discussed the wording of the tribute carefully. Now, as he spoke of his grandmother, the phrase 'stalwart and sensitive' had come from the Queen herself. Like the Union flag flying at half-mast over Buckingham Palace to mark the Queen Mother's passing, Charles's uninhibited and public expressions of emotion were another legacy from Diana.

'The family now understand,' says one influential Palace adviser, in a reference to the missteps of September 1997, 'that it is no longer sufficient to issue a statement of regret, then go grim-faced to church.'

Charles's voicing of feelings on his mother's behalf suggested the possibility of a fruitful new partnership. The gift of the late Queen Mother had been to amalgamate stern duty with outgoing emotion and tenderness. These are not always compatible qualities, and the two extremes now find themselves embodied in the differing characters of Elizabeth II and her eldest son. Kingship may not be on the cards for Charles – the current sturdiness of the Queen suggests she has inherited the longevity genes of her mother – but the prince may yet find a role in acting as the emotional foil to his stoic parent and sovereign, and perhaps even in opening some path to the workings of her inscrutable heart. The strengthening of the teamwork between monarch and heir will certainly be crucial to the future success of the figurehead family of whom British society ultimately asks little more than to be dignified, unified and caring.

The principal consequence of the Queen Mother's death was that her daughter finally had the stage to herself. On the eve of her seventy-sixth birthday, Elizabeth II at long last became the matriarch of her clan and of her nation, overnight an older woman but also imbued with added authority and appeal. The parallels with Queen Victoria became clearer still. The diligent and conscientious Elizabeth II might not yet be Britain's longest-lived monarch, but she is already the monarch who has travelled furthest and has put in the most hours of work. As people pondered the deaths of Princess Margaret and the Queen Mother in the spring of 2002, the fear was expressed that the summer's Jubilee celebrations might be dampened. On the contrary. Her Majesty's loyal subjects appreciated their unique Queen the more, and even the vocal minority who were not so loyal could see how her unflinching integrity and steadiness were virtues worthy of celebration. As Elizabeth II approached her Golden Jubilee, she was finally coming into her own.

Royal Who's Who

Tracing the role of the British monarchy in recent history is sometimes complicated by the royal family's habit of adopting different names and even birthdays for public and private use, and of moving through a progression of titles. This was particularly common in the early twentieth century. Thus the father of Queen Elizabeth II was born Prince Albert on 14 December 1895 and was called 'Bertie' by his family; he was generally known as the Duke of York after his father gave him that title in 1920, but when he became King he took the name George VI (remaining Bertie to his family) and decreed early June as the time when his birthday should be officially celebrated. His elder brother, 'David' to his family, was known as Edward, Prince of Wales, from 1910 until 1936 when he became King Edward VIII; then, after his abdication in that same year, he became Duke of Windsor.

Queen Elizabeth II has been comparatively straightforward, retaining the same single Christian name (and nickname, 'Lilibet') all her life—unlike her sister who was described officially as Princess Margaret Rose throughout her childhood. But as Queen she has two birthdays. Born on 21 April 1926, she celebrates the occasion officially on one of the first three Saturdays in June (largely in the hope of better weather for fellow celebrants).

There follows below, therefore, a list of the principal characters in this book together with their main dates, titles and family connections. These are, on the whole, pursued chronologically in the text but have on occasions been abandoned for the sake of clarity. Prince George, for example, Queen Elizabeth II's uncle who was killed in the Second World War, is generally remembered as the Duke of Kent, even though he did not receive that title until 1934 when he was thirty-two, and he is usually be referred to as such here.

Certain other names and technical terms are also briefly explained.

ADEANE, MICHAEL (LORD) (1910–84): private secretary to Queen Elizabeth II 1953–72.

AIRLIE, DAVID, EARL OF (b. 1926): Lord Chamberlain to Queen Elizabeth II 1984–97.

AIRLIE, MABELL, COUNTESS OF (1866–1956): lady-of-the-bedchamber to Queen Mary; grandmother of David Airlie and Angus Ogilvy.

ALBERT, PRINCE, DUKE OF YORK: *see* George VI.

ALBERT, PRINCE CONSORT (1819–61): husband of Queen Victoria; great-great-grandfather of Elizabeth II and of Prince Philip.

ALEXANDRA, PRINCESS (b. 1936): cousin to Queen Elizabeth II; daughter of Prince George, Duke of Kent; married Angus Ogilvy 1963; two children.

ALEXANDRA, QUEEN (1844–1925): wife of Edward VII; great-grandmother to Queen Elizabeth II.

ALICE, PRINCESS (1885–1969): née Battenberg; mother to Prince Philip; married Prince Andrew of Greece 1903.

ALLA: *see* Knight, Clara.

ALTHORP HOUSE: Northamptonshire home of the

Spencer family since the fifteenth century. Diana, Princess of Wales was buried there on 6 September 1997.

ANDREW, PRINCE, OF GREECE (1882–1944): known as Andrea in his family, the father of Prince Philip.

ANDREW, PRINCE, DUKE OF YORK (b. 1960): second son of Queen Elizabeth II.

ANNE, PRINCESS, PRINCESS ROYAL (b. 1950): daughter of Queen Elizabeth II; married Captain Mark Phillips 1973; son, Peter Phillips b. 1977; daughter, Zara b. 1981; divorced April 1992; married Tim Laurence December 1992.

ARMSTRONG-JONES: *see* Snowdon.

BAGEHOT, WALTER (1826–77): editor of The Economist and author of The English Constitution, the basis of the constitutional theory taught to George V.

BALMORAL: Aberdeenshire estate of British royal family, purchased by Queen Victoria.

BATTENBERG: *see* Mountbatten.

BERTIE: *see* George VI.

BIRKHALL: Aberdeenshire house and estate near Balmoral where the Queen Mother stays.

BOBO: *see* MacDonald, Margaret.

BOLLAND, MARK (b. 1966): deputy private secretary to Prince Charles from 1996.

BOWES-LYON: family name of the Earls of Strathmore, family of Queen Elizabeth the Queen Mother.

BRABOURNE, JOHN (KNATCHBULL), LORD (b. 1926): married Lady Patricia Mountbatten, daughter of Lord Mountbatten, in 1946. Producer of such films as Murder on the Orient Express.

BROADLANDS HOUSE: home of Lord Louis Mountbatten in Romsey, Hampshire.

BURMESE (1962–90): Queen Elizabeth II's favourite parade horse, a black mare presented to her by the Canadian Mounties, which she rode at her birthday parade (*see* Trooping the Colour), 1969–86.

CAERNARFON CASTLE: north-west Wales, birthplace of the first Prince of Wales (later Edward II). Site of the investitures as Prince of Wales of the future Edward VIII (1911) and Prince Charles (1969).

CAMBRIDGE: English surname adopted by Queen Mary's family, the Tecks, 1917.

CARNARVON, EARL (1924–2001): racing manager and friend of the Queen, known as 'Porchey' from the title of Baron Porchester which he held until he succeeded to his earldom in 1987.

CHARLES, PRINCE (b. 1948): Prince of Wales; eldest son of Queen Elizabeth II.

CHARTERIS, SIR MARTIN (1913–99): private secretary to Princess Elizabeth 1950–2, assistant private secretary to Queen Elizabeth II 1952–72, private secretary 1972–7, subsequently Lord Charteris.

CIVIL LIST: annual grant by Parliament to the crown for the upkeep of royal household, first paid in 1760 in return for the surrender of the crown lands, traditionally fixed at the beginning of each new reign, but increased several times in the reign of Queen Elizabeth II. Last set in 1990, it is currently fixed at £7.9 million a year until 2010

CLARENCE, PRINCE ALBERT VICTOR, DUKE OF (1864–92): elder son of Edward VII; one of his

Christian names was Edward, so he was known to his family as Eddy; elder brother of George V.

CLARENCE HOUSE: adjacent to St James's Palace, this 1825 house has been the London residence of the Queen Mother since 1953.

COLVILLE, COMMANDER SIR RICHARD (1907–75): press secretary to King George VI (1947–52) and to Queen Elizabeth II (1952–67); cousin of Sir John.

COLVILLE, SIR JOHN ('Jock') (1915–87): private secretary to Neville Chamberlain, Winston Churchill and Clement Attlee; also to Princess Elizabeth 1947–9.

COPPINS: country home to the Dukes of Kent in Iver, Buckinghamshire; sold in 1973.

CRAWFIE (1909–88): Miss Marion Crawford, governess to Princesses Elizabeth and Margaret 1932–49; married Major George Buthlay 1947.

CRAWFORD, GEOFFREY (b. 1950): Australian-born press secretary to Queen Elizabeth II 1997–2000.

DAVID: *see* Edward VIII.

DIANA, PRINCESS OF WALES (1961–97): née Spencer, daughter of John, Earl Spencer and Frances Fermoy (later Shand-Kydd); mother of Princes William (b. 1982) and Harry (b. 1984); divorced 1996.

DICKIE: *see* Mountbatten, Lord Louis.

EDDY: *see* Clarence, Prince Albert Victor, Duke of.

EDINBURGH, DUKE OF: *see* Philip, Prince.

EDWARD, PRINCE, EARL OF WESSEX (b. 1964): third son, fourth child of Queen Elizabeth II; married Sophie Rhys-Jones 1999.

EDWARD VII, KING (1841–1910, r. 1901–10):

eldest son of Queen Victoria, great-grandfather of Queen Elizabeth II.

EDWARD VIII, KING (1894–1972, r. 20 Jan.–11 Dec. 1936): eldest son of George V, and uncle to Queen Elizabeth II; known to his family as David; Prince of Wales 1911–36; abdicated December 1936 and known thereafter as HRH Duke of Windsor.

ELIZABETH II, QUEEN (b. 1926): daughter of King George VI; married Lieutenant Philip Mountbatten 20 November 1947; acceded 6 February 1952; crowned 2 June 1953. Children: Charles (b. 1948); Anne (b. 1950); Andrew (b. 1960); Edward (b. 1964). Residences: Buckingham Palace, London; Windsor Castle, Berkshire; Sandringham House, Norfolk; Balmoral Castle, Aberdeenshire.

ELIZABETH, QUEEN, THE QUEEN MOTHER (b. 1900–2002): née Bowes-Lyon; Duchess of York 1923–36, Queen Consort 1936–52, Queen Mother from 1952; now lives at Clarence House, London; Royal Lodge, Windsor; Birkhall, Balmoral; Castle of Mey, Caithness-shire.

FELLOWES, ROBERT (b. 1941): private secretary to the Queen 1990–9; married Lady Jane Spencer, sister of Diana,1978.

FERGUSON, SARAH, DUCHESS OF YORK (b. 1959): daughter of Prince Charles's polo manager, Major Ronald Ferguson; known as Fergie; married Prince Andrew, 1986; two daughters, Beatrice (b. 1988), Eugenie (b. 1990); divorced 1996.

GEORGE V, KING (1865–1936, r. 1910–36): second son of King Edward VII, grandfather to Queen Elizabeth II. Became heir to the throne, after his father, following the death in 1892 of his elder brother Eddy, Duke of Clarence; married Eddy's fiancée, Princess May of Teck, 1893. Known as Duke of York until his father's accession in 1901, then as Prince of Wales until his own accession in 1910. Children: Prince Edward, known as David, later Edward VIII and Duke of Windsor (b. 1894); Prince Albert, known as Bertie, later Duke of York and George VI (b. 1895); Princess Mary, later known as the Princess Royal (b. 1897); Prince Henry, known as Harry, later Duke of Gloucester (b. 1900); Prince George, later Duke of Kent (b. 1902); Prince John (b. 1905).

GEORGE VI, KING (1895–1952, r. 1936–52): second son of King George V, father of Queen Elizabeth II; known to his family as Bertie. Duke of York 1920–36; acceded as George VI following his brother's abdication 11 December 1936. Married Lady Elizabeth Bowes-Lyon 1923; also father of Princess Margaret Rose (b. 1930).

GHILLIE: a Highland retainer skilled in stalking, fishing and outdoor pursuits.

GLAMIS CASTLE: home of the Bowes-Lyon family, earls of Strathmore, near Forfar, Angus, East Scotland.

GLOUCESTER, prince henry, DUKE OF (1900–74): third son of King George V and Queen Mary; known to his family as Harry; uncle to Queen Elizabeth II. Married Lady Alice Montagu-Douglas-Scott 1935. His elder son, Prince William of Gloucester, was killed in a plane crash in 1972. Succeeded by his younger son, Prince Richard of Gloucester (b. 1944), who married Birgitte von Deurs 1972.

GRACE AND FAVOUR RESIDENCES: apartments in royal palaces and houses on royal estates in the gift of the sovereign and usually bestowed upon retired royal officials or the widows of distinguished public servants and figures.

HENRY OF WALES, PRINCE (b. 1984): 'Prince Harry', second son of Prince Charles and Diana, Princess of Wales.

HICKS, LADY PAMELA (b. 1929): younger daughter of Lord Mountbatten (and thus a cousin of Prince Philip); married in 1960 David Hicks, interior designer.

HIGHGROVE HOUSE: home in Tetbury, Gloucestershire, of Charles, Prince of Wales, since 1981.

HOLYROOD HOUSE: palace of the kings of Scotland, now the Edinburgh residence of the Queen when she visits Scotland.

JANVRIN, SIR ROBIN (b. 1946): press secretary to Queen Elizabeth II 1987–90; assistant private secretary 1990–5; deputy 1996–9; since 1999 her private secretary.

KENT, MARINA DUCHESS OF: *see* Marina, Princess.

KENT, PRINCE GEORGE DUKE OF (1902–42): fourth son and fifth child of King George V and Queen Mary; uncle to Queen Elizabeth II. Married Princess Marina 1934. Children: Edward, today Duke of Kent (b. 1935); Alexandra (b. 1936); Michael (b. 4 July 1942, six weeks before his father's death in an air crash).

KENT, KATHARINE, DUCHESS OF (b. 1933): only daughter of Sir William Worsley; married Prince Edward, Duke of Kent, in 1961. Children: George, Earl of St Andrews (b. 1962); Lady

586

Helen Windsor (b. 1964); Lord Nicholas Windsor (b. 1970).

KENT, PRINCESS MICHAEL OF (b. 1945): daughter of Baron Gunther von Reibnitz; married Prince Michael of Kent in 1978, after a first, brief marriage to Thomas Troubridge was annulled. Children: Lord Frederick Windsor (b. 1979); Lady Gabriella Windsor (b. 1981).

KENSINGTON PALACE: Originally the residence of King William III and Queen Mary, the state apartments of this seventeenth-century palace are open to the public. The private areas have been divided into spacious grace and favour apartments housing most famously Diana, Princess of Wales, during her marriage and after her separation in 1992 until her death in 1997.

KNIGHT, CLARA: nurse to Princess Elizabeth; given the honorary title of Mrs by virtue of her senior position in the nurseries of Lady Elizabeth Bowes-Lyon and subsequently the Princesses Elizabeth and Margaret Rose; known to her charges as Alla. Died 1943.

LASCELLES, SIR ALAN (1887–1981): assistant private secretary to Edward, Prince of Wales (1920–9), to King George V (1935–6), to Edward VIII (1936) and to George VI (1936–43). Thereafter principal private secretary to King George VI until 1952 and to Queen Elizabeth II (1952–3). Known as Tommy.

LAURENCE, TIM (b. 1949): naval captain, married Princess Anne 1992.

LETTERS PATENT: a form of royal warrant by which, among other things, peerages and dignities are conferred.

LINLEY, DAVID, VISCOUNT (b. 1961): son of

Princess Margaret and Lord Snowdon, married Serena Stanhope 1993.

LORD CHAMBERLAIN: the senior royal official in overall charge of the royal household, controlling budgets and appointments, and also in charge of ceremonial.

MACDONALD, MARGARET (1904–93): nurserymaid to Princess Elizabeth from 1926, then her dresser in adult years. Known to the Queen as Bobo.

MACDONALD, RUBY: sister to Bobo; nurserymaid to Princess Margaret Rose from 1930; dresser to Princess Margaret until 1961.

MARGARET, PRINCESS, COUNTESS OF SNOWDON (1930–2002): sister to Queen Elizabeth II. Married Antony Armstrong-Jones 6 May 1960; divorced 1978. Children: David, Viscount Linley (b. 1961); Lady Sarah Armstrong-Jones (b. 1964), now Sarah Chatto.

MARINA, PRINCESS, DUCHESS OF KENT (1906–68): daughter of Prince Nicholas of Greece; married Prince George, Duke of Kent, 1934.

MARY, PRINCESS, Princess Royal (1897–1965): daughter of King George V and Queen Mary; aunt to Queen Elizabeth II. Married Henry Lascelles, later Earl of Harewood, 1922.

MOUNTBATTEN: name adopted by the Battenbergs in 1917 and by Prince Philip of Greece in 1947.

MOUNTBATTEN, LADY PATRICIA (b. 1924): elder daughter of Lord Louis (and thus a cousin of Prince Philip); married in 1946 John Knatchbull, Lord Brabourne. By special remainder she succeeded on her father's death to the

Mountbatten earldom, which will pass to her son Norton (*see* Romsey).

MOUNTBATTEN, LORD LOUIS (1900–79): Uncle to Prince Philip; known to his family as Dickie; Admiral of the Fleet, Earl Mountbatten of Burma. Last Viceroy and first Governor-General of India (1947–8). Married the Hon. Edwina Ashley (1901–60) 1922. Killed by an IRA bomb planted on his boat at his holiday home in Donegal, Republic of Ireland.

MOUNTBATTEN-WINDSOR: surname proclaimed in February 1960 for all descendants of Queen Elizabeth II needing a surname.

OGILVY, ANGUS (b. 1928): married Princess Alexandra of Kent 1963. Children: James Ogilvy (b. 1964); Marina Ogilvy (b. 1966).

PARK HOUSE: farmhouse on the Sandringham estate, where Diana Spencer spent most of her childhood.

PARKER BOWLES, CAMILLA (b. 1947): née Shand, married Andrew Parker Bowles (b. 1939); divorced 1996.

PHILIP, PRINCE (b. 1921): husband of Queen Elizabeth II. Naturalised British as Lieutenant Philip Mountbatten 1947, married 20 November 1947 and created Baron Greenwich, Earl of Merioneth and Duke of Edinburgh. Granted the style and titular dignity of a prince of the United Kingdom 1957.

PORCHEY: *see* Carnarvon, Lord.

PRINCESS ROYAL: style usually bestowed upon the eldest daughter of the sovereign, currently held by Princess Anne, previously held by Princess Mary, only daughter of George V.

PRIVY PURSE: treasury of the royal household.

ROMSEY, NORTON, LORD (b. 1947): son of Patricia, Countess Mountbatten, and heir to both the earldom of Mountbatten and to his father's title as Baron Brabourne.

ROMSEY, PENELOPE, LADY (b. 1954): wife of Norton Romsey.

ROYAL LODGE: house in Windsor Great Park bestowed by King George V on the Duke and Duchess of York in 1931; today the Windsor home of Queen Elizabeth the Queen Mother.

ROYAL STANDARD: the flag flown wherever the sovereign is, never at half mast. England is represented by three lions passant, Scotland by a lion rampant and Ireland by a harp. Wales is represented on the arms of the Prince of Wales.

SANDRINGHAM HOUSE: home in Norfolk of British royal family, purchased in 1861 as a country residence for the future Edward VII.

SIMPSON, WALLIS: *see* Windsor, Duchess of.

SMITHS LAWN: the polo fields in Windsor Great Park, said, by tradition, to be named after a gardener who could not spell (hence the lack of an apostrophe).

SNOWDON, EARL OF (b. 1930): Antony Armstrong-Jones; married Princess Margaret 1960; created Earl of Snowdon 1961; divorced 1978.

SPENCER FAMILY: since 1992 headed by Charles, Earl Spencer (b. 1964), younger brother of Diana, Princess of Wales. Diana's two elder sisters are Sarah (b. 1955), married Neil McCorquodale 1980, and Jane (b. 1957), married Robert Fellowes 1978.

STAMFORDHAM, LORD (1849–1931): known as Arthur Bigge until receiving his peerage in 1911;

private secretary to King George V 1910–31.

TOWNSEND, GROUP CAPTAIN PETER, DSO, DFC (1914–95): equerry to King George VI 1944–52; Deputy Master of Royal Household 1950–2; appointed Comptroller of the Household of Queen Elizabeth the Queen Mother 1952–3; air attaché Brussels 1953–6.

TROOPING THE COLOUR: the yearly military parade held on Horse Guards Parade, London, to mark the official birthday of the sovereign.

UNION FLAG: popularly known as Union Jack; the flag of the British Isles, composed of the red cross of St George of England, the diagonal white cross on a blue ground of St Andrew of Scotland and the red diagonal cross of St Patrick of Ireland. Wales is not represented.

VICTORIA, QUEEN (1819–1901, r. 1837–1901): Britain's longest-ruling sovereign and great-great-grandmother of both Queen Elizabeth II and Prince Philip.

WALES, PRINCE OF: title usually bestowed upon eldest son of monarch, borne in the last century by George V (1901–19), Edward VIII (1910–36) and Prince Charles (invested in 1969).

WESSEX, EARL OF: title created for the Queen's youngest son, Edward, following his marriage in 1999.

WILLIAM, PRINCE (b. 1982): elder son of Prince Charles and Diana, Princess of Wales. First in line of succession after his father.

WINDSOR, HOUSE OF: adopted as the official name of the British royal family by King George V in 1917.

WINDSOR, DUKE OF: *see* Edward VIII.

WINDSOR, DUCHESS OF (1896–1986): *née* Wallis

591

Warfield. Married (first) Earl Winfield Spencer junior 1916, divorced 1927; (second) Ernest Simpson 1928, divorced 1936; (third) HRH the Duke of Windsor 1937.

WINDSOR CASTLE AND ESTATE: in continuous use since 1066, the castle contains 1,000 rooms and commands an estate of 5,313 acres.

YORK, DUCHESS OF: *see* Elizabeth, Queen, the Queen Mother; Ferguson, Sarah.

YORK, DUKE OF: *see* George V, King; George VI, King; Andrew, Prince.

Acknowledgements

> '*Majesty* marked the end of the era of sycophantic reporting of the monarchy . . . In retrospect, however, it can also be seen as a time bomb. In due course books between hard covers were to damage the Monarchy much more than a brigade of paparazzi.'
>
> Ben Pimlott, *The Queen*, 1996.

This book celebrates a personal silver jubilee. It is nearly twenty-five years since I wrote *Majesty*, whose great success was a watershed in my life. I always regarded *Majesty*, published in 1977, as self-contained, not needing any sequel. Then, in the mid-1990s, it became clear that the sequel *was* the story. A new dimension was created by the breakdown of the royal marriages, the drama of Diana, and the consequent overturning of popular attitudes, in which uncritical adulation was replaced by censure and ridicule that were equally over the top. If a society chooses to cultivate a fantasy family, making fallible human beings the vehicle for its dreams and aspirations, the consequences will be pain for the individuals concerned, and disillusionment for those who expect too much. Royal seeks to put these events and feelings into context, bringing the story of the Queen up to date, but also going back into history to show how we, Her Majesty's so-called subjects, have been the shapers of the modern monarchy and have adjusted the institution to our communal wishes and needs.

593

As with the writing of *Majesty*, my debt to those close to the Queen has been immense. I am grateful to the serving members of Her Majesty's Household, to the staff of the Prince of Wales at St James's Palace, and to all those who helped me on an off-the-record basis. I am also grateful for the help of Dickie Arbiter LVO, Sir Guy Acland Bt LVO, Charles Anson CVO, Christian Bailey MVO, Godfrey Barker, Julian Barrow, Lord Bell of Belgravia, Lord Patrick Beresford, Anthony Bishop CMG OBE, Olivia Bland, Lord Brabourne CBE, Alison Brown, Lord Buxton of Alsa KCVO MC, Alastair Campbell, The Rt Hon. Lord Carrington KG GCMG CH MC, Christine Carter, The Rt Hon. Lord Charteris of Amisfield GCB GCVO, Lord Condon of Langton Green DL QPM, The Rt Hon. Viscount Cranborne, Geoffrey Crawford CVO, Brigadier Sir Jeffery Darell Bt MC, Peter Dimmock CVO OBE, Peter Edwards LVO, The Rt Hon. Lord Fellowes of Shotesham GCB GCVO, Helen Fielding, Sir Edward Ford GCVO KCB, Freddie Fox, The Rt Hon. Malcolm Fraser AC CH, Martyn Gregory, John Grigg FRSL, Joe Haines, Charles and Elizabeth Handy, Belinda Harley, Nicky Haslam, The Rt Hon. Lord Hattersley of Sparkbrook, The Hon. Bob Hawke AC, The Rt Hon. Michael Heseltine CH, The Rt Hon. Sir William Heseltine GCB GCVO AC, Lady Pamela Hicks, Patricia Hipwood, Major-General Sir Michael Hobbs KCVO CBE, Anthony Holden, Chris Holker, John Holroyd CB CVO, The Rt Hon. Lord Howe of Aberavon CH QC, Richard Reid Ingrams, Michael Jones, Kitty Kelley, Geoffrey and Jorie Kent, The Rt Hon. Neil Kinnock, The Rt Hon. Lord Lamont of Lerwick,

Roger Law, Simon Lewis, Patrick Lichfield, Magnus Linklater, Colin Mackenzie, Robin Ludlow, Sir Trevor McDonald OBE, Sir Brian McGrath KCVO, The Right Reverend Michael Mann KCVO, Iqbal Meer, Sir Oliver Millar GCVO and Delia Millar, Christopher and Cherry Moorsom, Jan Morris, Greta and Bryan Morrison, Andrew Morton, Anne Neal, Martin Neary LVO, Nanette Newman, Vivien and Michael Noakes, Richard Ormond CBE, Sir Michael Oswald KCVO, The Rt Hon. Lord Owen of the City of Plymouth CH, Eileen Parker, Sir Michael Parker KCVO CBE, Commander Mike Parker CVO, Sir Edward Pickering, Sir John Plumb, The Hon. Margaret Rhodes, Sir Denis Rooke OM CBE FRS FREng, Lord St John of Fawsley FRSL, Sir John Sainty KCB, Anthony Sampson, Sir Kenneth Scott KCVO CMG, Michael Shea CVO, Professor Alfred Smyth, The Earl of Snowdon GCVO, The Rt Hon. Lord Steel KBE, William Summers LVO, Lt-Col. Michael Tomkin MC, The Hon. Kate Townend, The Most Reverend Archbishop Desmond Tutu, Lucia van der Post, Lady Jane Wellesley, His Grace the Duke of Wellington KG LVO OBE MC, James Whitaker, Canon John White, Phillip Whitehead MEP, The Hon. Gough Whitlam AC, Professor Robert Worcester

For this book I was granted access to the Royal Archives, and enjoyed many happy days looking out from the Round Tower at Windsor across the green beauty of the Thames valley—and also studying some documents. The Royal Archives has two traditions that make it unlike any other library in the world. At eleven o'clock a bell summons all present to coffee and biscuits, where an informal seminar takes place, as researchers compare notes with each other and pursue research leads with the uniquely knowledgeable librarians. Then, when your writing is completed, the Royal Archives staff take over the worst chore of any book, checking every citation back against the original document, word for word—with nary an attempt at editorial control. So thank you for the coffee, biscuits, research leads and meticulous reference checking to the registrar Sheila, Lady de Bellaigue, her successor Pam Clark, to Frances Dimond, and also to the Royal Librarian Oliver Everett. The responsibility for mistakes remains my own.

The royal 'rat pack', which did not exist in 1977, has, in its inimitable way, also provided me with many fresh insights—not to mention festive evenings in bars and restaurants from Trastevere to Tasmania. So my thanks to the rats who have been such cheery companions to a mouse without a daily deadline, and who, when cheese factories have loomed, have even trusted me with the rota reporting duties. My particular thanks for the white wine to Alan Hamilton of *The Times*, and, to Robert Hardman, then of the *Daily Telegraph*, for leaving me a little of the red.

Another new development since 1977 has been the birth of the academic version of the rat pack—the 'Prof. pack'. In the last twenty-five years the survival and misfortunes of the British monarchy have drawn the serious interest of sociologists, anthropologists, political scientists and historians who between them have generated a body of profound and illuminating work. This book owes much to the published research and ideas of Dr Vernon Bogdanor, Professor David Cannadine,

596

Professor Peter Hennessy, Dr William Kuhn, Dr Philip Mansel, Professor Ben Pimlott, Dr Frank Prochaska, and Dr David Starkey, and I am grateful for the collegial insights generously provided by those whom I have met.

Outside academia I have drawn heavily on the work of the authors Sally Bedell Smith, Sarah Bradford, Andrew Roberts, Kenneth Rose, Hugo Vickers and Philip Ziegler. I am particularly grateful to Kenneth Rose, the doyen of royal biographers, for his friendship and for the generosity with which he has shared his expertise of all things royal. Hugo Vickers has been a most friendly colleague and sparring partner in numerous TV appearances, and has generously allowed me access to his moated archive at Wyeford.

Inspired by the work of Philip Ziegler, I have tried to give voice to the experiences and opinions of those without a public platform, but whose personal memories, collected for more than sixty years in the archives of Mass-Observation, provide a unique repository of the way that so many anonymous Britons have felt in their hearts about royalty—both for and against. Dorothy Sheridan is currently the director of this invaluable resource, now headquartered at the University of Sussex and I would also like to thank Joy Eldridge, Anna Green and Anna Nomikou who assisted my researches there.

Every biographer owes a deep debt to the keepers of the papers in which the lifeblood of history is to be found, and I have received particular help from: Alex Galloway, Clerk of the Privy Council; Rosy Canter, archivist at Madame

Tussaud's, as well as the artists of the Sculpture Studio; Warrant Officer Brian Smith and Major Mitford-Slade at the Guards' Archives, Whitehall; Captain D. D. Horn, MISM FRSA, curator of the Guards' Museum; Mrs Jackie Kavanagh of the BBC Written Archives Centre; Robin Harcourt Williams, archivist of the Cecil Papers at Hatfield House; John Underwood, information librarian at the Science Museum library; George Newkey-Burden, historical archivist at the *Daily Telegraph*; Elaine Hart, archivist and librarian of the *Illustrated London News*; Virginia Murray, archivist of John Murray, publishers; Martin Killeen, librarian at Birmingham University; the staff of the D. C. Thompson Archives in Dundee; and the archivist of Glamis Castle.

I would also like to thank the librarians and staff of the London Library; Cambridge University Library; the Wellcome Institute; the Bodleian Library, Oxford; the Public Record Office, Kew; Balliol College, Oxford; Lambeth Palace Library; the House of Lords Library; Reading University Library; the British Library, St Pancras; and the British Newspaper Library, Colindale—with the hope that this last institution may one day receive the fresh funding and revamping of the spirit that make both St Pancras and the PRO such exemplary national archives to visit.

Among private archives, the Hans Tasiemka Archive remains a pearl. Its unique collection of clippings, from reports on the Diamond Jubilee of 1897 right up to yesterday's headlines, has been as invaluable with *Royal* as it was with *Majesty*. I am deeply indebted to Edda Tasiemka and to her assistant Heidi Raj—and also to my industrious,

598

devoted and eagle-eyed mother, Vida Lacey, who, from Bristol, organised a royal cuttings agency of her own.

The credit for the book's outstanding picture section goes to Suzanne Hodgart and Michael Rand, my former colleagues on the *Sunday Times* Magazine, and to Adam Brown of B & B design. Thank you to Douglas Matthews for completing the index in record time.

I met the Australian historian Yvonne Ward over elevenses at the Royal Archives, and have derived immense benefit from her knowledge and advice, both in regard to Australian attitudes to the monarchy and her own field of expertise, the family life of Queen Victoria. My thanks to her, and also in the field of Victorian studies to Dr John Plunkett and Dr Lynne Vallone.

My friend Gerald Grant has been my standby in all aspects of royal knowledge, from counting the grandchildren and great grandchildren of Queen Victoria to correcting the details of the family tree, and the book has benefited immeasurably from his precision and care. I am also grateful for the transatlantic expertise and hospitality of Neil Letson, and for the ever-cheery help with some unusual research leads from Lili Agee and Joe Feinberg.

My thanks to Andrew Maxwell-Hyslop for his transcriptions and suggestions in the early days of the project, and to Nina Drummond for arranging some of my very best interviews and for transporting me to them in her garden van. I was lucky to have the research assistance of Bianca Roccelli for nearly a year before her talents were snapped up by television, and I am grateful to

Jacqueline Williams, my 'wife number two' from Saudi days, for organising the flood of clippings that attended the death of Diana, and then for coming to the rescue in the last hectic weeks to organise the book's reference section.

The reporter's instincts and flourishing republican tendencies of Moyra Ashford helped keep the manuscript honest and true, while supplying invaluable material from the Public Record Office. Moyra even found treasures in Colindale. In America my old friend and greatest ever editor William D. Phillips never let me lose sight of the meaning, while supplying wise counsel and solid support through some scarcely believable publishing misadventures.

My agent Michael Shaw steered me through these—and other shoals and quicksands—with his customary sense of direction, and when Captain Shaw was really sailing, his assistant Jonathan Pegg demonstrated how much navigation of his own he had mastered. The publishing mishaps, it must be stressed, did not happen in Britain. Little, Brown UK, have once again proved publishers of remarkable empathy, quality, and efficiency, and in these last hectic months of publication I owe much to the steadiness and support of Ursula Mackenzie, Viv Redman, David Young and to the super-cool copy-editing of Gillian Bromley. In the keen eyes department, special thanks to Elizabeth Dobson for her proofreading, and to the measured trouble-shooting of David Hooper.

In the longer term, I owe still more to Philippa Harrison, my original commissioning editor and publisher, to whom this book is dedicated. Normally I dedicate my books to my family, and for the last five years my wife Sandi and younger son Bruno have tolerated the half life of co-existing with my work and obsession with their customary styles of love and support. But with their permission, this one is for Philippa. She was my publisher all those years ago on *Majesty*. She commissioned my books on Saudi Arabia and Sotheby's, as well as my collaboration on *The Year 1000*, and she has been the unflagging supporter of this book from the start. More to the point, she was the creator of Little, Brown UK, the reinvigorator of Virago Press, and a galvaniser of the Publishers' Association—the Association's first ever woman president. For more than a quarter of a century she has been one of the most creative, humane and inspiring forces in British publishing, and I launch this book in the hope it may prove worthy of her.

Robert Lacey
London
December 2001